Cultural Formations of Postcommunism

Contradictions

Edited by Craig Calhoun, Social Science Research Council

Cultural Formations of Postcommunism

Emancipation, Transition, Nation, and War

Michael D. Kennedy

Contradictions, Volume 15

University of Minnesota Press
Minneapolis
London

Published by the University of Minnesota Press
111 Third Avenue South, Suite 290
Minneapolis, MN 55401-2520
http://www.upress.umn.edu

Library of Congress Cataloging-in-Publication Data

Kennedy, Michael D.
    Cultural formations of postcommunism : emancipation, transition, nation, and war / Michael D. Kennedy.
       p.   cm. — (Contradictions ; 15)
    Includes bibliographical references and index.
    ISBN 0-8166-3857-8 (HC : alk. paper) — ISBN 0-8166-3858-6 (PB : alk. paper)
    1. Political culture—Europe, Eastern.   2. Postcommunism—Europe, Eastern.   3. Europe, Eastern—Politics and government—1989–   I. Title.
II. Series.
    JN96.A91 .K45 2002
    306.2'0947—dc21

2002002300

12 11 10 09 08 07 06 05 04 03 02   10 9 8 7 6 5 4 3 2 1

Contents

Acknowledgments

My exploration of the cultural formations of postcommunism is a reflection of the University of Michigan's international and interdisciplinary culture. I first met transition culture through the University of Michigan Business School and its MBA Corps. The Center for International Business Education initially supported my study of that work and other similar efforts across the world. The William Davidson Institute at the University of Michigan has made the University of Michigan one of the leading nodes of transition culture in the world, and I have benefited considerably by its proximity and support for my work.

The Center for Russian and East European Studies (CREES) has been my principal research home in the making of this volume. My faculty, staff, and student colleagues assembled by the Center, especially those from Poland, Estonia, Ukraine, Uzbekistan, southeastern Europe, and southeastern Michigan, have been enormously important for the kind of work this volume represents. It is often said that administrative work takes away from scholarly effect, but my direction of CREES was certainly evidence to the contrary. It enabled me to appreciate the value of collaboration in the production of intellectual consequence like nothing else.

I would not have undertaken this volume, however, if I did not enjoy intellectual ties that pulled me beyond transition culture and its principal world region. The Program for the Comparative Study of Social Transformations has been one of the most important sites for extending my theoretical range, and for developing my passion to study the relationship between intellectual and social change beyond my disciplinary and regional roots. The International Institute, an umbrella for international and interdisciplinary work but also the site in which the epistemology and practice of global expertise can be recognized, has been a place apart, and the collegium that makes international and interdisciplinary work gel.

My disciplinary home in sociology has also been important. The discipline's anxiety over cores and boundaries has been enormously productive in helping me to appreciate the contested quality of any field's intellectual politics. Michigan sociology's measure of support for and openness toward a critical sociology that cares as much about public goods as departmental standings, and about international reference as much as American values, have shaped this work enormously.

Of course U-M's intellectual culture is enabled by the generous support of foundations outside of it. The National Council for Soviet and East European Research (NCSEER) provided support for my initial study of expertise, and its successor organization, the National Council for Eurasian and East European Research (NCEEER), supported my work on the Polish Round Table. The United States Institute for Peace also supported research on the latter's peace work. The Ford Foundation supported the CREES study of identity formation and social issues in Estonia, Ukraine, and Uzbekistan, as well as the International Institute's and my own efforts to rethink area studies, and especially the grounding, translation, and expertise underlying it. NCEEER also supported our work in Estonia, Ukraine, and Uzbekistan around environmental issues.

As this list makes clear, it is unlikely that I have satisfied the wholes of anyone's community. Nor can I be assured that I have satisfied the great number of individuals who have given me feedback on the entire manuscript—Valerie Bunce, Craig Calhoun, Tom Cushman, Jan Kubik, Rick Lempert, David Ost, Sonya Rose, Mark von Hagen, and other anonymous reviewers. I thank each of these considerate colleagues for their thoughtful comments. I especially wish to thank Lisa Fein for her heroic efforts to index the whole volume. The broader number of colleagues I thank for their readings of individual chapters may not find what they seek in the revisions they have inspired or in the other parts of the manuscript they had not read. However, I hope that all of my colleagues who have supported this effort recognize the seriousness with which I have engaged their ideas and valued their contributions, and the importance of extending our work beyond these pages.

I would not have managed such a juggling act if my immediate family did not support me as they have. From the dojo to the barn, from church to school, from North Carolina to Pennsylvania, we seem to be always on the move. But we do it together, and that keeps me intact. Thank you Liz, Emma, and Lucas for showing me the solidarity that enables my critical transition culture to work.

Introduction

Cultural Formations of Postcommunism

It is a cliché. The world was dramatically transformed in 1989, much as it was in 1789 or 1848. Political and economic systems and everyday lives were radically changed. Transition typically names this epoch whose two mantras—from plan to market and from dictatorship to democracy—anchored a new liberal hegemony in the world, and especially in Eastern Europe. Although the culture shaping this transition is more contradictory and complex than clichés and mantras suggest, 1989 does signal a change in global culture.

After 1989, we are much less likely to think about alternative, and desirable, futures in terms of the contest between communism and capitalism. Socialism is no longer capitalism's principal counterculture.[1] Instead, we are much more likely to think in terms of what kind of capitalism enables economic or sustainable growth, and, more specifically, what institutional forms of property and finance suit those goals best. The categorical difference between dictatorship and democracy, or open and closed societies, also animates visions, but the normative superiority of civil society, a system based on pluralism, legality, and publicity, became more secure after 1989 than at any other time in the twentieth century.

This never meant that the social conditions motivating challenges against capitalism and its democracies were superseded. Outrage over incivility and immorality can still mobilize movements or revolutions in the name of substantive rather than procedural rationality, in rage rather than reason, in resistance rather than reconstruction. Protests over the course of globalization from Seattle to Prague at the turn of the century suggest that the grounds for mobilization may even multiply, as movements coordinate their resources and articulate new global visions that connect their grievances. And within that process, alternative futures may be cast that promise to deepen the emancipatory potentials of civil society, even as xenophobic and violent visions also find fertile soil.

The movements that mobilize alternatives shape these potentials, but these possibilities are just as much, if not more profoundly, shaped by the sets of power relations and cultural sensibilities in which the movements struggle. Unfortunately Hegel is right about when Minerva's Owl flies. It is extraordinarily difficult to analyze systematically and deeply those contemporary conditions that shape these actions. However, it is possible to undertake such an effort for those periods that most immediately precede and shape the times in which we live. This volume is, then, a historical sociology of a time animated by the emancipation of 1989 and ending with the contradictions of a bombing campaign launched in the name of human rights. This historical sociology is not, however, only about the past; it is also about the broader cultures in which we make sense of events, trajectories, and power.

Cultures are bound in time. That is not always apparent, or emphasized, in a good deal of social science. In more "stable" societies, one can focus on the structure of a particular culture or set of social relations and assume its endurance or track its evolution over time. If the broader sensibility that informed originating questions does not change significantly, the historicity of social relations or cultures can remain unstated. It is far more difficult to overlook that historicity in Eastern Europe.

Studies of cultural systems and social structures have to attend directly to the region's radical discontinuities. This not only means, for instance, that one can document dramatic shifts in the mobilization of social movements. It also means that the *sense* of social movements is discontinuous. To study social movements before 1989 was central to understanding the reproduction and transformation of Soviet-type society. After 1989, "transition" structures research and interventions, and it figures movements in terms of their contribution to the institutionalization of markets and democracy.

This volume is also bound in time. I researched and wrote this volume across the 1990s. Unlike those who engage more enduring structures, I have had to contend with the lability and historicity of cultures and social structures. I thought, however, that as I concluded my revisions between the spring of 1999 and the fall of 2000, I could treat this as a more conventional historical study. I thought that the more generic conflicts and contradictions of globalization were beginning to diminish differences that set lands once ruled by communists apart. I also thought the postcommunist world ready for the broad reconstruction of transition's purpose that I propose here. After September 11, 2001, I think I may have been right about the former, but oddly wrong about the latter.

In some ways, the postcommunist world becomes much less distinctive in understanding the cultures of globalization. The principal antagonist is no longer socialism or communism; it is terrorism. The United States can find allies in the most unlikely of places in common cause against a particular network of terrorists. The Middle East and Central Asia have come into focus as Eastern Europe once did when transition was central to the global imagination. In that new regional focus, the postcommunist world's distinction fades. In this new globalization culture, countries with a communist past become much more like the rest of the world, seeking security against global terrorism. But in that commonality, a reconstructed sense of postcommunism might also have far more to offer.

In December 2001, as I review this manuscript finally composed the preceding January, I find both broader and more contemporary resonance than I would expect. My reconstruction of transition's sense may not only be relevant to the part of the world on which I have focused, but to a broader reconsideration of the cultures of globalization in terrorism's wake. In this volume, I explore how cultures work to hide the relationship between building global markets and the proliferation of nationalism and violence. I explore how cultures work to establish an equivalence across nations that ultimately distorts competent interpretations of and effective interventions in social change. I explore how cultures work to establish a linear sense of social change that distracts us from the power of events to alter the course of history. I explore how cultures help to erase the memory of solidarity and freedom from the point of struggle. I may have underestimated, before September 11, 2001, just how broadly the implications of my study can extend. Although I have focused on how these cultures work in the postcommunist world, I hope that their critical transformation might contribute to the reconstitution of sense in a new global culture defined by fear and uncertainty. In fact, it might be helpful to remember that significant parts of the world were, only twelve years before September 11, defined by the politics of hope and emancipation.

The Meanings of 1989

1989 means emancipation. In that year the communist monopoly on political power ended in the nominally independent countries of the Warsaw Pact—in Poland, Hungary, East Germany, Bulgaria, Czechoslovakia, and Romania. Albania's emancipation came later. Independent political parties were allowed only at the end of 1990, and competitive elections were held in the following March. 1991 is also relatively more important for Yugoslavia and the Soviet Union. Although the pace of change picked up dramatically in 1989 at the republican levels in these socialist federations, the Wars of Yugoslav Succession began in the summer of 1991 and the Soviet Union broke up by year's end. Czechoslovakia was the last multinational federation, dissolving peacefully into Slovakia and the Czech Republic after the summer elections of 1992. In comparison to Yugoslavia, the Soviet Union's end was also peaceful, although considerable violence preceded dissolution and thereafter has been concentrated on its southern tier in the Caucasus and Central Asia. In each of these cases, from Poland to Estonia and from Armenia to Croatia, many have understood the making of sovereign states out of socialist republics and federations to be moments of national liberation. Because of the violence, but even without it, others have understood these emancipations to be nationalist horrors.

1989 thus means contest, but not about the countercultures of capitalism and socialism. The contest rests in the meanings of nations and their nationalisms. This is most apparent in those places racked by war. What may be symbols of fascist or communist tyranny to one nation can be symbols of national liberation or multinational harmony to another. In 1989, many Serbs read the symbols of Croatian independence as reminders of Croatian fascism from World War II. Many Baltic Russians read the 1992 language laws pertaining to Estonian and Latvian citizenship as antidemocratic and nationalist, while many Estonians and Latvians could not read Russian-language road signs as anything other than reminders of an illegal Soviet occupation. These contests also occur within nations. Heroes and traitors to the national cause animate the alternatives of political contest. For example, more than ten years after the end to communist dictatorship, some in Poland sought to judge presidential candidates by their relation to the communist secret police and their truthfulness about that past.[2] Despite these contests around the nation, Croats, Serbs, Estonians, Russians, Poles, and other East Europeans, all, more or less, seek to adapt to a world defined by transition from dictatorship to democracy and from plan to market. In this sense, liberalism has triumphed.

Liberalism's meaning varies across the world, however, and most obviously between Europe and North America. Nonetheless, in distinction from communist rule and nationalist mobilization its connotation is clear. Liberalism is associated with pluralism. Its pluralism is manifest in the valuation of multiple political parties and social organizations, as well as in its belief that a market economy and private ownership of capital are the foundations for freedom and the open society.[3] But liberalism cannot do it alone. In the wake of communism's collapse, liberalism depended on compatible nationalisms to structure social change in Eastern Europe and the former Soviet Union. These nationalisms could be portrayed as the realization of embedded potentials, whereas liberalism's sense was obviously transnational, and part of a global transformation called "transition." While liberalism through transition thus realized unprecedented influence, it also depended on socialism or communism. Transition could only be understood *against* this newly anachronistic political, economic, and cultural system.

In scholarly circles, the term itself is quite controversial, but *transition* has a distinct advantage. It focuses one's sensibility on forward movement rather than explicitly engaging the system from which nations sought to escape. It is a term very well suited, therefore, to those whose expertise is oriented toward the future, such as those in economic modeling or business plans, even though the broader and even more futuristic term *emerging markets* might eventually overwhelm transition's competitive conceptual advantage. Other more historical and cultural scholars tend to doubt transition's intellectual sense, however. Anthropologists are among its most severe critics; the concept deflects attention from everyday life and those immediately past practices that shape it. For those with such a focus, a prefix serves well.

But even here there is significant variation among those who identify these societies with post-Soviet, postsocialist, and postcommunist adjectives.

Apparently a matter of rhetorical taste, the choice of adjective also suggests different analytical and political sensibilities. Post-Soviet is the least polyvalent, but it is also the most geographically constrained. It does not easily admit those societies beyond the former Soviet Union, thus constraining not only the spatial but the consequent political and analytical imagination. The other terms avoid that limitation, but they also have troubling connotations. The postcommunist label focuses on the end to a particular mode of rule but is complicated because it is also used to describe formerly communist groups—such as Poland's Union of the Democratic Left—by those who wish to identify these actors' connections to a problematic past. The postsocialist label looks more sociological, because it appears to focus on the social system. However, it also uses the name its former rulers and their liberal antagonists jointly applied, overlooking those efforts to distinguish socialism from the practices of communist rule. That is one reason why I joined many scholars in the 1980s to use "Soviet-type society" to refer to societies organized on the Soviet model,[4] but that term has not survived 1989 very well. Beyond the stylistic problem implicit in applying a prefix to an adjective already burdened by a suffix, postsocialist fits the mood of transition. It is appealing to those who engage transition because it asserts that socialism is not only gone, but that is what was there in the first place. In this rhetorically limited world, I prefer to use the postcommunist label. Although it travels between the analytical and political world poorly, I like to use it precisely because it reminds us that names are not innocent, and rather reflect complex webs of meaning implicated in the contest over the course of history. After all, transition, even more than our choice of a referent to follow *post,* has shaped that very course of history.

Transition can work, so it goes, as long as the socialist past is expunged and the nationalist threat is held at bay. This narrative plot admits particular discontents as it assimilates manageable problems into its larger story while expelling others. In so doing, however, it diverts our gaze from transition's own cultural power. Transition is more than restructuring inequality and institutions, and the culture of transition is not just an inequality-generating ideology imposed on an East

European reality. Transition is a culture of power with its own contradictions, contentions, repressions, and unrealized potentials. Beyond the scholarly value of explaining these dimensions of transition, I base this volume on my belief that transition's virtues can be strengthened, and its tragedies ameliorated, by making its culture more explicit.

I hope that this cultural study of transition proves to be useful, therefore, to those still engaged in transition work across the postcommunist world. I also hope that it might inform engagements of globalization cultures that tend to be more postcolonial than postcommunist.[5] Ultimately, I hope to demonstrate that embedded within transition are cultural configurations that contribute to a broader movement to reconfigure globalization as freedom, and to bring emancipation back to social science and the social imagination.[6]

This culture of transition moves and is transformed across sites and time. In chapter 1, I explain the origins of this culture in the transformations of the late 1980s in my exploration of the relationship among *perestroika*, Poland, and Hungary. I refashion the common relatively determinist tale of socialism's collapse and transition's necessity with a more eventful account written with emancipation's critical accent. I then turn to the structural logic of transition's culture, by drawing on mid-1990s documents from the World Bank in particular. I contrast that culture to interpretations and interventions organized around poverty in order to highlight transition's cultural distinction. I follow that semiotic account with a more ethnographic focus on transition's culture in business from the early to mid-1990s, notably in the provision of advice about how to make better capitalist firms in Eastern Europe, especially Poland. I demonstrate how the culture of transition clearly empowers some, and can be transformed to empower others. But this culture, as constituted, cannot empower everyone. By moving beyond its relatively comfortable location in the world of business, one can identify critical variations in the way in which this culture frames, but also ignores, different sensibilities of social change. By drawing on twenty focus group transcripts across ten sites in two countries, I contrast interpretations of social change in Estonia (the exemplar of) and Ukraine (the problem for) and transition in the post-Soviet world. A great deal of cultural work takes place in making sense of transition's culture in different nations, but much effort also goes into constituting the limits of transition. This is especially apparent in the exclusion of war from transition's imagined field. In chapter 6, I consider the principal cultural formations at work in the distancing, and implication, of war in the making of transition. With NATO's intervention in 1999 and the fall of President Slobodan Milošević from power in Yugoslavia in 2000, transition is no longer conceivably distant from war's effects. And, with that implication, transition changes its cultural field, and therefore requires substantial reconstruction. I propose just such a reconstruction of transition's sense in the conclusion, where the mantra from plan to market is replaced with freedom's extension.

This volume thus focuses on the past coherence and alternative potentials of transition's culture. I focus on its structure and practice through the mid-1990s, with an eye toward influencing its transformation more than a decade after communism's collapse across the region. By attending to the *ways* in which postcommunist possibilities and problems are engaged, we not only attend to the epistemologies shaping our inquiry, but we also help to inform the character of the social transformations themselves. By making explicit those complexes of norms, rules, practices, symbols, and beliefs underlying the interventions of both the politically engaged and the analytically detached, we can illuminate the ways in which culture articulates social change.[7] And, by making that culture explicit, we also become more aware of the conditions of our action, and perhaps, collectively, have greater control over the consequences of our interventions. I hope that by making the culture animating our activity discursively explicit, we realize greater possibility in the structuring of our common futures.[8] At the very least, by putting culture to the analytical center, the study of Eastern European social change is necessarily transformed. Consider, after all, how odd it sounds to name *transition culture*.[9]

Transition Culture

To many, transition culture is a contradiction in terms. Culture involves values, beliefs, symbols, and rituals, whereas transition is about a transformation of political and economic systems from dictatorship and economic planning to democracy and markets. Culture also implies something enduring, clearly bounded and held in common—a nation's history or language, for example—not a dynamic process that occurs across the world in widely differing circumstances. And if one is limited to these conceptions of culture—something in opposition to other spheres of action in the economy or polity, and something that is shared by an obviously bounded group—then transition culture must be an oxymoron.

Culture also has a broader reference. Social life is cultural because meaning is imbued in every human action and its recognition. People need to understand what "planning" is in order to change it, and need to know what markets mean in order to adopt the appropriate dispositions. In this sense, transition culture might simply mean that set of understandings involved in the transition from plan to market and dictatorship to democracy. I wish to suggest, however, something more ambitious in naming transition culture.

Transition culture is a mobilizing culture[10] organized around certain logical and normative oppositions, valuations of expertise, and interpretations of history that provides a basic framework through which actors undertake strategic action to realize their needs and wishes. That mobilizing culture, in turn, structures transition. Transition culture emphasizes the fundamental opposition of socialism and capitalism, and the exhaustion of the former and normative superiority of the latter. It values broad generalizing expertise around the workings of market economies and democratic polities. Culture and history are not especially difficult to understand in transition culture, and transition culture certainly does not privilege those who are expert in reading complicated and contested histories and cultures. Instead, culture is treated like a hunk of clay that can be reshaped, and history as a path that should inform postcommunist institutional design. Most certainly, culture and history are not recognized to be things that envelop the work of transition itself. Transition culture assumes that publics emerge from communist rule damaged, and need to be educated in the values of capitalism and democracy, even while those publics must choose the leadership to educate them. Elite agency and institutional design are the principal subjects of transition culture, while popular culture and history are engaged only to the extent they inform elites and design. Globalization is given, and it is only a matter of debate about what course it might take, and who will benefit most from it.

Transition culture is most obviously located in the world of scholarship and policy making. When academics and bureaucrats debate the priorities of floating exchange rates, particular property rights, or other relatively technical choices in making transition, they help to build a global transition culture. Although furious debate might follow particular disagreements about policy, these contests rest on broader assumptions about the kinds of expertise that are important and about the trajectory of global change. The drive to understand how to make capitalism out of socialism rests on epistemological foundations that elevate broad, generalizing, and comparative expertise about market economies while diminishing the value assigned to those who know how socialist institutions work and how local networks operate. Transition culture does not only live, however, in the halls of transitology, one of the culture's principal academic expressions. It also lives in everyday life, when, for instance, a self-identified entrepreneur in Eastern Europe accuses his employee of having a socialist mind-set. That encounter reproduces an imagery of who belongs to the future, and who to a past that must be transformed or discarded. It also exists in a discussion of political justice and minority rights. An argument over the proper citizenship policy, cast with global comparisons in mind, operates within a framework of transition culture. Those who lament the decline of the Soviet Union and its organization of national relations are part of the past the advocates of transition culture want to bury. Transition culture did not easily digest, for example, the restoration of the Soviet national anthem at the end of 2000.

Not only does transition culture operate in a variety of thematic areas and social spaces, but it also enjoys quite elastic boundaries of membership. In fact, it is better not to think in terms of boundaries at all. One should rather think of membership in relational terms. Before his boss, the hapless employee might not be able to claim much affiliation with transition culture, but before the Western representative of a lending agency, the boss might appear quite deficient when he approaches a loan without a recognizable business plan. And all three of them might be closer to the core of transition culture if they are negotiating with each other in a nation that is on the fast track to membership in the European Union. Likewise, the scholars who argue about postcommunist currency rates or property rights with no particular place in mind might exemplify groundless transitology, while those who caution about social pressures and political complications might appear to be ensnared in past thinking and distant from transition culture's domain assumptions. However, those who raise such concerns with an eye toward "educating" the public are obviously within the fold of a broader transition culture interested in implementation and not only abstract models. Both, however, are likely to identify as beyond the pale of transition culture those who use public outcry as an opportunity to mobilize violent demonstrations in Prague against the World Bank.

As these examples suggest, some actors have more power than others to define the terms and meaning of transition. Transition culture expects that the boss should have more influence than the employee in defining those terms, and the lender more influence than the boss. Although each area of transition has its principal experts—from human resource management to marketing to constitution writing to local government—transition culture writ large has its core in financial expertise and the organizations that allocate funds within nations and across them. To understand how those in this core interpret and act on the meaning of communism's collapse and sequel is to approach the center of transition culture. With their power to name opportunities and problems, to identify preferred strategies and dangerous paths, to fund research, and to provide fellowships, this core helps to establish the structure within which transition, as a global culture, operates.

Transition culture does not only reside, of course, in a global space. While financial transactions might be increasingly global in their network, transition involves significant change on the ground— in factories, polling places, public media, and elsewhere. Relational understandings of culture mean that cultural change takes place in encounters across space and power, and not only in the pronouncements of those who enjoy the greatest concentrations of capital or authority. We might look to those with the greatest authority to define progress in transition—those from the European Union who mark the timetable to accession or those from the World Bank who assign creditworthiness for a new loan—to define transition culture. But to understand transition culture as a lived practice beyond the sites of its design, one should explore its application, interpretation, and transformation beyond its core. In that process, one might even understand better those emergent formations that the core is unable, or unwilling, to see, and to move beyond the culture that bestows hidden power on transition's categories.

Moving beyond this core makes transition culture's articulation with the nation and with history more obviously apparent. Transition culture relies on a dynamic but directed tale, one implying movement and goal. The nation in Eastern Europe, however modern, implies a continuity of survival, of struggle, and of unrealized potential. Its identity is based on a history of contingencies rooted in narratives of tragedy and triumph. Transition's mobilizing tales are also told in languages other than English, and in those expressions they carry other plots that convey more, and less, than what those in the core of transition culture might recognize. Those plots are filled with alternatives and debates about authenticity that transition culture is unlikely to elevate, while the probabilistic and comparative reasoning associated with transition is less likely to find a home in those national narratives. The relations embodied in transition culture thus are amplified, diminished, and altered by their necessary implication in national cultures. In practice, these cultures of transition and nation are not distinct, for they realize their effect only in articulation with each other. I find it useful, however, to identify transition culture's structure so that the qualities of its various transformations across sites of its implementation become clearer, and the capacity of those beyond its core to affect its potentials becomes greater.

There are obviously other cultural dimensions that shape this articulation of transition and nation. Gender is fundamentally important in forming the meaning of transition, as are class and regionalism.[11] Although important, these other axes of difference and their cultural associations do not enjoy primary focus in this volume. I would find, however, extensions to them entirely compatible with this treatment of transition culture and its national articulations. This volume is only one small step in an effort to center the cultural formations of postcommunism.

Cultural Formations

I draw my sense of cultural formation from the work of Raymond Williams.[12] "Structure of feeling," or the ensemble of meanings and values as they are actually lived and felt, is one of his core concepts. It enables his sociology to focus on practice and everyday life and not only expressed values and structures of meaning. He is interested in identifying the "dominant and definitive lineaments and features" of durable cultural systems, but he finds that this methodology substitutes too often for the more historical analysis of interactions among a number of cultural elements. He argues that one should study these structures of feeling on their own terms, as well as in articulation with these more systematic belief systems dispersed across time and space

(129–35). I approach transition culture with a similar disposition, but because its structure is unrecognized, I cannot proceed without the outline offered in the preceding section, and the elaboration offered especially in chapter 2. That account provides an anchor with which transition culture's transformations through practice can be recognized. I also use that structural account to clarify how the discursive boundaries of transition culture's past, and of its field of reference, are constructed.

The past, notably tradition, is typically figured as part of "culture," but for Williams, tradition is not just the "surviving past." It is "an intentionally selective version of a shaping past and a pre-shaped present" (115). Tradition can, as the selectivity suggests, be part of any current culture reinforcing power or undermining it. Residual cultural elements are formed in the past, but their relationship to contemporary cultural practices must be refigured through practice (123). In this sense, transition's past is not altogether obvious.

On the one hand, transition culture often draws on examples from across Eastern Europe, and across the capitalist world, to provide instruction for how transition should be designed. It also draws on the legacy of national struggles and the regionwide emancipation from communism initially realized in 1989 for its normative power. One can find the global and local reference of transition culture throughout this volume, most notably in chapters 2–4 where I elaborate transition culture's manifest structure and practice. But the selection of tradition goes far beyond what is included. Tradition also depends on excluding certain fields of action.

Transition's tradition tends to draw more on capitalist experiences from across the world than it does on any nation's socialist past. Socialism is something to be escaped, repressed, and destroyed. To the extent tradition is something to be valued and recuperated, transition hardly seeks to reconstitute socialism, except as a nemesis that explains the limitations of transition itself. The socialist mind-set, for instance, is critical to the sense of transition, for it explains what must be changed, and why transition may not work as those without such a mind-set would expect. War is even more distant from transition, as I explain in chapter 6.

During communism's collapse and aftermath, wars took place across the communist world's southern tier, from Croatia to Tajikistan. The West focused on the Balkan Peninsula, but this attention did not imply much sense of Western culture or history. The emancipation of 1989 might be treated as part of the West's general history, where transition means a "return to Europe" or even to normality. The wars of the former Yugoslavia were treated as somebody else's history. Transition culture's power is evident in the likely response to any suggestion that war is implicated in transition, and transition in war. Those within transition culture will immediately disavow much connection, especially before NATO's intervention in 1999. It is obviously a question of *nationalism*'s wars, infected by communist practices and socialist mind-sets. Transition cannot be responsible for those wars, for its very sense exists in opposition to nationalism and communism, and thus nationalism's wars cannot be part of transition's tradition. Beyond substance, tradition is also selective about the *ways* in which its past is described.

To a considerable extent, transition culture depends on the imagery of collapse, socialism's systemic exhaustion. That allows, on the one hand, transition culture to ignore the expertise that might be associated with understanding how socialism worked. On the other hand, it also suggests that the agency in social change rests with those who are building a global capitalism, not with those who emancipated themselves from communist dictatorship. And, most intriguingly, this image of collapse completely distracts us from the efforts of men and women to assure that revolution would be peaceful, and that it might have been otherwise. Transition culture's approach to culture and history distracts us from the contingencies and historiographical contentions underlying its own making. To understand the binding and potential transformation of transition culture, therefore, one must also develop a sense of how transition culture's tradition was made out of a global heritage, constriction of emancipation, and casting of a barbaric alternative. One must reconstruct its tradition, but in such a cultural system as transition, one cannot stop with tradition.

Like many others, Williams identifies traditions and institutions as part of what might be studied in cultural analysis, but I am particularly drawn to his work because of his stress on "cultural formations." Formations are those "effective movements and tendencies, in intellectual and artistic life, which have significant and sometimes decisive influence on the active development of a culture, and which have a variable and often oblique relation to formal institutions" (117). This emphasis is also linked to a focus on practice, or "social experiences in solution primarily to emergent formations" (132–34). He understands these emergent formations as "new meanings and values, new practices, new relationships and kinds of relationship" (123).

This focus on, and language for, expressing those cultural moments that are not fully or completely institutionalized fits well with attending to a culture of transition. This sociology is especially well suited to looking for those cultural articulations that transition might produce in interaction with other cultural elements. Rather than reveal ideologies or cultural patterns that reflect that which is already well understood, Williams seeks with this sociology to identify sensibilities that are not well articulated, and to detect those cultural formations that are themselves foundational for the making of social change, but perhaps poorly recognized.[13] I draw on this approach for identifying transition culture in business practice (chapter 3), its national articulations with freedom (chapter 4), and its disarticulation with expressions of loss (chapter 5). Although this is but one approach to a cultural sociology of East European change, this contingent approach to cultural formations seems most appropriate, especially when it is tied to the kind of deep reading Williams himself suggests.[14]

Culture can also connote something far more static and reflective than the deliberate and labile projects of social intervention and cultural formations that I seek to explain. Methodologies follow these alternative orientations toward culture too. Concerns about the distribution of values, or the representativeness of dispositions, depend on visions of relatively fixed cultural formations. For instance, there is a great deal of research on postcommunist societies that depends on the imagery of relatively stable cultural belief systems that can be elicited through survey research, and whose sentiments can be mobilized by the right conjuring of symbols and stories.[15] Those who seek such generalizing knowledge about attitudes toward the market, freedom, or poverty in Eastern Europe in this volume will be disappointed. Such an approach to culture is, of course, not the only view on culture in the human sciences. Rather than fix some bounded entity and construct a picture of that entity with data that claim representativeness, I work with a different sense of culture, and methodologies appropriate to its elaboration.

Ethnographies focus on the elaboration of a particular conjuncture, a complex case, to illuminate larger issues.[16] Historical approaches to culture draw on a wide range of sources—from oral histories to archival resources—to construct interpretations of differently complex cases whose validity rests on the acceptance and challenges made by others who are knowledgeable about the case.[17] Those who seek to enhance the historicity of social movements and their capacities for effective intervention are less concerned about the generality of attitudes among movement participants than about the structures of understanding that limit, and might enhance, movement efficacy. This kind of research relies heavily on a variation of focus group methodology.[18] This volume should be read from within such traditions of cultural study that seek to fix the object of their inquiry with their research, and to enhance capacities to understand the rules and resources that influence capacities to intervene in the world, or in scholarship.

I do not recognize transition culture to be like other cultures, whether of nations, classes, or organizations. It does not enjoy such secure sociological boundaries as these groups. I trust that this volume will clarify why I move away from the enduring and bounded sense of culture, and rather why, at least in this case, it should be understood in such a way that its continuity across time and space is always problematic. The accuracy with which transition culture expresses the reality of social life is also hard to draw given that it does not seek to reflect reality, but to anticipate one that does not yet exist. If one believed in its teleology, one might, I suppose, work with conceptions of consciousness that are false and true, but given the power of unintended consequences in any social project, from socialism to transition, I have lost the confidence necessary to assign registers of truthfulness. Indeed, most have lost that capacity, for nobody *clearly* owns transition the way communist parties at one time owned socialism. At least transition has not yet found its Lenin. Transition's power comes rather from its lability and capacity to articulate with a wide variety of actors and other cultural formations. Indeed, one theme of this volume is that transition's ownership might itself be subject to contest, with consequent conceptual, and practical, transformation.

Transition culture is, therefore, most appropriately understood as a cultural formation. Although one might assess how its elements vary systematically across populations, one ought to begin by exploring the meaning of that cultural formation and its articulation with others. The theoretical framework and methodologies I have chosen for this volume reflect that ambition.[19] But they also reflect the intellectual traditions beyond Eastern European studies with which I have worked.

Power, History, and Social Change

In an earlier work, I identified critical sociology with the focus on power, praxis, and alternativity.[20] In this volume, I develop a more cultural argument. The cultural sociology of communist rule was relatively well developed, especially for facilitating emancipation from communist rule. The cultural sociology of postcommunism is much less developed, in large part because it is embedded in transition culture itself, while its more postmodern forms tend to diverge from institutional engagement. Critical sociology, and especially its social theory, could be implicated within transition, but their foci have not made them proximate. This distance is not, however, necessary, and is moreover counterproductive for developing transition's potential.

I understand critical sociology to be organized around "theory that is self-conscious about its historicity, its place in dialogue and among cultures, its irreducibility to facts, and its engagement in the practical world."[21] Its most obvious traditions in marxism, feminism, or postmodernism have limited resonance with most currents of social change in Eastern Europe, but its principal theoretical emphases are better points of critical engagement with transition than are the particular inequalities and political projects on which it has focused.[22] With more substantial attention to the conditions in which critical sociology is elaborated, its relevance to postcommunist social change should be considerable, and found in several theoretical emphases.[23]

Critical sociology is *immanent,* as it seeks to highlight recognized but unacknowledged phenomena embedded in history and social change.[24] With its emphasis on developing new concepts to highlight understudied phenomena, its theoretical orientation is rather at a *sensitizing* level, inviting new explorations rather than falsifying empirical generalizations or expanding an abstract body of axiomatic principles.[25] At the same time that it is sensitizing, it is also cumulative, seeking to refine intellectuality's normative engagement of the social world. It not only identifies the normative penumbrae that surround social phenomena, but seeks to identify those conditions and engagements that promise greater rationality and emancipation in that present.[26]

Critical sociology is also *hermeneutic* in its serious engagement of difference. Difference involves not only variation, but also the challenge of communication across potentially incommensurate life-worlds. Rather than presume a disposition of actor to exist across time and space, this theoretical approach begins with the presumption that cultural difference is significant. Consequently, translation is never simple, and hermeneutics is always necessary. There are, in fact, several hermeneutic moments involved in social inquiry, especially in cross-national comparative studies. First, there is the challenge of fusing horizons across cases to make comparison possible. Second, one must link those observed cases to the culture of inquiry. Third, in extending a theoretical tradition beyond the conditions of its origin, one must establish the possibility of articulating its questions with the everyday worlds it seeks to engage.[27] This is true for both theories of transition and critical sociology, but the latter is more likely to investigate the conditions of its possibility, whereas the former is more likely to ignore it or consider it a hurdle to be overcome. The successful articulation of theory with everyday life is important for both, however.[28]

Critical sociology is focused not only on difference, but also on the (partial) transcendence of difference. Some of the most fruitful work in critical social theory has been in search of that articulation between integrating visions and emphases on difference.[29] Jürgen Habermas's work on communicative competence, in which "comprehensibility, truthfulness, rightness and truth [form] universal presuppositions of communicative interaction,"[30] provides one of the most important efforts in that direction. This theoretical movement seeks to provide a normative and procedural foundation for the critique of social practices, by identifying the ways in which communication among actors is distorted by power and exclusion. In some ways, Alvin Gouldner's sense of intellectuals as a universal, if flawed, class rests alongside this sensibility, because he finds in their culture of critical discourse a historically emancipatory rationality.[31]

Critical sociology is also *comparative,* for it always, at least implicitly, is concerned with alternatives and how things might otherwise be. Given the terrific variety of postcommunist experiences, critical sociology in this region can also be comparative in a more conventional sense. To assume that any single society reflects the systemic quality of postcommunist social change undermines that comparative ambition, and the recognition of important differences among postcommunist countries. Of course, although there are many strategies for undertaking comparative study, critical sociology is frequently historical.[32] This comparative and historical sociology tends to treat differences among cases with thick descriptions rather than parsimonious accounts of significant variation. It is also likely to take the contingency of social transformations seriously, and events to be potentially causal.[33]

Most sociology, according to William Sewell, seems to rely on either a teleological or an experimental sense of time. Most of the sociology of postcommunist transformations falls into these two frameworks. Transition is typically deployed with the former sense of temporality. Sewell describes the teleological with its location of causality. It attributes the cause of "a historical happening neither to the actions and reactions that constitute the happening nor to concrete and specifiable conditions that shape or constrain the actions and reactions, but rather to abstract transhistorical processes leading to some future historical state."[34] Teleological thinking is, of course, not the only temporality in social science. Theda Skocpol's study of revolutions exemplifies the experimental side.[35]

Although some have criticized Skocpol for particular logical and evidentiary problems,[36] the more important point for us here is that historical cases cannot be considered either equivalent or independent as they are in an experimental approach. Each case is embedded in history, and accumulates conditions that prevent either equivalence or independence to be reasonably imagined. It is hard to imagine that the French Revolution is the same type of event as the Russian Revolution, and that the Russian Revolution had no influence on the Chinese Revolution.[37] Likewise, one cannot imagine, for instance, treating the revolutions that ended communism in 1989 as separate events, and likewise, one cannot consider the conditions of postcommunist war apart from the conditions of peaceful transition. Or at least one should not.

Sewell's *eventful temporality* is a very appealing alternative. Drawing on historical sociologists Marc Traugott and Howard Kimeldorf as exemplars,[38] Sewell directs our attention to the events that transform social structures. This attention does not assume "causal independence through time," as does the experimental method, and rather assumes that events might transform not only the balance of causal factors but their very logic (263). Eventful temporality is thus "path dependent," but it also works with "temporally heterogeneous causalities" that can change over time. And, unlike teleological temporality, the eventful embraces the possibility of global or radical contingency, one that might "undo or alter the most apparently durable trends of history" (264). In the study of postcommunist social change, wars are likely to be understood contingently, but transition is less so.

Comparative and historical sociology's emphasis on the contingency of change derives from its approach to the complexity of difference, on the one hand, and its eventful approach to causality, on the other. By retaining the complexity of difference, and emphasizing the mutability of causalities in conjunction, comparative and historical sociology is quite likely to search for how social transformations might have otherwise been, and how apparent consistencies are reproduced over time.[39] This concern for reproduction and transformation as well as the complexity of difference is rooted in a deeper notion of modernity's alternatives. The classic studies of comparative and historical sociology have focused on the distinctions among alternative modernities in communism, fascism, and democratic capitalism.[40] The making and gendering of the English working class, the mandate to rule, and the question of state making and capitalist dynamism were all focused on explaining not only how particular outcomes were reached, but how they could otherwise be.[41] In a word, they have focused on *alternativity* rather than variations on a modernizing theme. The discourse around transition is different.

Postcommunist Social Change

Like comparative and historical sociology, transition studies focus on the making of modernity. Unlike the former, transition studies do not seek to elevate alternativity but to end at least one version of it. The majority of transition studies focus on the making of markets and democracy out of communist rule, and thus seek to end, both analytically and by intervention, capitalism's counterculture. However, like marxism, transition studies tend to stand in the stream of history as they analyze the recent past and present in order to shape the future. But this is a different kind of theory and practice. It is about making policy, not mobilizing movements. It is about designing institutions, not crafting revolutions. It is also about changing our sense of possibility and of history. Transition studies are about elevating variation over alternativity in our approach to social transformations.[42]

This shift to variation is not only about the end to socialism, but also about the hegemony of liberalism. Liberalism has historically sought to minimize the challenge of difference in favor of the interchangeability of citizens and nations, and/or the desirability of commodifying and rationalizing more widely in order to facilitate the broadest exchange and markets. Despite claims to recognize the "diverse array of national histories, cultures, and political systems,"[43] the premise of transition is that markets and democracy are transportable and mutable to all conditions. The goal of transition then becomes the foundation for inquiry. This teleological sense of scholarship is empowered by a vision of necessity, and the urgency of possibility.[44] Consider these few words from the introduction to a World Bank study:

> This transition, which affects about one third of the world's population, has been unavoidable. The world is changing rapidly: massive increases in global trade and private investment in recent years have created enormous potential for growth in jobs, incomes, and living standards through free markets. Yet the state-dominated economic systems of these countries, weighed down by bureaucratic control and inefficiency, largely prevented markets from functioning and were therefore incapable of sustaining improvements in human welfare. . . . [This report] drives home the utter necessity of both liberalizing economies through opening trade and market opportunities and stabilizing them through reducing inflation and practicing fiscal discipline—and then of sticking to these policies over time. . . . [This report] is about how to unleash the enormous talents and energies of these countries' populations, and how to help them achieve their vision for a future of opportunity and well-being for all their citizens.[45]

This transition is not just about transforming institutions, therefore. To be sure, communications, finances, accounting, and legal infrastructures are all woefully inadequate, but the *culture* of transition rests on the organization of expertise and engagement around these lacks. They become the basis for understanding and intervening in the system.[46] Scholarship is devoted to explaining how these lacks are pathological and how they can be remedied. David Stark has called this approach "designer capitalism," and Valerie Bunce has recommended its grounding.[47]

Of course, focusing on the lack is not the only approach to studying transition. Institutionalists such as Stark and Bunce offer alternative perspectives on communism's end and postcommunism's alternatives.[48] In contrast to the more teleological transition studies, institutionalists emphasize the system's dynamics rather than its destination. They emphasize the influence of the past on the present, and of the distribution of resources on the future. For instance, Ákos Róna-Tas's central point is one that transitologists typically minimize: social transformations are made not only by the making of a private economy per se, but also by who gets that private economy and why.[49] However, institutionalists accept more or less transition's metanarrative: that the problem is to figure out how capitalism and/or democracy can be built. They are open to a wider variety of practices (recombinant property not private property) or actors (local political actors, not private capitalists) that might realize those capitalist and democratic transformations, but in their very debate with designer capitalists and transitologists, institutionalists join transition culture. Two volumes published in 1998 illustrate this engagement.[50]

Both Stark and Bruszt and Elster, Offe, and Preuss address social change in Hungary and the Czech Republic, and Stark and Bruszt also devote considerable attention to Germany and some to Poland. Elster, Offe, and Preuss consider Slovakia and Bulgaria. Both volumes emphasize the distinction of change in this region, elaborate some models of Soviet-type society, and compare modes of extrication from that system. They both undertake path analysis to consider the impact of the past on postcommunism's reform policies. Both volumes explain and evaluate the variety of capitalisms and modes of democracy being built in these societies. Elster, Offe, and Preuss address the distant past, constitutionalism, social policy, and the relationship between conflict and consolidation. Stark and Bruszt are focused on the more immediate past and on developing new concepts for superseding old dichotomies.

Both volumes, like transition culture itself, are interested in agency. And, like transition culture, they focus almost exclusively on the agency of the designers. Although designer capitalism is not embraced in either volume, the influence of its ideological frame is apparent. The principal agency theorized is that connected with the concentration of resources or the legislation of alternatives. While trying to distance themselves from designer capitalism's focus on blueprints from without, they remain nonetheless implicated in that field's relative neglect of those beyond the elite. This omission is hardly apparent within transition culture, however, as the debate between institutionalists and transitologists focuses on the principal agents enacting capitalism and democracy rather than on their relations with those for whom, or perhaps over whom, postcommunist institutions are designed. This relative neglect becomes especially apparent in marxism's critique.

For marxists, the novelty of postcommunist social transformation is less clear. Marxist accounts are more likely to emphasize the similarities between capitalism's transformations, and those of the "transition." The common problems facing the shift from a Fordist economy to a post-Fordist one, where a labor aristocracy is undermined and finance, or merchant, capitalism is elevated, are likely to be highlighted.[51] These cross-systemic comparisons are not central to the transition debate. Also, a marxist perspective is more likely to emphasize the commonalities in impoverishment and a weakening base for labor's mobilization across capitalisms in order to highlight the systemic distinction of capitalism itself. Such an approach tends to minimize the significance of *postcommunist* capitalism's difference from other capitalisms, as it diminishes the significance of socialism's legacy in understanding social change.[52]

Above all, however, most marxist accounts of postcommunist social change redirect our attention to other agents of change. The main actors in their narrative are not managers; at least workers and other actors within the firm play more than bit parts. Although the transition literature might emphasize the importance of low unemployment for transition's success,[53] the life-worlds of workers are unlikely to be central to the transition problematic. Where the popular classes are discussed, as in the fate of the unemployed and the poor in Elster, Offe, and Preuss, they are the object of state policy, not subjects implicated in the making of history, or path. When they appear with consequence, they are likely to be portrayed as reform's obstacles with inappropriate mentalities or traditions. By contrast, Burawoy and others in his tradition would much prefer to see that action theorized, perhaps to exhume "the positive potentials of socialism."[54] But in the struggle to recover socialism, marxists also distance themselves from the stream of history where alternative futures are set in terms established by the new liberal hegemony.

Postcommunist Class

Regardless of its distance from power and its sense of history, the marxist critique is right in an important way, and applies quite specifically to these two exemplary institutionalist volumes. Neither theorizes how class relations or power relations on a global scale shape institutions or their own problematic. The institutionalists' analytical problems are established from the point of view of an international culture interested in realizing globally syncopated outcomes in markets and democracy.[55] Ideology plays a fairly limited role in the larger institutional account of change, and is more likely to be seen as an obstacle to the democratic designers' desire, not as a force that shapes the design of institutions themselves. Instead, ideology is likely to be portrayed as something to be overcome in the supercession of socialism and the design of rational institutions.

Elster, Offe, and Preuss, for example, theorize that economic interests, political ideologies, and ethnic identities might be located on a "reconcilability scale" from greatest to least. They suggest that such a scale helps us to understand why multinational Bulgaria and Slovakia are more challenged than relatively monoethnic Hungary and the Czech Republic in the race to democratic consolidation. On the one hand, this axiomatic starting point reinforces the value of transition culture's emphasis on the generation of economic opportunities (and inequalities) with the consolidation of democracy. Transition might, then, not only provide an economic stake in assimilating to its culture. They suggest that it might also introduce an axis of conflict that works against fundamentalist ideological or identity politics associated with certain parties and ethnically organized groups. Regardless of the theory's plausibility, this approach also helps to legitimate the installation of capitalist property relations in the name of democratic stabilization. Not only does increasing economic inequality produce greater economic rationality, but it might introduce a mode of conflict that is more compatible with democracy and pluralism. This provides a significant bonus for joining the culture of transition, especially when violence and war are cast as its alternative.[56]

With their focus on design, institutionalists are obviously within a field of discourse that enables them to engage, and become implicated in, transition culture. Marxists remain apart to the extent that they explicitly disavow that focus on capitalist variations and prefer to recognize socialist alternatives in their class analysis. But not all class analysis is consigned to such a distance from transition culture, especially when it focuses on the elite and its ideology rather than the popular classes and socialist recollections.

Gil Eyal, Iván Szelényi, and Eleanor Townsley develop such a sociology based on a theory of the fourth new class project of the East Central European intelligentsia.[57] Their sense of social change is based explicitly on patterned attributes of economic, political, and cultural elites at different points of time, primarily in Hungary but to some extent in Poland and the Czech Republic, and to a much lesser extent, but for stark contrast, in Russia. Their sense of capitalism is based on the qualities of these agents and their theorized relationships to others, primarily within their class. Action primarily takes place through individual adaptation of elites with different forms of capital—when, for example, socialist technocrats and anticommunist opposition from the days of communist rule ally to find a new place as the hegemonic managerial bloc presiding over postcommunist capitalism.

The civilizational project of the East Central European intelligentsia serves as the spirit that travels through history to provide different versions of the intellectuals' mission. The authors' invocation of Bourdieu tempers any Hegelian temptation, however, as they emphasize the "dialectical interaction between agents (their dispositions, habits, biographies, collective memories) and their positions (in institutions, class relations, and networks)."[58] More specifically, the cultural bourgeoisie contributes significantly to a new "spirit of postcommunism," drawing on the idea of civil society and monetarism to produce a new ideology for the emergent power bloc composed of their alliance with technocratic managers, foreign investors, and new entrepreneurs.[59]

Although this class analysis is quite different from the focus of most transition culture, in its attention to the different forms of capital constituting different aspects of the elite, it also works within the sense of transition culture. Rather than explain the contingencies of history or the alternatives embryonic in paths not taken and popular cultures not recognized, this sociology rests on a sense of social change as adaptation. In these authors' words, "those who are able to adjust their trajectories to meet social change most successfully are those who possess the most diverse portfolio of different kinds of capital."[60] This sociology reflects quite clearly the sensibilities of the new elite, as they adapt to a global transition culture. Of course, this adaptation can also be more active, and more radically reconstitutive, as Stark and Bruszt suggest.

They attend to the emergence of new identities derived from the process of change itself, whether in the Round Table negotiations that initiated the Great Transformation or in the variable accounts actors must provide to explain different liabilities to various suppliers and customers. But although they acknowledge this creativity, their explanation for its formation is rooted in particular institutional conjunctures, and not in larger cultural formations. They do not address ideology, even though ideology is implicit, and powerful, in their own account. International finance is, of course, not ideologically innocent, and is implicated in shaping postsocialism's pathways. In order to understand *why* Hungarian socialists lurch from their path as the public's caretaker to the imposer of financial discipline or *why* the fourth new class project is based on adapting to global capitalism, one must engage the power of transition culture. To do that, one might pursue the marxist critique of "neoclassical" sociology by exhuming alternative visions within the popular classes. But one might also find that alternativity within transition culture itself. One can clarify the cultural conditions of its practitioners' action by attending to the senses of history the future in transition.

Postcommunist Eventfulness

Neither eventfulness nor historiographical contention is central to institutional sociology, much less to transitology, but they have not always been so important to comparative and historical sociology either. Among the most forceful critiques of much comparative and historical sociology from the 1970s were those that focused on an overreliance on historical interpretations that fit with generalizing theoretical ambitions.[61] The path analysis associated with institutionalist approaches runs the same risk as this early comparative and historical sociology.

Consider, for instance, the fundamentally different interpretations that Elster, Offe, and Townsley and Stark and Bruszt offer for the Czech "success" in transition. The former conclude that the political stability of the Czech Republic through the late 1990s depended on the personal qualities of its political leaders and was accompanied by weak trade unions. The latter argue that the success of the Czech Republic depended on institutions and conjunctures that restrain executive authority and enhance trade-union influence in decisions. It is frankly difficult to decide who is right in these contrasting accounts, but it is useful to see the same path produce different interpretations among institutional theorists. But it is also unlikely that these authors or other institutionalists will return to this particular conjuncture, for these contrasting interpretations, or the subsequent decline in Czech political stability, are not the institutionalists' primary concern. Events are not so eventful in most institutionalisms. Indeed, the greatest event of them all hardly seems contingent or productive.

Rather than unleashing potentials from within its history and social practice, for most transitologists and even some institutionalists, communism's collapse is primarily a point of departure at last enabling the maladapted to adjust to a global system. Indeed, the end to communist rule itself realizes its cultural power in large part by minimizing its own eventfulness. Valerie Bunce's institutionalist critique of transitology illustrates the complexity of this uneventful event in the production of transition culture.[62]

Bunce self-consciously distances herself from transitology,[63] embraces its academic opponent in area studies, and argues that to understand postcommunist institutions one must understand better the *socialist* institutions that ended communist rule and shaped its sequels. More specifically, she argues that communist-ruled Eastern Europe and the Soviet Union had subversive institutions that produced similar systemic pressures that ultimately led socialism to collapse. With the modernization of society and economic decline leading some elites to press for and others to resist reform, homogenized societies were turned into increasingly cohesive publics pushing the agenda. Understanding this region as linked through Soviet power is also important for explaining the contagion of collapse. The end to socialism was the result of these systemic pressures building, and meeting a remarkable political opportunity in which leadership succession, Gorbachev's ambitious attempts at reforms, and major shifts in the international system coincided. With Poland and Hungary taking the lead, and Gorbachev providing support, the risk to those who would protest declined in the other countries of the Warsaw Pact and led to speedy imitation. Widespread violence emerged only in Albania, Yugoslavia, and Romania, where "Communist elites had domestic control over the military and where Gorbachev's actions with respect to military deployment were largely irrelevant."[64]

Bunce stands apart from many of the qualities associated with transition culture and its academic expressions. Most obviously, she does not focus on postcommunist institutional design, and rather treats historical conditions as more complicated than pathways to the present. She argues that detailed knowledge about particular places is critical for understanding how rational choices can be made, and that theoretical arguments about social change must also be made with broadly informed comparisons at heart. Finally, and most significantly, she refuses to work within transition's typical field of vision. Rather than isolate transition's barbaric alternative and compare variations on transition's peaceful theme, she puts Yugoslavia's exceptionalism to the heart of what she argues. Like all the cases of transition, she argues that Yugoslavia's end to communism drew on a nationalism that redistributed "political power and economic resources . . . from the first to the next tier of the system."[65] Its distinction from the Soviet Union and Czechoslovakia rested in the relative position of Serbia in its (con)federation and the particular structure of the military, arguments to which I shall return in chapter 6.

Bunce offers both a concise explanation of socialism's end and an incisive critique of much transitology, but her work nevertheless reinforces some of transition culture's most powerful assumptions. Relatively few scholars today argue that socialism could have survived, but this assumption about the system's exhaustion does something more than bury feasible socialism. It distracts us from the eventful causality of opportunity structures and their cultural interpretations in explaining socialism's end. Bunce moves far beyond transition culture by posing the question about how institutions and opportunity combined to produce that systemic collapse, but she ultimately subordinates events to destiny, and in that, provides transition culture with a vital historical institutional supplement. She explains why socialism collapsed when it did.

With her attention to opportunity structures, Bunce recognizes the significance of events and their timing, but she can only theorize them as brakes or accelerators on a socialist jalopy headed toward the edge of a cliff. Events and their makers cannot steer away from the precipice, or, in Sewell's words, they cannot change causalities. Bunce writes out of bounds any kind of historical inquiry that would enable us to see an alternative future in which communism's systemic collapse fails to take place, or occurs in something other than the register of peace (where it occurred peacefully) or violence (where it occurred violently). But even within her account, this institutional determinism is not entirely settled. Her attention to empirical detail and historical contention leads, potentially, elsewhere. As I will argue in chapter 6, the violence of Yugoslavia was not so inevitable as the institutional side of her argument suggests. Even the peacefulness of Poland's transition is not so obvious, as I argue in the next chapter. However, beyond the historical debate it produces, the eventful disposition also leads to a kind of historical and cultural sensitivity that transition elides, and without which nationalism's study cannot manage.

In one of the most systematic studies of nationalist violence within the lands of the former Soviet Union, Mark Beissinger explains patterns of violence between 1987 and 1992 with models inspired by social movement study.[66] He identifies different structural explanations for this violence, both in the institutional relationship among territories, states, and nationalities, and in the cycle of mobilization itself. Equally important, however, is the openness of his epistemology to the significance of the conjuncture, and to the potential residence of violence in peaceful, if conflicted, change.[67] Like other scholars, Beissinger studies conflict by distinguishing its modes or intensities.[68] In particular, he finds important relationships between nonviolent and violent conflict within cycles of mobilization. That very relationship suggests that within apparently peaceful conditions, the presence or absence of violence might be explained by a critical intervention, not by an abiding social condition, institutional configuration, or historical path.

Violence thus can lie beneath an apparent sea of calm. It might emerge when conflict management fails or when accidents happen. This potential for violence, of course, is not easy to read. It certainly cannot be found in superficial appropriations of apparently peaceful cultures, or in histories that rely on the liberal path apparently taken. Instead of a theory of history focused on those variations produced by different policies and corresponding elites, this history depends on an inquiry that reads deeply into cultural formations and strategic encounters to recognize alternatives not taken. What might have enabled Yugoslavia's road to be more peaceful? What could have happened to make the end to communism in Poland, and perhaps by contagion elsewhere, violent? And what beyond the march to liberal markets and democracy could the end to communism have produced? This imagining of alternatives not only encourages us to problematize what is seen as necessary in the making of transition, but also enables us to read into the past different possibilities for the future, and different meanings of the contemporary. That, of course, produces a contentious scholarship that itself depends on a deep contextual competence to recognize what could have otherwise been, and what still might be.[69]

Postcommunist Contentions

Bunce's contextual expertise draws her to the complications of historical interpretation that transition culture typically overlooks. She emphasizes that history is by no means linear, and that violent conflict and coexistence are both part of the past of Yugoslavia, Czechoslovakia, and the Soviet Union.[70] Like Williams, she argues that history is "subject to constant and contested interpretations,"[71] but it is not only a matter of asking how politicians and others use these partial histories. Academics do as well. Bunce is quite aware of that, and moves deftly among the contending interpretations of Yugoslavia's war, likely to no partisan's satisfaction. But when it comes to those less contentious histories, built on emancipation and transition's foundation, she notes no major disagreements.

Bunce's account of communism's peaceful end is part of transition culture itself, where a socialist past is discarded by a homogenized and cohesive public rising up to throw the bastards out. Although there may be relatively little contention in Poland's late-communist and post-communist history in comparison to that of Yugoslavia, that is itself partially the product of transition culture. Significant contentions are involved in understanding Poland's end to communism, but transition culture's focus on the future leads most to overlook those disputes in order to manage emergent problems, without necessarily resolving old ones. As I shall argue in chapter 1, the making of emancipation is far more eventful than transition culture typically allows. That eventfulness is also central to making a postcommunist critical sociology. But that sociology and its eventfulness depend on a reading of change that stands in the muck of history, rather than riding above it on transition's current.

One is much more likely to stand in the muck of history when engaging nationalism, for the study of nationalism necessarily engages deeply contentious accounts of nationalist encounters. One people's nationalism evokes another, which in turn inspires others. Rogers Brubaker builds on this notion and suggests that we consider the intersection of nationalizing states, national minorities, and external national homelands as the triadic configuration generating struggles. He recommends that we study each position in terms of Bourdieuian "fields" of activity, of "differentiated and competitive positions or stances" that encourage us to review contest within fields as much as between them.[72]

This approach to nationalism embraces contentiousness, for it invites us to recognize in nationalism studies their own implication in its practical reproduction. However, by segmenting nationalism from other cultural fields, this approach also resonates with the privilege of transition culture's position. This is especially evident in Brubaker's application to the Wars of Yugoslav Succession, in which he fails to consider how Slovenia's "liberalism" helps to explain the beginning of war.[73] For Serbs and others sympathetic to their readings of Yugoslavia's end, Slovene liberalism was certainly one form of nationalism. Alternatively, one might also look to the end of the Soviet Union itself, and consider whether the violence called "nationalist" could deserve other, or at least additional, adjectives. As Beissinger notes in his discussion of the violence attending the Sumgait pogrom in 1988, there was a wider range of motives in the killing of Armenians than Azerbaijani nationalism.[74]

To implicate transition in nationalism's violence threatens to embed liberalism in a cultural field that is more likely to be constructed by transition's socialist and nationalist critics than its liberal advocates, however. Although I am not comfortable in much of that company, these questions are critical to recognizing transition's own nationalism, or at least its cultural grounding, which is itself the precondition for realizing transition culture's reflexive potential. It also helps to compensate for that liberal temptation to segment culture from politics and economics, and from scholarship itself.

Even as she critiques transitology and recognizes Slovene liberalism as nationalism, Bunce nonetheless reproduces another vital element of transition culture. Her culture is primarily supplemental. It is historical symbols that might be manipulated by elites or might resonate with opportunities. It is dispositions that are shaped by national positions. It is preferences that are shaped by changing circumstances.[75] She recognizes and emphasizes the significance of being able to read context—institutional, historical, and cultural—for making game-theoretical kinds of explanations, acknowledging that these details are all subject to competing interpretations.[76] But she does not recognize, or at least articulate, the culture in which her own argument is made.

It is, after all, not only a matter of evidence that makes interpretations more or less fitting. Resonance of particular explanations with the expectations of hegemonic cultural formations is among the greatest determinants of what arguments can become compelling. For example, the clear distinction between international social science and the nationalism of others is critical to the viability of a transition culture cast from nowhere. And that is why its name appears oxymoronic. However, even if transition culture manages to escape any nation's accent, it winds up shaping explanation and interventions in its own image, even when scholars argue against it. To offer the socialist critique, or to lead the nationalist charge, merely confirms that the intervention does not belong in transition culture's authoritative field. Although Bunce is liberal with her distribution of nationalisms, and implies a socialist sympathy, she does reproduce the power of the panoptic on which transition culture rests.

Apart from her location in the debate over area studies, Bunce does not make her own location in historical or national contentions evident. Her arguments about socialism and its collapse challenge transition culture's limited attention to the past, but they mainly serve as a complement. They suggest that design is important not only in capitalist but also in socialist institutions, and that detail enhances the capacity to design and understand the impacts of design. Transition culture should be able to absorb that point. It also should be able to absorb the significance of opportunities for affecting the speed of change. What might be more difficult, however, is that designs are more polyvalent than designers expect, and that cultural formations have more possibilities than transition culture leads us to recognize, either in the future or in the past. Katherine Verdery's *What Was Socialism and What Comes Next?* is quite helpful in that vein.

As her title implies, Verdery begins with questions about the nature of this socialism to be discarded and its intended sequel. She writes, "'privatization,' 'markets,' 'civil society' and so on are objects of investigation saturated with ideological significance; we must question rather than mindlessly reinforce them," and interpret these things through the lens not only of those who apply them but of those who experience them on the ground.[77] Like Bunce, she emphasizes the significance of knowing what socialism was to understand what comes next. For instance, understanding how competition among the authorities worked under socialism helps actors expect similar contests in the implementation of various privatization schemes. Her arguments about the way in which liberalism and civil society necessarily articulate with different nations and sensibilities of nationalism work along the same lines of argument I attempt in chapters 4, 5, and 6. Her other themes on gender, time, the elasticity of land, and the magic of money are addressed better in more specific arguments. However, her final chapter and overall viewpoint mark an important difference from this volume.

In contrast to Bunce, who in arguing against transitology none-theless occupies its panoptic position, Verdery grounds her writing in the people among whom she works. She stands in their stream of history. Although she does have her village, she moves beyond anthropology's stereotype. She also has written ethnographies of the state, of the courts, and of the very sites of transition themselves. But, like many anthropologists, she represents foreigners, outsiders, in their least competent manifestations. Their stories

> present socialism—quite contrary to its own evolutionist pretensions—as not the endpoint of human social development but a dead end on the far more progressive road to capitalism, to which they must now be recalled. This rescue scenario has two common variants: "shock therapy" and "big bang." The first compares the former socialist bloc with a person suffering from mental illness—that is, socialism drove them crazy, and our job is to restore their sanity. The second implies (*pace* Fukuyama) history is only now beginning, that prior to 1989 the area was without form and void. While the image of "shock therapy" represents Western advisers as doctors, the "big bang" figures them as God. (204–5)

To be sure, these images are distressing, and, as I shall argue, they are present. And they can lead to misrecognition, especially in those sites beyond East Central Europe and its urban lands where Western dispositions find easiest application. But it is misleading to present them as wholly exogenous to the postcommunist world, or as wholly misguided in shaping history. Medical and religious missions are powerful narratives with which to restructure societies in need of radical change. As the representatives of transition culture are wont to say, those who have followed the prescription of the radicals in transition culture are those who have fared best in making their worlds better. And those who make this case best are not only from the West, but are those who know how to speak both the languages of the nation and of transition culture.

Verdery prefers "an image that denies the notion of a progress . . . and purposely mocks the very idea of evolutionary stages" (205). Using feudalism as her metaphor, she focuses on the parcellization of sovereignty over the state's assets. It enables her to focus on who gets what and why, to use Gerhard Lenski's key question for studies of stratification.[78] This metaphor allows both the state and the Mafia to become central objects for study, rather than ones that get in the way of analyzing, and conducting, transition. But while this image denies progress, it also puts Verdery in a stream that takes her outside the more consequential agencies shaping change. With this language, she very effectively marks areas of major concern for everyday life, but it also means that she must stand with Burawoy and others who would rather remain in opposition to those who would shape transition.

Critical Transition Culture

Although my own scholarship has been powerfully shaped by all of the authors discussed in the preceding section, this volume's principal concerns are informed by the tradition of critical sociology described earlier. I value the engagement of scholarship with the practical world. In this sense, I share an important intellectual ancestry with marxist colleagues such as Michael Burawoy, whose scholarship highlights everyone's political edge. I am substantively closer, however, to the particular focus on the intelligentsia and the new class arguments made by Iván Szelényi, Alvin Gouldner, Zygmunt Bauman, and others.

Broader social movements associated with the working class and other popular forces were plausibly the principal agents of history during late communism, but in the first decade after communism's collapse that historical agency clearly lies among elites within nations and across them who design postcommunist institutions. Intellectuals have been at that core of such interventions. I appreciate the ways in which these agents of transition culture have used scholarship to guide social change, and the ways in which their institutionalist critics have encouraged us to move beyond the teleological reasoning that designer capitalism generates. To work among these elites and engage their culture, as David Stark, László Bruszt, and others have, is to stand in the stream of postcommunist history, even if it is a different kind of history. This is a history made in variations and not alternatives, guided by a sense of accommodation to necessity rather than of the fulfillment of hope. But this history is itself a cultural construction. It reproduces the sense of liberal destiny in guiding postcommunism's trajectory, and of adapting to a world that is not of anyone's making, which then, in turn, requires no cultural explanation. Such a historicity is certainly not compatible with the kind of sociology that recognizes the challenge of difference and acknowledges the value of theory that is irreducible to facts.

Bunce's historicity is a very important corrective to transition culture's predisposition toward historical ignorance. But path analysis and soft institutional determinism hardly challenge that sense of transition as a necessary course, rather than a cultural construction, in the making of desirable futures. Bunce certainly recognizes the importance of opportunity in shaping the timing of socialism's end, but her historical institutionalism poses few, if any, real alternatives or consequential contingencies. In this, her challenge to transitology becomes its invaluable institutional complement rather than its critical alternative. Beissinger's focus on cycles of nationalism and violence in making social change in the Soviet Union's end is more eventful, and more suggestive of the kind of historicity that underlies much of critical sociology. His work encourages us to see the eventfulness of that end, and the radical alternatives—in peaceful and violent confrontation— embedded within it. By treating communism's *peaceful* collapse as itself contingent, one is encouraged to revisit the inevitability of transition as communism's sequel, and of liberalism as communism's and nationalism's obvious antagonist.

Both Bunce and Beissinger highlight the lability of these cultural categories, even while transition culture depends on their categorical distinctions. Verdery pushes this cultural analysis further with her interest in understanding the pervasiveness and power of transition's key concepts. This approach to culture is especially important in the reading of political opportunity structures, for it enables us to appreciate that not only institutions, but also the discursive structures cutting across them, shape our sense of inevitability and possibility.[79] Socialism's end depended not only on the exhaustion of a system, but also on its cultural recognition, and agreement among antagonists. Its peaceful conclusion depended on the capacity of representatives of the future and of the past to reach accord on the conditions and trajectory of system change. A history organized around systemic exhaustion diminishes that sense of alternativity highlighted in recognizing the achievement of agreement. But agreement is itself remarkable given the polysemy of its key terms.

Transition culture depends on the simple translation of its key concepts, so that debates about how to realize competitive markets and democratic consolidation can proceed. Participation in transition culture requires accommodation to that common understanding, even when those basic ideas are themselves contested and filled with alternative meanings. It also requires that one embrace a certain panoptic disposition to explain why transition is necessary and good, even as one argues from a specific position and uses that location to enhance the generality of the argument. In this sense, transition culture aspires to be less hermeneutic than it tries to be universal. Its comparisons are shaped more by variation on a general theme than by the recognition of differences whose commensurability is in question. Whereas Bunce clearly works with this sense of comparison in her account of socialism's end and sequels, Verdery elevates the challenge of difference, and with it, the importance of recognizing her own location in the course of transition, and in Romania.[80]

Ethnography more easily resonates with a critical sociology that locates itself within and across cultures, while broader comparative studies like that undertaken by Bunce and Beissinger appear, of necessity, to occupy a stance beyond those places and times. These comparative studies, however, can address more explicitly that sense of radical contingency that an eventful sociology highlights, for their work can bring to the fore those alternative possibilities realized in other places that transition culture articulates within its own general theme. Burawoy's unbound ethnography aspires to similarly broad comparative themes by embedding its scholarship in a clearly marxist tradition of inquiry.[81] One might also, however, ground that critical spirit within transition culture itself, and practice an immanent, rather than socialist, critical sociology. In such a fashion, one can bring the broader scope of transition culture's vision together with a reflexive tradition of inquiry that recognizes the challenge of difference, and the importance of extending cultural formations to meet those events, or those locations, that do not simply fit. One can unbound ethnography within transition culture itself, and identify its potentials buried in practice and promise. With this volume, I propose just such a *critical transition culture.*

Each of the following chapters has its own intellectual biography, but each contributes to the critical elaboration of transition culture. Although not every chapter is so eventful in its reasoning, each one also relies on a particular comparative strategy. In chapter 1, I focus more on a historical comparative method to illuminate the alternative paths and mutual dependencies of change in Gorbachev's *perestroika*, Poland, and Hungary. I also develop a broader theoretical comparison, by contrasting the culture of emancipation to that of this transition I have just described. I continue that comparison of metanarratives in chapter 2, where I compare the structure of transition culture with the structure of approaches that emphasize poverty rather than opportunity. In chapter 3, I compare the structure of transition culture with its practice, and compare the various understandings East European managers and Western advisers bring to the making of transition within firms. Chapters 4 and 5 elaborate the comparison among focus groups in Estonia and Ukraine, considering not only national differences, but their locations within the framework of transition culture itself as an important basis for comparison. In chapter 6, I turn to the radically dissimilar—the Wars of Yugoslav Succession—in order to explore how they might more fruitfully be brought into the framework of transition culture itself.

In each of these efforts, my analysis seeks neither the demonstration of theory nor the macrocausal analysis of a limited set of cases to explain a particular outcome. Instead, I contrast contexts of social change in order to reconstruct the integrity of the cultural formations of postcommunism on which the technologies of transition work, aiming to extend the capacities of transition culture to recognize its own limitations and broader possibilities.[82] In the Conclusion, I reconsider the meanings and potentials of transition culture by focusing on its labilities in articulation with the nation and with practice, as well as with the possibilities of locating a concern with poverty and freedom in its emancipatory potential. Here, in the end, I theorize self-consciously from within the stream of transition's history rather than outside of it,[83] with the hopes that transition culture might realize its emancipatory potentials rather than stimulate its barbaric alternatives. But this grounding in critical transition culture requires some explanation.

The starting point for any sociology, according to Bourdieu, is in its own sociology: "all the propositions that this science enunciates can and must be applied to the subject who practices the science."[84] Only by understanding the rules, interests, and stakes of the intellectual field can sociology, or any other social science, begin to acquire the autonomy that science requires. Through that autonomy, Bourdieu suggests, sociologists have the potential to become the agent through which the whole of society can reflect on itself.

A good deal of scholarship presumes the view from nowhere. Indeed, this book is possible only because I presume to discuss postcommunism's cultural formations in general, and in distinction from one another. The sense of an international culture, or scholarship, is remarkably useful in this presumption, for it hides the networks that shape the cases and questions of scholarship.[85]

Were I to continue in that mode, I should begin with the historical riddle I seek to explain, and define the universe of my potential cases. They refer most obviously to those places once ruled by communist parties with dictatorial powers, but whose authorities and publics now struggle to introduce more democratic institutions and market economies. Contiguity is important, however. Even if Cuba initiates its transition by the time of this book's publication, I would not presume to make its experience central to this volume. Nor are China, North Korea, or Vietnam part of this exploration, even though many consider China to have developed a powerful alternative model for what ought to be transition. However, democracy is too important to the critical ambitions of this volume.

After establishing the field, I should then provide the abstract rationale for the selection of the cases that merit the most consideration in this volume—Poland, Hungary, Estonia, Ukraine, and the former Yugoslavia. For instance, I should lead with the contrast between Poland and Yugoslavia if I wanted to explain how ten years of political instability can lead to either peaceful or violent change in communism's collapse. If I wished to compare instances of violent and peaceful dissolutions of federal states, I should compare Yugoslavia with Czechoslovakia and the Soviet Union.[86]

This volume is not organized around any particular historical riddle, however. Instead, I seek to elaborate the general contours and critical potentials of transition culture, and to explore some of the ways in which this culture is transformed across sites in varying proximity to its core.

Poland and Hungary are among the nation-states with the greatest claims to this proximity, given that they are the historical leaders in the emancipation from communism. In general, the formally independent states of Eastern Europe have been closer to the core of transition culture, given that they enjoyed sovereign political infrastructures that the Soviet Socialist Republics lacked. Moreover, some of these states had experience with significant economic reform—notably Poland, Hungary, and Yugoslavia—relatively lacking in other communist-led states. Nevertheless, within the post-Soviet world, there has been considerable variation in terms of success within transition culture—with

Estonia among the most successful, and Ukraine among the least. Yugoslavia is, in some ways, off the map. It is rarely discussed in terms of transition, but rather in terms of war and nationalism. And that is why I find it especially important to include in a study of transition culture's contours and labilities. Russia is a case in and of itself. Not only does its military potential give it a capacity to alter transition culture in ways smaller states cannot, but its position as a regional hegemon makes its nationalism different from those of the smaller states around it. It serves as the cultural other with which the tale of transition is being written. But although these are appropriate post hoc reasons, my choice of cases for this exploration begins with a different starting point.

I have chosen these cases not only because they fit into a meaningful continuum across the range of transition culture, but also because I have worked, to varying degrees, with people engaged in these regions, whether as respondents, scholars, or political actors. I have tested my arguments about transition culture not only against data, but also in interaction with people who have informed, and transformed, my sense of transition culture while living through transition itself. These networks should not remain invisible, therefore. They are, rather, formative to this volume.

My greatest contextual expertise in the region rests in Poland, but I am not a Pole, nor even a member of its diaspora, much less one of those hybrid intellectuals about whom Homi Bhabha speaks.[87] I suffer for that, for I do not have that stock of knowledge one acquires by growing up within a national culture and digesting its assumptions. Nevertheless, my engagement with Poland dates from my study of the Solidarity movement of 1980–81, and my abiding interest in emancipatory praxis.[88] I wrote the first version of chapter 1 in the moment of emancipation itself, in the summer of 1989. It has been revised many times subsequently, reflecting my own growing distance from a full identification with the emancipatory praxis of Solidarity itself, toward a more "in-between" position, in between Solidarity and the communists. In fact, I have a sense that I am becoming something like Georg Simmel's stranger, familiar with these different positions but no longer so identifiable with any of them.[89] Being such a stranger poses certain limitations, but it also enables an unusual distance from this Polish history, enabling me to write about the end to communism in ways that others, and even myself a decade ago, could not manage. Writing about Hungary involves even greater distance, even as it makes me more familiar to mainstreams in sociology.

Much of sociology's comfort with historical sociology comes when comparative figures the whole approach. With the comparative label, one can refine sociological orientations in a number of ways, through the parallel demonstration of theory, contrast of contexts, macro-causal analysis, their various permutations, and still other methods.[90] In the first version of the essay on emancipation, I built on that disciplinary practice and sought to contrast the similar roles but different practices of intellectuals and civil society in these two leading stories of emancipation from communism. It also helped that the Hungarian transformation was so well developed in the literature, and that experts on Hungary are prominent in the area studies network in which I have worked.

Despite the apparent symmetry, this was not an evenhanded comparison. I wrote about Hungary from a distance my lack of Hungarian language and reliance on secondary materials imposed. I could not engage the same level of historiographical disputes that my Polish grounding allowed. This lack is generally not as problematic in sociology as it is in area studies or history, for sociology's focus is generally in the comparison of cases, and not the interrogation of contending histories within a single case. This sociological viewpoint encourages a broader regional explanation and more compelling general argument about the ways in which intellectuals and the culture of civil society structured the emancipation of 1989. But it also comes much closer to that panoptic view that international social science frequently claims to occupy, and on which transition culture itself tends to rely.

My analysis of transition culture's structure in chapter 2 plays in that very terrain, where I write from a position that claims only to analyze the artifacts and elaborate their underlying codes. This reading is, however, grounded in my distance from a generalizing transnational disposition that finds little to be lamented in the lack of knowledge about the language, culture, or history of an area of study. My concerns will be apparent when I highlight the tacit knowledge about culture and nations on which so much "hard" social science rests. It becomes even more apparent in chapter 3, where I return to that more familiar position of a stranger.

In the world of transition culture, I am clearly in between. I am between East European managers and Western business experts, for I am familiar with East European and especially Polish life-worlds, but I am American. I am familiar with the American cultural schema, and its business projections to a lesser degree. My years of association with the William Davidson Institute at the University of Michigan Business School and the broader community of business experts who have worked in Eastern Europe have made me increasingly familiar with the habitus of business experts. Their substantial activity in Poland in the first half of the 1990s made my Polish grounding all the more useful.

Were this volume to rest in Poland and its East Central European neighbors, my choice of cases would not require much explanation. Sociologists rarely justify their home nation as the object of study, and area specialists in particular nations can take their investment in contextual expertise as the point of departure. But broader comparisons require more substantial attention, especially when extending from Poland to Estonia, Ukraine and the lands of the former Yugoslavia, and not to Russia.

I was drawn toward Estonia and Ukraine (and Uzbekistan) by the opportunity to work with scholars from those regions, and experts on those regions from my own university, when we were awarded a grant to study identity and social problems in those three sites.[91] The terms of the grant structured the comparison—it could support research in any part or parts of the former Soviet Union *outside of Russia*. Our choice of sites was grounded in the array of area expertise we had at the University of Michigan. With those contexts in mind, we sought the rationale for their comparison. Contiguous comparisons are often the most sensible, and familiar, for identifying critical differences in otherwise broadly similar cases. We instead developed a project that focused on one critical similarity—transition from Soviet rule—and sought other forms of similarity across radically dissimilar sites. To what extent would the identity project and social problems articulated in the smallest and most successful (from the point of view of transition culture) post-Soviet state, Estonia, be similar to the second-largest, and economically troubled, Ukraine? In this volume, that project framing has posed most useful, for it has allowed me to move beyond the East Central European terrain with which I am most familiar, and the sets of conversations about Europe and Russia that are frequently implied in them. Moving to Estonia and Ukraine, and especially engaging those who have lost something with the end of the

Soviet Union, is an important complement to an East Central European disposition on cultural formations of postcommunism. My draw to Yugoslavia was quite different.

During my research in Poland in 1983 and 1984, I spent one month in Yugoslavia. While there, I attended one of the conferences organized by the New School for Social Research and the Praxis group. Yugoslavia seemed, at the time, a marvelous alternative to Poland. Its official intellectual world was more open, both culturally and intellectually. Its attempt to deal with a struggling economy seemed far more innovative. Yugoslavia appeared to offer great promise. My scholarly attention drifted away from Yugoslavia as the promise of Polish social change grew, but war's eruption in Yugoslavia drew me back. The wars erected a distance from transition that the mid-1980s would have denied if futures were always smooth extensions of the present. A growing number of scholars, both with contextual expertise and not, have invested in an explanation of this turn away from transition. But they rarely undertake this effort within the context of transition culture. Given the emphasis of my colleagues at the University of Michigan, and the importance of examining that which is overlooked, or repressed, in the elaboration of any cultural formation, the Wars of Yugoslav Succession became an obvious case to consider in developing critical transition culture.

Russia is another obvious case. Its absence as a distinct case from this volume is a product of the history of my own intellectual collaborations, but something deeper too. Transition culture has a deeply troubled relationship to Russia, and is in some ways defined against it. As I shall demonstrate in my discussion of the Wars of Yugoslav Succession, transition's relationship to the use of force is also complicated. Both the deployment and the threat of violence destabilize transition culture, and Russia's relationship to transition culture is based on the containment of its potential threat. I do not have the cultural capacity and analytical tools to explain how transition culture works in and around Russia. Nevertheless, one can see the shadow of Russia in transition culture's function across the rest of the region, as we shall see most clearly in discussions of Ukraine and Estonia. Nevertheless, I shall leave it to others to explain how the arguments about transition culture might be reinforced or transformed when Russia figures prominently in the cases, and the lens, with which the cultural formations of postcommunism are viewed.

There is a broader point to be made here, however, about the choice of cases and the place from which one writes. I write from a position that draws on my intellectual affinities with scholars in the United States and the University of Michigan, and my abiding and originating scholarly interests in Poland. I have had the good fortune to extend my range of cases, and spheres of expertise, through extraordinary collaborations over the past decade. Drawing on other cases could reframe the major arguments I make about transition culture. Writing out of Japan, Germany, or Turkey, or out of Vladivostok, Bukhara, or Gdańsk, could also suggest a very different account of transition culture. The context of inquiry, both from which and in which one engages transition, matters in both the interpretation of data and, especially, the character of questions. I attempt, in this volume, to make that grounding explicit, rather than hide it in the panoptic gaze of conventional international social science. But because I write from within the space I occupy, I can hardly make its own contours sufficiently clear. Hence, I need those who address this volume to read this work as someone might view one of Václav Havel's plays.[92] The work only realizes its goal when my attempt to ground transition culture in different spaces inspires readers and subsequent writers to revise my depiction of transition culture through their location in other spaces. That ambition reflects a different kind of science rooted less in a cumulation of findings than in the ever-widening hermeneutic circle that extends transition culture's meaning across sensibilities of social change and of social justice. Ultimately, therefore, I propose that transition culture's meaning change. Rather than a project of institutional change, critical transition culture should become a project of cultural transformation that affects as much the core of the vision as it does the periphery. To realize that ambition, however, one needs to reread 1989 from within that most ambitious of cultural formations: emancipation.

One

Emancipation and Civil Society

1989 is transition culture's genesis. At least it is its historical point of departure, but it is rarely its object of critical focus. When 1989 is addressed within transition culture, it is typically discussed in terms of pacts and negotiations on the way to capitalism and democracy. In this approach, analysts treat socialism as background, and focus rather on the strategies of radicals and reformers on both sides of the negotiating divide to maximize their interests in transition.[1] To rest, however, in a world of interests and choices without attending to the framework shaping preferences risks not only the theoretical power but also the interventionist consequence of transition culture. For Stark and Bruszt, Elster, Offe, and Preuss, and other institutional theorists, this means that analytical efforts should also focus on institutional designs and the historical paths that produced them.

Bunce takes this institutional mission directly to socialism's end. In fact, she goes beyond transition's path to explain the collapse of communist rule in and of itself. Nevertheless, she articulates transition culture's central premise with her theory of subversive institutions. These "systems were fated to end—whether in the 1960s or the 1980s" (142). Transition rests on socialism's fate. However, Bunce also goes beyond transition culture's assumption of socialism's unfeasibility by attending to the institutional environments, opportunity structures, and sequences of events that help to explain the collapse of communist rule.

Détente and the Helsinki Accords of 1975 made states directly implicated in the Cold War increasingly implicated in one another while it also increased the chances for socialism's *peaceful* end. "If the end (to socialism) had come in the 1960s," Bunce writes, "it would likely have led to a bloodbath" (ibid.). Instead, in 1980–81, the Polish opposition managed to mobilize civil society in Solidarity before a relatively weak communist regime indebted to Western bankers. Strikes in the summer of 1988 forced the hand of moderates in both the party and in Solidarity to negotiate a new arrangement of power that would allow the introduction of more radical political and economic reform. Hungary, with a regime even more fiscally indebted, but with a society less mobilized, followed Poland's example after seeing Gorbachev support the change in Poland and remain in power (66–70). This sequence bestowed certain demonstration and diffusion effects on the more closed socialisms around them, leading to the system's collapse across the region (133).

Bunce therefore recognizes the significance of events, but none of the events that are crucial to her story challenge the determinism she is able to draw from her confluent account of subversive institutions and political opportunities. For the most part, events speed up social change, or slow it down, but do not transform the logic of causal factors.[2] Events play into a narrative of historical necessity reinforced by public will. It is difficult, however, to articulate such a tale of necessity with an eventful sociology.

Bunce's interest in opportunity structures leads her to just such an eventful sociology. She argues that expanded opportunity structures redefine resources, groups, and sensibilities of what is and is not possible.[3] Sometimes she even poses events and sequence as potentially altering the course of history. She wonders whether the Yugoslav state might have survived if all-Yugoslav elections had preceded republican ones in 1991, and whether the Czechoslovak state might have survived if a new constitution had been in place before dissolution took off (14). But these reflections do not alter the weight of subversive institutions in her analytical narrative because possibilities are principally a distraction from a social science focused on explaining the institutionally configured path toward socialism's end. Such a tale, in which socialism produced reformist elites and an increasingly cohesive public that together ended an obviously anachronistic system, is a vital element of transition culture's tradition.

Raymond Williams describes tradition in general as "an intentionally selective version of a shaping past and a pre-shaped present."[4] Accounts focusing on socialism's end can work as tradition for transition culture when institutional practices and social relations are read as transition's prequel. To a considerable extent this makes sense, for those ending socialism themselves anticipated making broader markets and democracy. But they also expected more, and less. Many expected a future of broader empowerment and recognition for civil society. Most did not expect socialism's cataclysmic end. And few recognized what they had accomplished in practice, and modeled for the future.

One might thus change the meaning of 1989 if one views it with a lens ground to view something other than transition's tradition. If, instead, one works with hermeneutic sensibilities dedicated to the expansion of meaning and the recognition of historical possibilities, 1989 becomes central to the constitution of a critical transition culture with eventfulness, contention, and narratives beyond or diminished by transition culture at its empirical heart, and peace and the negotiation of difference at its theoretical edge.[5] But that analytical mission also requires 1989's retelling.

In what follows, rather than focusing on either rationally choosing pact negotiators or subversive institutions fixed on socialism's end and transition's destination, I propose to focus on those who constituted civil society as the subject of history and spokesman for transition's necessity. Not only does this focus on intellectuals and their culture of critical discourse do greater justice to contemporary debates and strategies over communism's *negotiated* collapse, but it also enables us to recognize important contributions that 1989 has made to the culture of emancipation and the possibilities of a critical transition culture.

Emancipation Culture

Solidarity's struggle against communist rule in Poland during the 1980s can be understood as emancipatory praxis. This analytical frame allows one to embed the strategies, resources, and normative penumbrae of a social movement within a larger narrative of struggle for freedom and human self-realization.[6] The emancipation of Eastern Europe in

1989 was not, however, so obviously a direct and intended consequence of this praxis, nor was it so obviously consonant with the main trends of revolutionary culture. It is, however, critically important to consider the making of 1989 within the culture of emancipation.

Emancipation has been understood as a double transformation for the oppressed—"from the position of presociological and prepolitical persons to become sociological and political actors, and in the creation of new options, based on rights, for them."[7] Emancipation of Jews, of Russian serfs, and of slaves made from the African slave trade was implicated in a larger politics of liberalizing modernization, where arguments over the rational and modern state guided a variety of legal transformations to produce emancipation.[8] To be sure, there was a popular movement in nineteenth-century Russia advocating the abolition of serfdom, but the final initiative came from Tsar Alexander II himself in 1861. And the Emancipation Proclamation of American president Abraham Lincoln was itself timed more by the effort to preserve the Union in Civil War than it was moved by the arguments of abolitionists. Historically speaking, emancipation has been the by-product of other transformations and not solely the consequence of popular struggle. One might understand the emancipation of 1989 within this tradition of elite proclamations of freedom and empowerment in order that their societies get on a faster track of modernization.

Although emancipation has that historical reference, it also has a place in more recent, and more critical, theoretical traditions. Emancipation has been the normative principle underlying a great deal of critical social and cultural theory, most obviously in the Frankfurt School and in various types of feminist theory. It also has been the abiding goal of revolutionary and other radical movements. Emancipation is embedded in a culture of revolution that cuts across the French, Russian, and Chinese revolutions.[9] The normative centrality of equality, the legitimacy of violence, the sense of direction in history, and the unity of revolutionary purpose and agency are some of those elements that have animated revolutionary struggles against feudal and bourgeois society, and have given shape to our notion of emancipation. Moving beyond the liberal connotation, emancipation in marxist thought draws our attention toward "the manifold development of human powers and the bringing into being of a form of association worthy of human nature."[10] Conceiving of the possibility of this greater and postbourgeois emancipation enables the kind of fundamental critique offered by marxist and other radical theories.

The transformations of 1989–91 do not appear to have much in common with this marxist vision. Like the emancipation of the Jews from a religiously demarcated polity, the emancipation of civil society from a communist dictatorship over needs has been dedicated to the creation of rights that enable citizens to become more autonomous and critical.[11] Like Tsar Alexander II, Mikhail Gorbachev came to see constraints on public discussion and other freedoms as brakes on economic development, and he initiated a major reform from above to empower his empire's modernization. As in the United States in 1863, war has accompanied this emancipation from communist rule, but it has been relatively constrained geographically. Indeed, one of the striking points about this emancipation is how peaceful it has been.

Unlike earlier historical emancipations, the emancipation of 1989–91 resembles the conditions of proletarian emancipation in critical theory. This emancipation did not extend already-existing rights to an additional class of subjects. It was premised on the emancipation of an entire society from subjugation by a totalizing state. It was premised on the notion that nobody was free prior to it, and that a fundamental change had to be made in order to enable all to be free. It was also based on a discourse of recognizing popular empowerment, rather than a liberal vision of granting freedom. Indeed, instead of the grantors retaining authority, civil society's representatives were supposed to win power with a mandate to overturn the ancien régime.

The emancipation of Eastern Europe from communist rule is challenging, therefore, for a cultural formation of emancipation to absorb. On the one hand, it bears a strong affinity to those historical struggles for liberal and bourgeois rights in terms of both goals and actors enabling emancipation, and thus anticipates transition culture itself. On the other hand, its totalizing resistance to a totalizing state suggests a greater affinity for the marxist tradition it most explicitly rejects. It had a revolutionary subject with revolutionary aims but with an antirevolutionary strategy. But the most innovative part of this emancipation rests in the location of its agency.

Although civil society, in its various forms, might be conceived as the emancipatory agent, I would propose rather that the agent of emancipation was the intelligentsia, on all sides of the political barrier. This was no conspiracy, but the emergence of a kind of culture of critical discourse identified by Alvin Gouldner as that peculiar framework of intellectuals whose universality was real, if flawed. Gouldner's recognition of universality was based on his impression that the disposition of intellectuals "subverts all establishments, social limits, and privileges, including its own . . . [and] bears a culture of critical and careful discourse which is an historically emancipatory rationality."[12]

We can find in 1989–91 the effects of this culture of critical discourse where intellectuals on both sides of the communist divide emancipated civil society. Intellectuals acquired this authority by constituting a particular position for themselves in a discursively unified civil society existing in opposition to communist rule but nevertheless able to negotiate with those communists. And in turn, communists managed to find a way to justify their negotiation with civil society, and even find a way to convince the skeptics in their constituency that dialogue—the intellectuals' class disposition—was superior to the use of force in the maintenance of power.

This moment of *negotiated revolution* is critical for the cultural formation of emancipation. This revolution culminated in the formation of transition culture, where the struggle of freedom for all became principally a contest to empower the responsible. The ultimate promise of this particular emancipation and its aftermath is not, however, entirely clear. The contradictions and contingencies of transition remain particularly significant, a quality that tends to be hidden by transition's own cultural formation. I believe, however, that through the juxtaposition of emancipation with transition, and of their cultural formations with each other, we might identify more clearly the potentials, and dangers, of this moment and the ensuing decade.

In this chapter, I make several cumulative points. First, I discuss the distinction of civil society as a core concept of emancipation culture. I argue further that some intellectuals in opposition to communism created a new form of civil society by suturing a wide range of practices into a common vision of opposition to communist rule. I turn next to a historical-sociological account of that articulation of civil society by elaborating the major initiatives in Hungary and Poland that motivated communism's collapse. I then consider the significance of Mikhail Gorbachev and his intellectual entourage in this emancipation. In particular, I argue that their international strategy of disarmament and European integration helped to create the conditions for East European emancipation through nonviolent Round Table agreements.

In this sense, civil society's emancipatory culture was not only about legality, publicity, and pluralism, but also about the value of negotiating difference peacefully. This particular cultural formation of emancipation was the product of the dialogical culture established by the articulation of civil society's intellectual representatives and intellectually engaged communist rulers seeking greater rationality and freedom through peaceful change. But all of this depends on the articulation of civil society.

Civil Society

Jean Cohen and Andrew Arato provide one of the most important foundations for the cultivation of a critical social theory of civil society. They begin with a working definition. Civil society is

> a sphere of social interaction between economy and state, composed above all of the intimate sphere (especially the family), the sphere of associations (especially voluntary associations), social movements and forms of public communication. Modern civil society is created through forms of self-constitution and self-mobilization. It is institutionalized and generalized through laws, and especially subjective rights, that stabilize social differentiation. While the self-creative and institutionalized dimensions can exist separately, in the long term both independent action and institutionalization are necessary for the reproduction of civil society.[13]

This is not the only definition of civil society. The ambiguities and transformations of civil society through translation, from *koinonia politike* through *die bürgerliche Gesellschaft,* are enormous, and complex. They have, however, typically been invoked in opposition to claims of unmediated glory, whether of the City of God, the state, or the state of nature.[14] In the struggle against communist rule and its occasional complement, and occasional antagonist, in nationalism, civil society's vision has emphasized several distinctions. It has articulated a different desirable end state, emphasizing the value of "differentiation" rather than the homogenization associated with either national or class-based liberation projects. Also, it has emphasized a different method for realizing change. Rather than revolutionary violence, again whether on the basis of national or class grounds, it has emphasized the importance of self-limitation and self-reflection.

However, like the great proletarian revolution, the agent of change was simultaneously the bearer of universality. Civil society, like the proletariat, should overthrow the system of domination and, in so doing, realize the conditions of its own immanent potential. Unlike the universal proletariat, however, civil society represented a different kind of utopia. It was already existing, in "normal" countries, and therefore it was "realistic."[15] It was a eutopic utopia.[16] Its reliance on a law-based framework could reinforce that imagined state of regularity that the proletarian-inspired politics of becoming under communist rule simply denied. Civil society thus can be understood as both the goal and the vehicle of emancipatory praxis, but one based on a self-limiting form of struggle, and a realistic vision of emancipation based on that which already exists elsewhere.

At the same time, of course, not only is civil society associated with the freedoms of capitalism, but it is also associated with its injustices, those forms of exploitation or oppression organized around class, race, gender, sexual orientation, repressive technology, and other axes of domination.[17] In those societies where civil society is taken for granted, its fundamental value can be forgotten. When communities are decimated by the freedom of corporations to relocate jobs and investment, civil society hardly seems central to the debate about social justice. When violence against women appears to emanate from within the intimate sphere itself, the value of preserving that boundary between public and private hardly seems sensible. When the civil rights movement must appeal to the state to end discriminatory hiring practices, civil society hardly seems to deserve protection from the intrusion of a reforming state. When core civic institutions prohibit gay men and lesbians from participation, the state may be the only recourse to justice. When civil society treats the biophysical environment only as a resource to be exploited rather than as part of human life that needs to be nurtured, legality, publicity, and pluralism hardly inspire.

This litany of injustice does not elevate civil society to the center of emancipatory praxis or critical social theory. Its normative penumbrae in the United States are rather, taken for granted, or more recently, associated with a critique of the interventionist state and bureaucratic government. It is not part of a critical discourse associated with emancipation. Instead of civil society, identity and difference tend to assume center stage in cultural studies and much of critical theory. Some of the most fruitful work in critical social theory has been, however, in search of the engagement between the integrating visions of civil society and the emphases on difference in identity projects.[18]

When integration lies alongside difference in the elaboration of critical theory, socialist traditions are not far from the center. When societal totalities, and not only escapes to freedom,[19] articulate visions of hope, socialism retains its position as capitalism's historic, and principal, counterculture.[20] The relationship between socialism and civil society remains, therefore, one of the most important articulations to clarify when emancipation animates social theory and social change. With such a charge, Eastern Europe itself becomes core to critical social theory, and the normative penumbrae of both civil society and socialism central to the sociological enterprise.

Where socialism is an ontologically absent, and only an epistemologically structuring desire, the significance of civil society is less likely to be recognized or appreciated. In Eastern Europe, where socialism has been a lived experience, the opposition between socialism and civil society structures the imagination of alternatives.[21] Even after communism's collapse and only in the shadow of monopolistic communist rule, civil society remains the foundation of emancipation.[22] Ernest Gellner articulates this opposition very clearly.[23] For Gellner, socialism was not, and cannot be, emancipation:

> The unification of the economy in one single organization and its fusion with the political and ideological hierarchy is not merely most inefficient: it also inevitably leads to both totalitarianism and humbug. In an industrial society, full socialism cannot but be totalitarian—and totalitarianism cannot but be socialist. To allow an independent economic zone is to leave an enormous breach in the authoritarian system, given the importance of the economy. To deprive civil society of an independent economic base is to throttle it, given the inevitability of political centralization. (164)

Gellner's first concern is pluralism (167). Of course, there must be political constraints put on the economy (170), but these political controls must be balanced by "an autonomous set of production units" (ibid.). Pluralism also should exist within a desanctified ideological order, where no one vision is unassailable. Positions of power should not be the most lucrative in society; rather, these should be found in the economic sector. And individuals should be modular—acquiring and disposing of identities as interactions demand, within a basic nationalist frame where all speak some kind of common language and have a common ideological referent. These are the preconditions for democracy, Gellner argues, and, one might say, by extension, for emancipation (189).

Although Ernest Gellner lived for years in the West, his roots in East Central Europe are apparent in his theoretical imagination. He is part of that imagined community of East Central European intellectuals who struggled to develop civil society not only as normative preference but also as a political option for emancipatory politics in the 1970s and 1980s. After all, civil society was not just a philosophical alternative to the kind of socialism that communist parties produced. It became the emancipatory vision of social transformation. For this vision of civil society to become consequential, however, it had to become embedded in social relations and transformative practices. This was the work of intellectuals, who were themselves the primary symbols of civil society in practice and in opposition to communism.

Not every society had prominent figures like Poland's Adam Michnik, Russia's Andrey Sakharov, Czechoslovakia's Václav Havel, and Hungary's János Kis, but at some level, there were always public figures in the anticommunist opposition who would claim civil society as their ideology.[24] There were some opposition intellectuals, somewhere, speaking the rhetoric of civil society—democracy, public sphere, rule of law, and so on—on behalf of the nation either within the country or abroad. Their identity with the opposition did not come, however, with the articulation of these themes. The construction of intellectuals and civil society as opposition depended on *where* these themes were articulated, whether their authors expressed them in an alternative public sphere understood as samizdat, the parallel polis or second society, or, in late communism, in a relatively "independent" press. The power of their words was elevated to the extent that the international public sphere, articulated through foreign governments, nongovernmental organizations, and the international press, would recognize their position as a defender of human rights and civil society.[25]

More infrequently, one could find social movements that articulated and embodied these ideals of civil society. Solidarity, from its 1980 inception through most of the 1980s, associated itself through its spokespersons with the articulation of civil society.[26] Slovene social movements were even more clearly associated with this dimension of democracy's celebration. They approximated the archetypal New Social Movement more than anywhere else in Eastern Europe.[27] Although not organized as social movements per se, mass demonstrations were also expressions of this civil society in opposition to communism, and were much more widely dispersed throughout the region.

The demonstrators' self-restraint and peaceful nature suggested a disposition of compromise that many took to be associated with democracy itself. The Hungarian demonstration of March 15, 1988, was exemplary in this regard, as were the "singing revolutions" in the Baltic republics in the late 1980s, and the East German demonstrations of the fall of 1989.[28] Commentators were disposed to put the civil society label on these demonstrations relatively readily.[29] In particular, they could compare these peaceful demonstrations to earlier protests that were associated with violence against party buildings, as in 1956 in Poznań or in 1970 on the Baltic coast in Poland, or against party members, as in the Hungarian revolution of 1956.

The economic side of the civil society argument was more complicated. On the one hand, the second or informal economy was even taken as evidence of a nascent civil society. Liberal commentators especially took this as evidence of at least the Lockean version of civil society, demonstrating that people could organize economic activities independent of the state.[30] Hungary was particularly celebrated in this regard.[31] More difficult for civil society theorists, or proponents, as the two were often mixed, were the labor movements. Of course, not all labor protests or movements were associated with the building of democracy, and especially of civil society's principles. As with most things in Romania, the labor protests in the Jiu Valley were difficult to identify as evidence of civil society's potential.[32] The only independent trade union of note in Hungary's transformation was one of scientific workers, although it was explicitly aligned with civil society rhetoric.[33] Solidarity was perhaps least difficult to align with civil society, given that it was not only a labor movement, but self-consciously a movement for democracy.[34] And, at least in 1989, the miners in eastern Ukraine and western Siberia were protesting not only on behalf of greater benefits for themselves, but also for more independence in economic activities, lending some credence to a civil society emphasis on economic activity.[35] For the most part, however, labor issues were left out of the rhetoric of the civil society project. In retrospect, one might suggest that it was a strategic omission, given the subsequent importance of economic liberalism. Nevertheless, one should not fail to recognize that, in some places, an independent labor movement was part and parcel of the emancipation associated with civil society.

The more obviously troubling element for civil society theorists and advocates was nationalism. Today it is an almost boring convention to compare nationalists and democrats, advocates of the nation with advocates of the rule of law, proponents of collectivism and proponents of individualism. But during the opposition to communism, civil society advocates tended to assimilate nationalisms. Of course, some nationalisms were always held at arms length—especially those propagated by xenophobic and fascist organizations. But if one looks at the rhetoric of the dominant national movements—Rukh in Ukraine, the popular fronts in the Baltic states, Solidarity in Poland, the Hungarian Democratic Forum—one finds a remarkable synthesis of emphases on both the nation and democracy. In cases where the modal synthesis was rather between nationalism and fascism, or nationalism and communism, as in Serbia, Russia, and Romania, democratically oriented national expressions seemed all the more compatible with civil society.[36]

As a cultural formation in opposition to communism, therefore, the intellectuals' articulation of civil society could draw on a number of social phenomena as evidence of civil society's vitality—social movements, mass demonstrations, the second economy, "democratic" nationalism, and the discourse of civil society itself in alternative or independent media. The power of this civil society depended, therefore, on the capacity of opposition intellectuals to unify, discursively, these various conditions, and to claim implicitly, through their representation, the right and capacity to articulate civil society's needs, wishes, or interests.

The proliferation of civil society's expressions, and of intellectuals' capacities to represent them, varied across societies. Poland was, across the board, the most "developed" in its expression of civil society; Hungary was not so developed on the broad social movement side, and certainly not so much in the labor movement, but its second economy and intellectual opposition were among the most developed. East Germany had an important network of opposition figures organized around churches. Czechoslovakia, especially the Czech part, had its prominent dissidents, but little else. Bulgaria had little in any regard, and Romania and Albania less, until 1990. The republics in the former Yugoslavia differed considerably, but Slovenia was clearly associated with the most developed civil society formation in terms of movements and communist leadership.[37] Within the Soviet Union, the Baltic states and Armenia had the most vibrant movement-based civil society, while the intellectuals in Moscow, and later in other centers, also became more visible and consequential in the development of a civil society alternative.

Although civil society was thus a cultural formation in opposition to communist rule, it was also a cultural formation shaped by, and enabled by, communists. It was difficult to appreciate this quality at the time of struggle, but in retrospect, the communists' restraint and inclination toward compromise with representatives of civil society marked the most pioneering and consequential of transitions in Poland, Hungary, Slovenia, and the Soviet Union itself. Of course, one would not look to Nicolae Ceauşescu, Erich Honecker, or Slobodan Milošević, but various commentators emphasized the increasing reasonableness of communist leaders, whether Gorbachev, the liberal wing in Hungary, or even Jaruzelski in Poland.[38] If they could compromise, then the possibility for a civil society transformation, one based on the rule of law itself, was ever so much greater. This kind of legal revolution was thus possible only because the authorities themselves wanted it, even if it was clearly intended to strengthen rather than weaken the Communist Party's position in the new society.[39] In some places, civil society clearly took the lead, but in Hungary and Poland, at least, the power of civil society rested in the willingness of communist leaders to negotiate with it. In the Soviet Union, by contrast, Gorbachev's direction was not derived from the mobilization of civil society, but rather from an initiative to recast the contest between capitalism and socialism. Regardless of the source of civil society's power, this cultural formation of emancipation from communist rule was made with the participation of communist leaders themselves.

Civil society was not just a social formation, but, significantly, a cultural formation. Within societies, and across them, the specter of civil society haunted communism as all of its manifestations were knit together in one emancipatory vision that ultimately would not be resisted. This unprecedented combination in part accounts for the power of civil society as emancipatory concept. Civil society gained counterhegemonic status because *intellectuals claimed that the variety of activities taken in opposition to communism were evidence of the incipient formation of civil society.* Their words became more than the profferings of intellectuals, not only because of the moral capital they acquired in their political oppression, but because they could claim to represent civil society in negotiations with communist authorities, a position reinforced by international media.[40] Of course, not all of the communist world would be drawn into the vision of civil society, and certainly that specter did not establish itself with the same strength in all places. However, civil society's vision was powerfully grounded in Hungary and Poland, and their struggles laid the foundation for the hegemony of civil society throughout the region.

The emancipation of Eastern Europe was an especially eventful politics. Polish struggles enabled the development of the first successful example of Round Table negotiations, concluded on April 5, 1989. The Hungarian authorities and opposition both learned from these Polish developments. The opposition formed the Opposition Round Table on March 22, 1989, approximating in Hungarian conditions that which proved successful for Polish Solidarity.[41] The Hungarian authorities also took the lead in some ways, especially in international relations. They tore down the barbed wire on their border with Austria on May 2, 1989, enabling East German citizens to escape to Western Europe. When the Hungarian authorities announced on September 11 that they would not repatriate refugees to their country of origin, East German citizens fled through Hungary for the West by the thousands.[42] The Polish electoral results of June 4, and the invitation to form a Solidarity-led government under Tadeusz Mazowiecki on August 24, 1989, dramatically expanded the notion of what was possible in Eastern Europe. Given the outcomes of the Polish negotiations, the Hungarian authorities themselves were moved to negotiate with the opposition. After inaugural speeches on June 13, the Hungarian authorities tried to use the Round Table to position themselves to win legitimacy through electoral means.

These democratic transformations in Poland and Hungary were not lost on the rest of the region. Emigration and demonstrations in East Germany during the fall led to the collapse of the Berlin Wall on November 9. Without hardline allies in Poland, Hungary, or East Germany, the Czechoslovak authorities were increasingly isolated, and the opposition felt increasingly empowered. Building on the examples of their neighbors, the opposition developed its own Civic Forum and negotiated its own revolution, culminating in the election of Václav Havel as president on December 29, 1989. In this context, Bulgarian authorities attempted their own *perestroika* from November 10 to December 14, which itself led to Round Table negotiations there in January of 1990. Romania's violent conflict between December 16 and 25, 1989, provided televised examples to the region, and to the world, of the violent alternative to communism's negotiated end. Keeping the transformation off the streets and at the negotiating table was a long-standing ambition even for the Poles and the Hungarians, who did not have the benefit of the Romanian counterexample. The initiatives of Poles and Hungarians provided the example for the peaceful transition of Eastern Europe, and the transformation of Eastern Europe provided the example for many in the Soviet Union who wished greater sovereignty for both nations and civil society.[43]

Intellectuals, Compromise, and Mobilization in Hungary and Poland

The principal agent articulating civil society as opposition was intellectuals—critical intellectuals. Their position, and their power, were themselves a kind of product of the Soviet-type system itself, however.

The Soviet-type system reinforced the prominence, already considerable before World War II, of the intelligentsia in Eastern Europe. As it enlarged the ranks of the intelligentsia with the expansion of higher education, it simultaneously made the *autonomous* intellectual scarce. As this kind of independence became a rarity, even an expression of bravery or cleverness, the value of the autonomous intellectual could be elevated in cultural politics.[44] Intellectuals, and their cultural products, could become even more consequential under communist rule than they were in precommunist times.[45]

Revisionism—the promise that the system could be reformed from within by working through the Communist Party—offered a marvelous strategy for the intellectual to redefine the communist project, and to elevate the intellectual's role in political authority. Although the revisionist hope was relatively universal across the communist world until the mid-1960s, two critical developments severely undermined it. After the repression of protests by students and intelligentsia in March 1968 in Poland, and especially after the Soviet-led invasion of Czechoslovakia later that year, many fewer critical intellectuals within the region, and in the world more generally, could find much hope in the transformation of Soviet-type society through the circulation of elites. In Poland, in particular, intellectuals became ever more clearly identified with opposition to communist rule, and it would be difficult, if not impossible, to describe intellectuals as being on the road to class power.[46]

In Hungary, by contrast, the intelligentsia appeared to some to be on the road to class power, at least through the beginning of the 1970s.[47] Although Konrád and Szelényi's thesis was certainly contentious, by the end of the 1980s this vision of communist rule may have triumphed.[48] At least the Németh government in 1989 called itself a "government of experts."[49] More broadly, one might interpret Gorbachev's vision of *perestroika* and the hopes of other reform communists to rest on the foundations of such a vision of rule by the intelligentsia. It is not clear, however, whether civil society would have realized its promise were it not for the move made by the Polish intelligentsia in particular to support the development of civil society in *opposition* to the authorities, rather than in alliance with communist reformers.[50]

The Polish politics of intellectual responsibility put terrific pressure on intellectuals to choose whether they would serve civil society or the authorities. The seeds for this kind of antagonistic politics could be found in the failure of revisionism in 1968, but the failure of Gierek's approach to professionalism was the final blow. The politics of Solidarity in 1980–81 assured that intellectual responsibility would lie with the intelligentsia's immersion in a civil society identified in opposition to the authorities.[51] Already in 1976, Adam Michnik and others insisted that working for change from within the system was no longer viable. Instead, civil society would have to be built in opposition to the authorities, where *kompromis* would not be *kompromitacja*—where compromise would not lead to co-optation.

The Hungarians were in a very different position. There was no vital civil society on which a strong politics of opposition could be built. The intelligentsia did not have the option of immersing itself in an already constituted opposition. The tragedy of 1956 destroyed the possibilities for resistance, according to János Kis. To cope with the demand Kádár made—that society "forget" its experience in return for material compensation—civil society withdrew into private life.[52] Under these circumstances, Kis wrote:

> Whether a privatized society identifies with its defeated struggles or tries to forget them depends decisively on what its spiritual leaders—writers, journalists, artists, historians, priests, teachers—articulate. They, after all, are in the position that, by virtue of their profession, their words and silence constitute a public statement. It depends on them to decide if they will provide symbols of loyalty and models of

endurance to be emulated. In Hungary, this stratum did not supply society with the instruments to enable it to remain loyal to its revolution while making peace with reality. Indeed, the selfsame intelligentsia evolved into the source and foundation of the consensus that insists that the cultivation of intellectual opposition is a 19th century romantic pose and inappropriate to Realpolitik.[53]

Kis sought to provide a different model of intellectual responsibility. Intellectuals should not only restore that sense of opposition, but also develop a strategy that would take into account the defeat of 1956. Kis insisted that "the resolution of the country's crisis is conceivable only in the form of compromise."[54] Hungarian society, he writes, has yet to come to terms with the total defeat it suffered at that time, and those in power have yet to overcome the burdens of their victory. The economic crisis that overwhelms Hungary in the 1980s is the crisis of the restoration regime that came into existence thirty years earlier.

> Today we must remember the restoration not just in order to regain moral integrity, but in order to understand the present political crisis of the regime. We have to analyze former (failed) proposals of conciliation in order to find a more effective compromise to our present and future (perhaps less hopeless situation). The events of 1956–57 develop from a moral issue into a political one.[55]

The Hungarian alternative represents one practice of emancipatory civil society among the intelligentsia, one far more dependent on developing a politics of negotiation than a politics of mobilization, which in turn emphasizes an intellectual focus on contingency and compromise rather than a focus on moral and fundamental oppositions. This emphasis is very clear in how Kis analyzes the politics of 1956.

Kis emphasizes the "accidents" that shaped the logic of 1956. For instance, had no Soviet tanks been introduced into Budapest on October 23, a new government under the aegis of the People's Patriotic Front might have been formed and a multiparty system could have remained a possibility.[56] Also, when the Kádár government took power with the aid of Soviet tanks, the Kádárism of that period could have been replaced by the retrieval of Stalinists or by a negotiated compromise with Imre Nagy.[57] Accidents, however, are not simply made by unusual conjunctions of force. They are also made by strategic decisions. Kis is especially impressed with the politics of the workers council movement in this regard.

The workers council movement survived the formal restoration of the Kádár government in Budapest on November 7. The peaceful resistance by the Greater Budapest Central Workers Council, formed on November 14, was the first exemplar of sophisticated compromise politics. The council gradually dropped its demands for the restoration of the Nagy government and a multiparty system, as well as the departure of Soviet troops, in favor of promoting the self-organization of workers councils as well as council access to an open public sphere.[58] The Stalinist wing of the party had grown increasingly strong toward the end of November, however, and provoked enough violent conflict to end the possibility of negotiations with politically minded workers councils. The Csepel Iron and Metal Works workers council led the second phase of resistance. It advocated a less political function for councils, and took the restored Kádár regime as its point of departure, not the ideals of the Hungarian revolution. But by January 8–11, the possibility of even this kind of compromise was ruined by the increasing hard line of the Kádárist government, and the violent suppression of a strike by that factory's workers. These compromise strategies might have worked, Kis thinks, had the international scene and internal conflicts been different.

In the struggle to develop a civil society alternative to communist rule in Hungary, Kis gave a great deal of emphasis to the cultivation of opposition responsibility among the intelligentsia through a sophisticated politics of compromise and negotiation. This kind of self-limitation and strategic action is, of course, one element of the tolerant politics associated with a developed civil society. A very different kind of self-limitation and strategic action on behalf of civil society was developing in Poland. This sensibility emphasized an evolutionary, rather than contingent, history in the development of civil society and opposition to communist rule. And that sense of trajectory was itself the consequence of the growing power of Polish civil society and its opposition, at least through the early 1980s.

In comparison to other East European societies, Poland had never had a shortage of opposition or a surplus of silence.[59] Indeed, this was partially a consequence of its 1956. For Poland, 1956 was initially a year of triumph, a time when Polish party authorities defied Soviet authorities, opened new cultural boundaries, ended experiments with agricultural collectivization, established better relations with the Roman Catholic Church, and legalized greater workplace democracy through workers' councils. Even if this "Polish October" led to disappointment a few years later, and outright rejection by 1968, it was a far cry from the total defeat that 1956 signified for Hungary's opposition.[60]

By 1980 in Poland, 1956 barely figured into the opposition's consciousness. The legacy of workers' councils and revisionist party politics was far less important to consider than the issues raised by the 1968, 1970–71, and 1976 events that made independent trade unions, the loyalties of intellectuals, and the making of civil society central to the transformative agenda. The development of the Solidarity movement in 1980–81 made those strategic emphases socially real phenomena. The politics of compromise that Kis advocated in the mid-1980s was morally reprehensible for many Polish intellectuals. In fact, it is only a slight exaggeration to say that the imposition of martial law on December 13, 1981, turned the Polish intelligentsia, writ large, into an opposition to Jaruzelski's regime. Poland established its "exceptionalism" with the militance and organization of its working class, which in effect transformed the politics of intellectual responsibility. It was not a matter of where one stood, but with which side one allied. This created the social foundation for a strong politics of intellectual opposition and opposition to any compromise that could resemble co-optation.

The contrast could not be clearer. In the late 1970s and early 1980s in Hungary, the opposition was relatively limited, and primarily involved intelligentsia and students. Samizdat materials, a private charity to help the poor, the beginning of a tolerated political opposition in the 1985 parliamentary elections, and an independent peace movement characterized the opposition in the first half of the decade. The environmental movement called the Danube Circle proved one of the most significant opposition activities by the middle of the decade. In Poland, the 9.5 million–member Solidarity movement, with its base among skilled workers in large factories and the support of the Catholic church, promised that the opposition would be socially broad, and not limited to the highly educated. This distinction would inform the way in which the politics of civil society and systemic transformation could be constructed. In Hungary, the politics of civil society depended on the intelligentsia's organizations; in Poland, the politics of civil society was based on the intelligentsia's immersion in the activities of other social groups. The Hungarian intelligentsia led by default. The leadership of the Polish intelligentsia was hardly guaranteed. But both movements for civil society ended up in a similar state.

The Hegemony of the Hungarian Intelligentsia

Although today the Polish case is treated as "exceptional," in the 1980s the Polish case established the baseline for asking why workers were not oppositional in other societies, notably Hungary.[61] The authorities of other communist-led countries may not have treated the Polish case as a baseline, but certainly considered its example a threat.[62] The Hungarian authorities themselves could frame their economic reforms in order to provide a "prophylactic measure to thwart the spread of Polish Solidarity-inspired labor activism."[63] Whatever the reasons for the implication of Hungarian workers in painting rather than dismantling socialism,[64] it is relatively clear that the intelligentsia, not the working class, defined the Hungarian opposition.

Two dominant currents of Hungarian intelligentsia made their negotiated revolution.[65] The populists were numerically the largest group, and the hardest to define formally. Five of its nine founding members were poets and writers. They identified their movement with the needs of the Hungarian nation, defined ethnically or racially. They generally spoke of a "third road" between capitalism and communism. The authorities had cultivated them as an ally, especially since the 1956 revolution, although by the mid-1980s the populists began to identify with some projects of the democratic opposition. The populists formed the Hungarian Democratic Forum (HDF) in 1987 and generally avoided technical programs for economic transition in favor of literary-emotional politics. They preferred "intuition to analysis, and literature to social science."[66] Until the November referendum on the timing of the presidential election, they were the most successful in Hungarian transition politics, having won each of the four elections in the summer of 1989. They finally won the spring elections in 1990 and, together with the Smallholders and Christian Democrats, formed the governing coalition in mid-1990. But, in the beginning of the revolution, they were the most closely allied with the reformist party leader Imre Pozsgay.[67]

The other significant group of intellectuals in the negotiated revolution was called pro-Western, democratic, liberal, and urban. Many had their origins in the Budapest School of critical Marxism, and many were of Jewish descent. From 1981, their main efforts were directed toward the independent journal *Beszélő*, but in 1988 they formed the Alliance of Free Democrats (AFD). Their program for institutional reform was generally considered the most elaborate and formally specified of all of the opposition. They were often allied informally with reformers within the authorities, especially reformist legal experts and economists. Many other political parties and social groups formed in the wake of the political openings of 1988, but these liberals and their populist opponents represented the dominant alternative tendencies in the Hungarian opposition. And that was reflected in the spring 1990 elections, as these two parties received the most votes.

The populism of the HDF reproduced the traditional form of Hungarian twentieth-century nationalism. Above all, it was concerned with the fate of Hungarian minorities living abroad. It also promoted the idea of Hungary being somehow special and in between East and West, deserving its own unique identity based on an independent small-holding peasantry. But, by 1989, its emotive program did not suggest as radical a transformation of the Soviet-type system as did the Alliance of Free Democrats, for the main question of institutional transformation was not based on cultural matters or agriculture's ownership. The Soviet-type system's main antagonist had become the institutionalization of a free market–based civil society, and it was the AFD that promoted this as an alternative to the Forum's populism, and as the means for the transformation of Soviet-type society.

This group had already begun to move down that liberal road at the beginning of the 1980s. Much as in Poland, civil society became the principal alternative politics of emancipation to that of nationalism. To struggle in the Soviet-type system for the rule of law rather than that of the party, for free associations instead of party-sponsored organizations, for freedom from censorship and a multiparty system, provided Hungarians, like Poles, with a coherent transformative strategy that did not have to elevate one's nation above others. György Konrád expressed this simply:

> We want that internal process with which East Central Europe is already pregnant; we want bourgeois civil liberties and an embourgeoisement that is not hedged about with prohibitory decrees. We don't want the authorities to have discretionary rights over us. We want constitutional guarantees; we want it clear that semi-freedom is not freedom, half-truth is not truth, liberalization is not liberalism, democratization is not democracy. We want no less than what the most advanced democracies already have.[68]

Unlike the Polish, however, this Hungarian project was not very successful in providing a program that mobilized those beyond students and intelligentsia. Both AFD and HDF were mainly composed of intellectuals. Two groups formed in 1988–89 illustrate this hegemony of the intelligentsia.

On March 30, 1988, thirty-two young intellectuals, students, and workers (though mainly law students) established Fidesz, or the League of Young Democrats. The Hungarian acronym was designed intentionally to resemble the Latin *fidelis,* to symbolize the group's aim and character. Fidesz was constructed as an independent youth organization that would fill the gap left by the party's youth organization. It was formed on the basis of an imagined civil society, with an ambition to make civil society more real. Following Hungarian postwar political theorist István Bibó, it argued that the law should be to control the state and its rulers, rather than to control the people. The opposition, it said, should take rights guaranteed by the constitution seriously, and thus treat the law as if it, rather than the party, ruled. On that basis, Fidesz used the constitutional guarantee of association to defend its formation. Its leaders were arrested, and legal proceedings were begun against them. But in the three months of trial, the group grew to more than two thousand members nationwide. They lost the trial, but ultimately they won. In January 1989, legislation was passed in the Hungarian parliament that guaranteed rights of assembly.[69]

As a movement of students and young intellectuals, Fidesz did not claim to represent other classes. The group was mainly symbolic and exemplary, hoping that through its own civil disobedience and pressure for the rule of law, others might learn how to exercise their own rights. Fidesz activists believed that civil society and the rule of law would represent the interests of everyone, so long as people could learn to exercise their rights. They ultimately would not only seek election to parliament but also try to promote a broader awareness of legal rights and possibilities among workers and especially peasants. Fidesz thus represented the new "classless" universalism suggested by civil society. For these young lawyers, the emancipatory alternative was a law-based society in which individuals understand their legal rights and are ready to engage them, and where people's economic needs are satisfied by their participation in a free market of goods and services.[70]

Given the experience of Polish Solidarity, independent trade unions might have suggested an alternative future for Hungary, but even they were overwhelmingly from the intelligentsia. On May 16, 1988, the first independent trade union, the Democratic Union of Scientific Workers, representing those who work in the nation's research institutes, was founded. It followed a similar strategy as Fidesz, by acting as if a legal state existed. Because the Hungarian constitution and labor code had no guidelines about the registration of unions, and because Hungary accepted the International Labor Organization's statements on freedom of association, the Union argued that it had the legal right to form.[71] Other unions of intelligentsia were formed in its wake, including those of filmmakers and teachers. The principal affiliates of the federative Democratic League of Independent Trade Unions, founded on December 20, 1988, also were white-collar unions. Blue-collar workers remained organized by and large by the old communist-led unions.

The hegemony of the intelligentsia in the construction of Hungarian civil society was apparent not only in the personnel of its associations or in the philosophies of its proponents. Hungary's negotiated revolution was itself derived from the interactions of this intelligentsia with party officials, in typically intellectual forms: conferences and publications.

The most proximate foundation for the negotiated revolution was Hungary's economic crisis. Although not so obvious as that in Poland or Romania, by the early 1980s Hungary was in a dangerous economic situation, with the highest debt per capita in Eastern Europe. But this crisis need not have laid the foundations for dramatic change. Tamás Bauer, one of Hungary's leading reform economists, argued that Hungary's economic reform depended on three conditions: (1) a crisis so profound as to convince both ruling elites and intellectuals that the command economy was failing; (2) the existence of a "more or less free intellectual community of economists"; and (3) "the readiness of both scholars and government experts to cooperate and make the necessary compromises."[72] Economic reform in 1968–72 had been shelved in Hungary, even if the reform economists themselves remained in their positions. Economic reform therefore depended on the autonomy of economists and the willingness of political authorities to respect their independent expertise. It depended on the restoration of the intelligentsia's traditional position of autonomy and authority. But the intelligentsia won this authority not because of tradition or special talent, but because of the dynamics of change in the party itself.

In the spring of 1986, Imre Pozsgay, then general secretary of the

Patriotic People's Front, requested that reform economists produce a report on the economic crisis. Published in 1987, this report, titled "Turnabout and Reform," documented the economic crisis and proposed solutions that were heretofore only discussed in samizdat form.[73] This report was used later by Károly Grósz to oust longtime leader János Kádár.[74] While intellectuals and their products were being "used" by political leaders in their own infighting, the opportunity was also created for intellectuals to realize greater autonomous power and influence.

In June of the same year, 1987, the democratic opposition published "The Social Contract" in *Beszélö*, in which it called for political pluralism, with an independent parliament and freedom of the press, although not yet a multiparty system. Later that fall, the populists held a meeting where they established the HDF. Significantly, Poszgay was there attempting to establish his base outside the party. In effect, a small group of party reformers had intended to use this mobilization of reform economists, populists, and democratic opposition to change the party leadership. They finally succeeded.

In May of 1988, Kádár was ousted as first secretary. Károly Grósz was but an interim leader, however, as his indecisiveness and inability to win significant improvements for Hungarian minorities living in Romania undercut his position.[75] Between the fall of 1988 and winter of 1989, the party reformers steadily improved their position within the party. Simultaneously, party rhetoric came to accept more and more the prospects of a multiparty system, even if still incorporating Communist Party leadership. But the opposition organized itself into a new body that effectively undermined even this radical reformist strategy of the communists.

The HDF, the AFD, Fidesz, and the Democratic Union of Scientific Workers and five other groups founded the Opposition Round Table (ORT) on March 22, 1989.[76] Although alliances among the "opposition" had been proposed before, this opposition alliance was more clearly the product of the opposition itself. The ORT was formed in order to assure that negotiations with the authorities would not be manipulated to allow the party unfair influence over the structure of the talks and their outcomes. Indeed, it even modeled itself on the Polish experience, and tried to create through the Round Table what the Solidarity movement created through at least a decade of social conflict.[77] In contrast to the popular perception of negotiations in Poland, however, the Hungarian Round Table could claim to represent formally less than 1 percent of the Hungarian population and was composed almost entirely of intellectuals.[78] Nevertheless, by September 18, 1989, the Hungarians had negotiated a more complete revision of the Soviet-type system than the Poles. The revision was finally realized with the fully open elections of March 25, 1990. Hungary's "weaker" civil society realized a more fundamental change than the better organized Polish one. That, however, was a consequence of timing less than degrees of mobilization or superiority of strategies.[79]

Thus, the foundation on which the party reformers thought to extend their influence—independent associations of the intelligentsia—became instead the vehicle of an autonomous civil society that would negotiate the establishment of a multiparty political system and inspire the dissolution of the Hungarian Socialist Workers Party itself.[80] How one interprets the party's role in its own undoing, and that of the system over which it ruled, is itself profoundly complicated, and implicated in a complex intellectual politics. To be sure, the communist authorities knew that they were undoing what existed, but they were not clear about what was replacing it.[81] I am, however, quite convinced by Tökés's argument that the reformist elements in the party were "the ultimate guarantors of peaceful transition and negotiated political outcomes."[82] It is very difficult to raise the question in the Polish environment, but it ought to be posed.[83]

Poland's Mobilization of Morality and Struggle to Negotiate

Solidarity's size and heterogeneity meant that it could represent very different things to different people. Certainly, once it evolved beyond a defensive strategy for self-organization and toward a program for institutional reconstruction, a lively politics within the movement was healthy, if not inevitable. But for the movement to survive as a total movement of civil society against the state, debate had to respect the anchor points of Solidarity's self-understanding in self-organization, equality, and self-management. In 1980–81, dialogue, both explicit and implicit, reproduced these values in this cross-class movement.

The imposition of martial law destroyed the possibility for that continued dialogue, however, and with it, the cross-class quality of the movement. The public sphere shrank, as most people retreated from politics. This sphere retreated unevenly, however, as the intelligentsia was more likely to remain actively engaged in politics than were workers. The distinction of the Solidarity movement then began to fade. The pragmatic construction of a political movement that embraces equality, pluralism, and self-management as a condition of cross-class unity depends on an open public sphere with broad cross-class participation and a coherent opponent. This breadth could not be preserved under conditions of martial law and its aftermath. This new uneven participation has several foundations and manifestations.[84]

First, the very condition of martial law presented new dilemmas for the opposition. Who would lead the opposition? Should it have a unitary or decentralized and federative character? Should it focus on dramatic actions and try to spark immediate reaction, or should it prepare for the long struggle, and build an underground society? Should its base remain workers in factory cells, or should it reflect the multiple associational character of a pluralistic civil society?[85] Although it presented dilemmas, martial law also reinforced the moralistic qualities of the Solidarity movement. The imposition of martial law was one more element testifying to the alien qualities of the communist authorities, and why they could not be trusted. The philosophy of civil society articulated by Michnik and others in the 1970s became ever more self-evident in the 1980s as the authorities demonstrated their distance from what Poles really wanted.

Second, the opposition fragmented into several currents. Aleksander Smolar identified the mainstream opposition with Wałęsa, Solidarity, and the Temporary Coordinating Commission (TKK).[86] Smolar called realists those who considered it ineffective to continue to press for Solidarity's relegalization, and advocated coming to terms with the system. Smolar recognized another wave as radical for its greater demands than that of the mainstream, pressing for some kind of political revolution in Poland. Finally, another tendency noted by Smolar was characterized by the politics of youth, who rejected old formulations and sought a new politics resembling anarchism more than socialist or labor politics. Intellectuals could be found in all currents.

Despite their illegitimacy among the politically conscious, the Polish authorities of course tried to shape the strategies of the opposition. They tried to divide Solidarity along lines of authority, for instance. They tried to divide the underground leadership from those leaders captured by the authorities. The TKK underground, however, remained staunch in its commitment to respecting the democratic procedures that established the Solidarity leadership, and thus insisted that

Lech Wałęsa was the only person who could negotiate on behalf of Solidarity.[87]

The Polish authorities also tried to divide the classes animating Solidarity, by treating workers and intelligentsia very differently. On the one hand, the authorities established new unions that promised to realize many of the employees' demands for which Solidarity struggled. These new unions were most unsuccessful among the intelligentsia and the fields they dominated: health, culture, and universities.[88] The authorities also treated workers more harshly than the intelligentsia for oppositional politics. When interned, members of the intelligentsia were generally housed separately from workers, and treated better. The opposition activities of workers were also more strictly curtailed. Strikes in enterprises were treated more harshly than actors' and writers' boycotts. Efforts by physicians, teachers, academics, and artists to establish a more open field of information and culture went relatively unhampered. The minister of culture even said that although the authorities did not support the underground press, they did not go out of their way to persecute it either.[89] It is not surprising, therefore, that workers' oppositional politics declined more dramatically than that of intellectuals. This unevenness had devastating consequences on the class character of the opposition.

The social distance between classes grew in this period. Many in the intelligentsia were angry with workers for having failed to mount greater resistance to the regime. Negative stereotypes of workers became more common.[90] Solidarity also began to be criticized for having been too socialist, too "workerist."[91] The response of workers to this criticism was ambivalent. On the one hand, they again began to identify the intelligentsia with their supervisors rather than with themselves. On the other, they began to rely more on the intelligentsia for maintaining the opposition.[92] For instance, Zbigniew Bujak, one of the members of the Temporary Coordinating Commission and leader of the Warsaw/Mazowsze underground Solidarity movement from 1981 to 1986, found most of his safe apartments among intelligentsia households.[93]

The intelligentsia thus realized its responsibility, but in the process also assumed greater autonomy from the existing factory-based movements among workers. The anchor points of Solidarity's self-understanding, in social self-organization, equality, and self-management, were no longer decisive in defining the programs of the opposition, as the intelligentsia was no longer dependent on workers. Drawing on the symbolism of Solidarity, if not its organization, intellectuals could now claim to represent workers, but only as they represented the Polish nation. But what kind of intellectual politics might claim the mantle of Solidarity?

The regime itself clearly tried to shape that choice. On the one hand, it treated most harshly those such as Kornel Morawiecki of Fighting Solidarity, Leszek Moczulski of the Confederation for an Independent Poland, and others who advocated some kind of revolutionary, even if nonviolent, politics. It lambasted the youth-based Freedom and Peace (Wolność i Pokój, or WiP) as traitorous to Polish society.[94] On the other hand, it also encouraged the realists by offering selective inducements for cooperation.

For those willing to cooperate with the regime, Jaruzelski established a "consultative council," with about one-third of its members from the regime, one-third from Catholic circles, and one-third independent intellectuals. The Solidarity leadership criticized that council, established on December 6, 1986, for the deliberate exclusion of Solidarity's intellectuals. Only a few prominent and independent intellectuals, notably Władysław Siła-Nowicki, Andrzej Swięcicki, and Andrzej Tymowski, joined it. But its significance went beyond its effect on Solidarity; Jaruzelski recalls that the reasonableness of this group convinced him that dialogue with Solidarity was possible.[95] In this sense, the meaningfulness of dialogue as an intellectual value was being spread to the party through such organizations. Co-optation could work both ways. Likewise, PRON, the Patriotic Movement for the Renewal of the Nation, was an attempt by the authorities to co-opt the opposition. It was also, however, one of the institutions where the value of dialogue, rather than the spirit of repression, could be promoted within the government.[96]

Nevertheless, it is apparent that as the authorities began to move toward dialogue, they also were increasingly interested in constructing a "responsible" partner, one that would respect Poland's system and geopolitical realities. The best example of their tolerance was their permission for the establishment in 1987 of the first independent, nonreligious periodical in the Warsaw Pact, *Res Publica*. Although still subject to censorship, the publication pursued its liberal-democratic themes vigorously.

The regime also encouraged another kind of realism attractive to members of the intelligentsia, among others. It facilitated the promotion of a new patriotic politics based on the spirit of entrepreneurialism. Although its promoters included several former worker activists, this agenda was also antiunion, arguing that the solution for Poland's dilemmas lay in the promotion of a free-market economy and private-enterprise system based on the multiplication of wealth, not in the continuation of workerist politics based on redistribution.[97]

In effect, with these activities the Polish authorities were trying to establish a new modus vivendi between themselves and civil society. But this new agreement was not based on broad public participation, as Solidarity had been. Instead, it was to be based on a skewed participation, with workers returned to narrow union concerns, and the intelligentsia once again established as the representatives of the nation. One might say that the Polish authorities tried to reconstruct the Polish opposition in the Hungarian image—with an opposition concentrated among a self-limiting intelligentsia. In so doing, communists ceased to treat the autonomous intellectuals as anachronistic in the hope that the realism of such intellectuals could restore some measure of public consensus for the Polish communist order. But this proved to be impossible without the restoration of Solidarity.

Some have suggested that the authorities imprisoned the more militant unionists, such as Władysław Frasyniuk, while allowing those more conciliatory figures, such as Zbigniew Bujak, to continue their underground existence, but this is certainly debatable.[98] It is a familiar delegitimating tactic among authorities: the outlaw is free because we, the omnipotent state, allow him to remain free. It is hard to believe that the regime would tolerate such an obvious blow to its own claims to competence if it could help it. Bujak remained for the most part in the capital city, and tried to change residences every two weeks for more than four years. His freedom was one of the principal goals of the underground movement: to show the weakness of the state, and the strength of the underground. He was apprehended only on May 31, 1986, when the underground tried to stage a major underground Solidarity congress one month before the party's own congress.[99]

The arrest of Bujak and two of his colleagues spelled the beginning of a new process, the move away from the politics of the underground and toward a politics of negotiating revolution. With the capture of the principal symbol of Solidarity's underground existence, those among the authorities who were seeking dialogue could increase their influence, and the authorities could begin their move toward a politics of negotiation. Of course, they tried to do it without Solidarity, as in Jaruzelski's Consultative Council. Solidarity insisted, by contrast, that negotiations could not proceed without it. This apparent stalemate was broken by more than deft intellectual politics.[100] Just as in 1980, when workers' occupation strikes and demands for independent trade unions established the possibility for a negotiated settlement leading to Solidarity, in 1988 workers' protest put the dialogue on a new level. In April–May and especially August 1988, workers in Gdańsk and in other places initiated a wave of occupation strikes demanding, among other things, increases in wages and Solidarity's restoration. This movement was not, however, initiated by Solidarity's activists. It involved a new generation of workers, who trusted few outside their immediate milieu.

The authorities were extremely apprehensive about this new wave of strikes, and feared that they could not contain them.[101] The authorities had to abandon their strategy for promoting a new realism, and turn to another realism represented by the old Solidarity leadership. This leadership was, by now, relatively trustworthy in comparison to these new apparently anarchistic youth. The authorities' only hope was that these former opponents could restrain workers from further strikes. In return, the Solidarity leadership demanded negotiations for Solidarity's legalization. At the conclusion of August 1988, the path was set for the beginning of the first negotiated revolution. It was also an opportunity for the intelligentsia to consolidate its leadership in social transformation.

Civil Society and *Perestroika*

In some ways, the civil societies of Hungary and Poland are radically different. In the former, intellectuals claimed representation of a civil society that was mainly a "do-it-yourself" second economy, but one that implicitly sought more than a good standard of living.[102] In Poland, intellectuals could not represent civil society without representing Solidarity. The movement's collective organization among employees and the sacrifice of millions of its members defined its distinction. Intellectuals were dependent on a collective subject in Poland; the Hungarians sought to create just such a subject. In Hungary, compromise with party reformers was necessary, whereas in Poland a moral compromise with communists was understood to be a contradiction in terms. In both cases, however, opposition intellectuals developed a vision of civil society and social transformation that was remarkably similar. That was in large part the consequence not only of the intelligentsia, but of the role of communists in shaping the political opportunity structure, beginning with the Soviet Union.[103]

Mikhail Gorbachev and his intellectual allies transformed the political opportunity structure shaping emancipatory praxis in Eastern Europe. Gorbachev began his reign in March 1985 with an emphasis on *uskorenie*, or the intensification of economic development. His February 1986 speech to the Twenty-seventh Congress of the Communist Party of the Soviet Union introduced the need for *perestroika* or "restructuring" and socialist democracy. On April 26, 1986, an explosion at the Chernobyl nuclear power plant in Ukraine released enormous amounts of radioactivity into the atmosphere, affecting not only Soviet but European life conditions. The importance of information about such a catastrophe, and its inadequacy for local and global publics, helped to create the conditions for *glasnost'*, or openness and publicity. Over the summer of 1986 through the following year, a new struggle for "truth" and "openness" in the public sphere ensued, mobilizing the intelligentsia in support of reform. This led, Ronald Grigor Suny argues, to the erosion of communist authority and the opening of national liberation movements *within* the Soviet Union.[104] Of course, it had great consequence for those outside too.

Jacques Levesque argues that *perestroika*, and the specific "ideology of transition" that accompanied the transformation of Soviet foreign policy, retained that Leninist arrogance of believing that it could reshape the world by correct strategic thinking and resonance with universal values in formation. After all, the world was becoming increasingly interconnected, and the Soviet Union needed a foreign policy that reflected this integration, rather than conflict, on the world scene.[105] Facing a condition of relative economic decline, Gorbachev also sought a new way out of the increasingly costly military competition with the United States. Instead of competing with the United States on the military front, Gorbachev sought to increase Soviet influence over and integration with Europe by pursuing a strategy of disarmament and negotiation. Through it, Gorbachev gained a legitimacy within Western Europe that the Soviet Union never enjoyed, especially since 1968, reaching its peak at the time of the fall of the Berlin Wall (159).

The Brezhnev doctrine, justifying socialist international interests over those defined by national boundaries and articulated in the wake of the Warsaw Pact's invasion of Czechoslovakia in 1968, was Gorbachev's principal resource, and obstacle, in the "new thinking" about international relations associated with *perestroika*. Through 1987 and 1988, Gorbachev made several specific references to a shift away from this doctrine, stating, for instance, that "foreign imposition of a social system or lifestyle through any method, and even more so through military measures, is a dangerous way of acting from the past."[106] To articulate this shift convincingly was difficult, for many in the West and in East Central Europe would have believed Gorbachev's initiatives to be disingenuous given past disappointments with revisionism. Nevertheless, the ambiguity proved useful for Gorbachev, for it contained a promise of new international relations that might coax the United States, and especially Western Europe, into closer collaboration with the Soviet Union. The main cultural resource in Gorbachev's international diplomacy was the promise of eliminating the Soviet threat to the West. Just as the autonomous intellectual's value was elevated by the threat of its loss, the value of this peace offensive was elevated because the West could not know whether the possibility of disarmament might be lost.

Within Eastern Europe, Gorbachev's ambiguity worked in favor of reform in the long run, but did not facilitate change directly. Gorbachev refused to interfere directly in *favor* of reform. He allowed Polish and Hungarian leaders to initiate their own reforms, but his refusal to support liberal allies in the Czechoslovak, Bulgarian, and East German establishments probably wound up delaying reform in these more conservative regimes.[107] Indeed, his refusal to engage them probably meant that communist control over transition was far more limited than what the communists might have desired.

Gorbachev insisted on allowing countries to determine their own fates. He and his allies in the Soviet Union could not imagine—indeed, refused to countenance—the possibility that such an initiative would lead to the end of the Warsaw Pact. He believed that his forces and those of other reforming socialists would retain their hegemony over the direction of social change (Levesque, *The Enigma of 1989*, pp. 81–83, 99). Quite the contrary happened. Eastern Europeans ultimately left the alliance with the Soviet Union, causing the collapse of the Warsaw Pact. The Soviets lost the only leverage they had to facilitate the wholesale integration of Europe, rather than its partial incorporation on West European terms (225, 244–46).

In this sense, the "ideology of transition," as Levesque calls it, prevented Gorbachev and his allies from seeing what would be the likely outcome of power's decentralization. Gorbachev could not have imagined that European integration would take place on the basis of socialism's collapse, resulting in the exclusion of most of the Soviet Union from "Europe."[108] Ultimately, Gorbachev's vision of peaceful integration, "our common European home,"[109] became the idea that enabled the victory of civil society over communist rule, and the re-drawing of European boundaries to the advantage of East Central Europe, and the potential disadvantage of "the other Europe." Leninist arrogance about knowing the future, and ignorance about knowing one's own society, coupled with civil society's articulation in opposition to communist rule, were critical ingredients in communism's negotiated collapse. But such a portrait of communist authorities' contribution to emancipation would be inadequate without two additional points: peace and the intelligentsia.

Just as in Eastern Europe, the intelligentsia in the Soviet Union played an extremely important role in developing the culture of emancipation from communism. Whereas the most obvious players in developing that initiative in Eastern Europe can be found among the opposition, in the Soviet Union one finds the intelligentsia developing in alliance with *perestroika* itself. After 1989, the intelligentsia, especially outside Russia, developed an oppositional stance toward Gorbachev, but until that time, their activities and movements were often constructed in defense of, or in alliance with, *perestroika*. *Perestroika* was conceived as a way of empowering the intelligentsia made in the Soviet-type system, but repressed by it (Levesque, *The Enigma of 1989*, p. 30). The "new thinking" associated with the development of Soviet foreign policy was itself a reflection of considerable intellectual activity in analyzing the course of world-historic change, and the possibilities for the Soviet Union to ride with it. One might say, here, that those Soviet intellectuals analyzing globalization were better at anticipating an international politics than they were their own domestic conditions. Nevertheless, emancipation culture at communism's collapse was built on the authority the intelligentsia acquired under communism's initial repression. It also depended on accepting the intelligentsia's claim to competence in addressing the needs of society, and of the world.

The value of the intelligentsia under communist rule has been an object of long-standing discussion, but the association of communist rule with peaceful change is a product of the late 1980s. From the violence of revolution itself, through civil war, communist purges, collectivization and mass famine, revolution from abroad, and duplicitous peace initiatives abroad while conducting domestic cold wars at home, communist rule has not had a strong association with a sincere peace. Gorbachev changed that. Gorbachev renounced the legacy of violence that had characterized Soviet rule. As Levesque argues,

> One could, of course, invoke the bloody repressions in Lithuania and Latvia in early 1991. Given the magnitude of what was at stake, however, these incidents were so minor that they actually tend to confirm my point. Even Western democracies are more willing to resort to violence to preserve their territorial integrity or existence. The refusal by Gorbachev and his entourage to use violence and repression are so striking that they reveal a fundamental option of an ideological character. It was so strong that even the putschists of August 1991 (emerging from among the right wing of his associates) did not dare open fire in order to prevail. Given Gorbachev's frequent declarations that he would not hesitate to use force if necessary, it must be noted that it is only in retrospect that the absence of violence became so remarkable. Gorbachev's declarations remained only political weapons. (20; see also pp. 133, 163–64)

In this sense, it was not just that Gorbachev allowed countries to go their own way, but that he and his associates struggled to transform the culture of violence that had been associated with communist rule. His renunciation of violence and search for peaceful methods of social transformation ultimately led to the loss of his own power base, just as it did for Hungarian and Polish communist authorities.[110] At the same time, however, their common renunciation of violence, after a long history of violence, enabled civil society to realize far more consequence than any of its proponents could have imagined before 1989. Negotiated revolution was hardly an evolutionary inevitability.[111]

Negotiating Revolution and the Contingencies of Change

This chapter has been organized around intellectuals and the making of the cultural project of civil society. With this emphasis on intellectual agents and civil society, however, I do not mean to exclude others from the story of communism's collapse, nor do I intend to suggest that other cultural formations were not important. Indeed, when it comes to negotiating revolution, the communists had to introduce new vocabularies and convoluted cultural formations for their own consumption to legitimate their explicit compromise with civil society and relinquishing of Leninist prerogative. General Jaruzelski, for instance, had to recognize the distinction between constructive and destructive oppositions, and later to accept that those who symbolized his unacceptable opposition—Adam Michnik, Władysław Frasyniuk, Janusz Onyszkiewicz, and Jacek Kuroń—might belong to the first rather than the second category.[112] Simply, there are many more secondary cultural formations that deserve elaboration in a complete history of communism's collapse; civil society is only the key concept around which we can understand the impact of communism's collapse for emancipation culture. Alongside the key concept of civil society, however, eventful sociology and its focus on contingency are key to recognizing transition culture's critical potentials.

When revolutions are understood in terms of grand social forces under the spell of logics of necessity, we may be distracted from the accidents of history or other reflections on contingency. For instance, by focusing on the emancipatory praxis of Solidarity and its implication in exposing the immorality or contradictions of communist rule, we can miss the contributions that communists made to enabling change or the compromises that enable systemic transformation if not moral purity. The Hungarian transformation, given its abiding emphasis on political negotiation and attention to contingent thinking in the development of strategy, is much less likely to lure the analyst into a deterministic, or even moralistic, approach to communism's collapse.

Attention to international conjunctures and the impact they have on the capacities of states to resist change are one way to elevate the significance of the unnecessary but consequential convergence of forces in determining critical situations.[113] But communism's collapse has not been understood, typically, in these terms, given that the world system of economy and states in which Soviet-type society was embedded was itself changing so dramatically that it was hard to imagine communist rule surviving an era of flexible production and on-time delivery. However, China suggests an alternative communist response to globalization, of economic reform without substantial political democratization.

Of course, communists began their negotiations with civil society under the impression that the Warsaw Pact would survive and that communists would remain in the driver's seat of transition. Put in these terms, it is obvious that there are gross alternatives in the making of world history, and communism need not have collapsed so completely in the Soviet Union and Eastern Europe. Attention to the contingent is more than just recognition of systemic alternatives in the making of world history, however.

Jadwiga Staniszkis recognizes the significance of contingency. She emphasizes that communism's collapse was the consequence not only of systemic contradictions of the old system, but also of "unique historical circumstances and chance phenomena."[114] In particular, she emphasizes that the special composition of the Soviet elites—globalists rather than populists—enabled the East European authorities to introduce a new technique for dealing with the system's contradictions in economic reform, and subsequently, the Round Table. Furthermore, it was important that Germany's unification and crisis in the Soviet Union took place relatively late in the transformation process, in 1990 and 1991, respectively, for if they had occurred earlier, transformations within Eastern Europe itself could have been arrested.

Staniszkis marks the significance of accident, but her theoretical argument retains a more structuralist vision of change. She relies very heavily on developing categorical distinctions of identity and interest, and using these positions (e.g., globalists versus populists, corporatist liberals versus social-democratic liberals) to map the dynamics of transformation and the alternative programs available to the opposition, and especially to the authorities. The narrative of accidents is used more to explain the formation of a new center and interests than to recognize how things might have otherwise been. Nevertheless, this attention to alternative strategies is critical to recognizing the contingency of the process. Indeed, one should recognize that while the communists moved toward negotiation, other strategies were likely being developed as well.

In the fall of 1988, it certainly appears that the Round Table was at most an option. On September 19, 1988, the "expert" government of Zbigniew Messner was dismissed and on September 27, Mieczysław Rakowski was nominated to be prime minister. Shortly after his accession, Rakowski suggested that Poles were less interested in a Round Table, and rather more in a well-set table.[115] The announcement by his minister of industry, Mieczysław Wilczek, to close the Lenin Shipyards on October 27, 1988, seemed in particular to have been designed to signal another kind of transition, one that at the least bypassed Solidarity. Some have even wondered whether it might have been designed to provoke a reaction that would have called for the imposition of a state of emergency.[116] Despite the recommendation of the more radical members of the National Coordinating Commission to call a general strike, the Solidarity leadership decided to avoid confrontation and resist playing into the hands of the authorities.[117] Rather than take to the streets and inspire the state of emergency, Solidarity used its elite channels to register protest, and avoid the provocation that might have enabled the communist government to tell Western financiers that civil society was an unreasonable partner in economic reform.

The authorities knew that if Solidarity were not recognized at the conclusion of negotiations, serious confrontations would be unavoidable (116). At the same time, however, they continued to hope that they could bring a "responsible" opposition into parliamentary elections, even while they conducted rather crude anti-Solidarity campaigns in the press, and even "brutal" repression of independent student demonstrations in the fall. Although the church had been involved in enabling negotiations throughout the 1980s, in November of 1988 it played a crucial role in enabling the possibility of dialogue at all (130). By the end of November, however, things began to change. A critical moment came on November 30.

Alfred Miodowicz, the leader of the All Poland Trade Unions (OPZZ), the communists' unions, arrogantly posed to the rest of the Central Committee his wish to debate Lech Wałęsa on television. He presumed that he would win hands down in a debate with this simple electrician. But Wałęsa, as often was the case, beat expectations and crushed Miodowicz. When Miodowicz praised the direction of the authorities, Wałęsa simply replied that "you are going step by step, walking, while the rest of the world is going by car" (133). After that interview, even Rakowski argued that Wałęsa had to be treated as a serious partner for discussion, much as the rest of the world acknowledged his indispensability (134–35). With that successful performance, Solidarity could not be portrayed as a destabilizing force. And with that move, Miodowicz and his forces lost a great deal of capital to block the legalization of their principal union rival.

Although Miodowicz faced a major setback, there remained abiding resistance at the middle levels of the apparatus to any legitimation of Solidarity.[118] Nobody, however, had the power to unseat General

Jaruzelski. Nevertheless, Jaruzelski was not 100 percent sure that he would win his bet when he and three other leading figures threatened to resign in January 1989 in the face of Central Committee resistance to legalizing Solidarity.[119] The negotiated revolution clearly depended on General Jaruzelski's personal authority among the communists, and his own consolidation of power within the party.

Within the opposition, Lech Wałęsa was Jaruzelski's equivalent, but Wałęsa did not enjoy the same kind of authority. Wałęsa had considerable difficulty convincing striking workers in August 1988 that it was appropriate to end the strike in return for a promise to negotiate about all things, including Solidarity's relegalization. There was considerable debate in the press about who should represent the opposition in negotiations with the communists, and whether there should be any negotiations at all.[120] Staniszkis, in fact, argues that the "Wałęsa circle" excluded the liberal and populist factions of the opposition for their radicalism, which in turn was a shift in the class base of the actors, from the working class in large factories to the intelligentsia and their "theoretical interests."[121] Those who advocated independence above all other issues were fundamentally opposed to this compromise. Indeed, there were some protests that this was a "disgraceful compromise with communists"; the All-Poland Conference of Independent Youth Environments was organized under the slogan "One cannot negotiate freedom";[122] others complained that Solidarity's negotiators and its candidates were not chosen democratically.[123] As Bogdan Lis warned, the way in which the decision to negotiate was undertaken threatened the Solidarity leadership with the loss of its social base.[124]

Nevertheless, the legitimacy of these protests was limited because those who suffered most in prison, such as Adam Michnik and Jacek Kuroń, and leaders of the Solidarity underground during the 1980s, including Zbigniew Bujak, put their entire reputation behind the talks. Equally important was the church, and indirectly the pope himself. The presence of Tadeusz Gocłowski, Bronisław Dąbrowski, and Aloyzy Orszulik during negotiations legitimized that part of Solidarity that compromised with the communists.[125] Indeed, the noncommunist left within Solidarity and the church might be seen as having a common interest in the mode of change itself. As Jacek Kuroń observed, if the nomenklatura were to lose everything in the transformation, there would be no chance that democratic transformations could happen peacefully.[126] Peaceful change, recalled Bishop Aloyzy Orszulik in 1999, was always to be preferred by the church when it was at all possible.[127]

The Church was absolutely critical to establishing the very possibility of the Polish negotiations. The Church was a "witness" to the negotiations, assuring them legitimacy, and indeed that negotiations would be honest. Andrzej Gdula, a negotiator for the communist side, said that ultimately it was Pope John Paul II along with General Jaruzelski who assured this peaceful change. Without the direct oversight of the Catholic Church, these negotiations could never have taken place, and most certainly could not have succeeded.[128]

At last, negotiations were officially begun on February 6, 1989, at Namiestnikowski Palace and lasted for two months. More than four hundred people participated in the various negotiations. There were three main tables—on political reform, on economic reform, and on organizational pluralism, which concerned primarily the legalization of Solidarity. There also were eleven subtables devoted to questions of the media, health care, mining, youth, and other issues. Negotiations were surprisingly easy on the question of Solidarity's legalization; but they were especially difficult in the political realm, for both sides recognized that they were negotiating the future political architecture of Poland. The negotiations themselves were obviously filled with uncertainties and clashes of interests. Many of the subtables produced longer protocols of disagreements than agreements, especially around youth, legal reform, health care, and mining. Nevertheless, on the most important issues around the political table, real compromise was reached.

Private meetings at Magdalenka, a resort outside of Warsaw owned by the internal security forces, and in a separate room in Namiestnikowski Palace itself, enabled this compromise.[129] These negotiations were critically important because they helped to "melt resentments" between the two sides.[130] As Janusz Reykowski emphasized, the party had to look at the opposition, and the opposition at the party, not as enemies, but as players in the same game struggling to maximize their own position.[131] Beyond creating this identity of players in the same game, these meetings also provided an important place to resolve deadlocks through negotiation. One of the most critical moments was a disagreement about the election of the president after the elections, a deadlock that seemed to defy compromise. Communist negotiator Aleksander Kwaśniewski spontaneously suggested that there could be free elections to the Senate in return for a relatively strong presidency.[132]

Notably absent from these sessions was Alfred Miodowicz, and his own intervention nearly undid negotiated revolution.

On April 5, 1989, the parties to the Round Table agreement assembled to sign the accords. Miodowicz insisted on speaking after Kiszczak and Wałęsa, to symbolize the importance of his own trade union in the negotiations. Solidarity would not accept this, and the televised ceremonies broke off for four hours. General Kiszczak then called General Jaruzelski, who advised that the authorities must support Miodowicz. Shocked at the decision, and worried about the consequences, Reykowski spoke to General Jaruzelski on the phone once more, arguing that such a break in negotiations at the last minute would destroy the chances for compromise with Solidarity and likely cause violence. Solidarity and party leaders discussed the problem for three hours, and finally, accepted the wisdom of Kant, as relayed by party leader Ireneusz Sekula.[133] Osiatyński reconstructs the story about Kant,

> who was walking once along a very narrow street in Kronenberg and was stopped by a stranger walking in the opposite direction. One of them had to give way to the other. "I never give way to a moron," said the stranger. "I always do," answered Kant and went to the side to let the stranger pass. "Why don't we try it now?" suggested Kwaśniewski when Sekula finished his story. "Why not?" said Geremek. They all agreed to the plan.[134]

The entire process of initiating negotiation, from the end of the summer of 1988 through April 1989, was filled with contingencies. There were several moments when deadlocks and fundamentalist thinking could have led to withdrawal from the strategies of compromise. And there were agents, among both the authorities and civil society, who would have used the occasion to claim proof that peaceful change, or compromise with the enemy, was impossible. To reach this kind of agreement in April 1989 was already extraordinary. The outcomes were unbelievable.

The Unexpected Triumph of the Intelligentsia

Solidarity's election campaign was based on a new organization, the so-called Citizens' Committees. No formal body elected this group, and certainly Solidarity's remaining trade-union base did not. They were, in addition, composed primarily of representatives of the intelligentsia.[135] Of Solidarity's 261 nominations, only 10 were of workers and 35 of individual farmers. In contrast, there were 22 professors, 50 engineers, 35 lawyers, 20 journalists or columnists, 16 economists, 14 teachers, 13 health-care employees, and 1 religion teacher.[136] These candidates chosen to represent Solidarity were not elected either, but rather were picked by Lech Wałęsa and his closest advisers, much as the Round Table negotiators were chosen.[137] At the time, the class base of the negotiators—intelligentsia—was noted by some as a problem, especially for their relative ignorance of workers' voices.[138] Their most effective campaign element was a photograph of each candidate with Wałęsa, below which was written "We must win."[139]

The ascent of the intelligentsia in postcommunist politics is not unusual, of course. Like the Polish Round Table negotiators, nearly all of the members of the Hungarian Opposition Round Table were intellectuals.[140] Also, in both late communism and postcommunism, in Hungary as well as across the Soviet Union at the end of the decade, the intelligentsia surged in parliamentary representation.[141] One can view the whole process of reform, whether led by communists or by the opposition, as a process by which the intelligentsia sought greater authority and to establish its own particular modes of decision making and policy making on communist politics and programs. In both Hungary and Poland, it was quite apparent that the intelligentsia and party reformers sought a way out of the impasse without allowing the streets to dictate the outcomes.[142] To the extent that the intellectuals bore what Gouldner called a "culture of critical discourse," they also bore the capacity to subvert their own newly found privilege. In many ways, they did, but this cannot tell the story by itself. One must understand intellectuals in their social context, and, in particular, in the structure of their dependencies and in the timing of their negotiations with one another, and with representatives of the communist past.

Poland blazed the trail toward the Round Table. The Polish negotiations served as a model for the formation of the Hungarian Opposition Round Table coalition of forces. Had Poland not already resolved its own negotiations on April 5, 1989, Károly Grósz and the Hungarian Politburo might not have begun their own Round Table negotiations.[143] Nevertheless, as a relative latecomer, the Hungarian Round Table had fewer constrictions placed on what could be negotiated, and therefore generated a much more radical reform than that which the Polish reform provided.[144]

Some of the important fault lines around which subsequent politics has taken place can be traced to the ways in which the intelligentsia established its leadership and reproduced, or transformed, its dependencies. Although there were several contingencies in the politics of reform and referenda that reconstructed the politics of Hungary's transition, one can see in the Hungarian Round Table negotiations the electoral process in the making, as parties jockeyed for position.[145] As Tökés puts it, "the Hungarian NRT [National Round Table] may be likened to a cooperative, yet competitive multiplayer game."[146] The Polish negotiations were not anything like that, and Solidarity's electoral success was not something that anyone anticipated.

General Kiszczak has said in no uncertain terms that the communists were not negotiating away their power.[147] They expected, rather, to legalize Solidarity as an opposition, make it co-responsible for economic reform, and then in another four years hold entirely free elections. Things did not turn out as they expected. The authorities anticipated that Solidarity would at most win 40 percent of the seats in the Senate, and not 99 out of 100 as it ultimately did. They did not expect that so few communists and their allies would get the minimum number of votes necessary to enter parliament in the first round of elections. They were shocked at how little support they won.[148] With the votes cast, and tanks rolling into Tiananmen Square in China, Poles waited to see whether the election results would be honored. Even some of those who negotiated for the communists were worried that the election might be annulled.[149] Instead, the electoral results were honored and the communists struggled to form a government.

With this terrific vote of opposition from society, even those formerly allied with the communists began to rethink their allegiances. The movement of Peasant Party and Democratic Party legislators away from the communists toward Solidarity, in fact, made the election of General Jaruzelski as president seem especially uncertain. Indeed, had several Solidarity delegates not absented themselves from voting, Jaruzelski would not have been elected president. Had he not been elected, some fear that the chances for peaceful change could have been lost.[150]

Finally, President Jaruzelski asked General Kiszczak to form the first government, but he could not; Solidarity delegates explained to him that they could not take charge of the economic portfolios in his government, and he could not form a government without them. The society voted for change, and to form a government with the old ruling alliance would be impossible. Turning to those magic words provided by Adam Michnik on July 3, 1989, in his newspaper *Gazeta Wyborcza*, General Jaruzelski ("your president") finally asked Tadeusz Mazowiecki ("our prime minister") to form the government on August 24.[151]

Conclusions

Through 1989, civil society became the new specter of emancipation haunting Europe's communist regimes. Rather than haunt, one might say it possessed them. It provided an extraordinary vision of social transformation for Eastern Europe's intellectuals, filled the public sphere, and animated the institutional formation of postcommunist societies. Poles and Hungarians on all sides of the Round Table embodied this specter, however. The Polish and Hungarian practices of civil society in the transformation of Soviet-type society helped to stimulate a cascade of social transformations that could not have been predicted on the basis of the apparent dynamics of communist rule. Certainly, one could have expected that communism would collapse, but there was no reason to think that it could have changed so peacefully. Intellectuals' culture of critical discourse created, however, just such a potential. An institutional determinism might have shaped the conditions of change, but the contingent practice of intellectuals within a cultural formation of civil society enacted the transformation.

Intellectuals led the transformation from all sides of the political table. Dissidents who spoke in the name of civil society found a means, through the form of the Round Table, to speak with compromise-minded communists on the other side. The communists, wielding the power of a state that most perceived to be weak but still potentially violent, negotiated with intellectuals whose claim to power was that they spoke on behalf of civil society. The weakness of the communists, in cultural terms, was evident in their inability to challenge their opponents' claim to representation. Civil society's power rested, in part, on the notion that it could be represented by intellectuals whose principal distinctions lay in what they wrote, and the suffering they endured for that expression of conscience.

Civil society was more than an ideological frame, of course. The power of Polish opposition leaders rested on the potential threat of demonstrations and social movements rising up and potentially destroying the nonviolent and gradual character of social change. The Hungarians did not stand atop a mightily organized civil society, but they did seek a means to resolve the huge economic problems that overwhelmed not only society but also Hungary's economic planners. Indeed, because some of the nomenklatura had already begun its shift to a new society, where political power was not so critical to assuring economic power and privilege, change could take place. The making of economic civil society indeed facilitated the peaceful transition to a system in which free elections and a free press could organize the Hungarian polity.[152]

Certainly, some political forces and individuals were more associated with civil society's tolerance and pluralism than were others. Some claimed the mantle of the nation more forcefully than others did. The most remarkable point in this transformation, however, was that the national discourse was itself changed. The culture of communication between authorities and opposition was transformed. The end to communist rule was infused with the spirit of civil society. More than anywhere else, in the Round Table negotiations the spirit of conciliation and peaceful but legal change overwhelmed the sense of postcommunist society's making. Not only did the Round Tables express a notion that "we are all Poles" or "we are all Hungarians"; it also symbolized that even communists could *become* part of the process by which civil society—the spirit of negotiation, tolerance, and compromise—would come to new influence in defining the meaning of the nation. This strategy of social transformation, based above all on a fusion of horizons across apparently incommensurate positions, opened the way to the open society.

This process was by no means inevitable, and indeed, it is not yet finished. The negotiated revolution in Poland and Hungary depended very heavily on what the Soviet Union would allow, whose leadership was itself in the midst of a profound rethinking of international relations and domestic rule. Indeed, one might argue that the window of opportunity for negotiated revolution was relatively brief. Was negotiated revolution only possible after *perestroika* began in 1987 and before the Soviet Union collapsed in 1991? Indeed, one might wonder whether the Soviet Union would have collapsed had Eastern Europe not itself already left its camp and provided the model for the Baltic states and others. This kind of counterfactual reasoning is always contentious, of course, but drawing attention to conjuncture is critical for recognizing historical alternatives. The particular contingencies I would especially highlight are those less grand and more mundane moments where deadlocks could have turned deadly, and where conflicts were turned into breakthroughs instead. They are critical to rethinking the culture of emancipation in the wake of 1989.

Not only did intellectuals remake civil society as an agent, and goal, of social transformation. Not only did they manage to assemble critical intellectuals, the second economy, democratic nationalism, labor movements, demonstrations, and social protest all under the same roof of civil society in opposition to communist rule. They managed to redraw the oppositions between civil society and communist rule and to draw communists into the making of democratic and peaceful transformation. Using profound intellectual skills—from invoking Kant's account of the moron to imagining the greatest of trade-offs between your president and our prime minister—intellectuals from both sides of the political divide redrew the history of the world and made the impossible possible: they negotiated communism's collapse. Civil society was thus more than a frame for mobilizing opposition; it enabled a discourse of compromise, which paved the way to peaceful, but fundamental, change. Intellectuals' culture of critical discourse and the emancipatory potentials of civil society could be joined in this historic moment of transformation.

Critics from the left and the right as well as in the heart of transition culture might object to this account. Those to the right might challenge my wish to call 1989 emancipation given that the former oppressors maintain privilege, and if not exclusive, at least considerable power. Emancipation requires justice, they argue, and those who committed crimes against the nation or humanity must be brought to trial. If the Round Table negotiations, and that compromise between "reds and pinkos" in Poland, allow former oppressors to escape justice, that cannot be any kind of emancipation. That is certainly a profound problem, and has been addressed substantially elsewhere.[153] Intriguingly, this argument stands to the side of transition culture, and tends to be located within a discourse of nationalism that has been marginalized by the dynamics of transition culture itself. I shall, however, return to this challenge in the Conclusion, so that it might be read in light of my analysis of the Wars of Yugoslav Succession and more extended treatment of the nation as a cultural formation.

Those from within the heart of transition culture would object that although politics and civil society might have been the main object in social conflict and roundtable negotiations through 1989, priorities had to shift. Developing a rational economy was at the heart of past discontent, and making markets is not something that can be built around a roundtable. It had to be constructed through the proper application of global expertise in consultation with those who know how to implement it. This communicative competence thus requires different partners in the dialogue. It cannot focus on those contaminated by socialism, but should mobilize those who know better.

Whatever the merits of attending to that logic of necessity in the design of institutions, I have written this particular history in a way that marks the distance of that design from 1989. Transition culture can very easily claim the authority of emancipation by focusing on the historical exhaustion of socialism, and its succession as socialism's logical opposition and normatively and functionally superior system. Also, when the principal advocates of transition culture are simultaneously among the heroes of emancipation, the continuity of voice, even alongside a change in partners in dialogue, means that the heroes' legitimacy can rub off on transition culture itself. Finally, when those who complain most loudly about the distance of transition from the meaning of 1989 also invoke a spirit that is radically exclusionary or nationalist, they help to reinforce the liberal sense of suturing a focus on markets to the legacy of emancipation.

Many of those who are left, those concerned above all with impoverishment and the radical increase in inequality under socialism's successor, suffer a double distance from the apparent premise of this book. Not only does the making of markets clash with most of the main tenets of emancipation culture, but 1989 can be read as the foundation of that injustice. The broader intention of this volume is to expand the meaning of transition culture in order to make it more attentive to, and responsible for, the injustices and inequalities attending its transition. But that must begin with rewriting 1989.

This writing of 1989 is designed to constitute a different legacy for transition culture. Rather than mainly a reflection of socialism's exhaustion, people made 1989 through negotiations. These negotiations were filled with unacknowledged conditions of action, and unexpected outcomes, and thus filled with contingencies of all kinds that could very well have led to violent confrontations and the hardening of oppositions between the past and the future. Instead, a culture of critical discourse was made in 1989 that was based on an inclusive vision of civil society, in which pluralism and difference were integrated into a common future for each nation, based on the rule of law and of democracy. To be sure, intellectuals were the principal progenitors of this negotiation, and their own culture was critical to its success. But their own sense of self was embedded in a sense of responsibility for their nation that had to be communicated convincingly to a public that could have rejected that claim to represent the future. Civil society, as the discourse of emancipation and the hope for the future, created a different kind of political responsibility than the making of markets in transition culture. Recovered, that discourse and responsibility might make a different kind of transition culture that focuses more on impoverishment than on the empowerment of the privileged. It could help to make critical transition culture possible.

Two

Transition Culture and Transition Poverty

Since the fall of the Berlin Wall in 1989, countries in Central and Eastern Europe and Central Asia have been undergoing a dynamic process of economic and social transformation in their effort to create market economies. Throughout the region, countries have varied in the pace at which they have been able to put in place the components of a successful transformation to a market economy—and in their economic performance.[1]

The making of the market, not the construction of civil society per se, became the central problematic of social change after communism's collapse. To be sure, civil society and the democratic, if not also efficacious, state animate many efforts and Web sites dealing with postcommunist social transformations.[2] But through the mid-1990s at least, broad social empowerment and the elaboration of rights took a back seat to discussions of macroeconomic policy and the empowerment of the responsible, typically rendered through the firm and found in the person of the entrepreneur. Civil society's relative eclipse is partially owing to its quality as a cultural formation.

Although certainly civil society has had its advocates who claim to know what it is, and what it is not, it is more appropriately understood as a *contradictory* cultural formation. Its various normative principles—private property, political and organizational pluralism, national self-determination, human rights, popular expression, procedural rationality, tolerance, and the rule of law, to name a few—are very easily drawn into conflict with one another. Although advocates of one dimension or another might realize their intellectual and political fulfillment in the technical expertise, interpretative exercise, or popular mobilization around any one of them, embracing civil society in its totality demands reflexive judgments to articulate its conflicting principles. This unstable quality is one of its most attractive features for critical social theory and opposition politics.[3] Recognizing that contentiousness is important for enhancing civil society's emancipatory potential, but it has not appeared so useful for consolidating postcommunist institutional change.

As discussed in the preceding chapter, civil society can be woven together to form a coherent cultural formation in opposition politics. During the 1970s and 1980s, East Central European democratic opposition intellectuals and their allies tied these principles together in the mobilization against communism and the negotiation of revolution. This "protoliberal" civil society would not, however, retain its influence when institutional transformation of the economy became the principal focus of state power and these opposition figures turned into state leaders.[4] The emancipatory vision of civil society had a strong cultural and ethical theory underlying it, but it proved difficult to elaborate in institutional terms. Václav Havel tried to develop that moral sense of civil society in his exercise of presidential power in Czechoslovakia, and later the Czech Republic. But even this exemplary public intellectual could not find a theory and practice of institutional politics that would allow him to generate the kind of civil society suitable for a "crowned republic."[5] Those with another vision, with a simpler and congruous institutional theory, instead defined the terms of change. Transition, whose sense is exemplified in this chapter's introductory paragraph, came to define postcommunist social change.

The making of the liberal culture and market economy in general, and in Poland especially, has been analyzed in detail elsewhere.[6] In this chapter, I focus on "transition culture," that global cultural formation made, in part, out of Poland's success.[7] Its structural formation may not be obvious, however, because its center is filled with contest, and its viable and attractive alternatives are difficult to see. In order to make its boundaries and qualities clear, I describe the underlying structure of this "transition culture" in the first part of this chapter. I follow that elaboration with a review of one of transition culture's principal counterpoints in order to highlight transition culture's alternative. Standing a bit outside of transition culture, this intervention focuses on poverty and on "human development" rather than the development of the market.[8]

I focus on the artifacts of transition culture and its discontents in this chapter, but the principal agents of my analysis remain "intellectuals." Although individuals such as Havel are undeniably members of such a group, transition culture's theorists and practitioners may not be so obviously intellectual. Transition's professionals are obviously intellectual in their capacity to create and apply knowledge with consequence, but intellectual distinction also has implied distance from power and autonomy from commercial institutions. Membership in transition culture implies an affinity with the most powerful transnational organizations in the world. The businessmen and women described in the next chapter are even less familiar to those who focus on intellectuals per se, given that their cultural products are typically unwritten and distant from traditional intellectual presentiment. As I have argued elsewhere, however, their capacity to reconstruct the global culture of transition in both knowledge bases and symbol systems in order to make their East European application effective and powerful suggests a great intellectual effect in practice.[9] In order to appreciate that intellectual innovation and effect, one needs to consider the global culture in which they are articulated, and the ways in which their knowledge production elevates and deflates different claims to intellectual achievement.[10] Transition culture is, after all, quite different from the cultural formation of civil society.

Liberalism and Transition Culture

After the imposition of martial law in Poland in 1981, economic liberalism was being developed as an alternative strategy for transforming communist rule. Like the emphasis on civil society, advocates of this vision rejected the communist monopoly on power. But, unlike Solidarity's visionaries, the economic liberals rejected the emphasis on politics. Before communism's collapse, Mirosław Dzielski and others looked at the second economy for evidence of communism's liberal alternative. Departing from Solidarity's vaunting of the working class, this view celebrated the entrepreneur and the middle class. Dzielski wrote, "The person who trades is the pillar of civilization, and in conditions of socialism also its heroic champion."[11]

Although they focused on economic transformation, these liberals also recognized that society itself must change. It was not sufficient to change property laws. Indeed, society had to rid itself of economic traditionalism and socialist residues. Like Poland's reformist organic intellectuals in the end of the nineteenth century, these liberals believed that society must learn that making money is good for the nation. It had to learn that socialism was the enemy of the nation that needed to modernize.[12] Liberals developed this point of view before 1989, but when they took power, its cultural value soared. This cultural formation allowed them to critique actually existing civil society for its inadequacies, and to initiate radical systemic change regardless of popular wishes.[13] While civil society demanded either the intellectual's immersion or at least subordination to civil society itself, the economic liberal could speak on behalf of a global culture of economic wisdom. Rather than wrestle with the contradictions of civil society, economic liberals could cut to the quick of consequential change. But even in 1989, this vision's power was not so obvious.

Radical economic liberalism was not apparent in the negotiations over the Polish Round Table agreements of 1989. Although there were negotiations over economic issues at the Round Table, they hardly addressed the economy in the same terms as what came to dominate economic reform in Poland just a few months later. Leszek Balcerowicz was appointed minister of privatization, and his version of shock therapy—a relatively cautious plan that used a wage tax rather than indexation and with a recommendation to delay the privatization of large state industry—became Poland's macroeconomic strategy.[14] Despite the fact that most of the Solidarity delegates and others were cautious about such a plan, thinking that a more mixed approach to economic transformation might have been better, Solidarity and its allies stood fully behind the Balcerowicz plan by January 1990. Liberalism won out over more social democratic and corporatist strategies that the regime might have chosen. This new regime, and vision, had strong allies in the emerging global system of knowledge and practice that was to facilitate the transition to market economies across the world. Poland's shock therapy was enabled by, and helped to produce, the new global formation I have called "transition culture."

I have described transition culture as a mobilizing culture organized around certain logical and normative oppositions, valuations of expertise, and interpretations of history. These qualities provide a basic framework through which actors undertake strategic action to realize their needs and wishes, which in turn structures transition. Transition culture is also, however, a community of discourse.[15]

Professionals associated with international financial organizations, ministers of national finance, and scholars whose work is animated by the opposition between plan and market form the core of this transition culture. Transition culture is not analytically homogeneous, however. It is rife with debates over the proper form of ownership, the right sequence of reforms, and so on. Those participating in transition culture are unlikely to recognize their commonality, because they focus on the culture's contentions. For instance, they are much more likely to recognize differences about whether fixed or floating exchange rates are best, or what kind of presidential system allows for the implementation of lasting reform. Beyond its academic contentiousness, transition culture is also rife with the politicized assignment of blame, as in the recurrent debates between the preeminent individual associated with transition culture, Jeffrey Sachs, and the preeminent organization associated with this culture, the World Bank. One cannot belong to transition culture, however, if one cannot speak the language of transition and be able to use in practice its core concepts. It is presumed, however, that one can learn the language of transition, especially if one can speak English, transition's lingua franca.

Although membership criteria are clear with regard to language and knowledge, there are no explicit boundaries organized around ascribed statuses such as nationality or gender. This culture is open to anyone. Transition culture is multinational. It thrives on the assimilation of those from outside the "Western" experience. It is improved to the extent that more people from across the world embrace its presumptions and act in such a way as to reinforce the power of its prescriptions. It even looks better when those who articulate transition culture speak with accents that come from Tashkent or Tirana rather than London or New York. Transition culture's liberalism also becomes more evident when women play roles that indigenous cultures might proscribe. Transition culture fails to the extent that it drives people away from the promise of freedom and opportunity embedded within the vision's promise and becomes obviously prejudiced in favor of certain ascribed statuses. Like the integrating vision of civil society that animated communism's collapse, transition culture is therefore expansive.

In many ways transition culture resembles the kind of system that Talcott Parsons identified as modern.[16] Emotion, especially involving nationalism, is suppressed in favor of more professional and civil affective neutrality. Tasks should be increasingly specified within a relatively delimited scope of obligations rather than dispersed in a culture of irresponsibility. Self-interest, rather than that of some putative collective, whether of the nation or of the proletariat, should organize interest formation. Above all, the tasks of transition are relatively universal, with particular applications nonetheless informed by general principles. One indicates distance from the core of the culture with appeals to national exceptionalism. Although there is an emphasis on achievement within transition culture, its antagonist is not so readily obvious in terms of ascription, but rather of communism's negative selection that ignored achievement.[17] Like Parsons's theory, transition culture adopts a panoptic vantage point, in which the evolution of societies can be recognized from a position that is beyond any of them. In this chapter, however, I do not focus on transition culture's critical elaboration. Rather, I emphasize the conditions of transition culture's possibility by elaborating those common assumptions in its narrative that enable contenders in debate to recognize one another as members of this community of discourse, whose positions deserve amplification or challenge.

The underlying structure of transition culture relies on a basic opposition: the future is a form of global integration based on the articulation of transnational organizations dominated by the West. The past is a form of inferior economic organization dominated by a Russian statist culture. Its explicit concerns are to create a market economy and democratic political stabilization. The culture's analytical rhetoric emphasizes the importance of global transformations and the comparative study of interventions in making social change. Cases are relatively equivalent, and future success of the laggards can be found in the exemplars' present. Its normative rhetoric emphasizes freedom and opportunity and the dangers of dependency. It focuses on the inadequacies of communist rule and its possible remedy through international support for the right-thinking indigenous elite. Its typical protagonists are entrepreneurs, consumers, and citizens, and its typical villains are those with a socialist or statist mind-set.

Transition makers use these narrative elements to redesign what is normal and what is deviant in societies moving from communist rule to capitalist markets. Their stories typically revolve around the inadequacies of existing institutions and mentalities. State practices, the organization of the service sector, the infrastructure of communications, the technology of accounting and finance, and legal infrastructures frequently are identified as inadequate. To resist their change is taken as evidence of belonging to the past or a dysfunctional present. These inadequacies then become central to the analysis of the system itself and the remaking of institutions. Their inadequacies or lacks become the basis for understanding and intervening in the system, based on knowledge of a desirable future. These stories about the normal and the deviant are cultural resources on which experts and entrepreneurs draw to legitimate their claims to competence in administering business, and to identify who is part of the past that should be left behind.

Transition culture is thus driven to be dynamic, and designed to provide solutions to problems within a basic relationship between a relatively technical Western or globalized know-how, sufficiently transportable in order to be transplantable, and a local culture that must be assimilated. This fusion is possible because the future, or at least the normative future, is known probably as well as the past. As Jeffrey Sachs, one of the most prominent figures in transition culture, has put it,

> Poland's goal is to be like the states of the European Community. Although there are submodels within Western Europe, with distinct versions of the modern welfare state, the Western European economies share a common core of capitalist institutions. It is that common core that should be the aim of Eastern European reforms. . . . The real reason for optimism lies in the fact that the endpoint is so clearly discerned.[18]

Although not all participants in transition culture are so bold about knowing the end point, this kind of future history is important to the structure of transition culture. The main points of contention are about how to get to that normal future. Indeed, some nations in transition may have already gotten there.

One can pronounce transition to be complete. Presidents can announce it as a sign of political accomplishment, and lenders can document it in a way to reassign nations to different categories for borrowing. Joining NATO, and especially the European Union, is an institutional signal that ascending nations are now "normal" and thus join the ranks of those who set the standard. By joining those ranks, a nation is less likely to be treated as the one whose structure must adapt to fit, and more likely to be able to challenge the biases in the larger structure denoting normality.

Transition culture is, therefore, a culture with a history within nations, and across the world. It was at the apogee of its cultural power in the mid-1990s. The financial crises originating in Southeast Asia in the summer of 1997 that spread to Russia and Brazil shook the confidence of those who would prescribe the world financial system, and empowered others to doubt their capacity to advise.[19] Transition culture also had to take off. Although one might date its height with the attitude of confidence and inevitability its promoters bore in the very beginning of the 1990s, it was only after Poland, Estonia, and other countries recovered from inflation and resumed economic growth that their demonstration of success made transition culture so powerful. The World Bank's systematic analysis, *From Plan to Market: World Development Report, 1996,* appeared in just this time.[20]

I rely on this document because, through its published form, it represents a relatively stable artifact and enduring product that reached a wide segment of transition culture's potential public. Although the World Bank and transition culture generally are part of a dynamic knowledge culture, and thus subject to change, I believe that the basic principles I articulate in this section are enduring, at least through the end of the 1990s.[21] I shall rely on it to elaborate the structural formation of transition culture beyond this fundamental opposition between the past and the future.[22]

A Narrative of Transition

At its foundation, the World Bank assumes the necessity of movement from state-dominated to market-dominated societies: "The deep inefficiencies of planning became increasingly evident with time."[23] It is necessary because the world has changed, and statist forms of economic organization, since the 1960s at least, have become outmoded. If societies do not shift from statist to market economies, they will fall further and further behind. This is a given. It is also a given that the transition will be difficult. "It is not simply the adoption or modification of a few policies or programs but a passage from one mode of economic organization to a thoroughly different one" (3). Societies vary, however, in the measure of pain they must endure.

To be sure, a society's institutional legacy will influence the measure of a society's pain in transition (16). History and geography shape what leaders can accomplish, and what they can try to accomplish (5). Nevertheless, and here the interventionist identity of the World Bank becomes clear, "firm and persistent application of good policy yields large benefits" (ibid.). Great leaders, as in Mongolia or the Kyrgyz Republic, can make a mark in places where institutional legacies are not conducive to reform. Bad leadership also makes a difference. In Ukraine, the leadership's preoccupation with national identity distracted reform (11). Here, then, the premise of agency in transition culture's structure is apparent: it depends on the quality of leadership, from the level of the firm to the county's president or finance minister, and its proper focus on economic reform. National identity is not a critical issue.

The World Bank happens to conclude that "extensive liberalization and determined stabilization" are the best policies, although that in itself might be contentious within transition culture. What is not contentious within transition culture, however, is the cultural logic with which the Bank reaches that conclusion. First, one must be a comparativist to find the best strategy for change; one must look across societies and take lessons from each country. Second, one must focus on redesigning institutions to ensure that these policies will be implemented properly. Finally, one must transform the culture of work and life in order that the policies and institutions work properly.

The institutional redesign is the most complicated and contested within transition culture. The World Bank recommends, in the broadest stroke, that policy needs to (a) reform enterprises and increase the importance of the private sector; (b) restructure social safety nets; and (c) clarify property rights. There are debates here within debates across transition culture, but probably the most fundamental debate is between those who would advocate what the World Bank calls the "all-out approach" versus the phased or piecemeal approach (9–10).[24]

This contest has also been cast in terms of those who care about people and their suffering, and those who do not. Given that the World Bank has been critiqued for its disregard for people's lives, the bank marks up front that the bottom line is "the quality of life of the people who live in these countries" (iv).[25] And indeed, it devotes some attention to gender inequality, poverty and public health. But it mainly introduces these materials as evidence for the value of the "all-out approach." It argues that people suffered under the old system, and that the poor implementation of reform leads to greater suffering for all involved. For instance, it is well known that life expectancy has fallen in many countries during transition. The World Bank points out, however, that life expectancy has increased in the countries that have implemented reform most successfully (18). Thus, although all suffer, those who suffer most are those who make transition least effectively. Hence, one must learn the lessons of transition.

Although the particulars of advice are most important, the basic structure of argument rests on broad comparison. Countries are set up in four basic groups based on the extent of their economic liberalization, private sector output, measure of privatization, and degree of institutional change and social policy reform:

> Group 1: Poland, Slovenia, Hungary, Croatia, Macedonia, Czech Republic, Slovakia
> Group 2: Estonia, Lithuania, Bulgaria, Latvia, Albania, Romania, Mongolia
> Group 3: Kyrgyz Republic, Russia, Moldova, Armenia, Georgia, Kazakhstan
> Group 4: Uzbekistan, Ukraine, Belarus, Azerbaijian, Tajikistan, Turkmenistan

Comparing groups, the Bank finds that those in Group 1 are generally best off. For instance, those who have sustained liberalization did experience, like others, an initial decline in growth, but then returned to rapid growth after three years (29).

Comparisons occur not only by general groups, but in very convincing specific stories. They show the trade-offs, for instance, between different strategies for privatizing large enterprises, eventually concluding that the Czech experience provides many lessons for those concerned with all of the trade-offs (56). More schematically, one can look at the lesson boxes sprinkled throughout the text. Here I focus only on those in which countries from Eastern Europe and the former Soviet Union are featured in specific cases, with relatively firm assignments of virtue or failure (Table 2.1).

I find three intriguing generalizations in these boxed comparisons. First, some countries are for the most part invisible; Romania, the former Yugoslavia, and Central Asia are rarely if ever mentioned, while the Visegrad countries,[26] Russia, Estonia, and Ukraine are commonly featured. This is in part a data problem; the unmentioned societies are

Table 2.1. Specific Exemplars of Success and Failure in Eastern Europe and the Former Soviet Union

Box Number	Success	Failure
2.1: Pricing energy	Hungary	Russia, Ukraine
2.4: Trade policy	Estonia	Ukraine
2:6: Redistribution through inflation		Russia
2.7: Financial discipline	Poland	Kazakhstan, Romania, Russia
3.1: Creditor-led restructuring	Poland, Hungary	
3.2: Coal restructuring		Ukraine
3.5: Environmental liabilities	East Germany	Poland, Czech Republic
3.6: Privatizing natural monopolies	Hungary	Russia, Czech Republic
3.7: Restitution	Hungary	Baltics, Bulgaria, Slovenia, former Czechoslovakia, Romania
4.4: Income transfers	Latvia	Hungary
5.2: Corporate law	Russia	
6.1, 2, 3: Banking reform	Poland, Hungary, Czech Republic, Slovakia	Russia
7.1: Corporate taxes		Russia
8.1: Mortality		Russia, Hungary

Source: From Plan to Market: World Development Report, 1996, World Bank (1998).

those with less available or poorer quality data. The consequence, however, is an implicit assertion that the places we know more poorly are less important for generalizing about transition. Those countries that are visible, either because they are bigger or because they are more "Western," are privileged in setting the contours of transition culture. Their experience becomes the foundation for the global culture. Central Asia and the former Yugoslavia are not so relevant. The war-torn are especially exceptional, and undeserving of analysis within transition culture's generalizing parameters.

Second, countries tend to be posed regularly as exemplars of success or of failure. Ukraine and Russia are frequently identified as failures, although Russia has one successful moment in these highlights. By contrast, East Central Europe and the Baltics are the exemplars of success. Even when their failures are highlighted, they are nonetheless implicitly praised for their initiative and experimentation. In that way, countries are assigned national characters in transition.

Third, specific topical lessons are also provided in the boxes. For instance, they compare Estonia and Ukraine in terms of trade liberalization. They show how Estonia's liberal policy enabled it to adjust to "Western quality standards" and boost its export revenues. Ukraine, by contrast, is evidence of failure. Its continuing administrative control over trade and prices led to isolation from world markets, declining exports, trade deficits, and economic destabilization (31).[27]

This particular comparison illustrates the general analytical strategy of transition culture. The success of Estonia and the relative failures of Ukraine are used to elevate the significance of agency and the World Bank's prescription for the future. Leadership with the right policy is central, and can overcome the barriers embedded in institutional legacy and geographical location. Even more fundamentally, however, the general structure of the discourse is that transition has general lessons for each country, and successful countries ought to be imitated by those less successful. Because history is not destiny, the less successful countries must learn from the exemplars.

National Characters in Transition

Beyond the analytical comparisons, each country acquires a personality, a "national character," within transition culture. Estonia, for example, is portrayed regularly as an exemplar. It leads Group 2 along with Lithuania, Bulgaria, Latvia, Albania, Romania, and Mongolia. Baltic societies were the only ones that were not nominally independent under communism to make this list; every other post-Soviet country is ranked in the third or fourth level. In terms of cumulative foreign direct investment inflows, Estonia leads Group 2 with nearly 15 percent of its 1994 GDP ($646 million) (64). By 1995, the Czech Republic was in the lead on most indicators, but Estonia was not far behind (14–15). By 1999, Poland replaced the Czech Republic in leading transition culture across most dimensions of its evaluation, but Estonia continued its upward ascent, reaching double digits in growth in real gross domestic product.[28]

Estonia's exemplary status is most apparent when one considers the narrative that accompanies the World Bank's introduction to the country. Estonia is "disciplined," quickly growing, Western-oriented, and privatizing (italics are mine):

> Estonia has adhered to *disciplined* fiscal and financial policies and has led the FSU [former Soviet Union] countries in pursuing economic reform. It continues to experience *strong growth* after its economy bottomed out in 1993. Its GDP is among the *highest rates in Europe,* and the share of industry and manufacturing in economic output has remained fairly steady. . . . Utilization of manufacturing *capacity had expanded* from 50% in mid-1993 to 60% in mid-1997. . . . As Estonia *successfully reoriented it trade toward the West,* manufacturing production for export accounted for 49% of all production toward the end of 1996. . . . Estonia's *privatization program made commendable progress* in 1997 as the government virtually completed its large-scale enterprise program, except for utilities. . . . *Nonresidents now hold between 30% and 40% of total assets* in industry and services. Finns, Swedes, and Russians are the largest investors. . . . *Small- and medium-scale privatization is essentially complete.* . . . Estonia also made some headway in *finding effective owners* for enterprises by promoting corporate governance rather than maximizing privatization revenues.[29]

Ukraine is a much bigger society than Estonia, the second most populous post-Soviet society after Russia. Ukraine's nearly 52 million people make Estonia's 1.5 million seem insignificant. But Ukraine's position in transition culture is one of exemplary failure, rather than success, owing to the poverty of its leadership.[30] Its cumulative foreign direct investment inflows were less than 2 percent of its GDP (64). In 1995, Ukraine's inflation rates stood at 375 percent, whereas Estonia's was only 29 percent. Its growth rate stood at −12 percent in 1995; Estonia had already bounced back from the posttransition slump and grew at 4 percent in 1995. Even by 1998, Ukraine had not managed to escape its negative rate of growth. Unemployment remained very low in Ukraine at less than 1 percent of the labor force. Estonia's higher rate, at about 3 percent, was construed as making progress toward the market economy (75). Even in discussions of the efficacious state, Ukraine fares poorly. In the World Bank's 1997 report, Ukraine is specifically identified in a discussion of policy making. All countries in the former Soviet Union apparently have "confused and overlapping responsibilities and multiple rather than collective accountability." Ukraine is taken as the exemplar of this too.[31] Ukrainian judges' dependence on local authorities for their housing illustrates that country's poor government.[32] The most compelling illustration of Ukraine's dubious distinction in transition culture can be seen in the World Bank's country portrait, especially in comparison with Estonia's. Ukraine has followed a difficult road with its unfortunate parliament, informal economy, high taxes, excessive regulation, noncompetitive and limited privatization, and poor reception among foreigners (italics are mine):

> The road to *privatization has not been easily traveled* for the Ukraine. Much of the private sector is an *informal economy,* making it difficult to estimate its scope. . . . Real GDP *decline was expected to reach* −9% *in* 1996, *which was an improvement* compared to the −11.8% in 1995. Inflation has also dropped below 45% a year, down from 182% in 1995. . . . Parliament approved the 1997 privatization program, which included 1,440 medium-sized firms. . . . *High effective tax rates and excessive regulation* have constrained the growth of the private sector. The informal economy is estimated at one-third to one-half of the total economy. Barter trade was 11% of all external transactions and also represented a high proportion of domestic trade in 1997. . . . The 1992 official large-scale *privatization effort began slowly, using for the most part, non-competitive methods* (management/employee buyouts, leasing to employees, etc.). The reformist government has been successful in passing a law regulating foreign investment, the introduction of the new currency (Hryvna), and the stabilization of the Karbovanets. These measures have led to increased direct foreign investment, which was US$1.2 billion in 1996, improving from US$780 million in 1995. *Parliament has been an obstacle* in moving toward mass privatization. . . . Participation by *foreign investors in Ukrainian privatization is not very attractive* due to the small amount of stocks sold through the Stock Exchange or investment tenders; the overall lack of transparency; and laws that preclude direct foreign participation in certificate auctions. Due to the *slow pace of privatization up to* 1994, progress with *industrial restructuring has been slow.* Other contributing factors are the failure to attract much outside capital in the early stages of privatization, and weak bankruptcy laws. More than 5,000 *strategic industries are excluded* from privatization in the transportation, defense, energy, communications, and agricultural sectors.[33]

Estonia and Ukraine surely have had variable success with transition, but the underlying presumption of universality not only of methods, but also of challenges, suggests a great deal about the relatively generalizing, rather than contextualizing, approach that is dominant within transition culture. Societies are evaluated not on the basis of their own contextually embedded challenges, but rather on the universal card of expectations shaping transition. This generalizing vision is especially apparent when it comes to studying attitudes and values. Where cultural or social issues are considered, as in the case of poverty, women, and work, specific cases are rarely presented in the boxes for others to learn. Instead, culture is universalized and assimilated into a basic conception of time underlying the movement from plan to market.

Transition's Cultural Transformations

The principal cultural problem with transition is associated with the past, and its legacy into the future. There is always the danger that the problems of the past will be forgotten, and that the public will slip back unconsciously and embrace that past. "The public must constantly be reminded of the reasons for change and informed about progress to date," the World Bank warns us (11). Social consensus is important, it argues, and extreme inequality tends to threaten that consensus (12). Later, it acknowledges that greater inequality is necessary in transition, but that economic growth and good social policy can compensate for some of those problems. Also, "mobility, or freedom of individuals to seek better options elsewhere," can reduce the problems associated with transition (66). Not only is the past a threat to the future, but so too is that past embedded in community. Societies must become more fluid and mobile if they are to realize transition's radiant future.

Future culture is entrepreneurial, critical, and self-reliant. The World Bank's tacit cultural mission, for instance, consists in figuring out "how to unleash the enormous talents and energies of these countries' populations, and how to help them achieve their vision for a future of opportunity and well being for all their citizens" (iv). This future culture is apparently an unevenly realized, but omnipresent, capacity across the postcommunist world. Of course, institutions are important for this. For instance, the World Bank emphasizes that judicial institutions must be developed, but beyond these limitations, professional ethics and "engrained cultural attitudes toward the law, help to explain why so few private businesses want to use the courts to settle disputes, particularly in the NIS [Newly Independent States] and East Asia" (93). Within transition culture, elements of indigenous culture can be a barrier to the future.

Education is obviously important for generating the right kind of disposition. Across the region, the World Bank suggests that education should be restructured so as to foster choice, autonomy, and accountability in society. That general reorientation, it says, must begin with the reform of the educational system. Among other things, these societies must focus on the following elements in that reform:

- *Knowledge:* Preserve the achievements of the old system but rectify the earlier underemphasis on social sciences (by which the bank means economics, management science, and psychology) and the law.
- *Skills:* Assist the movement from specific skills to broader and more flexible skills better able to meet the continually changing demands of a market economy.

  Strengthen the ability to apply knowledge in new and unforeseen circumstances.
- *Attitudes:* Strengthen the idea that the initiatives of workers and others are rewarded.

  Assist the understanding that employing workers (subject to suitable regulation) is not exploiting them, but giving them an opportunity to earn a living.

  Assist the understanding that business has its place in society and hence that profits are needed to provide an engine of growth.
- *Values:* In line with the changed relationship between the citizen and the state, encourage the understanding that citizens need to take responsibility for their actions, including their choices about education, work, and lifestyle.

  Foster the understanding that freedom of expression is an essential and constructive component of a pluralist society governed by consent. (126)

The World Bank finds a particular education most valuable, and it is exemplified in the document's final box: "Business Skills Training is good for business—for trainers and trainees." It is "based on learning by doing and helping local talent and stakeholders help themselves." The particular story of Mrs. Smirnova, from Nizhniy Novgorod, is inspiring. After learning international accounting methods, she broke up her firm into thirteen independent companies and developed a business plan that won international awards (139).

Throughout this World Bank volume, cultural transformation is the foundation of transition. The culture of the past is a threat—it might undermine consensus for transition. It might challenge the value of business or wonder about whether employment is exploitative. The culture of the future is potentially everywhere; it merely needs to be inculcated. Of course, this might be easier in some places than in others, but it appears to be universally possible. Without cultural transformation, one cannot reach that radiant future, for initiative, creativity, flexibility, and autonomy are necessary ingredients for success.

At the same time as it is foundational, culture is also undervalued. Despite the fact that the document acknowledges cultural and historical specificity, neither culture nor history receives the systematic comparative analysis that is allocated to policy prescription and institutional developments. Unlike the systematic analysis dedicated to markets and firms, cultural expertise is treated as a tacit kind of knowledge without necessary empirical inquiry. Why?

It might have to do with the professional competencies that are privileged in transition culture and in the World Bank in particular. Within transition culture, expertise in cultural analysis remains localized and apparently anecdotal, and ultimately subordinated to those whose substantive expertise is based on broad comparison and generalization. To elevate the challenge of cultural analysis could elevate expertise in local configurations above general claims, and problematize transnational knowledge claims and those whose disciplines are organized around them. But cultural analysis has its own limitations in its articulation with the central mission of an interventionist culture. Those who wish to emphasize the challenge of reading a culture, or of interpreting a contentious history, typically do not provide prescription-laden knowledge useful for intervention. Thus, cultural analysis tends to remain tacit and implicit because its experts tend to work beyond the culture with which transition culture works. But the problem moves beyond even that contest over claims to competence.

For transition culture to be powerful, and retain its "ownership" in transnational space, it must supersede localized peculiarities and establish its claim to competence in a broader global culture. Sustained cultural analysis could put at risk transition culture's claim to panoptic vision, however. It could require transition culture to acknowledge its own peculiarity, rather than assume its universality. But in that reflexive move, transition culture should enhance its critical capacities. Although I cannot argue that this volume significantly reduces the gap between cultural analysis and policy making, I do believe that it should clarify the conditions of transition culture's possibility, and critical potential. That clarification begins with theorizing the structure of its cultural authority.

In synthetic form, the structure of transition culture provides several ingredients that make it a powerful narrative for claiming competence. First, it is based on scientific methods and comparative research that enable it to claim a superior approach to policy making. Those who can draw on the discourse of transition culture can claim a wealth of scholarship based on global experience. Second, success or failure depends on strategic intervention. Those who know best, and who have sufficient resources, can be successful. History and culture are things to be transformed, and made to yield to superior knowledge. Transition culture therefore encourages leadership to take responsibility to introduce change that might be at odds with local practices. Finally, none of this can succeed without transforming broad cultural dispositions. The dispositions most in need of transformation are those afflicted with the socialist past, and some nations are plagued more than others with this socialist burden. Although certainly the core of knowledge production could learn from the indigenous, transition culture presumes that its sense can be altered in particular applications but not in its basic worldviews. Those attached to a global transition culture have knowledge, power, and the future on their side in institutional transformation. One might draw the structure of transition culture, and its oppositions as follows:

Plan	Dictatorship	Russia	Past	Particularistic	Bureaucrat	Dependency	Ukraine
Market	Democracy	West	Future	Comparative	Entrepreneur	Opportunity	Estonia

Of course, this reading of transition culture's underlying structure is not based on a representative sample of transition readings, although I have read broadly in this area. Also, the World Bank's own view evolves, most notably in its later attention to questions of state efficacy and governance.[34] I nevertheless propose that this cultural structure provides a community of discourse in which transition is effected. This is even apparent in the United Nations Development Program's (UNDP) counterpoint to the World Bank's assessment.

Transition culture focuses on institution making, especially of the market and its supporting structures. Its hegemony in development of course is not uncontested, within societies undergoing transition and within the international policy network itself. The United Nations Development Program, in particular, poses an alternative account of transition and a different set of indicators with which to evaluate progress. In the remainder of this chapter, I consider one UNDP global intervention, akin to *From Plan to Market,* into the transition debate.[35]

A Counternarrative of Transition

No region in the world has suffered such reversals in the 1990s as have the countries of the Former Soviet Union and Eastern Europe. The number of the poor has increased by over 150 million. To put this into perspective, the figure is greater than the total combined population of France, the United Kingdom, the Netherlands, and Scandinavia. National incomes have declined drastically in the midst of some of the most rampant inflation witnessed anywhere on the globe. Mortality rates have climbed alarmingly in some countries. In short, transition has proven to be a complex and traumatic process. (6)

This paragraph begins the alternative assessment of transition by the United Nations Development Program. It reflects the program's "main priority" in eradicating poverty. It also links its work to "environmental regeneration, the creation of sustainable livelihoods and the empowerment of women . . . good governance and peace building."[36] It reflects the possibility of thinking about transition in different policy terms, in different ways than what transition culture tends to offer.

Instead of beginning with an account of where communist-led societies must go, and assessing them in those terms, the UNDP begins its evaluation with what those societies have lost. Instead of emphasizing the basic institutional homogeneity of the West, the UNDP is much more likely to emphasize variations in its policies, with the implicit argument that one cannot imitate and adapt, but rather debate and assess what institutional profile is best for the country in question.[37] As in transition culture, the authors of the UNDP report attend to rates of growth, but they also focus on the mode of its allocation. They center inequality and human suffering in their story of the preceding ten years.

In global terms, "Eastern bloc transition countries are the only nations in the world to have recorded a decline in incomes during the 1990s" (6). Inflation was the primary culprit. On top of that, illiteracy—nearly eliminated under communist rule—threatens a comeback. Women suffer disproportionately, and some ethnic groups, notably Roma, are more victimized than others by the transition (18). Health conditions are also declining—"The FSU [former Soviet Union], which once ranked proudly among the forefront of international social advances, is the only area in the world to suffer a decline in life expectancy during the 1990s" (7). As in transition culture, of course, there must be some recognition of differences among transitions, but even here, an emphasis on what was lost remains in focus.

The UNDP report distinguishes between iron and velvet transitions, with the former involving particular suffering and the latter having a "relatively smooth" change (8). The classificatory assignments between World Bank and UNDP reports look remarkably similar: in the velvet category we find the exemplary states of transition culture—Poland, Hungary, the Czech Republic, Slovenia, and Estonia (ibid.). These same countries, plus Slovakia, earn high praise for their educational levels too (67).[38] Poverty rates also were significantly lower in these countries than they were in the non-Baltic societies of the former Soviet Union (12–13). Within the former Soviet Union, in fact, the Slavic countries have suffered the most pronounced reversals in economic fortune, even though Central Asia and the Caucasus remain, for the most part, poorer (14). Nevertheless, the UNDP does not let us forget what a difference communist rule made, even in the most extreme of comparisons. Poland and Tajikistan are at opposite ends of transition success, but Poland's people live only slightly more than two years longer than those of Tajikistan. Had these two been market economies, the experts estimate that that difference in life expectancy would have been more like six (12).

The UNDP values some of the same priorities as the core of transition culture. Macroeconomic stability—a reduction in inflation and creating the right kind of environment for effective markets—is critical. Economic growth is relatively more important than inequality per se; at least in general, poverty is more a consequence of diminishing output than growing income inequality (28). It is also important to create a strong private banking sector. The authors also recommend the establishment of clear property rights and price liberalization. Like transition culture, they emphasize the importance of transparency in regulation, and the importance of developing the right kind of infrastructure to attract foreign investment and capital. They also value the development of entrepreneurship in small and medium enterprises.

Like transition culture, this report is interventionist. It also argues that the right kind of social policies can ameliorate the worst kinds of suffering. It even argues that the point of documenting tragedy is to provide a basis for sound policy (ibid.). It identifies the value of allying international agencies, nonprofit organizations, and multinational corporations in addressing human needs. Indeed, the World Bank itself got specific credit in several instances—for instance, in assisting the Georgian government in developing a finance system to support labor-intensive microprojects (191). It is, however, quick to emphasize the *conditions* that enable growth and minimal policy problems rather than the value of right thinking and good policy.

For the UNDP, one of the most important conditions determining success in transition is the initial condition of the country at transition's start—level of development, preexisting markets, and degree of domestic disruption derived from the collapse of the USSR. In particular, although it praises the policy initiatives undertaken by the exemplary states, it also states up front that "this should not obscure the more intractable problems of poverty found in the countries of the FSU" (30). These societies tended to be more deeply dependent on the economic integration of the Soviet Union, something that was disrupted by its collapse. Moreover, their economies tended to be more highly militarized, overindustrialized, and less developed in the service sector (31). The other "condition" aggravating declines in economic growth is war (32). Although the World Bank recognizes the importance of prior conditions, its emphasis on policy and the exemplary tends to minimize its attention to prior conditions. The two reports also differ on the kinds of policy emphasis the state should undertake.

The UNDP highlights much more than the World Bank document the importance of what it calls "the credible state." Under this heading, there should be a greater role of public regulation in banking reform. The privatization agenda might have to be amended, in particular to attend to those conditions where the state should regulate privatization so as to avoid monopolies. The state must address public health and education, and in general develop a more systematic approach appropriate for the postcommunist era of global competition. More effective tax-recovery mechanisms are important. Welfare is obviously dependent on a more credible state, and it is especially important for societies in which poverty is an overwhelming problem. The state must focus more on the vulnerable through more targeted programs. Microfinance programs are important, but must be adapted to the appropriate macroeconomic conditions.

In some ways, the UNDP struggles to minimize its distinction from the core of transition culture. It emphasizes that most countries agree on the general direction of reform. But here the emphasis on agreement is more an attempt to influence, and broaden, transition culture's list of priorities than it is to accept the methods with which transition culture's principal proponents imagine change. This is most apparent in the debate on the role of the state in welfare provision featured in the UNDP report. Anders Aslund offers a quite unmistakable transition culture viewpoint. Simon Clarke offers an account that resonates more with UNDP emphases. I quote the debate at length to illustrate how the UNDP itself sees the difference.

> The transition economies have emerged as "rough and tumble societies" marked by gross income inequalities and rampant corruption. Expenditures on social welfare are already high as compared to Western European standards. . . . rising income differentials are not related to a lack of social expenditures. The problem lies in a redistribution of these social benefits. . . . In 1994 nearly 5% of social spending went to housing subsidies. As these benefits were regressive, the larger the residence the more benefits received. The homeless and needy did not receive any assistance under this scheme. . . . What then is a solution? It seems unrealistic to expect to reform so corrupt a system in so short a period of time. Therefore, the short-term solution should be to reduce current expenditures. . . . Who then should take responsibility for the poor? Some responsibility should remain under the jurisdiction of the state. . . . Pensions, however, might best be managed by the private sector as was done by Chile and Argentina. In the long term, reform is necessary in order to effectively weed out corruption. (Aslund)

> To blame the problems of poverty and increased income inequality on the corruption of the social safety net seems "Bolshevik" in nature given that the primary factors influencing the halving of income and doubling of income inequality has been the "shock-therapy" imposed on the Russian Federation since the beginning of transition. Corruption is a problem which has impeded the implementation of reform, but before it is effectively addressed, one must examine where it has flourished; the higher ranks of society. The most corrupt echelon of Russian society is composed of the same policy members looking to reform the social safety net. . . . The inadequacy of social transfers will not be eliminated by reducing funding, because the problem lies within the policies connected to the distribution of these services. . . . One way to address these problems of corruption is to increase the accountability of the private and public sectors by placing them under the jurisdiction of legal entities to monitor their activities. There is certainly room for improvement, but all of these

issues . . . need to be addressed independently of the private sector. (Clarke)[39]

To the extent that "shock therapy" is associated with the core of transition culture, Clarke clearly sets himself up as its opponent. He also is critical of the kind of "leadership" that transition culture often embraces, especially when transition culture must accept the embourgeoisement and corruption of the elite in return for their support of radical institutional change (see chapter 5). For Clarke, as for the UNDP, privatization is clearly no general solution, and although it is not a general solution for Aslund either, it is the state itself, mired in the Soviet past, that needs the most radical shock afforded by privatization.

Culturally speaking, one of the primary ingredients in successful reform policies rests, as in transition culture, on the consensus of the public. There is a slightly different emphasis in this report, however; rather than emphasize the significance of leadership's reminding the public about the reasons for change, the UNDP report emphasizes the broader societal and political alignments involved in reform. Success occurs in contexts where there is "strong national consensus on direction of reform," in which Poland, Hungary, the Czech Republic, and the Baltic republics are included (29). Tragedy is most apparent, intriguingly, not when there is "apparent national consensus in the other direction" (Belarus), but when there is internal or political conflict or violence. War thus enters the discourse of transition as something embedded in the course of political and economic change, not as something "external" to the movement from plan to market. The UNDP does not shy away from societies experiencing war or extended conflict. Rather than treat them as anomalies, the UNDP reminds us of the magnitude of difference between, for instance, "war-torn and impoverished" Tajikistan and Poland (13). Those countries that have suffered war—Armenia, Azerbaijan, Georgia, and Tajikistan—have suffered the greatest losses in real gross domestic product (16). Indeed, this approach to transition relies much more on the elevation of danger than it does on the celebration of example.

This different strategic use of examples produces a very different picture of transition. It is not just the fact that the UNDP and the World Bank have sometimes convergent but more often different thematic emphases. It is equally important that they have different ranges of examples. The UNDP does not ignore Central Asia, but rather takes Uzbekistan's Mahallah (a community-based Islamic organization), for instance, as something from which others might learn. Moreover, no country earns a particular reputation for leading transition, or exemplifying failure. Estonia and Poland do not typically point the way, for their initial conditions may not be appropriate for Russia and Ukraine. Conversely, although Ukraine is the only society outside of Central Asia and Azerbaijan with more than 40 percent of its population living below the poverty line,[40] Ukraine is not developed as a negative example (but it never offers a positive example either!). The character of their negative examples also is different; rather than illustrate the wrong way to design policies, they are more typically deployed as warnings about the consequences of not addressing social problems. Indeed, although the discussion of Polish pension reform appears rather historical and neutral, its implicit caution is greater— the failure to address this kind of reform can cause political turmoil, if not also bring down governments. Finally, the nature of the examples, and warnings, is different. They are not meant to be imitated, but rather to be illustrative for how societies must deal with the problems that face them within their own meaningful contexts (Table 2.2).[41]

This alternative approach to transition lies a considerable distance from transition culture's core message, despite its convergence on particular arguments about the value of economic growth or comparative analysis of social change. Instead of emphasizing the importance of the exemplary, it focuses attention much more on the dangers and problems of transition in particular contexts. Societies are not equivalent, although lessons can be learned from each of them. Indeed, even the war-torn offer an important caution: with insufficient regulation of transition, economic transition can produce political crisis, violence, and even war. Albania, in this regard, becomes exemplary as a warning of what might happen if there is insufficient oversight over the privatization of wealth.

This UNDP approach also does not have as clear a structure of oppositions as does transition culture. It privileges the market and entrepreneurship, but not with the same emphasis. Its emphasis on the "credible state" requires plans and bureaucrats to implement reforms that underlie effective market regulation, and its emphasis on prior conditions limits the degree to which one can imagine the entrepreneurial search for opportunity as an omnipresent potential. It also does not

Table 2.2. Boxed and Textual Exemplars of Positive Efforts and Relative Dangers in Addressing Problems

Box Number or Text Pages	Learning from Positive Efforts	Dangers Needing Address
1.1: Poverty, war, and peace	Poland	Tajikistan
1.2: Ethnicity, gender, poverty		Roma women in Romania
2.1: Reform strategies	Poland, Hungary, Czech Republic, Baltic republics	Armenia, Albania, Russia, Ukraine, Slovakia
2.2–3: Crisis lessons	Hungary	Bulgaria
3.1: Health-care reform	Russia/Hungary	Hungary/Russia
3.2: Health-care reform (53–58)	Czech Republic and Kyrgyz Republic	
4.1–2: Education reform	Lithuania	Armenia
Middle-class formation (79–84)	Russian Federation	Russian Federation
5.1, 4: Social assistance programs	Armenia/Uzbekistan	
5.5: Unemployment policy	Bosnia and Herzegovina	
5.6–7: Pension system reform	Kazakhstan	Poland
6.1: Sequencing price reform and reducing subsidies	Russia	
7.2: Supporting women in business	Russia, Hungary, Czech Republic, Slovakia	
Historical background (161–63) to small and medium enterprise (SME) and performance (165–69)	Hungary	Russia
Rationale for SME support (164–65)	Slovakia	
SME development projects	Russia, Romania, Slovakia	
9.1: Enterprise credit	Poland	
9.2: Social investment	Georgia	Russia

Source: Vladimir Popov, Paul Gregory, Catalin Zamfir, Carol Scott Leonard, Asta Sendonaris, Susan Linz, Stephen Batsone, Nada Kobeissi, Giovanni Andrea Cornia, Victor Rodwin, Harley Balzer, and Omar Noman, *Poverty in Transition* (New York: Regional Bureau for Europe and the Commonwealth of Independent States, United Nations Development Program, 1998).

diminish the importance of particularistic knowledge to the same degree as the World Bank. Instead, it emphasizes the importance of initial conditions far more than general comparative lessons. Hence, no particular set of countries can become the exemplars of success or failure for others. Russia's distinction, and challenge, appears regularly throughout the text, and the West's variation is highlighted, suggesting that it cannot be treated as a simple model for the rest of Europe and Eurasia. Above all, this UNDP report does not focus on the future while ignoring the past; instead, it seeks to remind us of what has been lost through transition, and what values from the communist past might be bequeathed, and preserved. Nevertheless, transition culture sets the terms within which the arguments against ignorance of the past and the homogenization of the West must be made.

Conclusions

Raymond Williams has written that cultural formations are those "effective movements and tendencies, in intellectual and artistic life, which have significant and sometimes decisive influence on the active development of a culture, and which have a variable and often oblique relation to formal institutions."[42] Transition is quite obviously grounded in its own cultural formation, and bears consequent power to shape the freedom of actors to choose. To appreciate its historical variability and practice-induced transformations, however, one needs to elaborate its more structural qualities. Hence, I have approached transition culture through a rather more semiotic approach in this chapter, emphasizing its enduring oppositions and principal methodologies as I analyze the artifacts of its exemplary proponents.

The structure of transition culture appears to be clear.[43] Transition culture is itself dependent on the cultivation of a eutopic utopia, based on that which already exists elsewhere.[44] From plan to market and from dictatorship to democracy are powerful and compelling oppositions. Transition culture's embeddedness in a project about making the abnormal normal and the undesirable desirable makes its cultural distinction hard to recognize. Hence, comparing it to a project with a different structure enables us to recognize the peculiarity of transition culture.[45] With the UNDP's redrawing of transition's picture toward problems, and what has been lost in transition, the larger narrative of postcommunist social change becomes very different. It does not focus on the future, and does not anticipate a holistic or systemic transformation that characterizes transition culture's core and the emancipatory culture in which civil society's mobilization against communism figured. Instead, this approach to transition suggests the importance of a dialogue with those left behind in the rush to the radiant future, and the value of engaging the past to retrieve what it might bequeath the future.

Although transition culture appears, in this structural reading, to ignore this emphasis on dialogue with the past and the elevation of the particular, I do not believe that it is necessary to the cultural formation itself. It would be difficult to discuss transition culture without the contest between the past and the future in play. Transition culture would not exist if the choice between anachronistic socialist and suitably capitalist practices were not an important, if not dominant, cultural schema. To that extent, I have identified its core structure, but if the meaning of a cultural formation emerges primarily in its historical variability, and in practice-induced transformations,[46] the impression of transition culture's durability might be an artifact of the method used to study it. I worry that without linking structural analysis to "culture in action," our identification of a culture's core and ephemeral qualities could have more to say about our theoretical lens than it has to do with the dynamics of the cultural formation itself.[47] By attending to culture in practice, one can assess how any particular structural reading resonates with different conditions of and perspectives within that culture's reproduction and transformation.

Attending to practice also makes it more difficult to make the standpoint of one's own analysis invisible. When culture's study is grounded in practice, one is more likely to question the position from which the analysis itself is conducted.[48] We improve our capacity to recognize the contingencies of cultural formations, and their conditions, by combining the explicit analysis of culture in action across various sites with an explicit elaboration of that culture's structure. We also extend the relevance of this cultural study to immanent critique.

As I have demonstrated, transition culture is itself predicated on change, drawing in new actors and addressing new problems in its ambition to transform the world and make markets, not states, dominate the world system. It is driven to transform, and only secondarily to reproduce itself. It draws widely on lessons from around the world, and from problems within its principal domain of action. Its culture is organized around a particular sense of systemic oppositions, historical necessity, and institutional prescriptions organized around a focus on a future and an escape from the past. And it can find exemplary action within postcommunist countries that reinforces the sense of transition culture.

That sense, however, can lead it to miss the principal challenges of postcommunist social change. It can overlook the huge contextual differences between Poland and Tajikistan, or even Poland and Ukraine. In its focus on learning managerial techniques, it can miss the persistence of poverty. In its drive to realize a future based on markets, it can miss the importance of civil society in its Central Asian manifestations, or its emancipatory practices from 1989. And even in the midst of its most successful moments, it can miss the nationalism that animates the contradictions of transition culture itself. For transition culture to become critical, the cultural formations of postcommunism must be explored for their potentials in the production of "new meanings and values, new practices, new relationships and kinds of relationship."[49] Then we might be able to consider whether emancipation's translation into transition could produce yet another translation that makes freedom, rather than markets, the driving question of postcommunist change. And with that consideration, one can demonstrate culture's centrality to transition's future. But that requires the analysis of transition culture in practice.

In the following four chapters, I address that practice in ever-widening hermeneutic circles of translation and interpretation. In chapter 3, I examine one of the smoothest extensions of transition culture into practice: into the world of multinational business and Western technical assistance in Poland and other advanced countries of transition culture. In chapter 4, I focus on Estonia, the most advanced post-Soviet society in transition culture, and consider how those outside of business have formulated the history of communism's end and postcommunism's start in transition culture's terms. In chapter 5, I focus on Ukraine, one of the most troubled countries in transition culture, to explore those few links, and more gaps, in transition's translation. In chapter 6, I explore the Wars of Yugoslav Succession to consider how transition culture retains its integrity by assigning tragedy to nationalism. By working across sites of practice, from places of apparently smooth translation to sites of profound disjuncture, I hope to clarify the contingencies and critical potentials of transition culture.

Three

Transition Culture in Business Practice

The cultural encounters between American business advisers and East European managers in promising companies, in transition culture's most promising nations, should be one of the places where transition culture finds its smoothest local translations.[1] As in general, the opposition between a socialist past and a capitalist future clearly structures transition culture in business practice. Nonetheless, transition culture in action is a culture transformed. The *meanings* of socialism and capitalism are changed in business practice, through the contest over claims to competence in directing firms. These meanings highlight the lability of transition culture's categories, and of the cultural formation itself. By investigating transition culture's dominant schema in the strategic behavior of those for whom transition culture is but one potential affiliation, we can see some of the ways in which the dominant cultural motifs of transition can be altered.

Although the more global formations of transition culture might easily discuss movement from plan to market without any particular place in mind, those who work to implement transition culture in business cannot ignore context. In the practice of transition culture, the importance of those with contextual expertise grows. Knowing the nation's history, the local second economy, and even the language of work becomes much more important for implementing transition in business than it is for discussing the rules and resources that set up transition culture in general. To be sure, one cannot assume that in opposition to the global, the local means the national. However, in a setting where emancipation has meant national liberation, and where global actors define cases as nations and localities as national markets, it is very easy for the nation to shape the meaning of locale, and the meaning of contextual expertise.[2] But not everyone values that expertise to the same degree, or in the same way. That value emerges in a contest of competencies over the direction of a firm's movement toward a radiant future.

Grounding Transition Culture

The business practice of transition culture engages contextual expertise in several different ways. It can appear as a benign form of local knowledge that must simply be assimilated to the global culture of transition. Global advocates of transition culture can view this local knowledge as a useful additive, assimilated in order for business techniques to become effective. For instance, when I asked one Western expatriate manager (944)[3] how he can be a marketing expert in a culture he does not know, he responded as a scientist might. First, the Westerner provides the conceptual guides and the indigenous fill in the details. Next, the marketing expert tests those formulations through research, and alters preconceived notions if necessary. He recalled that pizza delivery did not seem to work as a concept. People did not want it; at least they apparently preferred to go to the delivery stands and eat their pizza there. This was partly because they did not want to stay in their flat, he said, but also because they did not believe that delivery would really be free, or that it would really arrive hot. As a consequence of this learning, his company initiated a major advertising campaign to convince people that space-age technology keeps pizza hot. It was explicitly stated that delivery was free. With the proper concepts and research, he said, you can see that the indigenous market in any particular postcommunist society is "pretty much the same as the rest" (944).

Contextual expertise functions as a useful additive not only in the promotion of products, but also in the promotion of new ideas in firm practices. It is not only getting the ideas right, but making sure that claims about East Europeans can be backed up by an East European. For example, one American emphasized that it was really important to have an indigenous partner for each American adviser:

> That's indispensable if you want to be effective . . . because then
> when you go in and say you make a recommendation, you say the
> East Europeans are like this. Or like this. And then the local fellow
> can back you up, because they're East European. (979)

Contextual knowledge is thus sutured to Western experience not only because it can provide information, but also because it helps expertise become more persuasive when the indigenous can be used to convince their fellow nationals of transition culture's insight. Transition culture thus becomes more powerful to the extent that it can be translated into the variety of local contexts. With this deployment, local culture is an additive to making globalized business expertise powerful. Local culture is not always so benign, however.

Socialist culture is generalized across space in the structure of transition culture, but in the application of transition culture it is grounded in locales. It becomes a label with which an individual, or set of practices, can be consigned to the past to be superseded. Representatives of a global transition culture cannot, by definition, be assigned to this past. By contrast, locals must struggle to demonstrate that they are not a part of it. And given that this contextual expertise is one of their greatest assets in the practice of transition culture, they must figure out a way to elevate the value of their local identity while at the same time expunging the socialist past that might contaminate them in transition culture.

Americans have ready scripts with which they can identify the representative of socialist culture, the type of actor or behavior that does not belong to transition culture. One American was quite specific about what most needed change in local practice, and thus was a clear sign of the past infecting the future.

> They haven't learned yet to think about making a profit. I mean
> when we were there, we were developing a system to chart costs for
> them and it was the first time they were really thinking about "are
> we pricing our products high enough to cover our costs?" It was the
> first time they really looked and said, "Oh, we lost $12 million this
> year." That's a big deal, you know, especially when your sales are not
> that much. And a lot of things they do—they don't do the standard
> sort of cost analysis that we do here in the U.S. "Should we under-
> take this project? Should we do this?" They just, I don't know, they
> kind of do it out of their gut. (976)

The relationship between socialist culture and East European cultures is not, however, obvious to Americans.[4] For instance, some Americans presumed that the qualities associated with socialist culture might be more enduring qualities of a nation. One American, after praising the strengths of his East European colleagues, lamented that they

> would approach a situation saying, "This is a problem." You know, that would be the first thing that they would say. And initially it was frustrating for us because we are both a little bit more optimistic about things. And we'd say, "No this is an opportunity. If you're going to speak to people at the parent company, you have to be a little more positive and not say it's a problem, because that will put people on the defensive immediately." (979)

Another American sympathized with this East European disposition, but definitely saw it as a problem for business. She said, "It's easy to feel the way they do, to feel frustrated, to be downhearted, not to want to kind of problem-solve and move forward. I've been in that attitude myself. And I think it looks really unprofessional." She later ascribed this particular disposition to that nation's culture, itself produced by "being under someone else's rule for as long as they have, they have a very defeated attitude" (976).

East Europeans are quick to recognize this American cultural criticism. For instance, one East European recalled the American impression of her countrymen:

> When I asked them what they think about East Europeans, one of the things they mentioned was that they are not really ready for changes and to change things. What's really interesting is that everybody's complaining, and some people do try and change things, but a lot of people not. (984)

One could interpret this cultural critique of socialist and perhaps national cultures as simply an American or Western presumption and condescension. But this critique is also embedded in East European accounts of culture in transition. Some East Europeans are very powerful critics of the socialist disposition, and in many ways are better situated to recognize how it works. One East European manager specifically charged the East European partner of his multinational firm with trying to limit the joint venture's success. He thought the motivation for this interference came from fear. He believed that the joint venture's success might reflect badly on the accomplishments of the indigenous firm: "it proves that it is possible to do something in that company" (956). The most compelling example comes from another Westernized East European manager who reflected on the executive he replaced. The old boss had a completely different management style from Western management, and that style simply had to be transcended:

> I mean, my first board meeting I come in and—we go through agenda items, I run the board meeting and, well, he's there. And there is a, uh—what was it? The decree or the resolution of the board that needs to be signed. So I look at the resolution. Everybody signed it already. And the resolution says, "As of such and such date, the price for such and such an item in such and such store should go from this to that." And I said, "Why are we signing? Why is it so important that the board needs to sign this? I know nothing about this item, I know nothing about this store. It should be, I don't know, Sales Manager, or Marketing Director deciding and—signing off, and that's it. . . ." So what it meant was that all decisions, even the smallest ones, were taken by a team. So if something went wrong, nobody was accountable. So, no accountability. No risk taking. And that ran through the entire organization. . . . So, that was definitely something entirely inconsistent with the way the parent company would like to see the company run. Or any Western company, yeah. The fact that he [sigh] didn't really, had *never* been exposed to Western concepts regarding business management didn't help either. Because, you know, the parent company guys were talking a different language. (955)

This recollection indicates powerfully how transition culture depends, in practice as well as in structure, on a holistic imagery of socialist culture as a culture to be transcended, and against which an alternative must be imagined.[5]

It is difficult, however, to fix the relationship between this socialist culture and East European cultures. Westerners are more likely to extend the drawbacks of socialist culture to a wider range of practices associated with being East European. The Westerner is also more likely to presume the East European to be a representative of socialist culture until that East European can demonstrate that he or she belongs to transition culture. And as East Europeans demonstrate that membership, they must rethink their own relationship to what it means to be Polish, Romanian, or Hungarian. In the sections that follow, I discuss in greater detail how East European cultural practices are connected to socialist and transition cultures by East European managers and their American business advisers.

Transition Culture and East European Management

Transition culture is a transnational community of discourse organized around the question of how to make market economies out of centrally planned economies. It depends on the elaboration of a globalized business expertise that selectively adds local cultures into it, and defines itself against a socialist past that threatens to disrupt the present. Transition culture provides the collection of stories and images on which both foreigners and East Europeans can draw to make their own claims to competence. Foreigners and East Europeans are, however, unequally positioned before this culture. After all, it is the East European who must assimilate to the cultural formation of transition. As in the American firm of the 1970s, there is terrific potential for "homosocial reproduction," but this time along the lines of passports and linguistic difference. And like minorities and women in Rosabeth Moss Kantor's work, East Europeans are more likely than their Western counterparts to recognize these cultural elements shaping recruitment and promotion within transition culture.[6] It may also be a reason why American advisers have been hard-pressed to identify any East European manager as exemplary.

These American business experts typically praise the instinct or feel of their managers, but rarely indicate any particular respect for special business expertise.[7] One could imagine that over time, managerial skills could follow Western management standards increasingly, and experts would be more likely to find something to admire in their East European counterparts. I expected to find more such evaluations over time too because of the transition culture's disposition toward generalization and the elevation of the business leader. Overall assessments of the nature of the transition are very common (i.e., from production-centered to market-centered firms),[8] and managerial expertise is typically held responsible for failure and success of firms during transition. On reflection, however, it is very hard for anyone to offer overall praise for management.

The business advisers we interviewed often acknowledged that their East European managers were good in some specific area. For instance, some interns praised their hosts for their ability to engineer anything, but typically they were surprised by my question. They did not expect to find anything particularly exemplary (965, 985, 981, 976). One intern remarked simply that his managerial associates were simply "not trained to manage people" (961). Another said that her managers were so bad that they made workers irresponsible:

> [They] have this attitude that their workers can't think. This was a direct quote from one of their managers. He said we treat our workers like they're dumb. Which they do. . . . and because of that, the workers kind of react in that way. They don't think. (976)

Americans often came back from their experience in Eastern Europe with little appreciation for the managerial skills of their hosts. In this sense, Americans assigned socialist culture to "typical" East European management practice. The exceptions to this rule are the most illuminating, however, for showing how powerfully that cultural presumption works.

It appears easiest to recognize managerial accomplishment by looking for responsibility and dedication to work.[9] They appear to indicate the potential for managerial adaptation to the expectations of transition culture. For instance, one female manager said simply:

> A lot of the managers have to work ten, twelve, fourteen hours per day. It's becoming more and more normal. But it was not at all normal at the time that the parent company came. . . . So when the expatriate manager came, he had to start to do that with his example. So he was there from morning until night. Not *forcing* the managers to be there, but as they saw him, they started to think more about that . . . when I came there, I had small children. So I also *tried* to escape from work at four or five o'clock. But then I, I realized it's not possible to do it that way. And I found a baby-sitter for my children. I found a cleaning lady for my house. And practically I stay at work really from morning till night . . . eight o'clock till eight o'clock. (957)

One young East European who was also getting her MBA at an American university offered the most general accolade for particular East European managers. She criticized most of the East European management with whom she worked. The lower management was unable to comprehend the mission of her joint American/indigenous team, and the upper management was generally unsupportive. However, there were two managers who were

> very competent, savvy. They see the broad picture of where the company is. And pretty clearly understand what they've gotta do. You know, they have different opinions, because they come from different backgrounds. But very competent people. Now the other group of managers may be a more typical set of East European managers. (977)

These two cases were unusual in that they were both prepared to identify generally superior East European managers. Nevertheless, as they broke with the tendency, they reinforced the general rule undergirding transition culture's elevation of global over local expertise. Both women recognized the superiority of managers, or their practices, by comparing them to other East Europeans. They did not compare them to managers outside their nation, but instead drew on a narrative of "typical" East Europeans to set the standard against which to measure managerial accomplishment. There were, however, two other narratives throughout our interviews that challenge the assumption that East European culture is inadequate and that the remedy lies in global business techniques.

The Challenge of Transition and Specific Skills

As I indicated in the chapter 2, transition culture places a lot of stock in entrepreneurs and managers, and has invested heavily in their education. To the extent they learn superior managerial techniques, and to the extent they adopt the appropriate attitudes, transition will succeed. When transition has problems, therefore, it is very easy to place the blame on the managers themselves. One might also, however, focus on the difficulty of the transition itself, and of managing a firm within that process of change. As one manager recalled:

> It's so overwhelming, and so frustrating. Because those very basic, fundamental things that should be easy to accomplish don't happen. And you get frustrated. Because it puts you in the position where you feel sometimes professionally embarrassed. . . . You know, you—your boss comes, says: "Right, you know, two months ago we talked about the fact that perhaps in those, supermarkets, when we sell chips in big shipping cases we should put labels on them so that people, you know, like in club stores here—so people can see what's inside." Pretty basic. You still don't have it. Two months later. You, you would just take this and glue it on, right? It's pretty simple. And you feel stupid. Because you've been trying for the last two months [begins to laugh] to put it into the system. And everything possible on the way—failed. And it's, it's a daily occurrence. (955)

With this as a point of departure, one might argue that no manager is likely to be up to the task of managing a transitional firm. Every manager, before the foreign observer with limited experience in transition, is likely to be found wanting, and to be found "socialist" in some particular fashion. Hence, a socialist "infection" might not be limited to the middle-aged and elderly East European, but rather, to those who become too embedded in local practices, or responsible for how things work locally.

In the face of this difficulty, East Europeans and Westerners can collaborate in producing the imagery of an East European manager who has left the socialist past behind. This imagery depends on elevating particular kinds of skills as indicators of membership in transition culture. Those who possess these skills might be recognized as part of the radiant future of transition even if solving the problems of the firm is beyond everyone. And to claim that others lack those skills might consign them to the past beyond redemption. However, people in different locations have different claims to competence, and are likely to assign to others different kinds of limitations.

Americans were more likely to emphasize communications and presentation skills as their own special competence and the specific inadequacy of East Europeans (978, 977, 976). After praising the common sense of her East European manager, one American expert emphasized a fundamental flaw: they did not know how to work in a team, and failed to communicate between departments and levels of management. "Lack of communication, besides lack of money, that's the biggest problem at the company, and it's really really bad, almost zero communication" (984). Communication was indeed a problem other outsiders mentioned (958), although no East Europeans in this set mentioned it as a major issue.[10]

Both Americans and East Europeans used expertise in personnel management as an indicator of membership in transition culture, but in a fairly limited set of ways. Good managers figure out how to provide the right compensation to motivate their employees (979, 982, 952, 961, 978). They know how to stimulate individual responsibility for company success (955, 979, 952, 982, 978). They are also willing to fire unnecessary or irresponsible personnel (961, 965, 956, 952, 970). Only two East European managers emphasized that they would do more than fire redundant workers. They might retrain them (970) or encourage them to set up privatized firms (952), but otherwise the East European managers demonstrated their membership in transition culture by their readiness to dismiss employees.

Good human resource management skills are an especially powerful way for marking the difference between transition culture and the socialist culture that is to be left behind. No American adviser emphasized the inadequacies of East European management when it came to personnel management, however. By contrast, East European managers used this as a way to mark their difference from their own colleagues or subordinates. For instance, one East European manager recalled the surprise of his employees when he announced that he was closing down one department of the firm. I asked him, with intentional naïveté, why they expected him to defend that department. He replied:

> They felt that they, they knew me from the past time [when he was a director thirty years earlier]. That I was, let's say, a patriot of this company, [but] they badly understand what is pat—local patriotism. For me local patriotism is to earn money. For those who want to work, and not to defend those groups and machines which are worthless from the technological point of view. They are good for a museum. They [the employees] are too sentimental. I am *not* sentimental anymore. (952)

Beyond personnel management, marketing is the other commonly identified lack of managerial skills in transition culture. The compelling general story around which more specific stories are typically inserted is organized around two elements. Transition is about the move from the production-centered to the market-driven company. This transformation of the firm typically takes place within uncertain or difficult markets. Several respondents in our interviews used marketing to speak of how well they are doing, or how their managers are quite good. They spoke of their firm's success in doing market research or in their focus on a particular market segment useful for their product. They talked about becoming more customer-oriented. They introduced special advertisements and special slogans directed toward their upper-end clientele. In the most high-minded of these accounts, one person said that he sold ideas and not just goods (956, 982, 975, 967, 958, 969, 970). Only East European managers invoked marketing as a claim to their own distinction. It was also used, however, to indicate the limitations of other East Europeans.

One East European CEO complained about how his marketing department kept sending out "socialist-style letters" (952). The same East European managers who praised their own accomplishments in marketing could still point to others in their own firms who continued in a socialist style of sales, just leaving goods on the shelves and expecting them to sell themselves for their own qualities (975, 956).

Occasionally, East Europeans might invoke other markers of professional competence to distinguish the good manager from managers with socialist mind-sets or corrupt practices. One manager, for instance, emphasized his abilities to make projections, and the unwillingness of his former boss to pay attention to those data (980). The specifics are interesting, but the more important point here is that the focus on specific competencies is another, more refined layer of transition culture.

At the crudest level, transition culture presumes East European inferiority to globalized business practice. But because transition culture requires East European success, it must provide a means for the globalization of East European management practices and the assimilation of East Europeans. Because East Europeans are not *assumed* to be part of transition culture, as Americans and other foreigners are, East Europeans must have a means by which they can demonstrate their acquisition of transition culture. Because transition economies are so complicated and difficult, however, East European managers can rarely demonstrate their membership in transition culture in holistic terms, as Americans and other Westerners presume to do themselves. Westerners and East Europeans can identify those East Europeans with specific skill sets associated with marketing, personnel management, or communications as belonging to transition culture. One might refine the set of oppositions used to identify the structure of transition culture with an additional list of qualities associated with socialist, or capitalist, management in transition:

Plan	East	Past	Short	Instinct (at best)	Production-centered	Dispersed responsibility	Poor, if any communications
Market	West	Future	Long hours	Expertise	Market-centered	Accountability in focus	Communications priority

(with ~ between each pair)

This refinement of transition culture—the identification of *specific* inadequacies and the identification of particular professional skills they might acquire—reproduces transition culture. It continues to identify the solutions as resting outside Eastern Europe, and the inadequacies as residing within it. Thus, transition culture provides the means—the identification of specific skill sets that East Europeans can acquire—for "homosocial reproduction" to cross national lines. It allows the East European to leave socialist culture behind, and enter a transition culture dominated by those outside the country. But over time, the national ownership of this transition culture could come into doubt.

Language and Transition Culture

Within transition culture, the difference between Eastern Europe and other national cultures or global business practice tends to be minimized and subordinated in importance to the competencies associated with global business expertise, or the quality of leadership (see chapter 2). Even the most obvious cultural difference, language, is treated as a minor obstacle easily transcended.

Western experts rarely mentioned any problem associated with language barriers because translation usually appears to have been more than adequate.[11] For example, one internship team worked in a place where few spoke English. One person understood English well enough to "understand basically what we were saying" and, with a couple of locally supplied translators, "there was no problem with English" (965). Another said, "It didn't bother me that much. I mean at times, yeah, it would have been nice to know what they were saying, and you know, there were times when I felt like, you know, he would give a fifteen-minute-long answer and our translator's answer would be two minutes. And you're kind of like, what else was in there? It didn't really bother me" (976).

The ease with which linguistic difference is transcended comes out even more clearly when there *was* a problem with translation. One person recalled a problem this way:

> We were in this meeting, and we needed help with translation, with this manager. And I had asked the [indigenous] student if she would be comfortable translating. . . . I said, "If you would like, you can help us with the translation, and I would really enjoy it if you would." But, rather than speaking up and feeling confident and feeling part of the team in the meeting, instead of taking a break to do the translation for all of us, she was sitting next to me, whispering very quietly the translation. And I turned to her and I said—in the meeting, I said, "You know what, um"—then the other [East European] student, actually started to translate, even though he only speaks [another Slavic language]. . . . The languages are very similar, and he felt confident enough to, to *bridge* the language, and also to speak loudly for the whole group. (981)

Occasionally, Americans were more appreciative of the challenge of translation. One American recalled:

> There's a lot of words that we use in English business vocabulary that don't exist in the East European business vocabulary. And I'm

trying to think of specific—oh, one of 'em was, uh, performance measure. It didn't translate. And it didn't translate—you could come up with the word for performance, and you could come up with the word for measure, but when you put 'em together, it just doesn't exist, and it doesn't make sense in this language. 'Cause that activity hasn't occurred. Or like another one was resource driver, which was the technical cost-accounting term. There were several terms with action that doesn't exist in [this language] yet. And so the word doesn't exist. And so there was—I mean the local fellows were spending like, you know, like a *couple hours,* you know, or days, just like, What do we mean by this? And looking at the different words, and trying to come up with a combination of words that *best* conveyed what we would mean in English. (977)

Those in the middle, those capable in both languages, were more likely to mark the challenge of translation. Several people in the middle mentioned that much was lost in conversations that were pressured for one reason or another—many people talking at once, or in time-compressed settings (984, 958). But there was also more to it. Concepts were important, but the mode of interaction was important too. Sometimes it even fit the stereotype:

My American friends complained that something which would be said in one sentence in English—in the East European language it is like the whole story . . . and that we waste a lot of time on just talking, talking, talking, and very often, when asked a question, the answer was, "Uh, it's a difficult question." . . . And they started talking about history. [gives short laugh] And even once it was, this was an exaggeration because one guy started talking about history from the eighteenth century. He just wanted to give the background of East European history, why it is like this, but . . . [laughs] but he just asked a question about today. (961)

Admittedly, this East European adviser, like another (984), admired the Western way of "getting down to business." He found that he often shared the inclination to go into "unnecessary discussions, details, stuff like that," along with those who shared his East European origins. But sometimes American directness was downright counterproductive:

Americans would say, very straightforward, that, well, what you do is useless. [short laugh] Or, you know, not exactly, but something like this, that after that, that person would know that, uh, they have not good attitude, or, they know that their work is unnecessary. Uh, so, very often I had to soften this, not to make it that sharp. (961)

Another person in a similar situation said, "It wasn't just translating, it was a cultural translation, and I couldn't put it that straightforward for an East European manager as they put it in English." In such a situation, the American would not be able to get the information they needed, as their very manner signaled to the East European their lack of sympathy. But by using the language, and even "complaining for ten minutes in, in the East European way," this adviser could get what the team needed. As a summary recommendation, this adviser suggested:

> Sometimes they [Americans] do not understand that somebody's different, that, so, although they adjusted very well to the culture, uh . . . But they were impatient about it, they were very often upset that something is different, that somebody doesn't meet their expectations. . . . That things cannot be like here [the United States]. . . . they should have something like in their diary: "Reminder: you are in different culture." (961)

You are in another culture. Transition culture, of course, is about multiculturalism, but the distinction of cultures is minimized within its particular pattern of homosocial reproduction. Although the Americans rely on minimizing the distinction, East Europeans tend to be much more ambivalent about erasing those distinctions that elevate the value of contextual expertise. It is particularly important to explore the dimensions of this ambivalence, for some of the most important liabilities of transition culture rest here.

Negotiating East European Difference within Transition Culture

East Europeans can and often do embrace transition culture's presumptions about the superiority of global business practices and the relative insignificance of East European differences. One manager (957), for instance, said that there was nothing intrinsically wrong with the way the parent firm does business in Eastern Europe; indeed, she said, her firm is like any other in the rest of Europe because the company has its own culture that cuts across national cultures. She also said, in her excellent English, that the language of business is English, implying that English is not so much a national property as it is a functional one. The only thing that was slightly wrong, she said, was that some of the Westerners were too arrogant, talked behind people's backs, and snickered at the East Europeans as if they were dumb. She said that this was their greatest failing, and she recommended that managers should recognize that her countrymen can learn.

Manifest appreciation for any indulgence of national cultures runs alongside this praise for global business practice. On the one hand, Westerners demonstrate the universality of transition culture by demonstrating some interest in, and especially some capacity in, the local culture. On the other hand, East Europeans demonstrate their membership in this culture by extending their appreciation for this, sometimes relatively limited, accomplishment. One East European said that the Americans she worked with were "really well prepared" because "they had classes and knew a lot of things about my country. Some things about the history, some current things, what's going on in the country's companies, a little of my language, some basic words" (984). Another American recalled that "when we got out into the streets and things, we knew a little bit of the language, and people loved it" (979). Indulging the local culture goes beyond the production of collegial appreciation.

Certainly, for business to be done well, there must be some sense of the country's mentality. The East Europeans enjoyed telling stories about the foolishness of Westerners without the right cultural tool kit. One manager (956) told with relish of the marketing strategy for Wash 'n Go, the combined shampoo and conditioner. They spent a bundle on advertising, emphasizing just what a good deal it was to have a combined shampoo and conditioner. This was ridiculous, he said, because East European women did not use conditioner. Another manager recalled a second absurd commercial. When women on the commercial shout "This detergent is great!!!" her people don't get it. The manager said, "Our people are not like that. They don't think about things so enthusiastically" (957).

Westerners do not necessarily take these as examples of Western condescension or cultural inadequacy. Instead, like the pizza marketer at the beginning of this chapter, they will only take these examples as indicators that the marketing office did not do good work. East Europeans, however, can use it as a symptom of a more general problem. East Europeans should be more in charge. Indeed, the most "Westernized" East European manager argued that a Western manager could not be the marketing director, because "he must understand completely what the people need, and what the people think in that market." But she could not have done the job before her training either, because she knew "nothing about advertising, nothing about promotion, about pricing" (957). East Europeans can learn, however. Transition culture presumes that. It does not presume, however, that those at the core of transition culture need to learn how East Europeans think.

Within transition culture, therefore, we have contests over who is best suited to manage transition: Westerners or East Europeans. On the one hand, Westerners will claim "ownership" of transition culture. East Europeans can join transition culture by invoking the proper skills, but can rarely challenge Westerners on those grounds. On the other hand, they can invoke their knowledge of East European culture to elevate their own competence over their Western counterparts. The dispute can rest on the relative significance of knowing local culture for any particular task. Ironically, three of the central skill sets associated with transition culture—human resource management, marketing, and communications—all potentially elevate the importance of local cultural competence in ways that accounting or writing business plans may not. Consider the following examples in human resource management. Here, one manager laughs at his Western boss:

> One of our bosses decided to implement special incentives for their sales guys. And he announced that everybody who sells more than a certain number of products in one month will be given Ray-Ban sunglasses. You know? Ray-Bans! Can you imagine? Ray-Bans. And the answer was, We already have glasses. For him it was something special, you know. Completely, mm, upstanding. The best glasses. All around the world, OK. OK, yeah, very good. But this is not the best incentive for East European people. And the answer was, OK, give us a hundred dollars for that, and this will be better. (956)

Sometimes it reflects an awareness of how the delegitimated past mixes with the present, as when one manager discussed "employee of the month" awards:

> They come up with ideas. They're happy to receive money, this reward. But when you want to put their name and their picture on the board and say, This guy really did something, no. Because, it continues to be perceived as something negative, really. Because you are cooperating with authority. Cooperation with authority is not good by definition. Because it's been—and it's not only the communist system, it's also the, the history of our country . . . to defy authority, to fight authority was a good patriotic deed. So now if you, all of a sudden, are recognized by authority, it means—well, who are you? Which

side are you on? Even though, you know, we try to communicate and explain, you know, it's, it's pretty good for all of us. They are very skeptical toward it. In fact if you—I, I was just amazed myself—when you try to—when you take like corporate creeds—or mission statements. In English. And they make perfect sense, they're sincere and all this. You translate into our language—it sounds *terrible*. It sounds almost 100 percent like communist propaganda. (955)

Sometimes it does not take a profound awareness of taste or of the past, but just a good sense of how incentive systems work. For instance, one Westernized East European manager complained that the parent company insisted on a certain kind of compensation system that was completely inappropriate given the ups and downs of sales in the market, regardless of unit productivity (955; also 952). Limitations are even more dramatic when it comes to assessing resistance, and corruption. As one manager recalled:

> Well, you see, I came one year ago. And before me, the general manager was one guy from the West. And it—the management was practically only Westerners. And they did a lot of work, good work. But they didn't expect and they didn't know how strong is the East European resistance. They thought that they wanted to create this factory exactly on the image of the factory in their home country. But it's, it's impossible. It is different conditions. Different people. Everything is different. So they did a lot of work, and later on they entered into big problems. They couldn't move forward. And that was the reason for which they asked for, for a local to be the manager. (952)

And when we asked what he could do that the Westerners could not, he said:

> In front of the foreigners East Europeans behaved like good actors. They played their roles. It's much more difficult to play the role of somebody in front of me, or even in front of another East European. So, to have success, you have to make the appraisal of your staff. Proper appraisal. So, they made a lot of mistakes in, in placing people. They trusted somebody who was not worth trusting. When I cut the possibilities of doing the, the corruption in one workshop—reported the guy subcontracted to his colleagues and has paid more money than was necessary, and they were using company's materials, company's workers, and so on—when I cut it, the guy said, "Thank you, I will not work anymore." And despite that he was a favorite of the Westerners. They were very surprised. I didn't touch him. I didn't have any contacts with him. But I know that he is stealing the company's money. So I cut the possibility to do it. (952)

East European difference is obviously important to transition culture, but its significance tends to be minimized when expatriates are the managers of transition. It is simply a difference to be transcended. It is, however, usually the East European who transcends that difference. East European difference tends to become more significant when it becomes a resource in a contest over claims to competence. Under these conditions, East European difference tends to be accentuated when the promise of transition is not being realized, when East Europeans feel that they should be in charge and Westerners remain in that station.[12] In the following sections, I explore a few moments where East European difference is accentuated.

East European Competence beyond Transition Culture

In the early years of "transition," the contest between Western expertise and East European culture was likely about the degree of fit between Western concepts and East European reality. In later years, it has become a debate over who can manage the fit, and in what areas that fit is best realized. What can Westerners really teach the indigenous after years of transition? As one expatriate consultant with East European background said in 1994:

> We now have much less need to bring in outside assistance [because] the expertise of our East European consultants has reached such a level that they can do 90 percent of what the MBAs could do, and they don't need to be hand-held in terms of being introduced to this country. (126)

Estonian consultant Alexander Plotkin and Polish consultant Bogdan Siewierski have emphasized: "managers in transitional economies are no longer interested in the theory of how things ought to work, or how things work in developed capitalist economies. They expect more specialized knowledge and specifically-tailored techniques, expertise they can use to solve their particular problems. After all, managers say, we have learned so much in these last six years, we expect Western trainers should also have learned from our experience."[13] Are the areas of expertise in which Westerners might advise becoming ever more narrow and specialized? And if that is the case, does consulting in transition economies differ substantially from consulting in any other site? Presumptions of superiority, embedded in transition culture, will have to give way to a culture of consulting that is specific and indulgent to the client's interests.

Consulting is only one form of technical assistance in transitional economies, however. Multinational corporations are another common form for transmitting global business practice, but here, presumptions of superiority and inferiority, or at least chains of authority, are not so easily transformed. Transition culture smooths tensions that might otherwise be quite common in managing multinational firms, and this was reflected in many of our interviews. For instance, one East European manager said, "They practically taught us how to do the business—what's the way in an open economy, how to do the business; because otherwise we would die" (957). Training offered by foreign companies was often viewed as a key credential for success. An American recalled that "whether [the training was] good or bad [laughing], they would consider themselves to be more professional, and then much more marketable to get another job" with that training (979). Beyond the fact of this gratitude or the value of the credential, forces of homosocial reproduction also are at work in the elevation of global expertise.

It is difficult to really appreciate how "true" the following stories are, and to what extent psychological defense mechanisms come into play. Nevertheless, East Europeans often downplayed the contributions of Western experts. One manager, for instance, said that the advisers did not tell him anything he did not already know (967). Another suggested that the firm could have done the project on its own, but having the Americans on hand gave the added kick needed (955). Another simply said that the staff was so busy that it was helpful to have someone else do the project for them (969). Another manager said directly, "I would like to have the confirmation of the Davidson Institute. If I go back to my firm with the program, I think their hesitation on that program will be much less" (956). Another lamented that the parent organization refused to believe him about the appropriate accounting system, and so he hired Western consultants to do the analysis to convince the parent company. I asked why that was necessary, and he replied, in an ironic tone, that they would not listen to "an old socialist manager like me" (952).

This story is no doubt familiar to those who study the contributions of consultants. They merely provide an outside perspective that confirms the position of those who understand the situation from within. But in the case of transition culture, management's claims might be doubted because of the presumption of where expertise lies, and does not lie. In their contest with others, especially foreign management, East Europeans need the alliance of foreign advisers to elevate their own claims to competence, and to reduce the suspicion that their advice is flawed because of its contamination with socialism's past. There is, however, one area of expertise in which East Europeans have an undisputed claim to superior competence, but its relationship to the past limits its value in transition culture.

It is of course well known that connections matter a great deal in business practices across the world and that many network ties are critical to career success. In Eastern Europe, these connections are easily as important, if not more important, for the well-being of the firm. For example, one firm's principal problem was that it kept on losing bids. The Western experts focused on the costs of production, and neglected entirely, because it was outside the sphere of their competence, how bids were really won. Competitors constantly lost to one firm because its bids were lower than the real costs of production. The firm could do this because of its previous ties with the clients. On the basis of past practice, the firm would make up its loss with these clients by getting paid for additional goods up front, knowing that the client would never expect those goods to be delivered. In that way, the firm would make up the loss incurred through its low bid (952). Here, then, the Westerner would actually lose business owing to a lack of connections. But how does this claim to competence, to expertise, fit within transition culture?

The narrative of connections is also tied up in claims to competence and homosocial reproduction. Transition is about moving away from such particularistic ties and toward the rule of law and market. In the East European context, this sense of connections is typically disparaged as a relic of the past. If one has to hold on to an old manager, for instance, what better than to assign him a job like governmental relations (955)? The "old managers" do not miss this condescension, but given the power relations of the transitional firm, they do not pose it as a problem in multinational context. In my interviews, however, this problem occasionally exploded into the conversation. One manager recalled a story in which the parent company demanded that this manager use his connections to fix standards for the import of some factors of production:

> Deliveries to our country are completely signed that the product has
> to be delivered according to the country's rules, our country's stan-

dard. And they expect that because I am a previous president [of the regulatory agency], I can have everything [done] like that [as he rubs his hands against each other, like "chop-chop"]. So I told them, "Why didn't you sign the contract according to the official standard? I am not responsible for your relation with that agency!" [They tell me:] "Oh, well, you have to arrange it somehow." "How can I arrange it? How? There are rules, standards." [They say:] "Arrange the meeting with them." Well, I arrange for the dinner with the, with the president of the commission. "You know him! Go ahead, arrange it with him! You know American officials? You know how to fight for visa in the States? Well, it's the same way with the our country's authorities. Apply, for example, [for] valid documentation. Write a letter, attach the documentation, and wait for the approval." How can I arrange it? It's not Bangladesh or any other country in which you can go [slaps the table, as if slapping down a bribe], give the envelope and arrange it. Maybe some envelope maybe would be helpful, but it is impossible to arrange these things without following proper procedures. I told them, I can maybe, *maybe* I can accelerate something. But it is impossible to avoid the necessary actions. They [the multinational managers] don't understand it. It's a colonial attitude. They suppose that they are in the wild countries, in which the, the—all the administration is corrupted totally. And in which I have friends everywhere and I can arrange it in a way they don't want to, to think about. It makes me crazy sometimes. (952)

The significance of "connections" and the importance of this kind of activity for getting bids or favorable rates of taxation is usually recognized as very important, and something East Europeans are themselves most adept in doing. At the same time, however, this is perhaps one of the most difficult areas of expertise to place on a grid between socialist culture and transition culture. On the one hand, it is typically denigrated as a valuable form of know-how when we are talking about the transformation of business practices, perhaps because it is associated with the indigenous themselves, or because it does not fit with our notions of proper expertise. On the other hand, to think of it as so powerful as to determine how the economy really works can lead the Westerner to be charged with condescension. In short, this claim to competence cannot easily be implicated in the transition culture itself, and yet, it is fundamentally important in a firm's conditions of success.

Contesting Claims to Competence

In general, homosocial reproduction tends to minimize the significance of conflict within the dominant culture, within transition culture. It exaggerates the conflict with the antagonistic cultures—here, with socialist culture. But it also minimizes the conflict with East European local culture because East Europeans in multinational firms must rely on their foreign counterparts to receive confirmation as members of transition culture.

Of course, there were slight contests. East Europeans tended to value local knowledge more than global expertise. Americans tended to value communication skills more than East Europeans did. Americans tended not to see any difficulty in linguistic barriers. East Europeans tended to identify condescension in Americans. Americans found pessimism in East Europeans. In one case, the indigenous/foreign contest grew severe, and led to a virtual absence of communication altogether. But one should not think of the cultural contest as moving only along lines of passports and national cultures. Transition culture is consequential, and it has made an alliance out of foreigners and some East Europeans who identify socialist culture as the main obstacle to developing the firm. Indeed, in most multinational firms, I suspect that homosocial reproduction proceeds along these lines of transition culture more than it does along differences in language spoken. One cultural contest, however, goes beyond transition culture and should be considered as a case study in the movement of transition to critical transition culture.

When asking about the exemplary manager, we found only one firm where the chief was praised unambiguously by the lower management. One manager said that his boss was a good manager because he knew how to build a team, to have great relations, and not to have any rivalries. Everybody gives their all to the team, working at least from 8:30 in the morning until 9 o'clock in the evening (967). The other person celebrated his manager because that manager "understood that the business should be done by the local people who knew the market" (960).

The American advisers assigned to this firm were extremely critical of the management, however. Their criticism was similar to what I have already discussed. The advisers recognized the management's energy, but could not find anything exemplary. They could not identify anything they learned from the local management. One intern praised the management's energy, but they "needed to take a step back and see what they were doing and focus in on and pay attention to some of the details of running an operation." Their business was growing so fast that the management team did not "have control right now of all the aspects of the business, have the control that they ought to" (985). They also did not listen. This concern over openness is a common basis for praise, or criticism, of East European managers by those who would advise them (958, 976). Another intern said:

> The managers . . . would get sometimes frustrated in some situations . . . they weren't as open in sometimes talking about some issues. They sometimes believed their way was maybe the right way, and they weren't very open to getting some comments. . . . A few times we suggested, "Well, have you ever thought of this?" And, instead of listening and maybe working with us, they kind of would listen in for a few minutes and then say, "No no no that's not our way. Won't work in our market." (981)

As if to emphasize how unreasonable this was, she compared them to other managers:

> [The others] were very friendly, very open. Very much wanting to learn. If we had any information to share with them, they wanted it. I mean, whether it was right, wrong, whatever, I mean, they wanted to see it first, and talk about it with us, and they would say, "Well, what do you think? Do you think this is right for our market?" Even though I'd only been there for like [laughs a little here] two weeks. So I found that very refreshing. (981)

It is difficult to assess how typical this setting might be. The indigenous management team being critiqued had grown up together in the second economy. They were almost like family. Their business was growing very rapidly. One manager said that their success was enough to answer a question about managerial accomplishment. He said that in the first three months of their operation, they had nearly three times more output than their predecessor had had in the previous year. And then, in the following year, they were asked to double their production, a task they accepted from the parent firm. And they nearly doubled that (960). Rather than focus on techniques or methods for demonstrating competence, this manager pointed to results. The advisers took this very condition and pointed out that the rapid growth could hide managerial inadequacies (983).

The East European manager attributed the success of the firm to the fact that an East European ran the firm. Expatriates are poor in this job, because it takes a lot of time to understand the mentality of the market, and during that time, they make a lot of mistakes, and have a hard time recovering from them.[14] He specifically recalled his parent firm's mistake in relying on an expatriate manager to estimate the size of the potential market. The parent firm radically underestimated what could be done (982). From that and his previous experience, he drew some general lessons:

1. When locals and expatriates are mixed, the team is less effective in part because there are very different time horizons:

> Having both foreign and local managers creates problems, which is like a division of the team. To some degree, you always see them as outsiders, who are just coming to do, you know, something, you know, [that has a] higher priority. But, at the same time, they are not seen as the long-term partners or long-term colleagues. . . . But, at the same time, because I said they are seeing themselves higher, this uh—the team does not, I think, uh, cooperate. Maybe I'm wrong, but I don't think so.

2. In these mixed teams, condescension is typical, even when claims to competence are dubious:

> Sometimes the expatriates see themselves as the teachers for [the locals]. . . . I know that probably the, the business knowledge of Americans, of Westerners, is bigger than the East Europeans, in, in some areas. But at the same time, the understanding of mentality, or even the contact with clients, are not compatible. I mean, you can't compare what the expats can do and what the local can do.

3. The global corporation is too much like the past: there is no responsibility because everyone is too much obliged to the narrow vision of their own department, and too dependent on those higher up:

> So, even if they understand me, they are not independent, this is the problem. So, we should have support from the top management. I think, uh, they're always . . . this is always a problem with a big company. They are not flexible. . . . people work for the big company, but they work for their department. This is the problem, so . . . I work for my boss, and I . . . if he comes to me and says I have no problems, for me this is the most important thing. So, therefore I cannot agree with people from outside, even if they introduce logical arguments, but, OK, but my boss wants me to have a product. Some of the processes are, reminds us of forty years of the communists. I mean . . . it cannot be compared, because they are completely different systems. But something what can occur in a big corporation happened in the past in our country.

4. The global corporation needs a different strategy for its support of indigenous firms:

> [At the same time,] I feel that we don't have enough support in the beginning from our parent company. . . . I mean assistance, some kind of setup procedures, things like that. And it doesn't have to be done with another manager who works with the company. Could be done to some degree as a consultant, or someone who stays for a month or two or three, whatever, just to help and, you know, maybe give some advice. But not being seen as a decision maker . . . an outsider. Just to maybe help us, to help create the system. To put the, uh, procedures in motion. To establish criteria for, uh, you know, for getting your clients. . . . And but, but this is not a big problem.

Contesting this interpretation, one of the firm's American advisers complained that the company insisted on special treatment from the parent company when in fact that special treatment would not be necessary if the company had the right kind of expertise and was more careful in collecting data. More generally, this American found that the indigenous management was "stubborn and pigheaded" when it came to dealing with the parent company. He found that they thought they could do it all on their own, but they could not. From that he took a general lesson about the relationship between the parent company and smaller countries:

> One thing that you learn is that they [the indigenous managers] really need to learn, the managers in them because you see how they react, because they really need to be explained things in detail, to lead them along where they're going, and they need a charismatic leader, that they can trust. They don't need the financial people, . . . [they need] people who are not just willing to listen to them, and also someone who has the strength to tell them when they are wrong, and that they respect—that is what's really required. (985)

More critically:

> One of the general lessons is that they need to learn to take care of their own house before they start complaining about what everyone else is doing to them. So, martyrdom is not a good call at all times. And, to work with the corporate office, you can't always just keep saying what's wrong or else crying wolf too much can ruin your credibility. (985)

This particular set of interviews was among our most interesting precisely because it offered very different perspectives on what managerial accomplishment meant, and how that was dependent on the kind of expertise and reference groups one enjoyed. In this case, the East European invoked local success, the weakness of multinational bureaucracy, and an expertise based on a fusion of local knowledge with global business practices. In many ways, the East Europeans embodied the realization of transition culture's promise. On the other hand, their critics could identify particular weaknesses in the way that management team worked, and especially criticized their blame of the parent firm. Indeed, their Western critics could return to the socialist model and invoke particular images from it to undermine the East European managers' claim to competence. To be "closed-minded" and unsophisticated in financial planning are attributes of the socialist culture to be expunged.

The deviance of this case from my general analysis—the outright contest over claims to competence between foreign actors and successful local actors—suggests something extremely important about homosocial reproduction and transition culture. Transition culture's assimilation of local culture and opposition to socialist culture is not only about demarcating who is in and who is out. It is also about building up narratives of accomplishment and inferiority that, regardless of objective merits, can be used by differently positioned actors to identify who is best. Even in conditions of success, Westerners can undermine the claims of locals by identifying elements of that East European's practice that resemble the socialist past. If our East European informants in this section are any example, however, East Europeans can also use the narratives of transition to bolster their own claims to competence. In a terrific inversion, they could argue that the multinational is inadequate before the emerging market economy. Socialist culture is not an East European disease, but the result of an organization out of touch with the local market's dynamics.

Although this was only one case, one might suggest that it anticipates the future. Indeed, it suggests the very dynamic that Prahalad and Lieberthal recognize in their assessment of corporate imperialism. They argue that the successful multinational firm will move away from asking how it can export current business models around the globe, and instead inquire into how emerging markets might require rethinking the price performance equation, brand management, the costs of market building, product design, packaging, and capital efficiency.

Most important, this will require rethinking where to look when seeking managerial talent.[15]

Conclusions

József Böröcz has introduced an extremely valuable concept for understanding the dynamics of postcommunist capitalism in general with "fusion."[16] By this he understands the "creative reinterpretation of old and new elements, creating substantively distinguishable qualities of social experience." He uses the musical repertoire of Béla Bartók to produce the image. He cites the Hungarian pianist Zoltán Kocsis: "Bartók's oeuvre is a perfect synthesis between Central East European folklore and composed music in the hands of a superbly creative individual." Although the making of a new business class will unlikely be awarded the same kind of artistic recognition, the imagery of fusion might be one of the most useful metaphors for the analysis of management practice within transition culture. But the contest is over how the fusion of global business practices and more spatially grounded cultures is to take place.

Homosocial reproduction within the management of transitional firms is explicitly based on imagery of fusion, but with very different loadings on how the various elements are connected. Contextual knowledge provides details, connections, and legitimation, while the global part of the fusion process provides the viewpoint and conceptual framework in which to put all those details. The fusion is most obvious in particular areas where East European management is relatively inexperienced: marketing, personnel, and communications. As East Europeans acquire these forms of expertise, fusion would suggest that the contradiction between grounded and global knowledge will be erased, or superseded by a new class of East European business leaders. And in many ways it has.

This image of supersession, however, masks the continuing difficulty of assimilating East European experience in guiding managerial development and homosocial reproduction. To a considerable extent, East European assimilation to global practice works best when it avoids challenging global presumption, and flees that socialist past as quickly as possible. The East European manager who challenges global management practices risks being identified with the East European socialist past. Identifying any manager with that socialist past would mark him or her as inappropriate for transition, and outside the future.

As fusion takes place, however, global privilege in homosocial reproduction ought to decrease. Indeed, the relative weighting of East European local knowledge ought to increase, and the claims to competence in assessing firm practices might rest more with East Europeans. To what extent, then, will matters of homosocial reproduction within multinational firms approximate those conducted in any other part of the world where center–periphery relations characterize the encounters between parent and local firms? I would expect that it should. Indeed, one of the best markers of transition's completion may very well be when the West's claims to superior competence no longer invoke the rhetorics of an Eastern Europe defined by its socialist past. Or perhaps an even better marker of transition will be found when the East Europeans base their claim to superior competence on the traces of socialism to be found in the multinational corporation. And we have encountered that already.

By combining the structural analysis of transition culture with this analysis of transition culture in practice, I have provided further evidence that there is a transition culture at work, with the structural opposition of a socialist past and a global capitalist future at its core. I have refined the argument by showing that this is not only an institutional transformation, but also a cultural formation that empowers contextually ignorant international actors to offer advice to those potentially tainted by the socialist past. The cultural formation provides, however, means by which the East European can escape the pollution of socialism, by demonstrating particular competencies in sanctioned areas of transition culture. This study of transition culture in action enables us to see how, in fact, the structure of transition culture is preserved even as the members of that culture change.

As personnel changes, however, the elements of that cultural formation also change. The ease with which the grounded knowledge disappears from the global portrait of transition culture declines dramatically when transition culture is applied. The significance of contextual expertise looms much larger. Sometimes the fusion of contextual and global expertise is a perfectly compatible procedure. Other times the failure to recognize the challenge and accomplishment of fusion handicaps the implementation of otherwise reasonable projects. Transition culture's global citizens can be quite rude, and downright "imperialist." East Europeans can be tempted to remind universalism's representative that they are in a different culture, and not just a culture that is tainted by socialism. East Europeans are more likely to recognize these tensions and conflicts, but they are also likely to hide them from their employers and supervisors. But even as they hide them, they are also transforming transition culture itself. They are accumulating the expertise and claims to competence that might flip transition culture on its head, and claim new centers of expertise in remaking global capitalism.

Transition culture, with the resonance of global liberalism, feels much more powerful than civil society in the 1980s. Transition culture is not an opposition culture; it is hegemonic. Like other hegemonies, it is contested and far from monolithic. At the same time, however, the presumptions of this culture are clear and the illegitimacies readily apparent. Socialists are not welcome, and East Europeans, before the global presumption, must be careful not to betray any hint of old thinking for fear of being tarred with that label. In the context of multinational business and the World Bank's publications, socialists nevertheless must be imagined in the core of transition culture's practice as the other against which the future is to be understood. This does not mean, however, that transition culture in business practice is without important labilities. The most important lability rests in transition culture's ownership, and in the location of incompetence within it.

The view from nowhere is deeply woven into transition culture. It maintains that epistemology both through its rhetoric and through its efforts to recruit members beyond London and New York, in Tirana and Tashkent. It is difficult to see the viewpoint from where World Bank reports are written when our eyes are drawn toward those objective lessons from across the world. When we think about place, we think about cases, not about perspectives that are shaped by experiences. And we do not think about ownership as much as argument. By addressing transition culture in practice, in this most conducive of homes, ownership nonetheless becomes central to understanding transition culture's dynamics.

We can see more clearly the conditions under which transition culture might claim its view from nowhere, or from neutral space. Multinational companies, one of our East European managers reminded us, have their own culture. It is just that sometimes Westerners' condescension gets in the way. It is rarely so bad as those English attitudes toward the Irish during the famine of the 1840s,[17] but one manager did question whether imperialism might be the best term to describe how his local firm was treated by its multinational owner. For the most part, however, cultural tensions were not described in such combative terms. Nor were they so obvious. They rested in arguments over what kinds of expertise should be remunerated most. They rested in the criteria used to judge a sound decision. They even rested in the questions one poses. The parent company is likely to be more interested in extending its own models of products and practices abroad, whereas the East European managers are more likely to be interested in making them work over the long haul at home—at least until they are the multinational representatives.

Transition culture's practice here also reminds us that transition is not just about necessity. It is also about translation and transition's articulation with other cultural formations. At the height of transition culture, its global representatives were empowered to teach, and East Europeans were disposed to learn, about business. Both were uncertain about the degree to which socialism tainted East Europeans, and both acknowledged that Eastern Europe had much to learn. But even within these remarkably hospitable conditions, East Europeans were resentful of the presumption their putatively more worldly advisers brought with them. They typically hid that resentment, however, for assimilation into transition culture brought opportunities. Through that assimilation, and translation, transition culture was reproduced even as it was transformed. As the East Europeans embraced the logic of transition culture, and embedded it in their local practices, they made it more Polish or more Hungarian, more appropriate to a Gdańsk or Szeged. Sometimes, they even used their familiarity with transition culture to elevate their own expertise beyond that of those whose global location put them closer to the heart of transition. And with that, they signal the transformation of transition culture that is critical to its expansion across the world. For transition culture to work, it must articulate positively with that other hegemonic formation after communism, nationalism.

Four

Transition, Freedom, and Nationalism

Mart Laar, the prime minister of Estonia from 1992 to 1994 and chair of the Pro Patria coalition, said the following on May 2, 1995, when reflecting on the meaning of the preceding four years of independence:

> The most basic and vital change of all . . . had to take place in the hearts and minds of Estonia's people. Without a major readjustment of attitudes, the postcommunist predicament would become a trap, and the nation would never move forward to become a "normal" country with free government and free markets under law. In the era of Soviet-imposed socialism, most people withdrew into a kind of private quietism; associations seldom extended beyond small circles of relatives and close friends, and the public realm was dominated by the communist party-state and its enforced conformities. People were not used to thinking for themselves, taking the initiative, or assuming risks. Many had to be shaken out of the illusion—common in post-communist countries—that somehow, somebody else, was going to come along and solve their problems for them. It was necessary to energize people, to get them moving, to force them to make decisions to take responsibility for themselves.[1]

Mart Laar is an exemplary liberal from an exemplary post-Soviet country within transition culture. Laar narrates a story of necessity and opportunity that resonates with other stories of transition articulated across the globe. I chose this particular fragment, however, because of its emphasis on the making of a new subjectivity around freedom and responsibility. Laar highlights that which transition culture only assumes: the significance of cultural transformation at the heart of transition. Freedom and responsibility form the core of that transformation.

In this chapter, I focus on this kind of narrative within transition culture. Above all, transition is not just about the business of post-communist capitalism, even if the social relations constituting the market are its dynamic core. Transition is also about a larger cultural transformation in which the nation is deeply implicated, and whose translation into more local and everyday circumstances is profoundly variable. I begin this chapter by considering the larger problematic of transition's relation to the nation. Following that discussion, I turn to its implication in everyday life. In particular, I draw on focus groups conducted in Estonia and Ukraine during 1996 and 1997 to discuss how narratives of freedom and responsibility are articulated in recollections of social change.

Nationalism and Transition Culture

Ernest Gellner's *Nations and Nationalism* is the typical starting point for any account of nationalism. The first words of his book begin with its definition: "Nationalism is primarily a political principle, which holds that the political and the national unit should be congruent."[2] This political principle is an expression of political legitimacy, typically for one's own nation, which in turn can be used to challenge somebody else's nation. But this is not, Gellner argues, a quality of humanity. It is a modern invention, but one so powerful that it is hard to imagine someone without a nation today. Nationalism, the ideology, has become so dominant that it has come to define the world. Its power rests, of course, on the power of the state that stands behind it, but that is not all. Transition culture also reinforces nationalism, if in a much less obvious fashion. Therefore we must go beyond Gellner's famous assertion of nationalism's simplicity. He argued that the formulation of ideas in nationalism does not much matter because the ideas within it are so simple that "anyone can make it up almost at any time."[3] Even by itself, however, nationalism's cultural formation demands more.

Craig Calhoun's elaboration clarifies the variety of debates and objects of analysis that typically goes under nationalism's heading.[4] Nationalism is a political principle, but it is also an ideology that helps to produce collective identity or social solidarity. Those ideologies, however, vary from place to place. As Benedict Anderson has famously put it, they vary in "the style in which they are imagined."[5] In one place, language might do. In another, sacred places might be the key. In another, race could be critical. There is no essence to this nationalism, but rather a set of family resemblances that enable us to recognize this variety with a single word.[6]

Underlying all of this—the nationalist movements, the nationalist states, the nationalist ideologies—is a broader discursive formation around nationalism that shapes the way we think not only about nations, but about modernity itself.[7] Roman Szporluk follows Anthony Smith and other theorists of the nation to argue that

> the core doctrine of nationalism includes the belief that "humanity is naturally divided into nations"; that nations have their "peculiar character"; that all political power is derived from the nation; that "men must identify with a nation" for their freedom and "self-realization"; that nations requires states for fulfillment; that the nation-state has the highest claim to men's loyalty; and finally that the nation-state is the condition of "global freedom and harmony."[8]

This doctrine is not just a collection of ideas. It is a deep cultural schema that organizes the practices of this world, from the color-coded political maps that guide our vision of the world's diversity to criteria for membership in international organizations such as the United Nations. Nationalism is also implicated in transition culture.

On the surface, it looks like nationalism is only a problem for transition culture. Nationalism is used as an explanation for why transition meets rocky roads. For instance, one reason for Ukraine's relative failure, the World Bank explains, is that its leaders were preoccupied in the first half of the 1990s with questions of national identity.[9] Estonia's leaders were not indicted for their own nationalizing ambitions, however; their transition has been relatively successful. Nationalism is thus a problem for transition culture at a second level: nationalism's meaning, and evaluation, varies depending on its articulation with transition culture's priorities. To decide when nationalism is, and is not, a problem suggests a cultural dilemma that transition culture does not confront when its rhetoric rests on freedom's desirability and the market's necessity even when nationalism becomes a useful factor for explaining transition's limitations. However, this reflects a third-level problem within transition culture. Transition culture is itself embedded in the discursive formation of nationalism. As individualism is itself linked to nationalism,[10] so transition culture cannot do without nationalism.

Although transition culture itself is multinational and has global reach, its imagination is inescapably national.[11] As I demonstrated in chapter 2, transition culture relies on the exemplary and the problematic to structure its interpretation of social change and its mandate for action. For instance, Poland and Estonia can provide important lessons for Ukraine and Russia in terms of how to implement economic and social change. It thus is structured by that most fundamental of nationalist propositions: the world is made up of different and discrete nations, equivalent and each with its own destiny to fulfill. Although the practice of transition culture might minimize the significance of national difference in the fusion of horizons within the multinational firm, the structure of transition culture remains founded on the organization of national differences.

The distinction between exemplary success and failure also is neatly smuggled into accounts of national characters and the caliber of national leaders. Mart Laar's voice is therefore more important than many of transition culture's leaders from London or New York because Laar comes from Estonia, one of the major success stories of the postcommunist world. Transition culture's power grows to the extent it can claim that there are success stories out there on which other societies might model their own transformations. Although tables indicating inflation rates and growth rates might be sufficient for the analysts, the broader public appreciates the well-spoken and articulate representative of the nation, and of transition's promise. Laar offers that compelling voice. He does not emphasize what the United Nations Development Program (UNDP) would point out, however. The UNDP argues that comparing nations with very different initial conditions at transition's start (inside and outside the Soviet Union) and very different social environments (from NATO's embrace of Poland to the grasp of war in Tajikistan) is problematic. And that is obvious, but nationalism's articulation with transition culture allows its membership to overlook nonequivalence.

Transition culture also structures its comparisons among nations from the point of view of an international culture that is markedly "Western." By emphasizing the virtues of the Visegrad countries, three of which were ultimately brought within NATO first, and those on the fast track to European Union membership, transition culture also rewards those nations whose leaders emphasize their own Western status. Again, the UNDP report suggests an alternative, looking to exemplars within regional or national conditions, finding, for instance, the Uzbekistani Mahallah as an exemplar of social assistance. With its implicit Western reference, transition culture helps to develop nationalism in opposition to transition even as it denies the association. This distinction can be seen even more clearly by juxtaposing the World Bank's emphasis on postcommunist social change with a work that centers the problem of the Russian diaspora in the postcommunist world.

David Laitin focuses his analysis on the identity formation of the Russian-speaking population living in the former Soviet Union but outside Russia, especially in Kazakhstan, Ukraine, Estonia, and Latvia.[12] Of course, the analytical focus of transition culture concentrates on institutional change, but transition culture also presumes identity transformation. Mart Laar's speech exemplifies this. The identity shift for transition culture is apparently nonnational, but involves a shift away from *Homo sovieticus* toward the rational capitalist actor, from a dependent and withdrawn subject to one prepared to take risks and make opportunity for himself, his family, and his nation. Although Laitin's game theoretical assumptions also inflect his subjects with calculating dispositions that are part of the habitus of transition culture, his subjects' assessments of transition nonetheless are made within a framework that centers the nation.

For the Russian-speaking populations in Russia's "near abroad," the transition was not just about moving from plan to market, but of moving from a privileged nation within a large empire to becoming a minority within a new nationalizing state.[13] It involves a choice about where to live, what citizenship to embrace, whether to protest in peace or violence the diminishment of one's status, and whether to learn a new language. In Soviet times, Russian would have sufficed, but in the new nationalizing states, Russian speakers must decide whether to invest in learning the new language of state. And with this focus it is hard to imagine that Estonia's "nationalism" would go unmarked.

In comparison to Ukraine, Estonia's citizenship policies have been much more exclusionary.[14] Although Russians constitute close to 38 percent of the residents of Estonia, all of the deputies elected to parliament in 1992 were ethnically Estonian. In 1996, six deputies were Russian. Exclusion was not, however, based on their ethnicity, but on the timing of their arrival in Estonia—whether they or their forbears were part of the interwar Estonian republic, or whether they arrived as part of the illegal Soviet occupation. Some analysts have even argued that this legal-rational strategy to exclude Russians helped to reduce the likelihood of violent confrontation.[15] The Estonian government legitimated its exclusionary strategy with an appeal to legal continuity. By arguing that Soviet-era in-migration was a violation of that law, the Estonian leadership could claim to embrace the norms of civil society even while excluding a third of the population from political enfranchisement. In this way, the West's historic resistance to recognizing the Soviet occupation of the Baltics as legal enabled the Estonians to argue that this exclusion of Soviet-era immigrants was reasonable, a claim that the West accepted grudgingly.[16]

The World Bank's emphasis on the success of Estonia takes as a point of departure the very same structure that allows the Estonian authorities to normalize their exclusion of the Russian minority from political power. By highlighting the problem of how the Russian minority responds to its new titular states, Laitin shifts our gaze from the standpoint of an apparently neutral international culture based on the sovereignty of nationally grounded legal systems to one that privileges the problem of this new Russian diaspora. Rather than undermine the accomplishments of Estonian transition, however, this additional focus helps us understand why Estonia is so much more "successful" than Ukraine.

According to Laitin, the Russian minority is more likely to try to assimilate to Estonian ways than Ukraine's Russian minority might assimilate to Ukrainian ways, *despite* the exclusionary qualities of Estonian citizenship law. Estonia's greater stability and proximity to a valued Europe convinced many Russian speakers that to remain in Estonia was better than returning to Russia. They might have preferred, Laitin argues, a more consociational arrangement, but the nationalizing ambition of the Estonian authorities forced that off the agenda by 1993. Economic opportunities also helped to undermine nationalist reaction within Estonia, as Russians sought to assimilate in order to take advantage of the relative prosperity Estonia enjoyed by the middle 1990s. At the same time, however, regional inequalities and the concentration of disadvantage for Estonian Russians of the northeast suggest the potential for significant conflict. According to Laitin, if economic development declines, or insufficient geographical mobility concentrates misery in particular regions, a Baltic Russian identity antagonistic to the Estonian nationalizing project could be reintroduced, and thereby destabilize development and forestall transition's realization. Ukrainian conditions are far different. Although the Russian and Ukrainian languages are more proximate, the prospects for consociation, rather than assimilation, are much greater.

There are significant regional differences in Ukraine in terms of national identity.[17] In the west, Ukrainian is dominant in terms of both language spoken and national self-identification. In the east, Russian has historically been the dominant language of communication among both Russians and Ukrainians. Ukrainians from the west are among the most active in pressing for the Ukrainization of public life—in education, business, and affairs of state. Their success has been mixed, however. Kiev's public life and educational system has been shifting quite markedly toward Ukrainian; also, Russian-speaking Ukrainians have been shamed, through nationalism's power, to use Ukrainian in public even when their grasp of the language is inadequate.[18] Although Russian is more widely used globally, and more developed in a broad array of areas, nationalism's power convinces many ethnic Ukrainians that this should be their public language, and the language of instruction in schools.

The proximity of the languages does not make it difficult for Russians to understand the language after some exposure. They are therefore not so threatened by it as they might be by Estonian, which is within the Finno-Ugric family of languages.[19] Laitin thinks it quite possible that Ukraine will ultimately develop a policy that allows Russians in the south and east to live locally in Russian.[20] That depends, however, on diminishing the nationalist agenda.

Laitin believes that the Ukrainian nationalist agenda is more apparent to the Russian speakers than it is to the West:

> Ukraine presents to the world a civic agenda; but just below the surface seethes anger against, even hatred of, Russians. The West sees the civic face of Dr. Jekyll; the Russians are beginning to see the enraged one, Mr. Hyde. Which half of the double personality will prevail is a question that is deeply worrisome to Russians now living in Ukraine.[21]

Laitin's volume illustrates the nationalist dilemma magnificently. It highlights the difficulty of addressing future prospects without taking into account the significance of language, citizenship, and national identity formation. At the same time, it also shows how difficult it is to write about this neutrally, from some panoptic vantage point. He cites the following words of Ivan Drach, the first leader of Ukraine's most important social movement for national independence, Rukh:

> Russians, unfortunately, practically do not know the Ukrainian soul. . . . It is possible that we ourselves do not yet know fully who we are. Still, it is useful from time to time to inform the Russians that Ukrainians will never accept the myth of the "one thousand years" of Russian statehood . . . that St. Sophia Cathedral belongs to the Russian Church, that our 700-year struggle for the restoration of our own state is a whim of nationalists. . . . Only in the Soviet period half of the Ukrainian nation was physically exterminated. . . . Ukrainians from Russia and other CIS states suffered a terrible, relatively recent horrific *deukrainizatsiia*. . . . The elements of apartheid and national segregation among them were usual daily occurrences.[22]

Laitin uses this quotation to illustrate Ukraine's Mr. Hyde, its "xenophobic provocation." It is probably true that Drach's statement is outrageous for Russians. Indeed, it may be one reason it was printed in the Russian press. For those who take a Ukrainian national problematic as a point of departure, however, the statement's sinister quality is hardly apparent. Outsiders rarely appreciate soul. Within its cultural formation, however, it is critical to the collective conscience, as Durkheim observed in the beginning of the last century.[23] At the time of its introduction, Black Power was certainly read as a provocation by many European Americans, but its meaning can hardly be captured satisfactorily by interpreting it solely through white eyes. Laitin is not himself Russian, but his ethnographic experience and linguistic facility locate him within the Russian diaspora, first and foremost. The standpoint dilemma is even more apparent in Estonia.

Estonians continue to fear for their safety and existence as an independent nation-state. Fully 43 percent of ethnic Estonians in March 1996 *definitely* believed that "Russia is a danger to the independence of Estonia" and another 36 percent thought it *probably* was, while only 14 percent of Estonian Russians considered it likely at all.[24] Laitin's book is framed in such a way that Russian imperialism poses no major threat to Estonian existence. It is difficult to imagine a book written from within an Estonian, or even Ukrainian, national problematic that escapes the normative penumbra of, and anxiety over, national independence.[25] For example, consider one other fragment from Mart Laar's speech:

> Estonia is usually classed with Slovenia and the Czech Republic as having gone the farthest down the road away from socialist authoritarianism and toward democracy and a market-based economy. When we regained our independence, 92 percent of our trade was with Russia. Our industry and agriculture were a shambles. . . . Inflation was running at the rate of 1,000 percent a year, and in 1992 alone our GDP fell by 30 percent. Basic goods like bread, milk and fuel were strictly rationed. On top of all that, we faced challenges to our political stability from extremists of the right and the left, while rising tensions between the native population and a largely Russian community (that immigrated during the period of Soviet occupation) seemed for a time as if they might spill over into overt conflict. Today, all these problems are receding so rapidly . . . like distant memories. Estonia has changed beyond recognition. We have reoriented our economy, going from dependence on the East to trade with the West. Inflation has dropped, and exports are increasing. Extremists . . . have been sidelined. . . . Ethnic tensions have greatly decreased and a large majority of those residents who are not ethnically Estonian now support Estonia's independence.[26]

For Laar, transition is thus not only about making a self-reliant subject. It is also about assuring an independent Estonia integrated into Europe. Estonian Foreign Minister Siim Kallas said:

> Political and economic integration with the European Union has developed into a top priority in Estonia's foreign policy, and more and more in domestic policy as well. . . . We are a European people and we are able to keep our identity only by belonging irrevocably to Europe, only together with other nations striving for the same goal. To belong irrevocably to Europe and to take part in developing its future is something Estonia can do only as a full-fledged member of the European Union.[27]

Transition means a move to Europe not only for purposes of market development, but for Estonian national security. In 1996, for instance, the Estonian defense minister, Andrus Oovel, remarked that Russia must change its approach to analyzing threats.[28] In addition to seeing dangers to its security, Russia should also analyze the idea that it might represent a threat to other countries. In the week before the 1996 presidential elections in Russia, Boris Yeltsin suggested that the Baltic countries should join the Commonwealth of Independent States and, in late 1997, he suggested that Russia would provide "security guarantees" for the Balts (an offer that was unequivocally declined). Baltic independence is regarded by some in Russia as a threat, an affront, or an aberration: communist Gennady Zhuganov has said that Estonia "could not exist without being a parasite on Russia"; Alexander Lebed promised in 1996 that "if NATO expands into Estonia . . . this country will have no future"; Vladimir Zhirinovsky has declared that he will construct giant fans along Russia's border to blow radioactive waste into the Baltic states.[29]

Nationalism and transition culture work together in the most conventional of ways. Transition culture is not only about moving from plan to markets and from dictatorship to democracy. It is also about assuring national independence and security from the imperial ambitions of those from beyond the West. This, of course, means that transition culture works for most nations of the postcommunist world, given that most nations of the world are too small to have grand imperial ambitions. However, there are some nations—notably Russia and Serbia—that have a different resonance with transition culture. (I will discuss that point in chapter 6.) One more point remains to be developed here, however, in regard to transition culture.

Transition culture and nationalism are mutually implicated, finally, because transition can be hegemonic only to the extent that it can be articulated as being in the interest of the nation. And that interest cannot be expressed, effectively, by those who do not speak the nation's language. Those spokespersons must bear the nation's history in their family background. Only they can *know* what the nation needs, so nationalism argues. Nationalism demands that transition culture be articulated from *within* the nation.

With such an articulation, transition's liberalism offers its rebuttal to nationalism. Liberal ideology enables Laar to step, provisionally, outside of his "Estonian identity" to administer the treatment that might cure his nation of socialist maladies. His membership in a global culture embracing markets allows him to recognize those Estonian qualities that prevent Estonia from reaching global standards. Simultaneously, his Estonian identity enables him to claim, without ever having to say it, that he has Estonian interests at heart. Liberalism thus enters the nation as an alternative nationalism, while denying its acceptance of nationalism. Liberalism gains its transformative power by becoming national. Nationalism and liberalism thus fuse in the successful application of transition culture.[30]

At several levels, therefore, one might consider transition culture's implication within nationalism. First, at the global level, transition culture works within nationalism's discursive formation. The very logic of comparative social science, in whose epistemology transition culture runs, typically treats nations as the units for comparison. Nations can be exemplary in positive or negative senses within this global comparison. Transition culture typically treats nationalist politics, however, as a threat to the more internationalist disposition it promotes. For instance, protectionist policies on trade are anathema to successful transition. However, transition culture tends to evaluate nationalisms with reference to the priorities of transition culture itself, which themselves have a Western standpoint.

Second, nationalism evaluates the danger or desirability of a particular nationalism from a Western point of view focused on the movement from plan to market. For instance, open borders to trade are absolutely important, whereas more exclusive citizenship policies, a condition that affects minorities and not global trade, does not figure in transition's central problematic.[31] Ironically, that very disposition in Estonia has helped reinforce Estonia's own nationalizing ambitions. To celebrate Estonia's success in transition means to minimize the problem of its Russian minority. By building Estonia's reputation as a successful economy, transition culture helps to create those economic conditions that increase the likelihood that minorities will seek to assimilate. Thus, transition culture helps to reinforce policies enabling a peaceful, but nationalizing, Estonian state. At the same time, Ukraine, with its more inclusive citizenship policies, winds up having its nationalism charged with responsibility for transition's failure.

Third, transition culture works within nations, and not only across them. For transition culture to work, it must have its own spokesperson who can articulate the future of the nation in the language of the nation. Not only can this serve the global culture well by providing an exemplar, but it is also critical for the fate of transition culture within that nation itself. But this articulation must go beyond the language of business to address popular culture. It must resonate with the narrative of the nation's history, and destiny. Transition's priorities might find expression in the national tale, where freedom, for instance, allows the nation to join the rest of the world. For the small nation, such as Estonia, it must also be implicated in a tale of national survival. Transition culture in Estonia must mean national security to be successful.

Fourth, these tales of national security and transition resonate very differently across the postcommunist region. In some cases, notably in Poland, transition and entry into NATO go hand in hand, saying that this military alliance is but an assurance of economic and political community. In other nations, as we shall see in chapter 6, transition culture can be posed as a threat to national security. And, of course, within nations, different communities can interpret transition very differently. Some can see it as a fulfillment of their national destiny, while others can see it as an attack. In these cases, the panoptic position favored by transition culture is difficult to maintain, and can only lead to additional charges of nationalism in interpretation. A more hermeneutic disposition, where the challenge of difference is embraced in the search to produce a new fusion of horizons, is one way to recognize nationalism's embrace not only of the subjects of research, but in the point of the research question.

In the balance of this chapter, I shift the focus away from central texts, pronouncements of *prominenci,* and the engagements of transition's agents. Whereas most studies of postcommunist social transformation focus on the visions of designers, their hegemony depends not only on their leverage over institutions but on the ways in which their ideas can be adapted into popular culture.[32] In what follows, I examine how transition culture is implicated into the nationalizing narratives of everyday life in Estonia and Ukraine. Drawing on focus groups conducted in Estonia and Ukraine in 1996 and 1997, I explore how some major themes of transition culture—notably freedom, responsibility, and international comparison—fit with various assessments of change. In the following chapter, I draw on the same data to consider how particular social problems—notably environmental problems—shape narratives of the nation and of transition.

Narrating Transition and National Identity in Focus Groups

Good survey research can help us discern which social identities are significant in predicting support for transition and affection for socialism. But although survey research can help us understand the distribution of attitudes, it is less useful for helping us understand the narrative formation of identities in social transformation. Narratives are the stories people tell about themselves and others, and about social problems and other aspects of social life. Narratives are implicated in identity formation of all kinds, as was discussed in the introduction.

Janet Hart has usefully distinguished two types of these narratives: ontological, "the internalized stories which combine received historical, psychological and cultural messages, subsequently transposed into particular behaviors"; and mobilizational, "intersubjective, designed by their authors to establish and support collective values, and to encourage solidarity."[33] We can think about the narratives of the nation in both terms, stabilizing the identity of participants with appeals to an enduring and imagined community, and mobilizing, when that community needs to be preserved, or transformed, in order to survive or thrive. Transition culture is much more clearly a mobilizing narrative of identity formation, specifically designed to persuade and mobilize resources on behalf of a strategic end. Consider again Laar's stirring words about the cultural transformation represented by transition:

> People were not used to thinking for themselves, taking the initiative, or assuming risks. Many had to be shaken out of the illusion—common in postcommunist countries—that somehow, somebody else, was going to come along and solve their problems for them. It was necessary to energize people, to get them moving, to force them to make decisions to take responsibility for themselves.[34]

While it is important to know the statistical association between social identities and the assessment of transition, we can learn through the study of narratives how people construct the meaning of these years of transition, and in so doing, construct their own place within, or in opposition to, transition culture. We can begin such an inquiry by asking directly how well Laar's symptomatic mobilizing narrative of transition culture accounts for everyday understandings of social change. To what extent have freedom and responsibility shaped the narrative of transformation? And how has that narrative been implicated in the nation? One way to learn this is to conduct focus groups.

As an approach that is useful for learning about respondents' perspectives—both what they are thinking and why—focus groups are well suited for the study of how various forms of social identity influence the articulation of transition. This method allows for the formulation of identity and transition in the words of the subjects themselves. Although ethnographic analysis does the same thing, focus groups are usefully thought of as "concentrated bursts of data" in which for one and a half to two hours, a moderator facilitates a discussion among six to eight people of relatively similar social status.[35] This enhances the comparative promise of qualitative research: it allows for relatively controlled circumstances, with consistent, if not identical, interview schedules (see Appendix A), similar conditions of data collection, and tape-recorded transcripts.

Our interview schedules had three basic elements. The first section focused on improvements with the following open-ended question: "In what ways have these changes of the last ten years improved your life and the lives of people like you?" Asked to list on an index card the three most important ways things have improved, the participants were then asked to identify the most important improvement. They then discussed the improvements. A similar procedure was followed with a discussion of difficulties, in which people were asked, "In what ways have changes of the last ten years or so made your life and the lives of people like you more difficult?" Finally, we asked whether the issues discussed during the preceding discussion affected men and women differently, whether they affected people of various nationalities differently, and whether they affected people of various regions differently.

Although one could pursue these questions in a single republic, we pursued this exploration of identity formation and social problems in a comparative framework across radically different sites of post-Soviet change.[36] This comparative framework allowed us to go beyond national or otherwise localized frameworks that structure most qualitative social research in postcommunist society. We could thus explore the potential for finding similar narratives of transition that cross national spaces. In this sense, we hoped to escape the nationalist problematic that constrains single-nation studies, on the one hand, and those comparative studies that focus primarily on national differences (rather those organized along class, gender, nationality, or regional distinctions) on the other.

We collected and analyzed twenty-four focus groups conducted in ten sites in Estonia and Ukraine in order to investigate identity formation and the articulation of social issues, with a total of twelve focus groups per country.[37] We broke down these groups by gender, nationality, and education, in order to ensure relatively egalitarian discussion conditions.

These focus groups in Estonia and Ukraine were as follows:

Estonia

- Tallinn (the Estonian capital, mixed ethnicity/nationality): two groups of Russians, one all male and one all female, with at least some higher education; two groups of Estonians, one all male and one all female, with at least some higher education
- Narva (a provincial city in eastern Estonia; primarily ethnic Russian): two groups of Russians, one all male and one all female, with no more than secondary education
- Tartu (a provincial city in southern Estonia, primarily ethnic Estonian): two groups of Estonians, one all male and one all female, with no more than secondary education
- Tamsalu (a rural village in southern Estonia, primarily ethnic Estonian): two groups of Estonians, one all male and one all female, with no more than secondary education
- Sillamäe (a Baltic coast city, primarily Russian): two groups of Russians, one all male and one all female, with no more than secondary education

Ukraine

- Kiev (the Ukrainian capital, mixed ethnicity/nationality): two groups of Russians, one all male and one all female, with at least some higher education; two groups of Ukrainians, one all male and one all female, with at least some higher education
- Donetsk (a provincial city in southeastern Ukraine, primarily ethnic Russian): two groups of Russians, one all male and one all female, with no more than secondary education
- Lviv (a provincial city in western Ukraine, primarily ethnic Ukrainian): two groups of Ukrainians, one all male and one all female, with no more than secondary education
- Olexandrivka (a rural village in Vinnitsa, in southwestern Ukraine, primarily ethnic Ukrainian): two groups, one all male and one all female, with no more than secondary education
- Ivankiv (a city just outside the Chernobyl zone, mixed nationalities): two groups of Russians and Ukrainians, one all male and one all female, with no more than secondary education

We chose our focus groups with these four broad comparisons in mind:

1. We sought to compare highly educated men and women in capital cities (Tallinn and Kiev). In each city, focus groups were conducted for both native Russian speakers and the titular nationality.
2. We sought to compare those with secondary education in provincial cities with different "ethnic" markers. One set is known for its devotion to the national cause (Tartu and Lviv) and the other is relatively more Soviet (Narva and Donetsk).

3. We sought to compare rural sites, Tamsalu and Olexandrivka, in order to assess how those men and women of titular nationalities, with no more than secondary education, discussed the transition outside the city.
4. We chose two sites particularly known for their environmental problems—Sillamäe in Estonia and Ivankiv in Ukraine.[38]

We identified a range of possible participants through the use of informal networks in each of the sites. On-site investigators relied on information collected in a preinterview questionnaire and interview to decide the most appropriate combination of actual participants, assuring that they were both willing to talk in moderation and sufficiently diverse in terms of place of residence and occupation.[39] We recorded, transcribed, and translated all texts into English and coded the data (see Appendix B).[40] Their interpretation was not, however, simple.

First, one cannot figure these groups as representative in any formal sense. We therefore did not recruit focus group participants through random sampling techniques, nor do I claim any kind of distributional representation for my findings. We did, however, try to standardize our methods of data collection in order to facilitate more inductive and direct comparison across groups.[41] We could, for instance, compare directly the amount of explicit attention any issue might win in focus group discussions. Although hardly satisfactory by itself, this statistical comparison enabled us to recognize patterns in the data that might not otherwise be apparent. For example, although most area studies experts would not be surprised to find that concerns about standard of living were among the most frequently discussed issues in these focus groups, they would not expect to find regional identities to be more prominent than national identities in structuring these discussions of accomplishment and despair.[42]

One also cannot assume the same standards of replication sought in survey research where the reflections on interviewer effects are so carefully attended. Some focus group experts advised us that we should not worry; focus groups, they said, are sufficiently robust to defy slight variations in moderator practice. Some of our moderators deviated from expectations more than we expected, however.[43] As I discuss in the next chapter, some Ukrainian moderators introduced their focus groups with a reflection on Chernobyl's importance, whereas other Ukrainians, more faithful to the interview schedule, started the discussion without that prompt about the environment's importance in understanding social change. In this instance of gross moderator variation, we cannot simply compare lines devoted to the environment across focus groups. We also have to attend to the ways in which moderator comments were incorporated, or dismissed, in the narrative of the focus group itself.

Regardless of how a subject is introduced into a focus group discussion, one might still argue that if a group spent a lot of time talking about an issue, it was important to them.[44] This is not necessarily the case, of course. For example, men from Narva said that they had almost forgotten about corruption because it is so obvious. As one man stated, "The policemen are just pure corruption," to which another replied, "We just couldn't remember it because it is something that goes without saying" (4409–4412).[45]

Despite these caveats, I find the explicit enumeration of issues to be a useful guide. The unspoken problem is a naturalized problem. For instance, although Narvan men resented the corruption of their policemen, their focus on other issues suggests that corruption, while potentially important, is either less objectionable or more difficult to change or challenge than other issues.[46] At least in comparison to other more extensively discussed issues, there is no obvious cultural tool kit on which to draw in the critique of corruption's commonality.

Ultimately, of course, the counts only set the stage for more refined interpretations of what the numbers mean.[47] In particular, one should consider these focus group narratives as ways to learn how key concepts and issues articulated in other circumstances are addressed in various social circles. In this chapter, I bring these focus groups to bear on one of the most important elements of transition culture: freedom.

Focus groups are not equally concerned with freedom, but there are important patterns of variation in freedom's engagement. The nine groups that used freedom as a narrative most throughout their discussions were all from Estonia, across both Russian-speaking and Estonian-speaking focus groups. The men and women from the most economically and ecologically devastated places in Ukraine hardly, if ever, spoke of freedom, and the women from the ecologically damaged place in Estonia—Sillamäe—were also unlikely to talk of freedom (see Table 4.1).

These codes for freedom are not, however, evaluative codes. They simply reflect whether freedom is discussed or not. For us to assess the valence of freedom in these discussions, we must turn to a discussion of freedom itself. Nevertheless, this distribution of emphasis on freedom

Table 4.1. Percentage of Each Focus Group Discussion Devoted to Freedom

Focus group	Lines in focus group	Lines devoted to freedom	% of transcript devoted to freedom
Narva women	3,691	895	24
Tamsalu men	1,843	418	23
Tallinn Russian women	3,704	836	23
Tallinn Estonian men	2,590	571	22
Tartu men	2,838	458	16
Tallinn Russian men	3,762	457	12
Sillamäe Russian men	3,324	372	11
Tamsalu women	1,982	211	11
Tartu women	2,466	261	11
Lviv men	3,544	367	10
Kiev Ukrainian women	1,856	185	10
Kiev Russian women	2,161	204	9
Sillamäe Russian women	4,203	375	9
Kiev Russian men	2,289	198	9
Narva men	5,036	394	8
Tallinn Estonian women	2,706	198	7
Lviv women	3,132	167	5
Donetsk men	3,009	141	5
Kiev Ukrainian men	3,136	142	5
Donetsk women	3,829	147	4
Ivankiv men	4,283	157	4
Vinnitsa men	3,076	19	1
Vinnitsa women	1,909	8	0
Ivankiv women	3,298	7	0

not only suggests that Estonia is more "successful" in transition culture's evaluative discourse, but that transition culture's frames of reference, if not its valences, pervade the narratives of Estonian everyday life to a much greater extent than they do in Ukraine.

Transition Culture and the Open Public Sphere

When freedom is discussed in focus groups, it is often used to mark one of the accomplishments of communism's end. This kind of argument cuts across all nationalities and both countries. Members of the intelligentsia, the highly educated from both capital cities, were quite likely, for instance, to discuss the opening of the public sphere and the wider availability of information. Russian-speaking Igor, from Tallinn, remarked that "We have learned so much lately that we didn't even dream about before. As if an avalanche had fallen on us! [Moderator: An open society!] It is even difficult to absorb all this information. It wasn't like this before. . . . Formerly, we just knew that we were going somewhere . . . toward some radiant future. Now it turned out to be that we ended up in the wrong place" (368–86). Vladimir 1, one of the Russian-speaking men from Kiev, reinforced the conviction of his colleague from Tallinn:

> Since the collapse of our former country, many of the prohibitions that oppressed us have disappeared. You couldn't read literature, you couldn't obtain certain things. Everything was prohibited. How many works of art, that the whole world had access to, were hidden from us? If we had been able to study all of that before, we wouldn't have been robbed of our education. (522–33)

There is little difference in sentiment between that Vladimir and what a Ukrainian-speaking woman from Kiev, Iryna 1, said:

> I am a philosopher by training. Philosophy was one of the most ideological sciences. It was not free at all. And after all those changes . . . I could submit my dissertation on psychoanalysis, the most hostile branch of the social sciences, so much so that it was prohibited here. (430–38)

Although focus groups outside the capital cities were not composed of the intelligentsia, they too were concerned about the openness of the public sphere, and the fullness of the information presented to them. Even in the cities with relatively Soviet identities, Narva and Donetsk, one could find appreciation for the free flow of information, something not so prevalent during Soviet times. As Ira from Narva said,

> We learned a lot about the past, as well. Everything was hidden—the truth. It's also interesting how it really was and what they told us. It seems that this is also a big plus for our time, to put it one way. You can't live with lies all the time. You need to know how things really were. (529–37)

Andrei from Donetsk said very much the same thing about improvements over the preceding decade. The only improvement he noted was "freedom of speech and *glasnost'*, and nothing else" (406–7). He elaborated:

I read the newspapers. I find out all about public life. I never had access to that before; all we heard was anecdotes. Now I can even express any kind of criticism safely. And with *glasnost'*, everything that goes on in the government appears in the press. You can find out; they don't hide anything. Even about accidents and so on. Before, it was hidden. (415–25)

The value of this *glasnost'* is, however, not so clear across all focus groups. Some, like Valia, also from Donetsk, find that *glasnost'* brought little of value, because people were not prepared for it, and because "there is much useless talk and no action" (880–81). Indeed, Vera 1 develops her comrade's idea:

Our *glasnost'*, you see, it is unilateral. It is working more like gossip. Our leadership shows us this way. [It says,] "Well, this government was bad, and we are good." And by what virtue are they good, what have they done that is good? Relatively nothing good. In some time a new government will say, "We are good, and those who came before us were bad." That is all *glasnost'*. (900–912)

Glasnost' would sometimes find its defenders in such groups, however. In Ivankiv, for instance, one particularly Christian man (Andriy) and one man relatively appreciative of Soviet rule (Yuriy 1) argued quite heatedly about the value of Gorbachev's contributions to the open public sphere. After Yuriy 1 complains about how the West is turning Ukraine into a "banana republic" (2010) and how the elite has "sold out the state" (2075–76), Andriy replies:

Listen, listen . . . Soviet rule did not let you look deep there. Sorry, but you would not sound like such a hero if it were still Soviet rule. Now you have possibilities to see real life and you complain. You say it was better then—they told you that it was good and you believed them. You remember how they described the West in satiric magazines such as *Perets*? They were saying it was hell. That is how we used to live—we did not know life in other countries. We lived in a vacuum, we did not see any way out. You did not know; all that you thought was that it was okay. And now you are free to see all that. It is like the case with Gorbachev: he opened the country to the world and they cursed him. (2090–2109)

Yuriy 1 replied to Andriy that the people were right to curse Gorbachev, to which Andriy responded that without Gorbachev, Yuriy would not know anything about the dealings of the elite. At that point, the moderator tried to defuse the situation, and brought others into the conversation.

Freedom of information and the open public sphere were thus not so much a product of communism's end as a result of Gorbachev's leadership. This at least was the case for those who lost their country with the collapse of the USSR. Gorbachev's *glasnost'* was, for some of our respondents, the only positive public event to have happened over the preceding decade, and for a few, it was not positive at all.

Others did not date the opening of the public sphere with *glasnost'*, but rather with the end of Soviet rule itself. In Tamsalu, a rural region of Estonia, Monika finds that the open public sphere not only makes life more interesting, but it is critical to the diagnosis of society's well-being:

> I imagine that now we have better and more correct information about the things in the world. First, because journalists are free to talk about everything. In a word, all kinds of things are happening which would have been unthinkable before. I imagine, previously an analysis was carried out somewhere so that this would not always get to me correctly. Now it's not like that.
>
> MODERATOR: Tell us, thanks to what is this so?
>
> MONIKA: Thanks to freedom.
>
> SEVERAL VOICES: "Yes, freedom."
>
> MONIKA: All kinds of things happen. We have handicapped people as well. It is acknowledged and it is written about. Formerly, they didn't exist. (608–36)

Urmas from Tartu reinforces this vision of a new information age in his description of one of the virtues of independence:

> I think freedom of speech and legal access to information is most striking. Before you could always listen to that crackling Voice of America and get hold of some newspaper. But it's important that you can do it legally. You can say what you want. If you find you have a different opinion, then you can have the right to express it. Before, there was this continuous feeling of craziness. If you didn't want anything to happen to yourself, then you had to shut your mouth. You could certainly find ways, especially if you had some kind of responsibility. Access to information is important. Then you can draw your own conclusions. People feel that they have freedom. (529–47)

Here, freedom of information and Estonia's freedom from Soviet rule are neatly tied together to fulfill the accomplishments of transition. But Estonia's open public sphere is not celebrated unambiguously. Enn from

Tartu, for instance, notes that some social problems do not find space in the press anymore:

> But have you noticed that now that we don't have censorship any-more, several of Tartu's problems don't reach the columns of *Pos-timees*? And here they write about the life in Tallinn. Several social problems of Tartu are published in the Tallinn's paper, *Päevaleht*. I've spoken to some authors. Tartu's paper doesn't take an interest in several subjects. And since Tallinn's papers don't accept everything about Tallinn, that stuff will be published in *Postimees*.
>
> MODERATOR: Do you consider it a violation of the freedom of speech?
>
> JÜRI: To a certain extent, of course. . . .
>
> URMAS: I think there's another aspect too. The thing is that all news-papers, *Postimees* included, have declared that they want to become the most readable newspaper in Estonia. But if we only take the problems of Tartu, it won't sell very well. It won't sell throughout the country. (696–729)

Both Monika and the men from Tartu reflect the transition culture problematic quite nicely. The end of Soviet rule certainly created the conditions for an open public sphere, but it could not solve all prob-lems. It merely, but significantly, allows one to identify problems.[48] The commercialization of information is certainly a critical issue that limits discussion. Significantly, however, the Tartu men addressed this problem entirely within the problematic of an independent and market-driven Estonia. Although there is an implicit invocation of the Soviet past in the critique—at one time, the press responded to local concerns and was not driven by concerns over market share—any virtues of the Soviet past remain relatively invisible.

For Russian speakers, however, those times are treated more ex-plicitly, and with greater ambivalence. Indeed, Russians are especially likely to lament the loss of time and the cost of reading in this new open public sphere. Irena says that "we used to subscribe to five maga-zines and four newspapers, now I don't even get one. Naturally, the only one we can afford is the one my husband buys" (1871–75). She generalizes this to all of Narva, finding that today, despite the wider openness of information, the people of Narva are "mentally poorer" (1886). Freedom has produced vulgarity, dirt, and shameful and dis-graceful things that are now "normal" (1970).

Some of the Russian speakers in Estonia's capital Tallinn began with a similar disposition as the Estonian speakers in noting the fears of Soviet times. Following up on Yelena's recollections, Lililia, notes the "absence of ideological pressure, freedom of conscience" (438) as one of the improvements. But Svetlana hesitates:

> I wonder, if you were to remember those times, were you really afraid of something? [Yelena says yes.] Really? It is strange. As far as I am concerned, I have always, including now, felt the same. . . . I have never been deprived of the feeling of inner freedom. Perhaps, sometimes I would indeed abstain from saying too much, perhaps there were certain restrictions . . . but among my friends I was never afraid and never felt any pressure. I was ironic about newspapers and whatnot. (454–71)

This produces a fascinating discussion about the meaning of this new freedom. They all read Solzhenitsyn when he was forbidden reading, passing the photocopy among trusted friends. Now, when freely available, nobody reads such books. Although they note that they could read a wide variety of officially prohibited authors before *glasnost'*, it was still difficult to get a hold of authors such as Bulgakov. Gorbachev changed that. Svetlana was satisfied to say, "People used to adjust. Not that we lived in hypocrisy all the time, but we simply sometimes abstained from expressing our opinion, preferring to express it rather among our close friends" (645–51). Natasha then takes the conversation to another level:

> I think that no society is free from ideology. That pressure is gone, but new pressures have appeared. In the same ideological sphere . . . [Svetlana: "And I think such pressures are even heavier for us now."] . . . Absolutely right! I also want to say that this new pressure is much heavier than the one we used to have. Because that one dealt with a very specific category of people, while this pressure extends to everyone. Even to those who have nothing to do with ideology! (658–74)

Here, one of the most significant points about the transformation of ideology after communism's collapse becomes apparent. During Soviet times, there was a clear distinction between ideology and the real, between dogma and life; after communism's collapse, ideology is much more fluid, much more pervasive, perhaps even much better connected to social relations.[49] After communism, it cannot be easily sidestepped. In the new open society, irony offers no escape. Indeed, it requires new skills to deal with the flood of information. Detachment no longer suffices. The exchange between Russian-speaking Igor and Vladimir in Tallinn illustrates this magnificently:

> VLADIMIR (responding to Igor's celebration of the flood of information): I don't know, I'm not sure. If you watch TV programs in Estonian or in Russian, they are just full of scandals, and nothing else. There isn't really that much information!
>
> IGOR: No, that's not what I meant.
>
> VLADIMIR: Well, it's a point of view and you are free to express it.
>
> MODERATOR: I apologize. This is an opinion, so everyone has the right to express it.
>
> VLADIMIR: Yes, public opinion can be manipulated in different ways. You can either keep silent, or, just the other way around. . . .
>
> IGOR: No, this is on a different level of opinions. There have simply become more opinions. There is the possibility of sorting out these opinions now. Formerly, there was nothing to sort out. (388–415)

The public sphere's opening thus requires that the subject develop a new capacity that was not cultivated under Soviet rule. With freedom of information comes the responsibility to judge its quality. And that combination resonates powerfully with transition culture.[50] Freedom requires not only responsibility, but a new level of critical thinking.

These alternative portraits of the open public sphere offer some substantial differences. There are a few, like Ivankiv's Yuriy 1, who find little appreciation for such freedom of speech. The man who brought *glasnost'* also brought an end to his country—the Soviet Union. There are more people who appreciate the public sphere's openness, but to a limited degree, and they can be rather cynical about its value. Too much of the open public sphere is devoted to vulgar materials, gossip, or propaganda. But even here, relatively few are cynical. If it is discussed at all, most people find value in this openness. They appreciate the opening of the public sphere for what it can tell them about the past and the present. There can be disagreement about the date of its emergence—whether it was a feature of *glasnost'* or of independence from the Soviet Union. Nevertheless, for most people, the opening of the public sphere is one of the positive features of transition. There are, nevertheless, a few who question the value of all of this free information. For some Russian speakers, there was a certain freedom in an ironic detachment from ideology, and the new times offer little room to escape freedom and its responsibilities.

The Gender of Freedom

One of the most common ways of talking about freedom is to emphasize the freedom of "opportunity" after communism's collapse. On one level, this is readily seen across the transcripts as a freedom of choice in consumption. The women of Tartu resounded about the question of improvement with the celebration of choice in consumption:

> AIRE: Now you have freedom of choice. Everything is available in stores, we can choose everything ourselves.
>
> KADI: It depends on your own resources.
>
> ELLU: No lines.
>
> EVI: An abundance of goods. (196–204)

Although one's resources constrain choice—a point rarely left unstated[51]—many people, especially women (Narva women, 1030–45), celebrate freedom of choice (Narva men, 825–45). Even for those Russian-speaking women who live in ecologically fragile and economically devastated conditions, the women of Sillamäe find virtue in the freedom associated with communism's end. Zinaida said, "the medical system has become more free: now there's a choice of doctors. Earlier there was only the local doctor, and he didn't want to send us to Tallinn for examinations. Now it is much easier." To which the moderator replied, "So again we can say: opportunities. Right?" Zinaida confirmed, "Yes. Opportunities. We can go to any doctor now." Nina then reinforced the point: "Yes, before, you had to go to the local doctor, whether you wanted to or not" (1055–71). Thus, even for those who might identify problems associated with the Estonian nationalizing state, freedom can still be a real value of post-Soviet Estonian life.[52] Andrei 2 in Narva described this freedom in terms of expression:

> I would describe this feeling of freedom not as a feeling of freedom but as the possibility to express one's personality. A space of self-expression has been enlarged in let's say every field. A wider scale of accessible possibilities in production, in private life . . . (642–50)

Pavel, from Donetsk, identifies the same kind of freedom, and elaborates in terms of work opportunities:

> Well, before, education was . . . Let's say you graduated from technical school as a locksmith or a stonemason. You would be a stonemason and work as a stonemason your whole life. Now, you graduate

as a locksmith. You're not a good locksmith. You go to courses to learn to be a salesman. That is to say that before, if you had a diploma, that was it. You were already stamped with that stonemason's diploma. And now you can be whatever you want. (515–28)

Russian-speaking Anya from Kiev agrees that there is a newfound freedom in the world of work. During Soviet times, her husband was not allowed to moonlight legally, she said. Now,

> my husband has three jobs and I also earn some additional money. My husband works in a college, a university, and a small firm. No limitations are put on him anymore. I consider that a big plus. . . . I work as a department head . . . I am able to take on the people I need. I can hire the person who works best, and not have to keep on the person about whom I have been told, "He will work here," while whether he can think or not is unimportant. . . . Overall, both work and daily life have become much more free. . . . All the same, I am still an inert person. I watch my female friends, who even at my [advanced] age, have successfully accommodated themselves to life and requalified themselves.[53] But I distract myself with my dacha, where I spend pleasurable time. (533–75)

Nadia, also from Narva, takes the argument about self-expression further. Influenced, perhaps, by a culture of emancipation, Nadia went so far as to call it self-realization. She said that after communism's collapse, "it's possible to realize one's abilities. That is, it's possible to organize an enterprise, some private business, and so on. That way, you can prove yourself, even if you don't have an education" (325–31). Tania added that "My children have the opportunity, first and foremost, to realize their own abilities" (335–37).

In general, women appear to be more likely to speak about the transition in terms of their family, much as Tania did. Opportunity is not only a question for themselves, but also for their children. Recall the Ukrainian-speaking philosopher from Kiev who wrote a dissertation on psychoanalysis. She identified the defense of her dissertation as the most important and positive thing that happened to her in the preceding ten years. She was quick to add, however, that had her child been born in the decade, that would have merited first place otherwise: "Having a child is important for any woman, of course. At the time when it happened, it was the most important thing for me" (441–44). Iryna 2, another Ukrainian speaker from Kiev, in fact managed to tie together her appreciation for freedom in communism's end with the greatest joy of her life, the birth of her child:

The birth of my child and the sense of freedom are connected things. I am not sure if I would have been brave enough to have children out of wedlock in the old system, because they did not like such things in schools, and I worked in a college at that time. . . . You were lucky if they did not throw you out, but they definitely would have started to educate you, so to speak. . . . It was awful—Komsomol meetings—I remember them very well. My child was born in 1990. It was the worst time for my child and me, both emotionally and financially. However, now I am very happy that I have a child. When you come home tired after all the troubles at work and see her . . . Well, my child and freedom are closely connected. (449–69)

Women's ties to children are apparent across all conditions of life and assessments of transition in our focus groups. Those connections figure prominently not only in terms of their own family, but also in terms of the kinds of work, and possibilities for freedom, that can be found within it after communism's collapse. Monika, a kindergarten teacher from Tamsalu, had this to celebrate about communism's end and freedom's arrival:

Formerly, we had fixed plans I had to fulfill. We had "potty plans" we had to fill in as to whether they pooped or not. That's just not important . . . [now] we can express our own opinions and put them into practice. I don't have such strict limits, I'm not so enclosed [anymore]. If I attend courses somewhere, I can come and use this knowledge immediately. It's not like in April I definitely have to celebrate Lenin's birthday. (272–84)

Not all women appreciate all of these freedoms. In particular, Anya from Kiev feels different from other women. She is not so connected to her family, and she has lost something important in her work with the newfound freedom:

I have worked for twenty-six years and I know my job. Now I am occupied with petty work that nobody needs. My dissatisfaction with my job reveals itself at home, in how I relate to my husband and daughter. My work has always meant a lot to me. There are women who only think about their families. I, unfortunately, was raised by the Soviet system and I gave a lot of time to my job. I thought first about the Motherland, and then about myself. Because of this, now sometimes I am overwhelmed by a feeling of not being needed, not being in demand. It's horrible. (659–75)

From the same Russian-speaking focus group in Kiev, Tatyana followed Anya's lament with the assertion that "lack of certainty about tomorrow . . . those words could be written by any woman" (679–80). Of all the women in the focus groups, she spoke most directly, and forcefully, about the gendering of transition. Indeed, with regard to freedom she noted:

> It seems to me that we have changed over these past ten years. I am speaking now as a woman. It seems that freedom of choice has appeared everywhere. That which was formerly condemned now appears openly, for all to see, even if in personal [i.e., romantic] relations. There is more freedom in the professional sphere as well. I have understood that, strictly professionally, I can do many things. We had all acquired a Soviet psychological makeup—this thing is allowed while that is prohibited. Now everything has become more open (481–96). . . . The changes for the better are very closely tied to the changes for the worse. For example, "freedom of choice in everything." But, what does that mean? I think that women have suffered like no one else. Why? Because women are before all culture, science, art, and medicine. You see, all of these professions are filled by women. At the same time, these are the fields that are practically not funded now. My husband works, which means that I can allow myself the luxury of not working while I look for a good job. But how many women are obligated to work at low-paying jobs or to get new qualifications, like Anya, for example?[54] But the years are passing. You see, these ten years we are talking about are the best of my life, and they happened during the cataclysms occurring in our country. And it turns out that I'm already thirty-nine years old and I can't insinuate myself into certain situations, because those situations demand someone who is, say, twenty-five. (616–43)

Tatyana inspired a lengthy conversation about gender discrimination in the workplace. The women of Narva also spoke a great deal about these opportunities, especially to prove oneself. But like the Russian-speaking women of Kiev, they noted that it was not for everyone.

> IRENE: Not everybody is capable of making a decisive action. The most important thing is that a person is able to break himself, to offer himself somewhere; but we're still not ready for this.
>
> IRA: Right. Right.
>
> IRENE: Our generation, in any case. We're not used to it, we weren't trained for this.
>
> IRA: We're used to being appreciated for our deeds.
>
> NATA: That we should be appreciated. Not that we should prove ourselves, but that they should see how good we are.
>
> IRA: We don't know even how to sell ourselves. (442–61)

These women did not explicitly say that men are better situated than women to realize the opportunities to be found in freedom, but the terms of their discussion did not frame the opportunities as their own. Rather, opportunities appeared to be mainly for their children. Among the Estonian-speaking men of Tallinn, however, the explicit gendering of this opportunity was taken up. Juri pointed out how the newfound freedom of opportunity is making life more difficult for women in Estonia:

> Even women not involved in business have a hard time getting to any position, even to a mid-management position, in comparison with ten years ago. At that time, they had a certain position with a certain salary. I feel that this freedom is abused to the detriment of women—that they don't get the same wage for comparable work. And . . . I don't have experience, but I have heard it from the media. (2238–49)

Aarne, however, rebukes him about his positive portrait of the Soviet past. In those times, he said, "they taught women to do the kind of work they shouldn't have been allowed to do" (2252–54). Juri relented and agreed. Toomas L. and Toomas K. then took the gender of freedom into another problem.

Toomas L. said that he was "really pained by the decrease in the Estonian population" (2179–80). Toomas K. observed that with the greater freedom to act, and the greater freedom to decide when to have a family, the size of families will decline. Hannes confirmed his colleagues' academic wisdom with his own experience: "I've experienced that personally. At the end of the eighties, my wife and I didn't have anything else to do besides have babies. But now there are other things to do" (2210–15).[55] Although gender promised to become prominent in the discussion among these Estonian men, it was quickly subverted by the anti-Soviet and Estonian national discourse. Indeed, even among women, gender rarely served as an explicit master signifier for any discussion.

The Kiev Russian focus group was the only group where gender literally organized about one-quarter of the discussion. Tatyana was in large part responsible for articulating a vision of gender that enabled the group to identify problems in its terms, including the much-vaunted freedom associated with communism's collapse. For the most part, however, the nation dominates the discussion, especially in Estonia.[56] Even though Tallinn's Estonian-speaking men might identify job discrimination as a problem, the issue could smoothly shift. Instead of recognizing women's disadvantage, women's freedom becomes a problem for the nation. For some men, women's freedom is potentially dangerous. In other cases, however, freedom might serve the nation, especially when the nation's future can be identified with transition culture and the realization of the entrepreneurial spirit, as in western Ukraine.

Nations of Freedom

Two men from Lviv exemplified the link between the promise of the nation and of transition. Zenoviy and Stepan were especially convincing about the virtues of freedom in the new system. At a certain level, their ideas seemed to genuinely embody the virtues of transition culture. They refused to support the idea that things had gotten worse in any way over the preceding ten years. They may have gotten more complicated, but certainly not worse. Zenoviy said that life had improved "spiritually" (1160–62). He elaborated:

> We are learning, and this is hard physically, psychically, and morally. [It is hard] morally only because I've already lived for forty-five years and much of that time is lost. Because there was no private property, there was no chance to open my own business, to prove myself not just for material reasons, but to prove something to myself in life (1171–80) . . . to prove to myself what I am capable of. (1196–97)

Stepan adds: "That you are somebody. And not this education that I was taught in school where they tried to prove to me that I was nobody. I just didn't agree with that" (1199–1202).

Stepan and Zenoviy embed this pride in entrepreneurial freedom in a larger narrative about the distinction of their region's identity. Stepan initiates a conversation about Lviv's leading political role in the anticommunist and pro-independence effort as well as its economic ambition:

> STEPAN: Politically, we were the first, I mean our region. Still, why can't our region be made into a kind of [economic] independent zone, like they have in Poland, in Europe? For example, when we had the New Economic Policy, it was in the Odessa region. And now in Odessa, they want to make this economic zone, you see?
>
> VOLODYMYR: The Galician zone.
>
> STEPAN: And economically, the Lviv region hasn't even made a step toward an economic [zone].
>
> ZENOVIY: Kiev won't allow it. (2943–?)

Zenoviy subsequently embeds that regional difference in a different psychology, in fact linking the Ukrainian—understood as western Ukrainian—mentality to the Baltic one:

> I think we are more adaptable, our psychology is not as corrupted in comparison with the central and eastern regions. We are more adaptable to such difficult conditions. We Ukrainians, all our lives, have been individualists. Therefore we are in a better position, because, I repeat, our psychology is not so corrupted. Let's take, for example, the Baltic states. They have moved more quickly to the market economy. (3269–81)

Of course, not everyone in that group finds the western Ukrainians so exemplary. Myron, for instance, laments:

> Lviv could be in a better position, but our people don't want to produce anything. They are used to buying everything abroad, bringing everything from there. Even so, they could produce something now, disregarding the difficult situation, but they don't want to. They say it is easier to bring it from abroad. They have lost the habit of work, they don't want to think. (2943–3006)

Even in this criticism, however, the Ukrainians "lost" the virtuous disposition that they once had. Clearly, socialism is cast as something imposed on them, something alien, something that must be overcome. Socialist dependency may be more compatible with those in the center and east of Ukraine, but certainly not in the west. Opportunity seeking and self-reliance are thus cast as something that is embedded in the Ukrainian way, as well as something that can be learned. For the men of Lviv, their close neighbor, Poland, shows the clear value of private property. They note that Poland facilitates the proper disposition toward work with its respect for private property and its provision of technical equipment such as tractors that Ukraine does not provide. In short, people have the opportunity to work in Poland; in Lviv, they say, "we aren't given this opportunity" (671–72). Who exactly deprives them of this opportunity is not clear, however. Someone, somewhere, prevents the fulfillment of their personal, and national, destiny in transition culture.

Transition culture's core problematics, if the World Bank's publications are any indication, are less likely to blame others for entrepreneurial limitations. Certainly, these problematics can identify inhospitable infrastructures and unhelpful tax systems, but transition culture seeks to cultivate a disposition in self-reliance that tears down those barriers to transition even before the political economic environment is right. In this regard, men from Estonia are more exemplary than those of Lviv. The Estonian men from Tallinn suggest the sophistication, in fact, of transition culture. In identifying improvements over the preceding ten years, Ain summarized his basic point by saying that there has been a broadening in opportunities to act:

> I've formulated it like this: the increasing freedom to determine your life and actions and fulfillment. The level of freedom, not freedom itself. You clearly can't have outright freedom. Of course, the improvement of the economic situation is also connected with the broadening of opportunities. But although it hasn't improved for everyone, there's still a small group of people for whom the situation has improved or is improving. If something is concerned with the improvement of living conditions, then it doesn't apply to everyone, only to a certain group. It seems to me. . . . But a level of freedom and the fact that people can move in the direction that they most desire exist without doubt. How many use it and can use it and how many are ready to use it are questions in themselves. We can talk about freedom, we can sing about freedom, we can shout about freedom, but when we attain freedom, all of that doesn't mean that we'll know how to use it. There aren't very many who know how. In analyzing these things, we definitely have to differentiate those who stepped into this society relatively unimpeded, who don't have experience of the past. They have a much easier time utilizing this level of freedom than those who already have a certain experience which hinders them. (399–441)

Toomas K. takes this point one step further:

> The economic situation is related to the enterprising spirit in the case of people like me. How much I earn depends on that. How much I feel like doing. Actually this transition from one society to another has left many people waiting for the state to do something for them. They continue to wait. With increasing freedom comes responsibility. If I take out a loan—I can simply get one now, you can simply get fifty thousand from Hoiupank—I have to look ahead and take responsibility so that I can do something with it and pay it back. So this theoretical opportunity of freedom doesn't necessarily mean that everyone can use it and know how to use it. Some are simply left waiting. (478–98)

Ain and Toomas K. could very well be colleagues and friends of Mart Laar. They speak the same language and share a habitus. They are highly educated Estonian men from the capital city, ready to recognize that the Soviet past impaired people's capacities for self-reliance.

Although never explicitly stated, it is implied that Estonians are more likely to be unimpaired by that past than are Russians, and that the young are less affected by it than are their elders. Nobody is automatically responsible; that discipline is exceptional, and that is what produces society's inequalities. The resonance with the World Bank and transition culture is remarkable. Also interesting, however, is that this disposition is not limited to the highly educated Estonian men of Tallinn. One finds a similar critique of "dependency" in Sillamäe, a place decimated by environmental pollution and economic dislocation:

> IGOR: Well, in the past, all the decisions—not all, of course, but most of them—were made by "them." You had only to appear at your job, do it, and go home. What happened afterwards—whether you could go somewhere or not, buy something or not—that all depended on "them." Whether they allowed it or not. Nowadays, basically everything is . . .
>
> MODERATOR: Nowadays it depends on . . .
>
> IGOR: On your own decision. That is, whatever I want; I think, I plan how to do it, and I work toward it—in general, anything can be done. (403–20)

This remark occurs *despite* the radical criticism of the Estonian nationalizing state. It is still possible for these Estonian Russians of the northeast to show their attachment to Estonia, to emphasize that they are *Baltic* or *Estonian* Russians. As in Sillamäe, in Narva the group's introduction begins with a discussion of where people were born, and to what extent they might, then, feel as if they were a "native." Within this context, Estonia has a positive connotation. Sergei, for instance, worked in Dushanbe, the capital of Tajikistan, after his graduation from school, but:

> In 1985, when *perestroika* began, I felt the political situation in Tajikistan—an attitude toward the Russian-speaking population in Tajikistan—because I spent all my life there. So I decided to make a change and to move closer to Europe, to civilization, to move to the west, to Estonia. (224–34)

Although they complain about how much of a problem Estonian independence has made for their relationship to family and friends who still live in Russia (1482–1519), the Narvans also emphasize their distinction from other Russians. They are more "Western" in their "culture, mentality, and way of life." Andrei 1 points out that "they are Russians, but they became more civilized in Estonia." Andrei 2 amplifies this by saying, "It's a general approach to problem solving. Not just to grab an axe and a sword, but to try to solve [problems] somehow" (2528–55). They are also aware that Russians in Russia do not consider them to be Russian at all, and that they themselves, after living in Estonia for some time, cannot manage to live somewhere else (2561–69). Indeed, they seem to appreciate Estonian rather than Russian border guards much more (2857–3032). After a discussion of how one-quarter of the Narvan Russians supported Estonia's independence initially, Sergei emphasized just how Estonian, how realistic, Estonian Russians have become, and why there is no conflict here as there is in Karabakh:

> Because of the turn of character, because of the high cultural level of the Estonian people, because of their national specificities, such as staying calm, being reasonable, being cautious in actions . . . and those Russians who were either born here or who live here for a long time—they already have these typical Estonian features. (2617–30)

Vladimir 2 is a bit more cautious than Sergei; he amends Sergei's account of the peace of Estonian–Russian relations:

> We had Karabakh here, blew up at the time of Gorbachev. At the same time, the Supreme Soviet of Estonia began to think about separation. Well, while they were separating—we were living. Knowing that Karabakh had already blown up, that it was burning, but . . . Under the condition that freedom would come. Freedom to act was given to everyone. Mart Laar told himself: "If you want to live good—you've got to go for it! Salvation for those who are drowning is in their own hands." By the way, now everybody lives according to this principle. And why there was no military conflict in Estonia? The youth rushed to make their living by any means. Just to have something to do. The means were not important. Robbery, blackmail, rackets—you could say that 100 percent of them abandoned politics. (2652–75)

It is clear from these exchanges that Russians are themselves divided about their place in Estonia, but even in the northeast there is reason for hope, much as Laitin also found.[57] Whether they become part of it by adapting to Estonian culture, or adapt by "making a living by any means," is no doubt a variable. But they seek to be part of that Estonian future. This is, however, most clear in the capital city, for there, even as the Estonian and Russian speakers disagree about the direction of transition culture, both groups articulate the present within the basic structural framework of transition. They both articulate the future in global terms.

Opening to the World

The spatial imagination of the men from Tallinn was relatively well developed for those in capital cities. The Estonian-speaking men were especially likely to elevate the significance of regional inequalities within Estonia, but both focus groups devoted a great deal of time to a discussion of the international comparison. Opening to the world— knowing one's own place by comparing it to other places in the world— is a very important part of transition culture and something very well developed in Estonia (see also Sillamäe men, 349–52), and especially in Tallinn. But this global articulation is used to very different ends, with very different foci.

The Estonian-speaking men were quite oriented toward international affairs and comparisons—in fact, emphasizing just how important the international reference is for having an open society. Returning to that emphasis on the public sphere, but with an international spin, Toomas K. said:

> In my circle of work, this communication with foreign countries is essential, considering we've lived for so long like lonely mice in a cage and seen just a remnant of the world. We haven't been able to compare ourselves with others. Comparison is very important. If we don't see what others are doing, it's like a sack race. (813–22)

This communication, then, realizes one of the traits transition culture implies: the reduction of national difference. Ain points out that a new logic has emerged in Estonia, because "we have the same system as most of the world now," and "conditions start to assimilate because of similar traits in the systems" (1036–45).

Russian men also used the comparative method to assess Estonia's state of affairs, but for them the distance between Europe and Estonia was perceived as far greater. After mentioning that he too has traveled, Alexander 2 said:

> I haven't seen anything like this anywhere. Such sharp contrast between those who are absolutely supposed to carry the main burden of taxation. There are rich and there are poor. If you stumbled in this life, you are done with, you are poor! That is the problem! Thus, I think that the main problem is sharp inequality in society, inequality that should not exist in a European state. (622–34)

Typically, the Estonian-speaking men used the advanced countries as positive lessons for Estonia. Sometimes, however, they used the experiences of these other countries to relativize their country's problems. They argued, for instance, that all countries face a loss of security (1727–41). Like Estonians, those in Japan and the United States suffer increased stress and lack of time (1794–1810). The comparative method with advanced countries was even turned back to the discussion of regional inequalities within Estonia. Hannes uses Finland's experience as an example to argue that the state must intervene in regional inequalities because international investments flow much more obviously into capital cities because of their relative ease of communication (1092–1103). International comparison is also used in reference to other post-Soviet countries, but here the comparison is used to signal appreciation for what has not happened. Things are much worse, these men note, in Lithuania, Latvia, Belarus, and Ukraine (1604–20).

The Russians have a much different attitude toward the post-Soviet world and its former clients. For example, Stanislav said, "For me, the worst of all in this whole story of the collapse of the empire is that I lost access to Eastern markets" (739–42). Indeed, he accuses the Estonian government authorities not only of ignorance in matters of trade (one should not put up boundaries to discourage trade), but also of setting up a racket (862–900). Basically, the Estonian government ruined a great deal of industry because it destroyed the market—whether in the east or the military market in Iran and Iraq—that formerly made the Estonian Russians' businesses so successful (1081–1164). This policy is not even sensible from an economic point of view, they argue, because there are so many Estonian businessmen who work with Russia, which leads to an interesting debate about the appropriate role of Russia in forcing this opening of trade (2126–95). The role of the West in affecting their lives is also discussed at some length.

Unlike the Estonian men, who simply take it as a point of departure, the Russian men want to debate the breakup of the Soviet Union. Rather than treat Soviet rule as somehow abnormal, and therefore deserving of extinction, the Russian men suggest a conspiracy of the United States and the West more generally in bringing down the USSR (1177–1276). The West does not fare much better with them, even when it provides investment. An American company manages Alexander 1's successful firm, but he is quite critical. All they produce goes to the West and nothing to Estonia. And in five years, he warns, the advantage Estonia has in lower wages will be lost, at which time the company will relocate and seek cheaper conditions of production elsewhere. Alexei lamented that everything is governed by economic expediency (1799–1848). Their attitude toward the European Union is also very critical and skeptical (2569–83).

More generally, one might say that transition culture itself elevates the value of international comparison. Given Estonia's relative success among post-Soviet countries in making that transition, transition culture has likely encouraged such an international disposition, especially among the highly educated.[58] The Russian men, however, point out just how skewed that international reference of transition culture is. It appears to be driven not so much by neutral economic questions as by politically motivated pro-Western and anti-Russian practice.

This is especially clear in terms of freedom to travel. People from Narva are especially likely to note the problems in visiting their friends and relatives in Russia. This is one of the worst changes for many Narvans. Ira says, "It's very difficult to go see them [relatives and friends in Russia]. And friends don't visit—everything was easier before, wasn't it? They'd visit on holidays—it was pretty normal to go visit someone. Now you can't do that. Now you need all this time to get documents in order to travel. Of course, all this keeps people apart. Our ties are falling apart" (2180–89). And the Estonian state is not solely responsible for the problem. Vladimir 1, also from Narva, notes that "the majority of problems are still created by the Russian side and not by the Estonian one"; Vladimir 3 and 4 agree (2857–63). The women emphasize that the Estonians do not have this sense of isolation. Indeed, unlike these Narvans who feel isolated, because they want to visit Russia regularly and they cannot, the Estonians are not at all isolated. "With their Estonian passports, they're not isolated at all," Nadia notes. She knows the Estonians well.

Estonians mark their freedom of travel as one of the great accomplishments of transition.[59] As Aarne from Tallinn thought about another improvement derived from the changes of the transition, he remarked that there is a greater opportunity

> to expand yourself, develop yourself, study, even within the border. The choices are simply greater than only Moscow, Petersburg, Riga. From today's standpoint, all of those places are open to us. But there's also Harvard University and Oxford—all of the other places

like that, which we couldn't even dream about before. Opportunities to expand yourself and educate yourself have certainly increased (673–84). . . . Maybe, certainly the fact that Estonians have a lot of travel opportunities and Russians might have restrictions makes for different opinions between nationalities. They only have the chance to travel to Petersburg. (697–703)

While the Estonians debate the degree and direction of this internationally open society, the Ukrainians are much more constrained in their vision of the world. Poland offers the model for west Ukrainians, whereas those in Donetsk refer to what happens in Russia. The Russian and Ukrainian speakers of Kiev hardly speak of the international comparisons. They speak only occasionally of international commerce—for instance, when the Ukrainian-speaking men tried to identify who is to blame for the limited foreign investment (2316–2442). Vladimir 2 even lamented that "Independence fell on Ukraine out of the blue. There were no cadres here. They were gathered in Moscow . . . all those cadres, the entire elite, got educated there. We don't have an elite. We don't have a basic culture. I mean in Ukraine" (958–70). To a considerable extent, these Ukrainian narratives remained rooted in Ukraine and in the Soviet past, even as they struggle to see the future. A big nation, Russia's "most favored Lord"[60] from Soviet times, Ukraine may be less well situated to become part of that global culture that is transition.

Conclusions

In this chapter, I have elaborated the dimensions of transition culture's lability. A structural reading of transition culture in the terms of this chapter's key concepts might have produced a figure like this:

$$\frac{\text{Plan}}{\text{Market}} \sim \frac{\text{East}}{\text{West}} \sim \frac{\text{Past}}{\text{Future}} \sim \frac{\text{Nationalism}}{\text{Globalism}} \sim \frac{\text{Unfreedom}}{\text{Freedom}} \sim \frac{\text{Dependency}}{\text{Responsibility}} \sim \frac{\text{Ideology}}{\text{Reason}}$$

However, this structural reading, though consistent with an ideology of transition, misses important transformations of transition culture in the national narratives articulated by our focus groups' recollections. Indeed, this kind of figure draws our attention away from the labilities of postcommunism's cultural formations.

Transition culture is more international or global than that past against which it sets itself. It favors a model of cultural transformation toward reason, responsibility, and openness that knows no national boundaries. It favors a mode of state regulation that is open to trade and commerce. Freedom is its catchword. At the same time, of course, transition culture remains nationalist. It is not the same nationalism that transition culture critiques, but transition culture cannot escape nationalism's discursive formation. It accedes to important elements of that nationalism.

Transition culture sees the world in terms of nation-states. It identifies positive and negative exemplars with nation-states. Its spokespersons make transition culture legitimate to the extent that they are of the nation. They represent transition culture more to the extent that they identify with the West, for transition culture's standpoint clearly does not rest in Russia. This much we could see in chapters 2 and 3, but in this chapter we can see that transition culture has broader application than to business plans and marketing strategies, and that its nationalism can work in unexpected ways.

Nationalism is apparent in discourses over self-reliance and responsibility. For example, some west Ukrainians tried to make the case that their entrepreneurial passion is tied to the regional distinction and collective individualist psychology of Ukrainians. Maybe not as good as the Balts, and maybe being held back by somebody in Kiev or elsewhere, Ukrainians still struggle to throw off the shackles of socialism, they argued. The men of Lviv clearly aspired to membership in transition culture, but they expressed it in the language of nationalism. One can find the same rhetorics of responsibility in Estonia, but without the same elevation of West over East.

The Estonian- and Russian-speaking men of Tallinn were especially prolific about the dispositions that are celebrated in transition culture. Even in the provinces, Estonians and Estonian Russians, especially the men, sang the praises of self-reliance and ambition. To be sure, the Russian speakers resented the nationalizing state, but their identification with a sober and problem-solving Estonian culture, which is itself assimilating into a transition culture combining global awareness and local initiative, was striking. Also striking, however, was how differently they translate that global awareness. While the Estonian speakers tended to normalize their country's problems with such a vision, the Russian speakers used that very same global awareness to critique Estonia's trajectory. It is not normal, they argued, for Estonia to refuse to recognize our Russianness and to discourage trade with and travel to Russia.[61] Hence, though the bias in transition culture is obviously Western, its principles can be used to critique that very bias. The value of critique is greater, however, when private troubles can become public issues.[62]

Most of our respondents found terrific value, for instance, in the openness of the public sphere. Estonians were likely to fuse that openness with the end of Soviet rule, but Russian speakers were likely to look to Gorbachev's *glasnost'* for the beginning of freedom in speech and press. Some, however, find this new era less appealing, given that, along with additional information, one also finds a superabundance of smut and scandal. Some Russian speakers went beyond lament to recognize a new ideology. In the old system, they argued, there was an inner freedom that ironic detachment could preserve. In the new system, freedom brought a new disposition that cannot be escaped. It is not said exactly what that new vision is, but that might be part of its power. That new ideology is unnameable, and hard to demarcate. In the old system, ideology could be recognized for its distance from reality; in the new system, ideology and everyday life resonate in ways that make inner freedom more difficult.[63] Still, for many Russians especially, it was there and "weighty." Thus, although freedom might be associated with the market and the future, and ideology with the plan and the past, some of our subjects found a new kind of unfreedom in the present, and an intellectual quality lost in the past. Russian speakers were more likely to offer this critique of smut and ideology. Once again, it appears difficult to interpret even the opening of the public sphere without attending to how it affects, and is understood in, different national communities. Even the capacity for critique appears to be shaped by national orientation.

Conditions of life obviously constrained freedom too. While celebrating freedom of choice in consumer goods, most people followed with a lament that of course not everyone can afford that choice. Although opportunity abounds for the realization of oneself and one's dreams, not everyone can manage. These freedoms are obviously constrained by class and gender, but they are not discussed as much as one might imagine. Gender is especially underplayed. Only one group really fingered how much more limited women's freedoms are, and how that which has been called freedom has led to discrimination against them. Inequalities of class and of gender clearly diminish freedom. Perhaps one of the greatest unfreedoms rests in the inability to articulate the conditions that limit freedom. If freedom is the core of transition, clearly we must go beyond its political and economic impediments to recognize the ways in which cultures work to empower and disempower different groups and different forms of freedom.

Transition culture does not focus on those freedoms denied by material inequality, given that one of the elements of the past to be relegated to history's dustbin is socialism's rhetoric around equality. Self-reliance and responsibility are supposed to take the place of state interference and individual dependency in establishing the conditions of one's livelihood. Attending to those freedoms denied by gender inequality may be polluted less by association with socialism, but feminist concerns within a postcommunist world also suffer in a cultural formation inflected by discourses of national emancipation. Nationally framed emancipation can, sometimes, be articulated with gender critique,[64] but this typically feeds into a society where the distinction between tradition and emancipation is drawn with a thick line. Turkey was such a place at the end of the Ottoman Empire, where one of the most effective arguments against Islam was one based on the critique of its gender practices. But where tradition and emancipation cannot be so ideologically opposed, the gender problematic is harder to elaborate, as is the case in most of Eastern Europe.[65] The articulation of transition culture and nationalism therefore makes it *more* difficult to articulate some of freedom's constraints. But this limitation is not intrinsic to transition culture.

Already, this hermeneutic sociology of transition culture across various regional, national, and gendered communities of discourse suggests critical labilities in the formation. First of all, transition culture can be translated into everyday life, and not just into business. It has been remarkably integrated into the narratives told by the Russian- and Estonian-speaking men and women of Estonia. Second, the narrative of transition culture becomes more powerful to the extent that it rejects its pretension of globalism, and articulates with national narratives that can themselves acquire multiethnic spokespersons. Estonian culture is not only appealing to Estonians, but also to Estonian Russians. Estonian Russians can then translate global transition and Estonian national identity into a discourse of Estonian-Russian rights and victimization. They can contest nationalist transition within the recognizable boundaries of transition culture. Transition culture *can* embrace national difference. Indeed, for it to succeed, it must.

Beyond this, however, these focus groups also bring some hope for the more critical potentials of transition culture. Some people have a remarkable capacity to identify the *constraints* on freedom that transition culture brings. Sometimes, these constraints appear disconnected from national narratives, as in the critique of the media's commodification and the loss of local news. More typically, however, these critiques of freedom have national articulations. Russian speakers are more likely to point out the limits of transition culture's freedom, whether in terms of free trade with Russia, in the mentalities of freedom's subjects, or in the gendering of freedom. But these critiques draw on the socialist past and an eastward gaze in ways that transition culture hardly embraces. For transition culture to cultivate its critical capacities, it might do well to address more effectively its socialist past. But it must also take care not to get stuck in it, for looking toward the past easily invites narratives of loss and ressentiment rather than of direction and empowerment. For that reason, it is quite useful to engage transition culture not only on its own conceptual terms, such as freedom, or its own preferred sites, as in business practices or in Estonia, but in those substantive and geographical areas where transition is most challenged.

Transition's translation is much less pervasive, or effective, in Ukraine, especially in its ecologically and economically devastated areas. Another narrative of transition, or at least of transformation, is more evident there: one of loss, both realized and anticipated. To be sure, these narratives are embedded in deeper narratives of gender and the nation, but their direction, and coherence, are not so clear. Perhaps that narrative uncertainty derives from their grounding in reaction, rather than in the engagement or direction provided by the cultural formation of transition. But for us to address that directly, we need to take advantage of that great emancipatory promise of transition. Under Soviet rule, many problems did not exist because they could not be named and discussed in public. In postcommunist Ukraine, there are plenty.

Five

Environmental Problems, Civility, and Loss in Transition

Transition culture is not the only cultural formation informing and interpreting change in communism's collapse and aftermath. As the United Nations Development Program (UNDP) report suggested, one could understand this period as a time of terrific loss and impoverishment. The elements of this analytical narrative can also be incorporated into a much more obviously political one. The Communist candidate for president in the 1996 Russian elections, Gennady Zhuganov, organized his campaign around such a narrative of loss. He said:

> the road we have traveled for the past five or 10 years. On it we have lost our country, half our national wealth, the dignity of a great power, the respect of the entire world, and our confidence in a future for each one of us . . . lost several million of our fellow-countrymen . . . our fellow citizens killed in the 200 wars and conflicts unleashed on our native soil, dead before their time, or not born at all . . . they have stolen our faith in our own resources and our ideas of ourselves as a great power. We are being taught to accept promises of humanitarian aid, handouts of secondhand clothes, and advice-cum-orders from abroad on what we should be doing and how we should be doing it. . . . For the first time in Russia's 1,000-year history, mothers and fathers feel guilty for leaving their children a half-destroyed, untidy home. . . . And I am ashamed that I was once in the same party as the turncoats, destroyers and traitors of the Fatherland who currently

rule in the Kremlin. But there is another road . . . Russia's road to itself, a road to spirituality, prosperity, plenty and dignity. It is the road followed by countries against which the rest of the world now measures itself. These states live by the simple rule that the welfare of their citizens comes above all else. We simply need to shrug off our slumbering unreliability and depression, pull ourselves together, be ashamed for what we have done to our own history and the world of our forefathers and say to ourselves: We are Russia, we are a great people, and there is no power on earth that can conquer us. Believing in ourselves and starting to act—that is what we want.[1]

Zhuganov's 1996 campaign was an exemplary threat to transition from the most problematic country within transition culture. Because of Russia's size, position in military affairs, and anxiety over its international status, transition culture has had to treat Russia differently than every other society, without, however, being able to address its problematic status directly.[2] The global allies of Russian proponents of transition apparently accepted as necessary, if regretful, extraordinarily problematic behavior by Yeltsin and the oligarchy that ran Russia. Yeltsin's bombing of parliament and arrest of his opponents in 1993, wars in Chechnya and threats to its sovereign neighbors, and extraordinary corruption in privatization are regrettable, but apparently acceptable.[3] The West, one observer finds, expects only a "presentable" Russia, not a reformed Russia.[4]

Rather than focus on transition culture's assessment of Russia, or elaborate the critique Zhuganov and others offer for transition culture, I continue the hermeneutic themes developed in chapter 4. Here, however, the hermeneutic gap is much greater. In chapter 4, I considered how transition culture's principal themes, notably around freedom, could be translated into nationalisms of various sorts. Here, however, I consider a theme that transition culture denies, but that is clearly dominant in some parts of the postcommunist world: loss.

Hermeneutics connotes more than translation. It reminds us that the fusion of horizons between different standpoints always leaves something out. Although translation's practitioners and theorists recognize the enterprise as complicated work that involves hermeneutic exercise, those who depend on translation tend to see it as typically sufficient and relatively unproblematic. Indeed, transition culture, as I argued in chapter 3, relies heavily on translation while simultaneously minimizing the hermeneutic dilemma. To consider loss in transition requires that we elevate the dilemma. Beyond relating the meaning of the words, hermeneutics seeks to understand the contextual meaning of those expressions and elaborate the larger cultural relationship between life-worlds in which those articulations are embedded.[5]

One could translate the woes of those who suffer in transition by emphasizing their inadequacies before transition. If these dispossessed subjects of transition embrace Zhuganov and other opponents to liberalism's vision, transition culture's proponents can dismiss their despair by assigning them to the status of the unredeemable and the enemy. I would propose, however, that despair's articulation requires that the challenge of translation, and the hermeneutic dilemma involved in it, become much more important. Discourses of freedom and opportunity might be variations on the theme of transition culture's universalism, but the articulation of loss is embedded in a life-world radically incommensurate with the vision of the future that transition culture promotes. To expand its reach and to maximize its inclusion, transition culture needs to cultivate a greater capacity to listen to those who are marginalized from its radiant future, and thus attend to the hermeneutics of loss in transition.[6] Drawing on those same focus group data discussed in chapter 4, I consider in this chapter how those who emphasize the pervasiveness of problems, rather than the realization of freedom and opportunity, articulate transition.

Transition Culture and Socialist Civil Society

Zhuganov's invocation is compelling because it centers victimization and injustice. It resonates with a broad array of people and not only with those who live in Russia. It is also, however, peppered with "moral messianism," Ernest Gellner's term for one of civil society's most dangerous alternatives, where the social order is sacralized, power is concentrated, and consequently economic dynamism and liberty potentially denied.[7] Whether or not this vision, and communist leadership, would be so dangerous is hard to say from a "neutral" point of view. Certainly, from the viewpoint of transition culture, it could be deadly. And from the point of view of the newly independent and liberated states of Eastern Europe and the former Soviet Union, it is a cause for concern. A Russia lamenting its loss of empire is not a Russia encouraging civil society at home or in its "near abroad."

Of course, Russia is not the only imagined community anxious about the adequacy of civil societies for national destinies. Drawing on in-depth interviews with parliamentary elites, Elżbieta Skotnicka-Illasiewicz and Włodzimierz Wesołowski found Polish deputies from Christian and Peasant parties to be anxious about Europe.[8] It is understood as a potential threat to Polish national identity. Europe is debauched, they claim, and Poland retains, or should retain, its traditional moral and spiritual values.[9] These nationalists construct the nation as a particular moral community with common interests. In such a framework, the elaboration of national distinction becomes quite important. By contrast, liberals from both the postcommunist party and post-Solidarity parties understand Europe as a "configuration of civil societies."[10] These liberals view nations as pluralistic sites of interest formation among individuals and groups. Liberals tend not to elaborate the nation in ideological terms because *their own nation should not be peculiar.*

The major difference between Polish and Russian suspicions of Europe and of civil society rests in the problematic of the small nation. In the case of small nations, national "interests" depend on integrating with Western institutions that privilege the register of nations in the key of civil society. Although there may be Estonians, Poles, and Ukrainians who fear that both Russia and Europe might undermine the integration of the nation, the power of such a narrative articulating threat is tempered by another concern. The nation could still lose its independence. While anxiety over its superpower status still might animate Russia's international politics, concerns over its sovereignty appear paranoid, at least in comparison to the national security concerns of a Poland, Ukraine, or Estonia. Integration with a Europe of civil societies poses no great defense of sovereignty for Russia, but it is critical for the smaller nations. Consequently, transition culture promises more to "small nations" than it can to Russia because transition culture implies protection from the fourth Russian empire. For the small nation, transition and nationalism fuse. For those who envision empire, transition is a threat and Soviet times do not look so bad.

Appreciation for the Soviet or socialist past is anathema to transition culture. The World Bank explicitly enunciates its fear, worrying that the problems of the past will be forgotten, and that the public could slip back unconsciously and embrace that past: "The public must constantly be reminded of the reasons for change and informed about progress to date."[11] In this vision, civil society must be remade before it can become an asset in transition. If civil society can be roused by visions of victimization and injustice, rather than mobilized in self-reliance to seek opportunity, civil society might become a barrier to, rather than an asset in, transition.[12] Assumptions that civil society can be mobilized to oppose transition enable actually existing civil society to be more or less disregarded by transition culture's proponents.

In theory, civil society is important to transition culture, and in particular, to the World Bank's general conception of the efficacious state.[13] The leading forces of state reform are "farsighted" and "effective" indigenous leaders in alliance with international agencies that provide technical advice based on broad comparative experience. Local civil society plays a critical role, however. It can provide local expertise that translates international insight into locally appropriate practices. Most fundamentally, however, civil society must lend its cooperation to reform. The World Bank highlights compensation for the adversely affected and social pacts as critical elements of this cooperation.[14] In general, the World Bank argues, the state should be brought closer to the people. One should give people a voice, broaden participation, and have the state embedded in consultation (10–11). It argues that "an active civil society and a competent and professional bureaucracy are twin pillars of a constructive relationship between state and society" (160).[15] Regulation, for instance, is superior when it is "light." Light regulation requires, however, civil society's invigoration (67, 71).

Civil society in the former Soviet Union, and even in Central and Eastern Europe, was invisible in the World Bank's 1997 report, however. Positive examples of an efficacious state from the region were also hard to find. The Czech Republic's transparent privatization was praised (6), but its appearance was the exception that proved the rule. The Commonwealth of Independent States (CIS) never provided a positive example. Most of the positive lessons came from East Asia, Europe, and North America. Africa was frequently invoked in the discussion, but it rarely provided positive examples. The African problematic did focus on the question of legitimacy and state–society relations, but in the postcommunist world, state–society relations were relatively ignored. Why?

Of course, there might be a mundane issue explaining the uneven attention. Those who study Africa may be more likely to be engaged in the problem of state–society relations than are those in Eastern Europe and the former Soviet Union, where institutional design, not state–society relations, is the principal focus.[16] But this uneven focus itself has an underlying cultural foundation. One cannot ignore civil society—or at least that segment of society beyond the state—in sub-Saharan Africa because modernization theory's transparent failure and the alien quality of the colonial and postcolonial state have made engagement with society beyond the state and elite intellectually, and politically, necessary.[17] On the other hand, institutional designers might feel justified to ignore the disposition of civil society in postcommunist societies because it is peopled with insufficiently modern, or still socialist, subjects.

One of the principal challenges facing transition culture is to rethink the place of civil society within it. It is too easy to read the project of civil society through the lens of those "insular elites" who make the transition in spite of the wishes of a civil society with a "socialist mentality." It is too easy to rest with the "backward culture" notion of civil society. It is too easy to trust that state reform and institutional change will reconstruct the mentalities of the populace to produce the entrepreneurial, critical, and self-reliant civil society that rests at the foundation of transition culture's hopes. It is too tempting to say that Estonia provides the model of the appropriate civil society, demonstrating that in fact transition can be embraced in popular culture, and in that fashion criticize the Ukrainians and Russians for their own inadequacy. Although Estonia and Poland are nation-states, they are not the same as Ukraine and Russia. Nationalism gets in the way of thinking about transition—not only in terms of Ukrainian and Russian nationalism, but also in terms of that nationalism that equates Ukraine and Estonia, Poland and Russia. They are not the same kinds of nations.

Nevertheless, one does need to develop a comparative method with which to examine how nations, states, and civil societies are, and are not, similar. Rather than begin with the presumption of national equivalence, one might compare how similar social problems are articulated in different locations, within and across states. The focus groups discussed in chapter 4 are quite helpful to that task, especially if we read their narratives first through the problems they articulate, rather than from the demographic positions they represent, or the languages in which claims are made.

Social and Environmental Problems

I understand social problems to be phenomena acknowledged as not only undesirable, but also a consequence of social relations and potentially remedial.[18] Social problems might include poverty rates that could be lowered, environmental degradation that could be halted or reduced, and gender or ethnic discrimination that could be alleviated. Of course, others might understand these same phenomena not as social problems at all, but rather as conditions of human existence, the price of transition to a market economy, or a condition of national survival. These phenomena are then understood as less problematic because they are treated as inevitable or necessary.[19] The contest over the definition of social problems is thus dependent on the cultural formations framing their various interpretations.

To some extent, the end of Soviet rule was a story of social problems.[20] Soviet rule was assigned responsibility for a variety of problems, from assaults on national cultural survival to crises of economic rationality to endangerment of the environment.[21] The promise of post-Soviet society was a promise of normalcy, an end to some social problems and perhaps the acquisition of new ones.[22] The identification of problems and the normative standards used to evaluate phenomena thus depend on the narratives in which they are embedded. In this sense, instead of beginning from the point of view of how representatives of different nations, or classes, articulate problems, we might ask instead how the articulation of problems constitutes identities.[23]

Although one might begin in any problem area, I believe that one could profitably begin with environmental problems. Although economic problems are by far the "dominant" issue structuring narratives of change in our focus groups, that subject area is not a productive lens with which to rethink the transition culture project. After all, one major critique of the socialist mentality is that the individual entrepreneur, or civil society writ large, fails to assume sufficient responsibility for economic problems. Also, the UNDP's critique agrees with the basic transition culture point that most problems are derived from limited, or negative, economic growth. Transition culture is not only hegemonic in discussing the conditions of economic accomplishment, but by focusing on economic problems first, one reinforces the dominance of transition culture's assumptions about the primacy of the economy. Other things become secondary, including the recognition of actually existing civil society. A focus on the environment suggests something different.

There must be a productive partnership between the state and existing civil society to address environmental problems, even within the

logic of transition culture. The World Bank itself identifies civil society's partnership as critical to making the state effective in this arena. It
also argues that the public discussion of environmental problems is
fundamental to their resolution. On top of that, there was considerable mobilization of civil society over environmental issues during late
communism, especially in Armenia, Ukraine, and the Baltic countries.[24]
If there is such a dynamic partnership to be constructed in post-Soviet
societies, one might expect to find it in the environmental arena.

Of course, we also know that in post-Soviet life, ecological issues
do not merit the same attention they once did. In Estonia, at least, survey research indicates that ecological problems were associated more
with anti-Soviet attitudes than with concern for the environment per
se.[25] Russian, Armenian, and Ukrainian authorities even returned to
viewing nuclear power as one of the means to ensure their political
sovereignty, if not their ecological security.[26] In order to address this
area, we chose to conduct focus groups in two sites particularly known
for their environmental problems: Sillamäe in Estonia and Ivankiv in
Ukraine. Given the focus on environment in this chapter, I elaborate a
bit more about each of these places in what follows.

Chernobyl is probably the most widely known environmental
catastrophe associated with the former Soviet Union, and certainly
Ukraine. One of the best places to assess how this environmental disaster influences the discussion of identity and social issues is Ivankiv,
one of the district centers of the Kiev region, not far from Chernobyl
but outside the thirty-kilometer radioactive contamination zone. It
has the third degree of radioactive pollution, and is mainly an agricultural district with some manufacturing. Ivankiv is composed mainly
of Ukrainians. We assembled one focus group of Ukrainian men and
one of Ukrainian women. Participants of both groups had no more
than secondary education.

Estonia has no nuclear power plants, but experts consider its greatest ecological risk to be located in those nuclear power plants that surround it in Sosnovy Bor in Russia, Ignalina in Lithuania, and Loviisa
in Finland.[27] Without a plant on its territory, however, the possibility
for grassroots involvement in ecological matters decreases even if it is
very important to international commissions. There are, however, local
conditions that could produce significant environmental damage. One
place especially conducive to such activity is Sillamäe.

Sillamäe is one of two major sites of "military pollution." This refers to the contamination of air, water, and soil from military units, including the leaking of fuel pipelines at military bases, the dumping of outdated explosives and weapons, the scuttling of ships, and chemical and toxic pollution from various materials, including rocket fuels.[28] The most dramatic and central problem is, however, the existence of a radioactive waste depository.[29] Constructed in 1948, the Sillamäe plant originally processed alum shale for its uranium and deposited the waste on the marine terrace at Cape Paite. Since 1959, these "tailings," were deposited in a reservoir on the Gulf of Finland. Experts recommend that this waste depository no longer be used, and that a new one be constructed to enable the plant to continue its production of rare earth metals. They find a landslide at this depository to be quite possible, especially following an earthquake or major sea storm, and recommend that efforts be taken to halt erosion. Further, the residents of the town are affected by breathing the radon escaping the facility. Experts recommend that the deposit be covered with various materials. But how are these conditions, framed by expert assessments, recognized and appreciated by local actors? We rely here on two focus groups, Russian men and women[30] with no more than secondary education, and their interpretation of the preceding ten years.

Across all of the focus groups, the most explicit and prominent problems were associated with economic issues. The standard of living, which we understood to include general quality-of-life issues such as the price of goods and their availability, the availability and quality of infrastructure, and insecurity about the future, on average occupied more than one-fifth of the discussion. Related to that, but with a different emphasis, employment concerns and salary issues took up 15 percent and 6 percent, respectively, of the focus group discussions. Education was relatively important in this general area, commanding 9 percent of the discussion. The environment was less prominent. It occupied on average only 6 percent of the discussion, but it shaped discussion more than inequality and trade matters.[31] This is consistent with some accounts of environmental change that have emphasized how the environment may have been a stalking horse for other more salient dimensions of change such as independence. But, of course, the environment is more important for some groups than others.

As we expected, groups from sites of particular ecological destruction were more likely to spend time discussing the environment, and Ukraine was far more oriented toward ecological problems than

Estonia (Table 5.1). Only two Estonian groups address environmental problems to any degree, whereas all but three Ukrainian focus groups substantially addressed environmental matters. Ivankiv led the list in terms of explicit attention given to environmental issues. All of the discussion about environmental matters derived from Chernobyl.[32] Sillamäe men also devoted a great deal of time to the environment, but Sillamäe women discussed environmental themes considerably less, and only when the moderator introduced the issue toward the end of the discussions (women: 3214–3458; men: 2375–3126). The men from Olexandrivka also addressed the environment to a substantial degree. Thus, despite the pervasiveness of ecological problems in the former Soviet Union, the environment tends to emerge as an important theme only when ecological problems are localized. Although we did not always anticipate which sites had local environmental problems, it was only in those places of relatively considerable problems that the environment was centered for both men and women of that place. Nowhere was the environment centered more than in our focus groups from Ivankiv (Table 5.1).

Environmental Crisis and Despair in Ivankiv, Sillamäe, and Olexandrivka

Both the women and men of Ivankiv emphasized the localized character of the crisis and the effect of the reactor's explosion on their home region and their very own conditions of life, but neither the post-Soviet state nor civil society seemed to deserve much appreciation.[33] One man, however, Andriy, expressed some pride in what an independent Ukraine means:

> Well, maybe it is a wrong word, but I would like to say, anyway, that there are possibilities now to be proud of your nationality. I mean, I remember the times when it was shameful to speak Ukrainian. Here in Ivankiv it was not a problem, but in Kiev . . . when people from here tried to switch to Russian and it sounded terrible. And there were a lot of people who laughed at us and called us "Seliuky" [country bumpkins] and other not very nice names. Now it is not like that. Of course, a lot of people still speak in Russian, particularly in Kiev, but there isn't that negative reaction anymore if you are on public transportation or in some other city in Ukraine. . . . All this has made me more conscious of my Ukrainian identity. I am proud of my nationality. I did not think much about it before. Not because I was small, but because hardly anyone considered them-

Table 5.1. Percentage of Each Focus Group Discussion Devoted to Ecology

Focus group	Lines in focus group	Lines devoted to ecology	% of transcript devoted to ecology
Ivankiv women	3,298	893	27
Ivankiv men	4,283	1,067	25
Sillamäe men	3,324	788	24
Olexandrivka men	3,076	380	12
Donetsk women	3,829	318	8
Kiev Russian men	2,289	157	7
Kiev Ukrainian women	1,856	125	7
Sillamäe women	4,203	238	6
Kiev Ukrainian men	3,136	156	5
Kiev Russian women	2,161	97	4
Olexandrivka women	1,909	67	4
Donetsk men	3,009	59	2
Tamasalu women	1,982	23	1
Lviv men	3,544	41	1
Tallinn Estonian men	2,590	12	0
Tallinn Estonian women	2,706	10	0
Tamsalu men	1,843	2	0
Tartu men	2,838	2	0
Narva men	5,036	0	0
Narva women	3,691	0	0
Tallinn Russian men	3,762	0	0
Tallinn Russian women	3,704	0	0
Tartu women	2,466	0	0
Lviv women	3,132	0	0

selves Ukrainian. "Ukrainian? Ah, that's a laugh," they used to joke. That was the typical reaction. Now people have become proud that they are Ukrainians and that we have a state. It is not perfect, of course . . . there are problems. (794–838)

In what would become a dominant exchange throughout this manuscript, Yuriy 1 disagreed with this presentation of national independence. He went on to talk, in Russian, about how multinational the Soviet Union was. Andriy had no vigorous supporters in his group, and even his appreciation for Ukraine was quite muted, as we shall see later. Support for Ukraine was also relatively passive among the women. Vira said that she had hope at the time of the referendum on Ukrainian independence in 1991, "but we were deceived" (3035). Still, Vira finds it "good that we live in Ukraine, and not in the Soviet Union" (3049–50).

Instead, the men and women of Ivankiv (and also of Olexandrivka and Donetsk [263–360]) had a hard time finding anything positive to say about changes over the preceding decade. The women laughed at the question (434), and then went on to talk about the birth of children or the acquisition of an apartment. Mykola focused his critique of the notion of improvements taking the Chernobyl disaster itself as a point of departure:[34]

> Well, what can I say about these years? There was nothing good, everything was bad. More and more people die. Young people die, middle-aged people die, thirty to forty years of age. The mortality rate is increasing. Especially cancer. How do I know? My wife is a nurse. She tells me that every year they have more and more cancer patients. They get more every year. What else? The bone problem . . . and eyes. It affects your eyes. . . . it all came after the explosion. Before 1986 or 1987, I never experienced such things. I was healthy. But then it all began—eyes, bones, pain everywhere. Impossible. It is not a single case. Everybody suffers, even young people. It is a kind of sickness. (1243–71)

Not all the hesitation about the virtues of the present derived from Chernobyl. Even Andriy, newly proud of being Ukrainian, said the worst thing was the economic crisis, and then the pervasiveness of violence, itself an effect of cheap Western cultural productions. "People," he said, "used to be better, kinder" (1342–43).[35] Nevertheless, the effects of Chernobyl were hard to forget.

Once a region for sanatoriums and produce, the area around Chernobyl can no longer support itself economically (men: 1273–93, 2189–94, and 3361–3437; women: 2156–81). The women cannot sell their produce, although to survive, the local women are forced to eat it (988–94, 2200–9). They even eat what are considered the most contaminated items, mushrooms and bilberries, not out of habit, but out of hopelessness (1929–2009). Hopelessness, apparently, is something they can get used to (men: 3057–85). Indeed, what hope there is rests on getting the kind of job that treats health as incidental to survival. Valeriy says that his job in the Chernobyl zone is a "nice job, but it is bad for health. . . . It is harmful, but as they say, money, money, money" (702–14).

Most of the men and women in the Ivankiv focus groups were personally tied to the Chernobyl disaster. Some of the women's husbands died as a consequence of the explosion (867–77).[36] Some of those who suffer health problems as a consequence of the explosion feel themselves to be discriminated against (men: 3091–3100, 3140–43). When going to the hospitals, the women said that doctors have given up on them. The doctors treat them as if nothing could help them (1413–44), or as if they are tired of the problem (men: 3127–28). One man said that they were viewed as a source of money, because the treatment for their problems is ongoing (3026–28). Even more generally, the men and women of Ivankiv feel oppressed on the basis of their Chernobyl association. Maryna also noted that prices appeared to be higher in Ivankiv than in Kiev, because "they think we have a lot of Chernobyl money so they illegally raise the prices" (1020–24). Vira went on to say, "The people who haven't visited us here, they think, that here in the 'Zone' we are being paid, so they can rip us off. But now they [the state] practically give us nothing" (1026–30).

On top of this particular discrimination, civil society itself is simply less sympathetic. In general, Andriy said, "People are more indifferent to other people's troubles" (3107–9). Maryna said something similar among the women: "People are wicked now. My work is a good example. People are reluctant to talk to you. You cannot talk with people, you cannot share your troubles or your joys with them. Everyone is hostile" (1498–1504). Although similar in this regard, the male and female focus groups appear to be rather different in their thematic structure.

Both men and women in Ivankiv mentioned the suffering of children among their concerns (men: 3019–20), but the women were especially emphatic and concrete. They said that 95–96 percent of the children are sick (2112); blood problems, high cholesterol, thyroid problems and dysentery, stomach and liver problems were specifically mentioned (2129–33, 2091–2103, 900–901). Maryna was direct:

> It does not matter for me. I am worried about my child. She is growing in the Zone. Like a mom, I am very concerned about the health of my child. But my own health doesn't matter anymore. I've gotten sick, and I will get sick . . . the most important thing is the children. (1911–18)

Although the men are said to have suffered more, the women's discussion was more concentrated on health issues. A significant part of the men's discussion involved much larger categories of imagination, questioning, for instance, what the West could and should do with regard to the nuclear crisis (3556–90). Among the men, a debate about the virtues of the Soviet past, the Ukrainian way, and the importance of Ukrainian language dominated the transcript, as one particularly Soviet man (Yuriy 1) and another particularly Christian man (Andriy) animated debate over the virtues of the West and of Soviet times.

Among the women, ideological contention was hardly evident. Language was not an issue in their region, they said (3166). This relative absence of ideology was not a reflection of the women's passivity. For example, they challenged the premise of the moderator's question about the virtues of the Ukrainian way by saying, "You will probably not like this, but life in the Soviet Union was not so bad for us . . . we were used to it. We did not live so badly" (2939–45). The men agreed. Indeed, Valeriy was relieved when the moderator turned away from improvements over the past ten years and went to problems:

> All right, then, here you go. I would like to talk about the [Soviet] Union. I think life was simpler in the Union, personally for me. I don't know about other people. Now, when Ukraine is separate, I do not see anything good. (1454–60)

This stimulated a major discussion about how much better Soviet times were, and how much better people could live. Back then people got paid with a currency whose value was stable, and not subject to the devaluation of inflation. But now, only some people have money. Valeriy shouted, "They have things and we do not! Why is it like that? Why is it impossible for me?" (1671–73).

There are, however, different ways in which the past can be appreciated. After Andriy and Yuriy 1 agreed that the nation is at fault for voting into office self-interested and incompetent rulers, their accounts of the past diverged. Andriy emphasized that the Soviet state was "built on force. It was all based on oppression, on secrets and prohibitions. That's how the Soviet Union ruled" (1755–59). In response, Yuriy 1 demanded that Andriy explain what was so awful, "what kind of violence did Soviet rule do to you?" Andriy responded about a moral kind of violence that denied respect for being Ukrainian:

> When I was small I was embarrassed to speak Ukrainian, although I wanted to. It hurt me that I could not. But you, please, do not think that your Russian offends me somehow. Not at all. In a civilized so-

ciety, I think every person speaks the language they want and is respected for that (1776–84) . . . you know how it goes in the United States of America? There are many nations there. They are all with their traditions, their backgrounds. But our country [the USSR] was based on different principles. The decay started from up there. It is the same as Russian tsarism. The wrong principle from the very beginning. They used to tell us that everything was OK, but the very root of the state was rotten. (1790–1801)

Yuriy 1 refused to engage the problems of the Soviet Union, but again redirected his critique to Ukraine, and especially its leaders. The best strategy to defend the Soviet past is to focus, apparently, on the Ukrainian present. Then one can suggest how things could be different by stating how the Soviet past was better. For instance, "The USSR used to produce many things under Stalin. And many items were for export. We had planes and tanks and lemonade and ice cream . . . It was all exported" (2215–19). Yuriy 2 added, "I would add that we have huge unemployment. It was not like that before" (2234–36).

What is to be done? The dominant speakers in the group said that Ukraine needs a strong leader. Yuriy 1 thinks "we need Adolf Stalin. More concretely, someone like Pinochet." Andriy countered and asked what Stalin led to. Yuriy 1 simply said that we need "one man responsible for everything, a dictator" (1986–96). Chile and the Soviet past provide the reference. Andriy would rather put his faith in God and "love your brother as yourself" (4060–61), but he too expressed the need for a leader. "There is something specific in the nature of our nation," he said, "that without a leader you don't get anywhere. It's been like that for centuries" (2652–57). Beyond the search for a leader, nobody articulates any narrative of transition that promises hope. Although both find virtue in the state's position on nationalities, praising a social peace that does not exist in the Baltics (2912–45), independent Ukraine, whether state or civil society, does not offer much hope. In the women's group, Olena said that at least during Soviet times they believed in something; "we must believe in ourselves, in our spiritual values that have to develop. We must believe in something" (3102–5). They must believe in something, but what?

Ivankiv's discussion of the environment contains many themes that are reflected in other focus groups—the regionalization of environmental problems, the gendering of concern over health care, and the subordination of environmental and health concerns to economic survival. Thus, although certainly Chernobyl had something to do with the generation of Ukrainian consciousness, by now it is also a source of differentiation among Ukrainians in terms of who has suffered most directly and who has not. It is also a source of nostalgia for the Soviet state. Although that state produced the problem, it was also more attentive to the suffering that it caused. And although Soviet civil society may not have been empowered, at least it cared more for its citizens than Ukrainian civil society apparently does.[37] Corruption in civil society, and not just in the state, undermines the capacity for an efficacious civil society and the vision of transition. The Soviet state and civil society appear relatively appealing by contrast.

Transition culture's hope that civil society might forget the past and remember reasons for change is completely unrealistic in Ivankiv. Although the Soviet state caused the crisis, the post-Soviet state does less for civil society. Indeed, it drives civil society to desperate solutions. Environmental concerns are subordinated to crude economic survival. Women in Ivankiv disregard the health implications of the food they grow and consume. As Olena said, "It is better to die of radiation than of hunger" (2208–9). The postcommunist economic crisis not only helps to absolve the Soviet-era leadership for the ecological catastrophe it made; it also can make it possible to ignore environmental danger entirely. This is the lesson of Sillamäe.

To be sure, the members of our Sillamäe focus groups were aware of their Russianness. This was evident even in the Russian Estonian moderator's introduction to the men's focus group, in which he invited the participants to identify themselves, not only in terms of their work or family, as in other places, but also in terms of where they were born. They responded to the invitation with clear markers of whether they were born in Estonia or in Russia. Most were born in Estonia, and some of them had citizenship. Their identity is not, however, simply as Russians, or as Estonian citizens, but very much as Russians of the northeast. As Victor L. said:

> Estonia has abandoned the Russians who live here in the northeast. There are practically no jobs here, no salaries, nothing. You live as you can. And you can fix the situation yourselves. . . . [speaking as he would imagine "Estonia" to speak] You, Russians, live here as you want. In other words, die out. It's your problem how much you earn. Or you can leave for Russia. [The moderator asked then if he did not feel any support from the state, to which he replied:] There essentially is none. (1690–1709)

A subsequent exchange indicated the depth of their suspicion toward the Estonian authorities. They wondered whether they were not trying to undermine their local firms on purpose. Pavel even noted that Tondi Elektroonika had a branch in Tallinn and one in Sillamäe, and although it does not work at all in Sillamäe, it at least works, if poorly, in Tallinn (1738–42). They are astonished at this disregard for microelectronics given that Hong Kong's success was built on it (1765–80). They are critical at the level of the enterprise too, because the same "party comrades" who ran the firm before now just set their own salaries without constraint (1845–70). Economic conditions are clearly terrible, and the authorities, both Estonian government authorities and former party leaders, are to blame. But these critiques are different from those in Ivankiv. Like Ivankiv, concerns are organized around work and employment opportunities. In contrast to Ivankiv, however, the men from Sillamäe criticize what they call a "give me" attitude, a "psychological habit," that is associated with being from a Soviet-era closed town that "could get practically anything" in consumer goods, and that "somebody has to come to the rescue" (2283–85). This criticism of passivity extends to the environmental theme as well, but only among men. Sillamäe's women were quite different in the thematic structure of their discussion, and their overall mood.

The women of Sillamäe were quite different from all of the focus groups. They were, on the one hand, clearly the most pessimistic and hopeless. The following reply to a question about problems over the past ten years is indicative of the group's mood:

ELENA: And even if we've written "unemployment" and all these other problems—they are problems, but just for us, personally. And my personal problems no longer interest me at all. I have stopped living as a human being. I only think what I must do for my children. My personal interests have died. . . . [later] I'm thirty-three, and I have no life.

HELEN: I agree with Elena, we are just lying in a swamp.

NINA: We have already outlived ourselves.

ELENA: Yes. We are only victims, now. Only through . . . We'll be like bridges to carry our children into the future. That is, we are the sacrifice, we are practically not people. (3058–78, 3103–19)

The women were not primarily concerned with environmental issues. Economic problems, drug use among their children, and other more apparently immediate concerns overwhelmed their narrative (the women of Ivankiv registered similar concerns about their children [1697–1873]). The women of Sillamäe knew of radiation problems, but they did not think about them in the context of their daily lives. Irene 1 said, "We've simply gotten used to it. . . . we are being poisoned every day and in the end we forget about it" (3253–71). They had so many other problems that environmental issues were the least of their concerns. Employment and economic issues were so overwhelmingly important that the focus group participants viewed the Soviet past with approval, even in terms of environmental degradation. They recalled that hazardous jobs in the factories paid higher salaries to compensate for the health risk. But now there are no such preferential wages, and life conditions are so bad that hopelessness reigns. As Elena said, "At the present moment, we aren't too worried about it [the environmental problems], because there's not much difference between being alive and dead" (3442–44). Hopelessness with regard to economic problems clearly overwhelms environmental concerns. Transition depends on hope, for civil society cannot act without having a sense of efficacy. The women of Ivankiv and Sillamäe had none.

The men of Sillamäe were not nearly so pessimistic as their female counterparts. Some of them seemed to be aware of, and engaged with, the environmental problems. They were not as negative as the women about the environment either. They even felt that the environment was "cleaner" now that they have stopped reprocessing uranium (3079–3162). The men nonetheless did note a couple of problems: they sit on a uranium lode and the radioactivity from it, especially in the exposed oil shale areas, is a problem (but some wondered whether the radioactivity from the sun was worse! [2893–2948]). Another more potentially disastrous problem is the storage of the waste from uranium processing. In fact, it is a point of concern across the Baltic Sea region. People from Sweden, the Netherlands, and other countries have expressed their concern and have offered support and advice. But the focus group participants were not well informed or even concerned about these issues (2403–47).

Accompanying this disposition to discuss environmental problems was a much more strategic approach to political issues. Although both men and women were disenchanted with postindependence politics, the men were not nearly so resigned to their fate. Instead, their criticism was laced with a notion of how things could be otherwise.

Although the men lamented that "public opinion isn't considered in anything" and that "they're [the authorities] used to telling us fairy tales and they go right on telling them" (2552–53, 2655–56), the men could point to alternatives. They noted that although environmental conditions were worse in Kohtla-Järve (2495–2511), the local officials in Kohtla-Järve were more open and concerned with environmental problems. In Sillamäe, one man said, there is a kind of silence, where people are passive and the authorities take no initiative (2638–69). Another said that the issues will never be dealt with adequately until the tailings "blow up" (2869–70).

The women had a different approach to dealing with their principal crisis—their children simply living for fun *("kaif")*. The children, they say, have no principles, which for them was provided by the Komsomol. This communist youth group may have been a bad idea, but "a bad idea is better than no idea at all" (2431–32). The key for these women, at least in terms of finding a potential solution, rests in inculcating spirituality, whether that has to do with religion or with intellectual culture (2402–2966). But that had nothing to do with the environmental crisis and attendant health problems in the narrative. It was a sign, however, of their search for hope.

As one would expect, then, those who live around sites of ecological catastrophe are much more likely to weave into their stories significant tales of ecological problems. At the same time, however, the overall dominance of economic issues structures even these stories, either by being interwoven with the environmental theme itself, as in Ivankiv, or by overriding ecological concerns, as among the women of Sillamäe.

Given the relative insignificance of environmental issues outside of those zones of ecological catastrophe, one could very easily conclude that environmental problems were, in fact, a surrogate for nationalism and that ecological consciousness is a luxury of advanced industrial societies, or a consequence of a community's devastation. There was, however, one other group that discussed environmental themes substantially more than average: Olexandrivka men, whose comparison with their female counterparts invites our reconsideration of the gendering of environmental concerns.

In some ways, these Olexandrivka men are quite similar to the men of Sillamäe. In both cases, region was the overwhelming source of identification. Of course, most regional references did not concern ecological issues. For instance, one Olexandrivka man complained about how his region has not been paid wages for a year and a half, but people in Kiev and the miners rebelled after only three months of waiting and got their wages (1141–50; a similar concern was registered among Ivankiv men [2550–64, 2667–73]). Another man complained that local government in Dniepropetrovsk extorted money to gain the right to sell apples in that region (2012–18). Regions compete with regions, and their poor community has poor chances in the new economy. Discussion of the environment was clearly structured by this regional emphasis.

The men's group was far more likely than the women's group to discuss the environment. The men of Olexandrivka devoted 12 percent of their discussion to the environment, but the women only 4 percent. As in Sillamäe, where the environment was clearly not the dominant concern of either men or women, men were far more likely to incorporate it into their stories. To understand why this is the case, one must look to the focus group narratives themselves.

The men of Olexandrivka discussed Chernobyl only after the moderator's prompt (2301–2678), and then turned the larger crisis into one much more specific to their region. Vasyl 1 said:

> They created the Chernobyl fund and they put some of our money in that fund, but we don't have anything against that. But we have also suffered. Our village is situated in a polluted zone and we live off the land. We pay into this fund, but we don't get anything from it. But that is the way things are. Chernobyl is a general tragedy and we will pay. But there are a lot of instances where it ought not to be necessary to pay. . . . They take a lot of money for that fund, but where does it go? What do they do with it? No one knows. (2355–71)

Right out of this discussion of Chernobyl and the regional inequalities associated with it, the men turned their discussion of the environment directly to local concerns, and how the past led to the environmental problems of the present. Indeed, the ecological consciousness of this group, in comparison to all others, was quite impressive. Vaso began the discussion of local conditions this way:

> The ecological problem is such that we don't know how to protect either the environment or ourselves. When we do something, we don't know what effect it will have. Will it help the situation or harm it? We polluted everything. (2424–30)

The men focused especially on the chemical problems resulting from pesticide use and water pollution as a consequence of sewage seeping into the rivers. In some ways, they noted, conditions are better today because they no longer have the money to buy the amount of pesticides they used to use. But although some varieties of mushrooms have returned to the forest and the men might breathe a bit easier as they work, there are now so many pests that their crops are at risk. What is more, the soil has accumulated so much poison that one could not switch from growing apples to a more profitable strategy for planting grain. The community cannot adapt to the market economy because the ecological crisis prevents it. As in Sillamäe, the community's adaptation to transition is disabled by the legacy of the Soviet past, but unfortunately for transition culture, that past does not look so bad by comparison.

Lamenting the Loss of the Soviet Union

One of the most compelling ways to establish distance from the Soviet past, and appreciation for transition culture, is through the fusion of national emancipation and transition culture's project. This was quite obvious among Estonians, but it was also apparent among the men from Lviv and the people from Kiev. There, freedom could be tied to intellectual openness, national emancipation, and entrepreneurial opportunities. But where there are no great compulsions to know the truth about the past, to take advantage of market openings, or to take pride in being Ukrainian, the appeal of the past looms large. Consider the lamentations of Olexandrivka.

Ethnicity was not so important among women or men. The men said there are no problems in Olexandrivka along those lines (2215–45), and though the women discussed the Ukrainization of language at some length, it was not an especially compelling issue for any of them (1490–1605). Both men and women were extremely negative about Ukrainian independence. Both invoked the Soviet time as a positive point of reference. For instance, the women of Olexandrivka said:

> We are living terribly . . . right after the onset of independent Ukraine. From 1992, 1991 . . . there are all these "Kravchuchky,"[38] no matter where you go, there are these Kravchuchky, no matter where you go, and when we went to Moscow, everyone asked, "Why did you separate from the Soviet Union. You had it good." Perhaps, I'm not right. (258–88)

One might think that those who suffered from Soviet policies around the environment might blame the corruption, or incompetence, of those times. But instead of blaming that Soviet past, the people of Olexandrivka, Sillamäe, and Ivankiv blame current strategies for change. To be sure, the men and women of Sillamäe, Ivankiv, and Olexandrivka do not celebrate the Soviet time without criticism, but at least then, it appears, sacrifice was compensated. Today, the political authorities appear to ignore sacrifice and indulge themselves, and civil society is mean and brutish.

Like Sillamäe and Ivankiv, Olexsandrivka was relatively hopeless. Together, the women queried their moderator about what they should do if "nothing comes to mind" about improvements, and they can imagine only changes for the worse (193–97). Later, Olena said that the only "change for the better" that she can identify is that she still hopes things will get better (580–82). The following exchange among men in Olexandrivka shows how difficult the premise of improvement was to get across:

> MODERATOR: The first block is "Turns for the better." I want you to think of positive changes in your life connected with considerable social, political, and economic events that took place in Ukraine. Which events have influenced you most? Positive developments, I mean now. Later we'll talk about negative moments, but now let's talk only about positive changes. You may write down at least three positive changes. It can be some ordinary thing. Birth of a child, for example.
>
> VASO: Difficult to say.
>
> MODERATOR: Yes, but not very, I hope. There were some good things in your life, weren't they?
>
> MISHA: Excuse me, but I don't think I understand the question. You said a birth of child. Could you give some more examples?
>
> MODERATOR: Well . . .
>
> MISHA: Just to make it clear. We are probably not able to answer your question.
>
> MODERATOR: Still, you see we are interested in general problems, such as Ukraine's independence. For example, do you think proclaiming independence of Ukraine influenced your life well? You will write it down. If you consider this to be a negative factor. Well, presidential elections, for example. What do you think? There were a lot of various events for last ten years. . . .
>
> MISHA: And what about turns for the worse?
>
> MODERATOR: We'll write about bad things later in the next block.

MISHA: OK.

MODERATOR: Now we are considering turns for the better. Please, write it down.

VASYL: I have nothing to write.

MODERATOR: But was there something? I just can't believe that there was nothing for ten years that influenced your life positively. . . .

VASO: A lot of people in Olexandrivka started their houses before *perestroika*. They have built a lot of houses—a street. But from *perestroika* on, nobody wants to work.

MODERATOR: No, you are talking about negative. Let's do it later.

This emphasis on the negative was not limited to these places of ecological and economic catastrophe. Even in Lviv, where national independence is presumably more valued than it is in other parts of Ukraine further south and east, the women had a hard time recognizing improvements. In fact, four of the women explicitly stated that there were no such improvements (371–420). In Donetsk, one woman, Yelena, expressed her despair most powerfully:

> Now you don't know how to behave. The old has gone, and the new hasn't yet come. . . . And we live only for today. If before we saved something, then they have taken away what we have saved. It has lost its value. Now you survived a day and that is good. What will happen tomorrow we don't know. We don't have an extra kopeck to . . . save for a rainy day. And a rainy day has now become very expensive. And I fear for our children. I'm bringing up my daughter, and if, God forbid, I should pass away, I don't know what would happen to my child. I have fear. (1104–26)

With such despair, what vision of the social transformation is available? One that only reinvents the past to become a vision for the future: the reintegration, perhaps reincarnation, of the Soviet Union.

A narrative of loss can inform a vision of the future. The Estonian speakers rarely spoke of anything that they missed from Soviet times, but some Ukrainian speakers, and certainly Russian speakers, could recall what they missed. Embedded in their tales of present woe grows an even more fond recollection of Soviet times, and resentment for its end. As Tonia from Olexandrivka said, "Everybody is unhappy with the secession from the Soviet Union" (1112–14). Galia said:

> Who could know there would be that kind of division? At that time they agitated for us to vote for independence. The people at the top broke the country apart, but it's the common people that suffer

(1134–49). [Tonia added:] They agitated in the following way. The dough at the bottom was Russia while Ukraine was the top part where all the sweet things are and if one divided the pie, we could live well in Ukraine, and without us Russia would go into decline. But the opposite happened. (1154–62)

Gorbachev is to blame. "He started the disintegration" (1255), said Liuba. And Liuba is not alone. In many of the post-Soviet sites we can find regret for the loss of the Soviet Union. As Valia from Donetsk said:

> I think it is very bad that they have split up the Union. They have separated Ukraine from Russia, Russia from Uzbekistan, and so on. That is to say I understand it this way: here is my hand with five fingers, cut one finger off, it will be painful for the other four, for example. . . . The breakup of the Soviet Union has led to nothing. It has been painful for everyone. This breakup—it hasn't become better for any country in a moral, material, or spiritual way. (1007–24)

Vera 2 added later, "I would like it if we were all together [in the Soviet Union]. First of all, I didn't vote for separation. I always [wanted] us to be together." The moderator asked her if the troubles she mentioned earlier came from the breakup of the USSR. "Yes, I think so. It is worse for me" (1182–93). Valia makes the point even more strongly:

> I join in the opinions of people sitting here. That health care has declined and everything. But I, as a mother and a woman, am worried about these politics of contemporary life. They have deprived me of being a woman. To feel like a woman. To feel like a mother. To feel like a citizen of my Union. It is as if I hold it in my hands. And no matter how hard I hold on, our [present] government takes it away from me anyway. . . . on whatever level, whether you were a scrubwoman, or somebody else, still you felt [in Soviet times] like a human being. That was taken away from me. (1238–56)

Attached to these tales of loss are accounts of the breakup. There are no narratives of systemic collapse among those who miss the Soviet Union. Instead, they tell tales of conspiracy and theft. Oleg from Donetsk explains:

> When the Soviet Union was being formed, the communists knew what to do. An enterprise would be here, parts for it were made in one republic, a third republic made others. After the breakup, all this production was ruined. So many people lost jobs. And the result is incompetence. The tsars have simply ripped it apart, why should they obey Moscow? Everybody wanted to be a little tsar. Look how

many tsars have appeared. What did we care if we were governed from Moscow or Kiev? But it makes a difference to them—either Kiev obeyed Moscow, or now it doesn't obey anyone. Now it is its own tsar. And whatever it wants, it brings to itself. It rakes in everything. (1382–1405)

Not everyone narrated the breakup so clearly, but there is a powerful thread running through the tales of loss: those who have power today have undeserved privilege, and this is one reason for the crisis that afflicts the masses. Besides the challenge of building a new system, the new elites are not constrained by anything and they take what they want. Proverbs are plentiful, especially among the Russian speakers, and they can be helpful. Summing up this point, one man from Donetsk said, "The fish rots from the head" (1046–47). It is not clear who the head is, however.

Vova thought that a new group has come to power, but things are still done in the same way (1477–81). Like Vova, Sergei finds that a new group grabbed control in the power vacuum that emerged after the collapse of the Communist Party. He said, "The democrats began to feel they were above the law, and they started doing all these things. That is, they didn't expect to stay in power for long. They started grabbing everything for themselves. They were working for themselves, they weren't interested in the needs of the people. They just want to rake it in" (1646–56).

Andrei from Donetsk saw it a bit differently. He said, "There are no real authorities. It used to be that they did what they said. If an enterprise lagged behind, they put all their resources behind it and they did it. And now we have nobody, everyone is his own master. A factory director is his own master" (1619–25). Nevertheless, "those who were in power before *perestroika* are living well. Precisely those who were in power. When the party money, the state money, disappeared, they created start-up capital and went on from there. And those who were nothing before became nothing [paraphrasing the 'Internationale'—those who are nothing will become everything]." (781–91)

These tales of undeserved power and privilege could inspire class-based mobilizations. Indeed, it might be argued that Ukraine carries within it the potential for a class-based revolt, given the relative insignificance of national distinctions in the articulation of loss. I would, however, put the national distinction at the heart of the matter, for nationed interpretations of Soviet times shape the degrees of freedom with which class can organize transition's interpretation.

Where tales of national oppression during Soviet times, and national emancipation in post-Soviet times, organize interpretations of power and privilege, it is difficult to use Soviet times as a positive point of reference. For Estonians, this need not even be articulated because it is self-evident. Among Ukrainians, however, it is not self-evident. Andriy's relative isolation in his Ivankiv focus group made this quite clear. Although he emphasized that at least now he can feel pride in being Ukrainian, this did relatively little to combat the sense of economic and ecological crisis among his fellows from Ivankiv. In this sense, the Ukrainian national democrats may be right to argue over the struggle for the Ukrainian soul: a narrative of the nation's survival, and destiny, may be the only cultural barrier to a revaluation of Soviet times during transition's crisis. For those who can articulate Soviet times through a narrative of orderliness and relative equality, tales of present-day power and privilege can be woven within a tale of loss and politics of movement back to the future. Russia may not be the only nation that finds the Soviet Union's national anthem stirring, and deserving of restoration.

The Narrative Implication of Civility's Loss

To center the nation's position during Soviet times as the principal frame for articulating transition and loss implies greater fixity and determinism in the cultural formations of postcommunism than I intend. I would rather propose that everyone experiences some kind of loss through transition, but its expression is variably encouraged and suppressed by the cultural formations in which they are embedded. The way in which the women of Lviv talk about the loss of civility may be the best example of this.

Like their male counterparts, the women of Lviv were more ready than their counterparts to the east to identify improvements in general, and even within their region. They spoke at great length about the changing infrastructure in Lviv and the introduction of finer shops with more expensive prices. But like women across the focus groups, they discussed problems with banditry, worry for their children, and declines in everyday civility. Although they suggested that things are like this across Ukraine, they emphasized how bad it was in Lviv proper. Tetiana recalled her work as a tram driver:

You arrive at a tram stop and someone gets on. I mean like this: someone says a little bit in Russian, then they attack this person immediately. They almost start fighting. I work there, so I know. You can see it in the shops, at your job. One can say that there is no respect for each other in the last few years. People, regardless of their age, whether they are thirty, fifteen, or sixty years old, they have become, if I may say it without being rude, like animals. Precisely this has become very very very very bad here in Lviv. (2170–2203)

The loss of civility is introduced with the use of Russian language and the dilemma of the Russian-speaking minority in a nationalizing part of Ukraine. Rather than introduce a rebuttal, as the Christian Andriy might have challenged the rather Soviet Yuriy 1, Tetiana's lament inspires the other women in the focus group to augment her point. Ohla adds more to this negative portrait of Lviv:

I think that people live the worst in Lviv oblast. The people here . . . Here there is a very widespread . . . I can't even express it. Look at the Khmelnytsky oblast, there is nothing like that there, look at Vinnitsia oblast, there is nothing like that. And here, here is the worst depravity, here we have the biggest racket. It is horrible. Lviv oblast is the worst. I think so. (2346–56)

Olia confirms this with her portrait of another region:

Let us take the Ternopil oblast. If you go in a tram there or in trolleys, everybody is addressed in a very human way, from the soul. It is very pleasant for you if someone says "Sorry" or "welcome," or "Let me pass through," or whatever. And here, we don't have that, because if you get on the tram they bark at you, "Are you getting out?" So you don't want to speak to them ever again. Just that kind of purely human responsibility isn't to be found here right now. (2376–90)

Nobody challenges this relative assessment of Lviv. Apparently the women agree that Lviv's civility is worse than in other parts of Ukraine. Where the contest might emerge, however, is in terms of how this loss of civility might be understood. Maria, in fact, defends Lviv's incivility by framing it as a sign of progress. She simply says why Lviv is so rude:

It is the Lviv oblast where people live best. Look at the way people dress, what kinds of houses they are building. They are living better here than people in eastern Ukraine. There they build houses like "a boot" [simple and unpretentious]. If we look at this from a different point of view. The more a person possesses the more malicious he or she becomes. Why are they kind? Because they have little. They are not striving for money, they live according to what they have. And here everyone is competing with each other, not to be worse than he is. (2398–2414)

The women of Lviv illustrate something quite powerful about a tale of civility's loss. Although most focus groups, and especially those of the women, will identify the increase in rudeness, if not downright danger, on the streets, the women of Lviv were better prepared to repress that point. Their national narrative, and their identification with the region, encouraged them to suppress their resentment for the change. The loss of civility might be a necessary evil in the construction of a new order. To acknowledge that Soviet times produced greater civility in everyday life is to evoke a nostalgia that hardly fits with either transition culture or narratives of national emancipation. And yet it is a loss that can be widely felt across national boundaries, and across divides of language and class.

Incivility is one of the most important social problems through which one might examine the cultural formations of postcommunism. Unlike economic equality, whose value might be challenged by liberal economics, and unlike ethnic relations, whose accounts are powerfully shaped by national standpoints, civility's value is relatively uncontested. Its principal dilemma rests in its association with a Soviet past, and relative incompatibility with transition culture's future.

Transition culture emphasizes the importance of cultivating self-reliant, opportunity-seeking, critically thinking people, but it does little to talk about the cultivation of civility or spirituality. In our focus groups, especially among the despairing women in crisis, there is a definite search for meaning. The women of Sillamäe were extraordinary among our groups, devoting 12 percent of their discussion to the question of spirituality and religion. Elena began that discussion with the identification of the problem with youth today:

> It's simply that the only point of living for them is to have some kind of fun, that is, to find some pleasure where they can. They call it *"kaif."* What else is there for them? Compared to drugs, even sex means nothing to them. That's just a passing fling; they don't really understand what sex is. But drugs—they're so pleasant, cheap, and quick. What else do they need? Only *kaif.* After all, what's the purpose of life—pleasure, right? The more money you have, the more pleasure. . . . It's a lack of spirituality that leads them to these vicious pleasures. (2402–61)

Elena suspects, however, that the root of the problem is money. Parents must go out to work, she says, and it leaves the children without "human contact" (2527). This leads to a more general discussion of what Helen calls "spiritual education" and how things have gotten worse.

> HELEN: Now it's worse because in the past we had these organizations, there was some development. Because seeing beauty gives a person at least some sense of religion . . . at present all spirituality and religiosity are centered in the family. If before there were some attempts being made from outside, now . . . it's only within the family. . . . It wasn't just limited to the family, everything wasn't tied to the family. A person would get some spiritual education at home, but then he'd also pick things up outside somewhere. But now there's only the family. Outside, there's only low-quality information.
>
> MODERATOR: The family can't cope with it, right?
>
> HELEN: Yes, the family can't withstand it. (2625–72)

Elena goes on to speak of other families' crises, and this leads to an extensive discussion of how religion and spirituality address the crisis. To be sure, there has been an explosion of evangelical religious groups in Sillamäe, but the women debate whether this formal religion helps address the problem. "Not everyone can become believers," says Irena 1 (2689). Narva's women also lamented the loss of civility, security, and values in transition. Nata said:

> The ideals that we learned in childhood have vanished. By ideals I mean those that we've believed in since childhood. We can say Lenin, the party, the Komsomol, right? And all of a sudden—boom! Everything's ruined in one move. Everything we grew with turned out to be lies. . . . I'm not for bringing the Komsomol back right now, not at all. Young people have simply fallen apart. They don't know what to do, or what to believe in. . . . now there's simply nothing. (1252–1306)

Ira and Svetlana 1 extend the problem beyond children. Svetlana 1 says that life values have been changed; Ira replies:

> IRA: Today, even an honest man, upstanding, intelligent—as you've pointed out—is in the background, right?
>
> SVETLANA 1: He's the most unhappy.
>
> IRA: Has to be pushy.
>
> SVETLANA 1: He's the most unhappy person.

IRA: Pushy, like they say, "cool," right? There are other ways to put it . . . decisive, yes. Maybe not very honest, because otherwise you can't earn anything. . . . Look at the movies. . . . He can hit back, to smash someone's face—there's an ideal. Our children, by the way, build on these ideals. (1496–1524)

Instead of the loss of civility being an unfortunate by-product of transition, it becomes a direct effect of the West's negative influence. Svetlana 1 sums it up: "It's just gotten worse in the last ten years. That's what I think. People will become completely impoverished. Impoverished in general—morally, materially, then, for survival" (2752–57). Nadia adds mental impoverishment to this list, but she also anticipates a better future. She believes that "a group of moral and honest people is going to come about. They're there, these people do exist" (2840–42). Hope resides, for these women, in the resurrection of morality, spirituality, and civility. But it does not come from transition. It might come, however, through the recuperation of those values made under Soviet rule for the society that transition breeds. But that can only be part of it.

Recognizing War and Peace in Transition

By design, our comparative study of identity formation and social issues avoided societies embroiled in war. But this did not mean that questions of war and peace were missing from the focus group discussions on social change in Estonia and Ukraine. Indeed, peace in Estonia, and especially in Ukraine, was one of the greatest values to be found in the decade since Ukrainian and Estonian independence from Russia. The Ukrainian-speaking women of Kiev enunciated this quite clearly.

Liudmila identified one of the changes for the worse as "the fear of armed conflict." The moderator asked her why she identified that as one of her three greatest problems. "I compare the situation with what is going on in Russia, in Chechnya, in Yugoslavia. I see that Russia is our neighbor and it is fighting." Svitlana 2 added: "And looking for an enemy all the time," to which Valentyna responded, "Thank God we are separated from Russia." Svitlana 2 replied, "Yes, I told my husband, 'If this were Russia, you would be in the first ranks to be called up.'" Valentyna begins to say, "It is Afghan—" (meaning Afghanistan all over again), but is cut off by the moderator.

The moderator asks whether Ukraine might be the attacked or the attacker. Most imply that Russia would be responsible. Iryna 1 said, "Our neighbor Russia is wicked and active." The moderator becomes involved in the discussion at this point, stating that "Our country, our people, can be involved." Iryna 2 adds, "in some kind of conflict." Valentyna expresses her fear: "If they want, it is their business. God save us from being refugees like the Serbs." After stirring up this passionate discussion, Liudmila tries to introduce more balance: "History shows us that Russia is very good at wars and expansion. However, almost all families consist of Ukrainian and Russian members. It is a factor of stability." Others join in the chorus, extolling the virtues of multinational kinship, and generally conclude that cousins would not fight one another. Natalya summarizes by saying, "A Muscovite would not fight against Chechnya if he had a brother there." But then Liudmila adds, "It depends on his government." And Iryna warns, ominously, "And our government may provoke a war" (975–1045). Here, for some reason the moderator misses the cue and moves on to another subject.

Although these women were the most forthright about their anxieties, they were not alone. Anna, also from Kiev but from the Russian-speaking group, found the declaration of Ukrainian independence to be quite a positive thing in this regard: "I have two sons and the problems of Afghanistan and Chechnya are very worrisome and painful to me as a mother" (422–25). Another Russian-speaking group, in Donetsk, found the same. Lidia said:

> And I hope that our independence, for example, will provide me with the opportunity, when my son grows up, and it's time for him to join the army, that it will allow him to stay in Ukraine. Because there is a war right now in Russia . . . And they usually take all of our [men] from Donetsk and the Donetsk region to all possible . . . Well, to Afghanistan, to go to war and all. . . . I hope that our independence will provide my child with the opportunity to serve safely in Ukraine. (667–679)

Yelena added:

> I, for example, voted for independence first of all because I felt sorry [for all those guys who went to Afghanistan], how many of them have perished. And now, when I look at those Circassians . . . Chechens . . . , for example. It would be horrible if now, for example, we were a part [of the Soviet Union], and our boys were killed there. (696–705)

In Lviv too, Liudmyla broke the ice about identifying improvements by praising President Kravchuk's order, that "everyone drafted from Ukraine be returned to Ukraine to serve in Ukraine. I reckon that our children should serve in Ukraine" (454–58). Later, Olha and Liuda agreed that this was fundamentally important, and an improvement of the past ten years (878–96).

The women in Narva were the only group in Estonia to mark this improvement. Many of those women had boys of draft age, and this stimulated broad conversation. They expressed their relief that their boys would not have to serve in the Russian army. Svetlana 1, Tania, and Svetlana 2 all had boys ready to serve. Svetlana 1 said, "It really is the most important question for any mother," and consoled the other mothers with her observation that at least those going into the Estonian army will remain in Estonia. Irene added that that is better than "sending the boy off to Abkhazia, Chechnya, or something like that, Karabkah and so on" (832–939). For the Estonian-speaking groups, this improvement need not be mentioned because it is an assumed value of Estonian independence. For the Russian speakers, however, it is a value that is inconsistent with their feelings of loss, although another interpretation of the state of military affairs can resonate with those feelings of loss.

Apart from one of their number, the men of Olexandrivka found that shortening the period of mandatory service in the army was not such a good thing—there are too few serving in the armed services and there is a lack of discipline (571–648). Yuriy 1, a former captain and political officer in the Soviet army—the man from Ivankiv who longed for Adolf Stalin—also was quite critical of the Ukrainian state for its irresponsible support of the army and the navy (2041–81). Indeed, he found that "they're doing everything to ruin the armed forces" (1963–64).

Although questions of war and peace were not that prominent in the discussion groups, it is also clear that some citizens, overwhelmingly the women and especially mothers of military-age boys, find themselves to be at risk. In more positive terms, independence from Russia creates a better chance for peace. Some of the men worried about the loss of military capacity, but military affairs were hardly mentioned at all in the male groups. One man, Serhiy V, from a Ukrainian-speaking group in Kiev, was an exception. He issued one of the most profound statements around these matters, and indeed, about the success of Ukrainian transition:

The most important thing in Ukraine is that we have social peace. You can hardly find a country in the former USSR where there hasn't been a war. An armed conflict, we could say. Starting with the Baltic states, ending with Russia. There were conflicts in all the former republics. There is a war in Russia that they call a regional conflict. A civil war. Here, thank God, it is quiet. I think it has been the policy of our country since we got independence. We may criticize it, but it is all right in this respect. There are divisions in Ukraine, for example, western and eastern Ukraine. The eastern part of the country is more pro-Russian while the western regions are more European. But they manage to listen to each other and to solve problems in a peaceful way, not through conflicts. (1078–1100)

For these people from Estonia and Ukraine, one of the positive elements of *their* transition was their distance from war. They genuinely feared widespread violence and war as the hellish alternative to what independence from the Soviet Union, and from Russia, has meant. The Soviet war in Afghanistan lives in their memory, and the first postcommunist war in Chechnya was proximate. One of the greatest openings for transition culture in those societies beyond Russia rested in transition culture's apparent association with peaceful change. Ironically, and unfortunately for transition culture, that international peace is not apparently linked to civility in everyday life.

Conclusions

It is tempting to read these tales of despair as articulations of a crude socialist mentality antagonistic to transition culture. One might also read these longings for the Soviet Union's integration as threats to national rights, or privilege, and therefore voices to be discounted, ignored, if not outright repressed. If one were to take the structural logic of transition culture to heart, this chapter might be read as a litany of problems without solutions. It might be more productive, however, to unpack this imputation of socialist mentality and Soviet nostalgia to see what lies within it, and what might be recombined to integrate with a new vision of national destiny and transition's hopes. How might a different hermeneutics, based on another fusion of horizons that respects actually existing civil society's wishes and needs, reconstruct a narrative of loss in transition? On the positive side, might that different hermeneutics provide a better cultural foundation for a transition culture organized around the expansion of freedom and not only the making of markets? On a more threatening note, to deny that something was lost in transition is to invite too many people to be alienated from the critical potentials of transition culture.

One very powerful narrative underlying the sense of loss is the yearning for rules, orderliness, and responsibility. This theft of state property by the new ruling class and this danger on the streets posed by the newly dispossessed and hopeless youth are hardly necessary ingredients to any transition culture or national destiny. It may be, of course, that titular nationalities are less inclined to listen to the needs of those who speak another language, and to appreciate their fears and concerns. It also may be that those who cannot speak the language of self-reliance and opportunity seeking will not get a fair hearing, because their woes will be seen only as an anachronism that a new generation will supersede. However, transition culture and those who despair are seeking in common a rule-based order that appeals not only to efficiency and global markets, but to fairness, decency, and dignity. To the extent that those who articulate a project of national emancipation find a way to model civility in the government and in the public sphere, and legislate that respect in the schools, trams, and streets, they might find that Soviet nostalgia could be replaced by belief in a nation's future in transition.

Some Estonian Russians represent that very kind of hope. Sergei from Narva believed that "the euphoria of a small state" (1873–74) would eventually subside, and Estonian leaders would come to develop a more reasonable approach to their large Russian minority. The men of Sillamäe also embodied some hope in the institutions of civil society in partnership with a global network of actors interested in assuring the well-being of a larger ecological system. Alexander from Donetsk says we need to wait three or four generations, and "only then will Russia or Ukraine be a great nation" (1520–23). Yelena, also from Donetsk, argues that the breakup of the USSR was not the most terrible thing. For her, "everything depends on how we put the economy of the country in order" (2193–94). But who is to put it in order?

To the extent that transition culture fails to provide that sense of hope through legality, desperation can lead to other sources of order. Nobody else was as extreme as Ivankiv's Yuriy 1 in his articulation of Adolf Stalin as his vision for the future. That lack of extremism is one sign of hope. At the same time, it was striking that he met so little resistance in the articulation of this desperate vision. Even his nemesis in the focus group, the Christian Andriy, ultimately agreed that Ukraine needed a strong leader. After all, he said, it was in the national character. In Donetsk too, the future seemed to depend entirely on the character of the leader that Ukraine earns. If the national vision fails to provide that order, might imperial memories inspire? Or worse, might xenophobic fantasies mobilize?

Men are more likely to offer these grand solutions in transition, national emancipation, and great leaders. Men, it seems, tend to parade their despair, and articulate visions in which others take responsibility. The entrepreneurial spirit is one exception, where men embrace their own self-realization as a model for the nation's salvation. But this is not a language available to those who articulate despair. Women, by contrast, tend to privatize and absorb that despair. They are responsible for their families, seek hope in their personal ties or spiritual revival, and ask why the public sphere makes their duties more difficult, rather than more possible. I am not in a position to recognize whether their concern for spirituality is likely to result in a more efficacious civil society, and whether it might infect the state with responsibility. For transition culture to realize its promise, however, the community of civility needs to accompany the opportunity of individualism in the cultivation of hope. Otherwise, Western entrepreneurialism could be reinforced by the violence of Western popular culture to construct a different, and less peaceful, vision of the future. And, of course, examples of such violence are not only to be found in fiction.

The men, and especially the women, of Estonia and Ukraine looked at the wars in the former Yugoslavia and along the southern tier of the former Soviet Union with alarm. But for independence, their sons could be at war in some distant part of a past, or present, Russian empire. Even for those who appreciate little about transition, social peace is a great good to have been won. The relationship between transition culture and violence is not so obvious, however. Crime and symbolic violence within civil society have certainly increased within postcommunist societies, even if the violence of war has varied across them. Peace is clearly one of the central issues a critical transition culture ought to address. To date, however, transition culture has managed to insulate itself from responsibility by assigning violence to socialism and nationalism.

Six

Transition Culture and
Nationalism's Wars

On July 11, 1995, Srebrenica, one of six "safe areas" supposedly secured by United Nations Protection Forces (UNPROFOR) in Bosnia-Herzegovina, was attacked.[1] Bosnian Serbs entered the city and took it over from the 450 Dutch national UN troops assigned to protect it. NATO aircraft launched two strikes against the Serbs, but relented and accepted the takeover when the Serbs threatened to kill thirty-six Dutch troops they held as hostages.

A Muslim enclave of some forty-five thousand people, many of whom were already refugees from other parts of Bosnia, was destroyed. The Serbs forced some twenty-five thousand people to move to Tuzla, another safe area, in a process that has come to be called "ethnic cleansing." Another twenty thousand people, mostly men, were missing. Serbs took four thousand Muslims to a nearby stadium with the claim that they were to be interrogated as possible war criminals. Other Muslims fled to the hills to try and make it to another Muslim area. And still others were taken during the night of July 11 and had their throats slit, much as a knife is used to slit the throat of a goat.

Women and girls as young as twelve were also taken. Some were raped. Two, twelve-year-old Mina Smailović and her fourteen-year-old cousin Fata Smailović, returned several hours after being forced outside by Bosnian Serbs wearing United Nations uniforms. With blood from the assault covering them, Mina cried and said, "We are not girls anymore. Our lives are over. We don't have a life anymore." Later that night, her cousin Fata hanged herself with a scarf.[2]

The Bosnian Serb military leader of this incursion into Srebrenica, Ratko Mladić, justified the takeover by saying that the enclave had not been truly demilitarized and that Bosnian Muslims had used it as a base of military action. The United Nations spokesman in Zagreb would not contradict this claim.[3]

At that moment in the mid-1990s when transition's cultural formation was finally formed, its alternative from hell overwhelmed the European southeast. In the words of the International Commission on the Balkans, "The civilized world was shocked, then horrified, and soon outraged. At the same time, it was perplexed and divided."[4] It was the "hour of Europe," in which diplomats exercised their mediation only to see agreement after agreement violated. The United Nations sent its peacekeepers and the United Nations High Commissioner for Refugees helped to support millions. But this was all inadequate, especially before the violence that had become standard operating procedure.[5] Mark Danner identified five steps in this procedure, renewed in the spring of 1999 in Kosovë:[6]

1. *Concentration.* Surround the area to be cleansed and after warning the resident Serbs—often they are urged to leave or are at least told to mark their houses with white flags—intimidate the target population with artillery fire and arbitrary executions and then bring them out into the streets.
2. *Decapitation.* Execute political leaders and those capable of taking their places: lawyers, judges, public officials, writers, professors.
3. *Separation.* Divide women, children, and old men from men of "fighting age"—sixteen to sixty years old.
4. *Evacuation.* Transport women, children, and old men to the border, expelling them into a neighboring territory or country.
5. *Liquidation.* Execute "fighting age" men, dispose of bodies.[7]

By the end of the Serb campaign, approximately 850,000 Kosovar Albanians left Kosovë. But ethnic cleansing is not only the result of Serb violence. In the month following the July 1995 Allied Rapid Reaction Force air strikes against Serbs, Croatia launched a massive military operation to take the Krajina region from Croatian Serb forces. Between 150,000 and 200,000 refugees were forced to evacuate their homes and go to Serbia.[8] And after the 1999 NATO attack on Serbia, the Kosova Liberation Army (KLA) established a new and powerful presence in Kosovë, with new accounts of terror inflicted on innocents filling the media. Timothy Garton Ash exemplified Western reporting with this report from the end of January 2000:

> Many Serbs fled to Serbia when KFOR [the NATO-led military force MDK], marched in last June. Most of the rest have subsequently been driven into Serbian enclaves by intimidation and outright terror from returning Albanians. Particularly among the younger generation of Albanians, who have known Serbs only as remote oppressors, there is a growing intolerance of all ethnic others (including Roma and Muslim Slavs). People under thirty make up more than half the population and young Kosovars manifest a thirst for revenge that sickens not just foreigners but also many among the older generation of Kosovars, who still have personal memories of peaceful coexistence with the Serbs. Just before I arrived, an elderly Serb professor was lynched by a mob celebrating the Albanian "flag day" in Pristina. There used to be some 40,000 Serbs living in Pristina; now there are just a few hundred.[9]

The injustice was overwhelming not only because there were new victims. Serbian Orthodox Bishop Artemije, who earlier protested the oppression of Kosovar Albanians, said on July 15, 1999, that such treatment of Serbs in a pacified Kosovë was even worse:

> Now the Albanians are oppressing Serbs and are committing the same crimes against Serbs and other non-Albanian communities that were committed against the Kosovo Albanians in the time of Milošević's regime. But these recent crimes occur in the time of peace and with the presence of KFOR very often right in front of their eyes! Undoubtedly, the wartime acts of kidnapping, rape, murder, and the massacre of innocent people and the burning of their homes and their religious sites . . . are horrendous crimes. But in our opinion it is a much greater crime to commit and allow similar criminal acts after the peace has been established.[10]

But what do these horrors have to do with transition?

Tales of transition are very different from war stories. There are very different actors and plots. Transition has a story line of heroic reformers and entrepreneurs working with supportive states and international actors to produce a variant of that which already exists in the West. It has its demons, but for the market to be confident, those demons must be part of the past already in the process of being buried. On the war front in southeastern Europe, however, demons are everywhere, and heroes are hard to find. At least war heroes do not cross national lines easily, whereas entrepreneurs of any nationality serve as models for others in transition culture. Some of war's victims might cross borders, but in their new locales, these refugees can become burdens, or even threats, to their host country's stability.[11] Although there are victims in transition, their role is marginal because their suffering can be superseded in the making of a better tomorrow. For those who write about war, victims are at the center of a story written to motivate external intervention, or are distributed across story lines to signify the quagmire that external actors would best avoid. Quagmires rarely configure transition culture's analysis.

Allthough these narratives are vastly different, and the problems organized by the narratives poles apart, war and transition are nonetheless deeply intertwined. This became politically obvious after seventy-eight days of NATO air strikes against Serbia in the spring of 1999, but the articulation of transition culture and what could be called nationalism's wars developed throughout the 1990s into a vigorous, but contentious, field of scholarship. *Within* transition culture, however, the wars were hard to see.

War outside Transition

Why haven't these wars been at the center of transition culture? After all, through the media and increasingly through the flood of refugees, victims of these Wars of Yugoslav Succession overwhelmed the West's sensitivities. Although the Vietnam War was the first war to enter American living rooms through television, these wars arrived at the height of the global information age. TV gave us the feeling that we knew what is going on; we saw the refugees on TV, we heard them speak, and we witnessed their devastation. And not just on TV. There were scores of books, academic and popular, from histories of Bosnia, Kosovë, and Yugoslavia to personal memoirs, which allowed us to get the details, the inside story, what happened, why it happened. The Internet allowed us "direct" access to those who suffered; throw up the right Web page and you can get the latest news, and the contending opinions.[12] And then there were the movies, getting us inside the war, making us feel trapped, much as others were trapped. One could feel the hopelessness, the inescapability, the cycles of unavoidable violence, much as the Macedonian-born, London-based photographer

Alexander discovered in his home Macedonian village in *Before the Rain*.[13] But what kind of knowledge is this?

In a certain sense, we knew the victims of these wars better than we knew the victims of transition described in chapter 5. The experiences of transition's victims were relatively marginal to the main story of building markets and democracy for, the story goes, their lives were but a bridge to the future when the next generation sheds the burdens of socialism's past. By contrast, the victims of war were in the spotlight. But the meaning of their publicity is not so apparent.

Inspired by French postmodern philosopher Jean Baudrillard, Stjepan Meštrović argues that this war was "simulated." Television news and entertainment helped to blur the boundary between real and simulated, or fact and fiction. Consequently, he argues, the extensive coverage of this war in the media led the rest of the world to think of the catastrophe as just another crisis, one they "know," but one from which they were comfortably removed.[14] He writes: "the television camera does not really bring one closer to reality. It actually distances the viewer from what Simmel called the aura of the object."[15] Even when it comes to the mass rape of this war, he argues, one wonders whether the "real sexual brutality committed during the Balkan War of the 1990s blended all too easily with the fictionalized sadomasochistic fantasies that became increasingly popular in the postmodern world of the same time period."[16]

Meštrović finds, however, that this was not just spectacle; the West sided with Serbia.[17] Even at the time of his writing, most observers would not have agreed with Meštrović's ultimate conclusion. The West rather obviously sided with Croatia and Bosnia rather than with Serbia. Indeed, when American planes bombed Serbia in an apparent defense of Kosovar Albanians, it is hard to believe that anyone at one time believed that the West backed Milošević.[18] Nevertheless, Meštrović is, in a certain sense, right. Until NATO went to war with Milošević over Kosovë, the West treated Milošević as a potential partner, and therefore one who could not be a clear enemy. Where transition could identify its heroes and villains relatively easily, with socialism and its forces part of that past to be superseded, Milošević could not be overlooked until he was overthrown. With such complexity in the assignment of innocence and responsibility for war and peace, transition culture's practitioners could easily identify these wars as a thing apart, even as it appropriated the potentially distinct emancipation of 1989 as its historical foundation.

In 1989, with the more or less peaceful collapse of communism, the world was filled with hope for a new world order in which democracy and freedom could be the watchwords of the century's end. Transition culture was built around that hope, as Europe and North America looked toward Eastern Europe to confirm that the "European way of life" of democracy and civil society was universal.[19] Looking at southeastern Europe after 1991 was hardly a mirror in which to gaze, however. It was better to view that war from a distance enabled not only by the television camera, but also by the familiar trope.

Yugoslavia's nonalignment with the major power blocs of the world system, its integration into both world economies, and its "self-managing socialism" had been presented as clear alternatives as well as important comparisons to what Eastern or Western Europe had. And they were meaningful comparisons. In the 1960s and 1970s, and even through 1989, Yugoslavia was as "European" as any communist-led society, and in many ways, it arguably was better developed for "transition" than those now more frequently identified as East Central Europe.[20] But with these wars, most of the lands of the former Yugoslavia became profoundly "othered."[21]

These places embroiled in war were distanced from "the West" with the familiar trope of Balkanization, itself the "synonym for a reversion to the tribal, the backward, the primitive, the barbarian."[22] When southeastern Europe became the Balkans, it was no longer Europe, no longer part of that universal "us" with which transition culture writes the future. The bounty of books and films that came out with the war, often using the familiar travelogue genre, put the rational and civilized Westerner in the position of being normal, so that the wild and irrational Balkans could be understood, by their being inexplicable.[23] Yugoslavia was of course no panacea before the wars, and those who watched it closely knew that there were profound contradictions threatening to alter the road of Yugoslav development. Many scholars now claim that they foresaw war, but few predicted that mass rape and liquidation would be its standard operating procedure.

Ethnic cleansing, mass rape, hostage taking, and genocide overwhelmed symbols of universalism and progress and made southeastern Europe profoundly different. This shift in broad cultural orientation became clear to me during an introductory sociology class that I taught in 1995. As we discussed the latest news reports about ethnic cleansing, we were reading a textbook, published only in 1991, whose author said the following about war:

> Some of the chief ambitions of the past that led to war in the past, particularly the acquisition of new territories, have become less relevant in the contemporary world. Modern societies are today much more interdependent on a global level than ever was the case before, and for the most part, their boundaries are fixed.[24]

Both factors—the disinterest in new territories and the sanctity of borders—were violated in the former Yugoslavia, even though the post-Yugoslav nation-states were highly interdependent. Communism's peaceful collapse reinforced a Western sense of late modernity's interconnectedness and peaceful trajectory, but communism's violent sequel offended that very disposition and the presumptions enabling that optimism. Whatever their potential analytical or empirical connections to more peaceful processes of postcommunist social change, postcommunist wars disabled the global ambition articulated through transition culture, *but only if wars were part of its process.* Transition culture's practitioners could ease any distress by distancing the wars from the culture's universal hope, and its agents' responsibilities. If *transition* were based on adaptation to a new *global* order, *wars* were based on *their* nationalism. However, there are reasons to think of these processes of peaceful and violent change in greater proximity than this discursive division would suggest.

Transition and nationalism's wars began within the same world conjuncture. They had common origins in the struggle by communist leaders and civil societies to redefine their place in a world transformed by the end of the Cold War and an expanded Europe and Western alliance. They took place in contiguous lands. Citizens of peaceful transition treasured the mode of their transformation especially when they could recognize their proximity to war. Finally, both transition and war worked within nationalism's discursive formation. However, nationalism's lability enabled transition culture's practitioners to distinguish their national identifications from those that produced war's horrors. That distinction needs to be explained, and not assumed.[25]

In war's explanation, as well as in its engagement, nationalism tends to become a fixed agent, overtly and overly responsible for its horrors. In transition, nationalism remains invisible. By overlooking the nationalism of its own cultural formation, and by relying on *others'* nationalism to define *those* wars, transition culture's practitioners apparently and provisionally solved the problematic relationship between transition culture's own universal and expanding ambition and these wars' interruption of late modernity's hopes. Wars are nationalist, and transition culture is not. But, as I have argued throughout this volume, it is impossible to consider transition culture without viewing its nationalisms. In that reconfiguration, transition culture and nationalism's wars become newly proximate, and their comparison analytically productive.

This engagement of the Wars of Yugoslav Succession should be read as the companion historical bookend to chapter 1. Both chapters set the historical framework within which transition culture has been organized. Both chapters rely on various narratives of social change to organize their subject. Both chapters analyze the analytical strategies authors use to constitute the history that is part of transition culture, and that which is beyond it. Of course, transition culture has much more to pick from in emancipation, for 1989 gives transition culture its legitimacy in the exhaustion of socialism and the public acclaim for its liberal sequel. When it comes to the historical constitution of transition culture in war's proximity, its practitioners must do what they can to establish transition's distance, and innocence. Nationalism's discursive formation works well.

Nationalism's War

Many powerful arguments have been organized around nationalism as the dramatis persona of the Wars of Yugoslav Succession.[26] For instance, although the International Commission on the Balkans recognizes the significance of change in the international political environment, the proximate cause for failure rests in nationalism's "hijacking" the democratic process.[27] One might, however, look to Gale Stokes for one of the most coherent and concise accounts that explain the beginning of the Wars of Yugoslav Succession.[28]

The root cause for the tragedy of Yugoslavia rests, he argues, in Yugoslavism itself. Building on pan-Slavic ideas, the Yugoslav communists were advantaged by having the internationalism of marxism, the Partisan struggle against the Nazis, and Josip Broz Tito, an unquestioned leader, as resources in the remaking of Yugoslav identity. Socialism could overwhelm nationalism only "as long as the communist movement remained strong" (114). But its own strategy for decentralization through self-management—both political and economic—

undermined the socialist alternative. Nationalism could overwhelm decentralized socialism. Tito's death on May 4, 1980, marked the end of several forms of Yugoslav integration—not only the end of this leader's life, but also the passing of that Partisan generation that could inspire so much. Economic decline in the 1980s made matters only worse. The main story for Stokes, however, comes through a narrative of national mobilization:

> The road to civil war began in March 1981 when Albanian students took their demands for better conditions at the University of Prishtine to the streets. . . . Their demonstration touched a nerve of Albanian patriotic feeling, and over the next month anti-Serbian demonstrations demanding that Kosovo become a Yugoslav republic became so massive that the federal government sent in troops. (121)

Stokes then narrates the tale of Kosovë's importance to Serb national identity and politics. Among other reasons, Kosovë's importance rests on its place in Serb martyrology. In fields close to Pristine, Serbs lost a battle to the Ottomans in 1389 that was immortalized in epic poetry, signifying the Serbian fate to forever die for freedom but be denied victory (122). This aspect of Serb identity has managed to crowd out most other rhetorical legacies, especially its liberal ones. By the mid-1970s, the imagery of this victimization was critical to the revival of a new ideology of Serb suffering. Under the patronage of Slobodan Milošević, head of the Serbian League of Communists since 1986, this ideological frame established the Serbs' victimizers as Tito and his successors (124). This "religio-romantic" claim to Kosovë territory and Serb identity clashed with the Albanian claim to Kosovë, itself based on the 90 percent Albanian majority in the province.[29]

Stokes also introduces the political-economic problem. Kosovë was an extremely underdeveloped region of Yugoslavia—Slovenia was some six times more developed, and the per capita income for the region was about 28 percent of the average Yugoslav income in the early 1980s. Kosovë occupied a kind of "peripheral status" with mineral deposits and an export economy based on raw materials to the rest of Yugoslavia. At the time, Albanians perceived that the rest of Yugoslavia was exploiting them for their raw materials, even as the north claimed that Kosovë's underdevelopment was a consequence of its overpopulation and other inadequacies. The Kosovar Albanians received the lion's share of federal support for underdeveloped regions.

With such an economy, however, the University of Pristine's highly educated graduates found no jobs (122–23). The effect of these competing national claims and political-economic conditions led to nonnegotiable dilemmas:

> On the one side Albanians . . . wanted to have their own republic in the Yugoslav confederation; on the other side Serbs . . . [who] wanted to control more fully than the 1974 constitution permitted them. . . . The Serbian media blamed all problems on the Albanians, refusing to recognize that the Serbian police arrested over three thousand Albanians and killed more than one hundred Albanian protesters. On their side, the Albanians firebombed the ancient patriarchate at Peč and harassed Serbs into leaving the province (although the many stories of Albanian rapes of Serbian women seem to have been manufactured by the Serbs). (123)

Milošević used these dilemmas to establish a new vision to succeed the failing Yugoslav one. This vision was based on his domination of Yugoslavia, and when that failed, domination of a greater Serbia. Significantly, he drew on that same mobilization of civil society which in Poland and Hungary led to a liberal vision gaining hegemony. Milošević, however, turned mobilization toward a neo-Stalinist nationalist hegemony (126).[30] In March 1989, the Serb government imposed its control over Kosovë, at the cost of twenty to as many as 140 lives (ibid.).

By contrast, Slovenia's national discourse had been already attached more to a Central European than a Balkan regional identity, and its vital civil society and independent intelligentsia in the late 1980s made it appear more akin to Hungary and Poland than to any other region within Yugoslavia (127; see also chapter 1). Illustrative of this disposition, about one million Slovenes signed a petition protesting Milošević's actions in Kosovë, and one month after Serbia's consolidation of control in Kosovë, Slovenia held Yugoslavia's first open elections, deciding who should be Slovenia's representative to the federal presidency (127–29). Croatia followed Slovenia's pluralizing course by the end of 1989.

Ante Marković was the last hope for a unified Yugoslavia. He became prime minister in March 1989, and by January 1990, he had institutionalized a series of radical economic reforms to create capital markets, privatize small businesses, curb inflation, and other initiatives. Stokes notes that Marković enjoyed wide support in foreign circles, from "George Bush through Mikhail Gorbachev to Pope John Paul II"; but from within, the non-Serbs saw him as a centrist, and the Serbs attacked him by drawing on both populist and socialist rhetoric (131). The International Monetary Fund (IMF) and the World Bank tried to keep the Yugoslavs together, but "by early 1990 emotions in Yugoslavia had reached the point at which economic arguments ceased to have an impact" (132). The first clear step indicating the end of Yugoslavia came when the Slovene delegation walked out of the January 1990 party congress of the League of Communists of Yugoslavia. The Slovenes and the Serbs had radically opposed visions for the future of Yugoslavia. Bosnia-Herzegovina, Croatia, and Macedonia supported the Slovenes (ibid.).

The Slovenes and Croats had open elections later that spring. In Slovenia, the liberal forces, which included the liberal Slovenian communist leader Milan Kučan, won. Here, liberalism and nationalism joined. In Croatia, however, the liberal forces associated with reform communists failed—perhaps because of liberalism's realism. Those liberals argued that Yugoslavia must be a federation given that Croats live outside Croatia, and Serbs outside Serbia; the alternative, one of their representatives warned, was civil war. The nationalist leader Franjo Tudjman, by contrast, called for a "Croatia within its 'historic and natural boundaries . . .'" (134). Tudjman won. After his election, he fanned the flames of Serbian apprehension, resulting in their own declaration of secession and wish to unite with the rest of Serbia. Violence ensued, and Yugoslavia began its long and violent death (137–38).

The other four republics held elections toward the end of 1990. Milošević and his party won handily, though fared poorly in Belgrade and other major cities. Montenegro's victors threw in their lot with him. The results in Bosnia-Herzegovina reflected the national split in the country—with each party getting its share, and the presidency going to Alija Izetbegović of the Party for Democratic Action (based in the Muslim community). Macedonia's significant number of Albanians put their representatives in parliament, but the winning party evoked nationalist Macedonian memories. The reformed communists did not fare so badly, and one of their number was elected president by the Assembly.

Kosovë's autonomy within Serbia had already been stripped. In February 1990, Milošević sent in police forces to suppress Albanian protests and riots demanding free elections. In July 1990, the Serbian population supported a referendum to write a new constitution, the effect of which would be to link Kosovë to Belgrade even more closely (136). On the same day, the Kosovar Albanian parliamentarians declared that Kosovë would be independent of Serbia and a republic of Yugoslavia. Under the leadership of Ibrahim Rugova, a man inspired by Mahatma Gandhi, the Albanians undertook a new strategy of non-violent resistance, establishing an alternative society complete with "political structures, schools, and even hospitals."[31] Stokes concludes his story by pointing to impossibility: "The situation in Kosovo remained at an impasse: a small minority of self-righteous Serbs fully in control by force of arms, the large majority of frustrated Albanians dispossessed and hostile" (136).

It was not the Albanian–Serb conflict, however, but the conflict between Serbs, on the one hand, and Croats and Slovenes on the other, that made Yugoslavia ultimately untenable; the former wanted greater centralization (but without non-Serb meddling in Kosovar affairs), the latter greater confederation (but not for Croatia's Serbs). The spring witnessed fighting between Croatian and Serbian forces in Croatia, and intervention by the Yugoslav army. On June 25, 1991, the Slovenes declared independence, and the Croats immediately thereafter. Yugoslav troops intervened, but Slovene forces proved more resistant than expected. After a few weeks, the federal troops left Slovenia, and the Yugoslav army took the side of the Croatian Serbs in the conflict within Croatia.

The Germans moved the entire European Union to recognize the independence of Slovenia and Croatia by January 15, 1992. Those who voted in a referendum on independence in Bosnia on February 29 and March 1, 1992, also found independence to be the preferred option. The disaffected Bosnian Serbs, however, refused to vote in this election, and both Serbian and Croatian nationalist forces accelerated their drive to seize separate territories. Bosnia was divided by force, and populations were relocated through terror. And that led ultimately to the attack on Srebrenica, where this chapter began. One of the critical questions, however, is why the Kosovar Albanians remained relatively peaceful. Stokes writes:

> The Albanians in Kosovo have been remarkably restrained in the face of extreme provocations by the Serbs, perhaps because they are poorly armed and know that the Serbs will not hesitate to massacre them. But with unemployment in the 40 percent range, with education at a

standstill, and with no governmental functions reserved for them, it remained in doubt how long they could maintain their moderate stance. Together with their conationals in Albania and other parts of Yugoslavia, the Albanians constituted a population of about five and one-half million, more than the Croats and almost three times as numerous as the Slovenians. How long could it be before they attempted to assert that position in the Balkans to which ethnic politics seemed to entitle them? (143)

The crisis Stokes anticipated finally came true in the spring of 1999. One should be surprised that it did not happen much earlier. If it were not for the determined nonviolent leadership of Ibrahim Rugova, war would have ripped Kosovë apart much sooner than it ultimately did. Rugova offered Milošević an incredible opportunity to reach a peaceful solution on the Kosovë question, but, at least according to Warren Zimmermann, Milošević "squandered" the opportunity. By 1998, the Kosova Liberation Army (KLA) mobilized substantial numbers of supporters ready to take up arms to realize the independence of Kosovë and, in the process, assassinate Serbian police. The Serbs' "terrorist" designation for the KLA rests in this guerrilla military strategy, but it is difficult to accept the simple charge when Serb forces committed mass murders against the population they accused of harboring the armed resistance.[32]

For those who emphasize the nationalist argument, it is hard not to assign principal responsibility for the war to Serbia, and Milošević in particular. Croatian nationalism and Tudjman's aggressiveness can be recognized and critiqued[33] but the Serbian side typically set the dynamic. As Sabrina Ramet emphasizes:

> there is nothing comparable, in Croatia, to the kind of apartheid and "ethnic cleansing" to which the Albanians of Kosovo have been subjected. And although there are some striking similarities to the ideologies of Milošević and Tudjman, most particularly when it comes to Bosnia, they have treated both their political rivals and their ethnic peripheries rather differently. . . . To the extent that one may judge Serbia to be more fully in the grips of nationalism, one may conclude, in that event, that although Croatia's path to democracy is strewn with obstacles, Serbia does not seem to be on that path at all.[34]

Nationalism clearly plays a role in explaining the crisis of Yugoslavia. Although some might use this as sufficient explanation, it clearly is not. In the deft hands of Stokes and other superior analysts, one can see that other factors fall into the explanation—the decentralization of Yugoslav socialism and the coincidence of economic reform with austerity, among other factors. Nevertheless, when nationalism becomes the dramatis persona in making tragedy, liberalism can pose as its clear alternative. Stokes writes powerfully about that, especially in another essay.[35] Stokes discusses the potential for pluralism in Yugoslavia after war by invoking American legacies of pluralism and by looking to Germany and Poland for examples.

In order for Germany to overcome its Nazi heritage, it had to be occupied and its political infrastructure destroyed. It also had to develop a "pluralist discourse of remembrance" in which painful memories and wrong steps in historical development would be confronted and engaged. The Poles exemplify this pluralism in international politics, accepting "responsibility for their own nation's past," recognizing error, being able to apologize, and refusing to blame others for all their ills.[36] The root of the opposition between this progressive politics and that of nationalists, Stokes argues, is in nationalism's intolerance for pluralism:

> The principles of openness, democracy, pluralism, and market became the founding dogmas of the European Community, so that when the revolutions of 1989 occurred, pluralism was recognized throughout Eastern Europe as the only viable sociopolitical model. It is just the openness of pluralism that both the Communists and the nationalists cannot abide. The ideal of the homogeneous people is their device to fend off the radical indeterminacy of pluralism, the assertion of the democratic states that it is process that is important, not ends. . . . This is why pluralism and nationalism can never be fully compatible.[37]

As an explanatory motif, therefore, nationalism works when a clear alternative in liberalism's values can be recognized. It takes one more element, however, for it to become the player in tragedy: when it can be embedded in a larger metanarrative of history, especially apparent in another essay Stokes wrote with other experts on Yugoslavia. They emphasized that the "homogenization of nations through population exchanges, refugee flight, border adjustments and massacre are a dominant characteristic of the modern experience."[38] Yugoslavia, thanks to Yugoslavism, is simply, tragically, late. It denied modernity and preserved a structural problem left unresolved through the twentieth century. Yugoslavia's wars were not derived from the transition to markets after communism, but rather embedded in the making of nationalism's modernity.

This focus on war and nationalism is subtly implicated in transition culture. It is embedded in a historiography for which transition to markets and democracy offers an alternative to war, and not its explanation. Even better for transition culture, however, the passions of nationalism are such that democracy and markets could do nothing to stop war's horror. Transition is innocent. Europe is distant, North America even more so. Liberals need not look at themselves when explaining these horrors. The Wars of Yugoslav Succession, when nationalism—in opposition to liberalism—is in play, hold a critical function in transition culture: the unspoken, but deadly alternative to markets and pluralism. But the tale might also be told differently, with liberalism and transition featured much more prominently. Nationalism will not disappear, but its opposition to liberalism might not be so stable, and its innocence before war might not be so convenient.

Transition, Nationalism, and Militarism

Bogdan Denitch has argued in several books and essays that the crisis of Yugoslav socialism and its subsequent breakup are a manifestation of the conflicts and contradictions attending state socialism. Across the region, he argues, the reality of the market and its ideology have flown apart, producing distress for those distanced from the enrichment that capitalism promised. He also argues that the abstractions of liberalism and the market need to be developed in real East European conditions, and succeed, or else the vacuum will be filled by nationalism.[39] When this is combined with uneven regional development, as it was in Yugoslavia, the contradictions are explosive. In sum, Yugoslavia's failed market socialism produced a nationalism that is a potential danger for the whole of Eastern Europe and the former Soviet Union, because it is derived from the contradictions of state socialism and unequal regional development, not ancient ethnic hatreds. It is a real alternative future, and not something limited to the Balkans.

Valerie Bunce also interprets Yugoslavia's violent end through the lens of socialism's contradictions, or, as she calls it, its subversive institutions. With their terrific concentration of power in the party-state and weak and dependent society, socialist institutions divided and weakened the authorities, homogenized society, and made it more cohesive and powerful. When leaders die, especially those of the stature of Tito, differences among elites are magnified in the contest over successors, and over the course of socialism's economic and political reform.[40] In the course of socialism's collapse, power devolves from the first to the next tier of the system in general, which in federal states such as the USSR, Czechoslovakia, and Yugoslavia means an end to the federal state.[41] For Bunce, therefore, any explanation for Yugoslavia's end begins with the subversive character of socialist institutions, and continues with Yugoslavia's specific institutional framework to explain the violence of its dismemberment. Bunce emphasizes the institutional location of the military in her explanation of communism's violent sequel. Based on her comparison of the relatively peaceful breakup of the USSR and Czechoslovakia with that of Yugoslavia, she argues that where the military is included in the breakup, and where the resources of the center are relatively limited, there is a greater likelihood of violence.

Violence is also the result, however, of failing to recognize militarism. The International Commission on the Balkans reported: "The EC [European Community] foreign ministers who tried to negotiate cease-fires in the summer of 1991 found it nearly impossible to understand that there were political leaders in Europe who would not hesitate to use military force, or that, for the Serbian and Croatian leaders, war might be a deliberate, 'rational' choice."[42] Militarism, beyond socialism, liberalism, and nationalism, is therefore critical to understanding postcommunism's violent alternative. But, of course, this is not an unprecedented argument in the sociology of war and peace.

At the height of the Cold War, C. Wright Mills argued that "the immediate cause of World War III is the preparation of it."[43] He devotes the rest of his book to a discussion of militarism and its attributes and causes. Mills found Russian and American ruling circles to be gripped by a military metaphysic, in which all policies and the world itself were understood in terms of a national security defined in military terms. The economy itself, while not at war, increasingly becomes defined by military priorities resulting in what Mills called the Permanent War Economy. The public became apathetic and dominated by "crackpot realists" who could not see the bigger picture and instead could only focus on the next step in a logic that would lead to war. Some twenty-five years later, E. P. Thomson found another militarist logic, but one even more dangerous that he named exterminism. Exterminism dominated both Soviet and American economies and polities, originating in imperialism but given life by the weapons system associated with the bomb.[44] After the Cold War's conclusion, Sam Marullo relied on a similar approach to explaining the likelihood of war, identifying the social and cultural forces and economic and political processes that encourage war and militarism within the United States.[45]

But the Cold War did not produce World War III. Some argue that American militarism in general and the Reagan military buildup in particular were essential to producing the collapse of communism and the end of the Cold War.[46] Fearing that such an argument could justify militarism in other circumstances, others, such as Marullo, would rather look toward other factors, such as the resurgence of civil society, to explain communism's collapse. These debates are clearly important, not only for historical sociology, but also for contemporary global politics. If Western military superiority was the central feature responsible for ending communism, might it not also do the same for nationalism? Shouldn't liberals stand fast against nationalism and use violence when necessary? This was one important conclusion of the International Commission: "diplomacy not backed by force is tantamount to hollow gesturing. It is the punch of power that lends conviction to the suasion of diplomats. Where it is lacking, the well-meaning are left to the mercy of the reckless, and brute force, rather than reason sustained by might determines the outcome of conflict."[47] Although there is terrific conviction in this statement, its sense is bound up within a certain kind of nationalism that finds Western might critical to peacemaking, and Balkan militarism to be merely degenerative. It depends on the arguments of "democratic peace" theory where democracies, regardless of their military capacities, do not start wars or go to war with one another.

Democracies may not start wars, but others have argued that an arms supply and militarized economy by themselves increase the likelihood of war.[48] Proximity to other wars and recent wartime experiences also increase the likelihood of mass violence. For example, the Soviet invasion of Afghanistan and the internationally supported resistance movement there made Tajikistan, and other countries touched by the Ferghana Valley, more at risk of war than other postcommunist countries at a greater physical and cultural distance.[49] Although Yugoslavia was not in any special proximity to hot wars, it did have the largest standing army in Europe, and its emphasis on guerrilla-based defense strategies made arms broadly available and widely distributed.[50] Albania's own political crisis in 1997 vastly increased the arms supply available to the KLA, and helped to produce the violent alternative to Rugova's nonviolent movement for Albanian rights.[51]

Beyond the availability of arms, the end to the Cold War itself helped to produce the tragedy in Yugoslavia by undoing one of the key institutions integrating Yugoslavia: the Yugoslav People's Army (JNA).[52] The JNA built itself up as an organization that was prepared to defend itself against invasion from one or another bloc. But with communism's collapse in the Soviet bloc, and the wish by some Yugoslav republics to join Europe, the JNA ceased to be perceived as, or arguably to be, an all-Yugoslav institution. It rather identified with those forces that wished to stop Slovenia and Croatia from leaving the Yugoslav state, and thus aligned with Serbia. The JNA itself perceived European policy to be designed to split Yugoslavia down the middle, with some republics belonging to East Central Europe, and some to the Balkans. In this sense, to act to defend Yugoslavia meant to take the side of the Serbian republic, which itself could not be viewed as all-Yugoslav.[53] The "fall of the wall" meant, in other words, to rebuild, if not a wall, at least a fence, through Yugoslavia.

Militarism's contribution to war thus cannot be appreciated without its implication in nationalism's global articulation. First, in the beginning of the decade, Europe was unprepared to recognize that some actors would use military force to realize their political aims. It defined such violence as beyond the European ken. To the extent that nationalism and militarism were identified in opposition to European integration and peacefulness, Slovenia's nationalism could be identified as European, whereas Croatian and especially Serbian nationalism would be identified as barbaric, as non-European. Bunce captures this sentiment in her emphasis on the pervasiveness, and variety, of nationalism:[54]

> Thus what differentiated the Slovene from the Serbian party was not nationalism, because nationalism and even secession for that matter, were central to the project of their respective political leaders. . . . in both cases the Communist Party moved toward the public, with nationalism serving as the bridge. . . . nationalism in the Slovene context was linked with reform and an exit from socialism and the state. By contrast, in the Serbian context, nationalism, socialism and opposition to reform were joined together, and two options were considered for the future of the state: recentralization of the existing state, or, failing that, expansion of Serbia to embrace the totality of the Serbian nation.[55]

Serbs, distinguished in the Balkans for never having been "effectively defeated or humiliated" since the end of the eighteenth century, stood alone.[56] The means for Serbs to realize their national mission rested in the redrawing of republican boundaries, by force if necessary. By contrast, with their Western support, the Croats through 1995 and the KLA after 1997 did not, could not, stand alone, even if they were not so obviously democratic and peaceful as Slovenia was understood to be. Their militarism nonetheless could be constructed as only responsive to a much more aggressive, and dangerous, Serbian militarism. But what are the origins of that Serbian militarism? What made Serb nationalism so violent? One can turn to a history of Serbian national identity. One might also, however, understand that history better by defining the place of Slovenian nationalism and European and Western policies in transition.

Global Origins to Nationalism's War

The dominant view of Slovenian nationalism, certainly within Slovenia, and more broadly across Europe, has been that Slovene leaders have always struggled in peaceful, democratic, and pragmatic ways to resolve their own needs within the constraints of the system in which they found themselves.[57] They offered a way to democratize Yugoslavia when they insisted on confederation within Yugoslavia in January 1990. Slovenes showed their multinational solidarity when they offered support to the Kosovar Albanians when the Serbs stripped the latter of any governmental power in July 1990. The Slovenes provided leadership in the European style when they held their referendum on peaceful secession in December 1990. Their declaration of independence on June 25, 1991, and the subsequent attack by Yugoslav forces only confirmed what their previous moves indicated: the Slovenes could not be a part of such a Yugoslavia.[58] This remarkably peaceful and legalistic orientation, Minnich argues, is partially the outcome of Slovene learning under Austrian and Serbian monarchies: that "self-determination is possible only through responsible participation in existing political structures."[59] Clearly, Slovenia belongs with the rest of the erstwhile Hapsburg empire in Europe.

Slovene politics *may be* virtuous in comparison to the politics of other peoples of Yugoslavia, but this underlying sensibility of liberalism versus nationalism also enables us to ignore how Slovene liberalism, and that of the West more generally, is itself implicated in the making of war. Susan Woodward offers a powerful, alternative, account that emphasizes both the responsibility of international organizations in making this war happen as it did and the significance of that most liberal of Yugoslav nations, the Slovenes, in making it so. Woodward certainly is no fan of nationalism. But rather than assign it only to those who commit genocide, she finds responsibility more broadly distributed. The major actors in Woodward's account include the nationalist leaders themselves. She does note the differences between neofascist leaders such as the Serb Vojislav Šešelj, and democratically inclined reformist communists such as the Slovenian president Milan Kučan, but she avoids using these distinctions to explain. Instead, she emphasizes how leading Yugoslav actors from all sides played some kind of nationalist card in ending Yugoslavia, and in making the war happen. The principal focus for Woodward is the collapse of authority, not the rise of nationalism.[60]

Nationalism was not the only alternative to Yugoslavism, of course. There were other actors in each of the republican elections that could have offered less nationalist options, but the sets of relations in which they were embedded pushed them to more and more nationalist strategies. This is obvious, for instance, in Macedonia, where the "center-left" president, Kiro Gligorov, was pushed, by the dynamics of the Albanian–Macedonian conflict, to side with more radical nationalist Macedonian parties in a bloc against Albanian parties, even while he tried to co-opt more moderate Albanian actors into the government (342, 357–60). But significantly for Woodward, it was not just domestic actors that forced this outcome.

The Yugoslav war operated in a global system. The center collapsed because the identity of the federal state—nonaligned and privileged in Western loan making—was destroyed with the end of the Cold War. Also, European states and the Vatican facilitated the exit of Croatia, and especially Slovenia, with promises of speedy recognition and sooner entry to the European Union (149, 158–59, 175, 205–10). With these not-too-irrational nationalist strategies, these Croatian, and especially Slovenian, republican leaderships developed their own strategies to make cohabitation within the Yugoslav federation impossible. Of course, many of these strategies were downright democratic. When the Slovene government supported its oppositional youth movements in critiques of the army and in support of the Albanian movements, it articulated the emancipatory politics of civil society identified in chapter 1. At the same time, however, it also had the consequence, whether intended or unintended we do not know, of exacerbating the republican conflicts in the region. The eventual exit of the Slovenes and Croats forced the other republics to declare their independence too, even though they were not as "prepared" with developed civil societies and alternative politics. And without the Slovene and Croatian presence, the counterweight to Serb domination declined. In this sense, although arguably more liberal and democratic in their nationalism, Croat and especially Slovene nationalisms were also more lethal since it was these nationalisms that most immediately destroyed Yugoslavia. And it was the destruction of Yugoslavia, Woodward argues, not the attacks of Serbs, that explains the crisis that has become Yugoslavia.

"Nationalists" are therefore those who accepted the definition of these wars as wars of irreconcilable ancient hatreds. Nationalists are international actors who recognize republican boundaries as sacrosanct. Rather than encouraging and empowering those who might have mobilized along other formations of identity, or along principles of class or civil rights, nationalism's international actors recognized above all else the national identities of these actors, and accepted domestic nationalists' definitions of the conflicts (169–70). Even the sanctions against Serbia played into the hands of nationalists by undermining the possibilities of democrats and others to popularize their message, while confirming the claims of nationalists who portrayed the world as being against Serbia (293). Moreover, to recognize the three national parties of Bosnia—Muslim, Serb, and Croat—as the representatives of the Bosnian people meant that the category Bosnian itself had no place (298–302). And despite their protests against the nationalism, these same international actors did not follow the implications of their commitments: they virtually invited local actors to respond only to nationalist mobilizations and the struggle over territory, most obvious in their failures to distinguish human from national rights (147).

These nationalisms around the Wars of Yugoslav Succession were implicated in diaspora politics and the domestic politics of other nations too. Germany was especially important in this. Having just celebrated the right to self-determination in its unification with East Germany, the Federal Republic put self-determination above the sanctity of boundary maintenance (153). With the support of important Catholic constituencies and the pressures of the largely Croatian *Gastarbeiter* community, and the familiarity of Germans for the Croatian tourist areas, the support of Germany for the Croat and Slovene moves for independence was powerful and consequential (185–89).

Even the international portrait of the struggle was importantly a matter of identity formation. Those who won elections in Croatia and Slovenia could portray themselves as the victors of a democratic process in opposition to communists from Belgrade (152). Woodward further maintains that Croats provoked attacks on Dubrovnik, the ancient city, in order to increase world outrage at the Serb-led JNA (182). Bosnians used UN-sponsored safe areas as staging grounds for assaults, and allowed attacks on those safe areas to garner them more resources from international actors (320–22). In this sense, Croats and Bosnians could accumulate resources by using the media to portray the inhuman brutality of their opponents. Bosnian and Croatian Serbs, losers in this global media campaign, simply resorted to their own force of arms (208–9). Finally, UNPROFOR's neutrality itself reinforced nationalism's wars. In order to safeguard the provision of food and medical supplies, it had to respect whatever authorities occupied the territory. But in so doing, it conferred upon those authorities state-like legitimacy, and reinforced the point that military control of territory is really what mattered.

Woodward's interpretation is not only compelling because it seeks to place the Wars of Yugoslav Succession in a larger systemic theory, but also because she moves to the ground to operationalize her meanings of the nation and Yugoslavia. Although she does not have the ethnographic style of an anthropologist, her message would resonate: that international policy makers not only were operating with contrasting agendas with their interventions, but also operated without a good sense of the local meaning of the nation (197, 205).

Although in the West the coincidence of nation and boundaries might be imaginable, in Yugoslavia, the sanctification of the right to self-determination could not be promoted as legitimate if it foreclosed the right for the redrawing of the former Yugoslavia's internal boundaries. Given that Serbs in Croatia and Bosnia, and Croats in Bosnia, never considered themselves minorities, but rather nations with equal rights, their newfound minority status was clearly a demotion, and even a threat (228).[61] Ironically, constitutionalism, thought to be one of the foundations of transition, worked in much the same way to facilitate war.

Constitutional Nationalism

Constitutions and the rule of law are critical elements of transition culture. For transition to work and for civil society to defend itself from the tyranny of the state, laws must be transparent and there must be a capacity to enforce them.[62] Precisely because laws can be contradictory and interpretations multiple, there must be some central authority and body of law to which conflicting positions might ultimately appeal. By relying on the constitution as a supreme arbiter, civil societies can find the principles with which to organize their consensus. As sociological theorist Jeffery Alexander put it:

> Civil society . . . means trust in the universalistic values that abstract from any particular society and that provide critical leverage against particular historical actors . . . it is this very separation from the endorsement of particular arrangements that makes democracy possible. Because the ultimate loyalty of citizens is to overarching rules rather than to the outcome of any particular game, policies and office-holders can be changed. . . . It is constitutions that codify these universalistic rules, in a legal form that authorizes democratic succession and political dissent.[63]

Constitutions may also, however, configure dissolution. Robert Hayden maintains that the Wars of Yugoslav Succession are themselves produced, and reproduced, through constitutionalism.[64] The roots of this dissolution, he argues, rest in the 1974 Yugoslav constitution and the efforts by the (then Socialist) Republic of Slovenia in September 1989 to make the federal constitution irrelevant to Slovene national self-determination.

Throughout the 1980s in Yugoslavia there was a growing consensus that the 1974 federal constitution would have to be amended. Practice indicated that the federal constitution was supreme over republican legislation, however. For example, republican legislators typically appealed to the federal constitution's contradictory principles to justify changes in republican constitutions. That acknowledgment in practice shifted in the summer of 1989 when Slovenia introduced constitutional language pertaining to the sovereignty of the Slovenian nation (36–37). The federal constitution itself proved inadequate to the Slovene challenge. The Constitutional Court of Yugoslavia only had the right to offer its opinion on republican legislation's convergence of republican with federal law. Unlike American federal law, there was no way in which, constitutionally, the federation could enforce the superiority of its law over republican law. At least this was the Slovenes' argument; their refusal to accept the supremacy of the federal constitution ultimately wrote the rules by which other republics would respond to Yugoslav central authority. Even before their declaration of sovereignty on July 2, 1990, the Slovenes thus practically made Yugoslavia a consensual union of sovereign republics in 1989. In the summer of 1990, Slovenian and Croatian experts drafted a model that reflected this confederal arrangement. This proposed constitution weakened federal authority even further than the 1974 document, for no federal organ was given "clear authority to do anything meaningful" (62).

Why bother with such a confederation when international treaties among sovereign republics would have realized much of the same? Hayden argues starkly that "the model looks to have been a carefully constructed constitutional fraud, which seemed to promise the creation of a structure for a new Yugoslavia, but that instead took care to ensure that no viable institutions would in fact be created" (64). It could satisfy international actors who wished to see Yugoslavia survive, and the publics of Yugoslavia who wanted national sovereignty but some kind of continued connection with other republics (64–65).

With the fall of Yugoslavia, constitutional nationalism came to define the new order. The Croatian constitution of December 1990 epitomized, for Hayden, the constitutional and legal privilege of one ethnic nation over another, but all the republics had some element of this nationalism, at least in their preambles. The Serbian constitution was different from the others, however, for it was designed to elevate the power of one man, Slobodan Milošević, while it directly attacked minority self-rule in Serbia (68–69). With this elevation of nationalism to the heart of constitutionalism in the former Yugoslavia, even that state with the greatest multicultural history, Bosnia-Herzegovina, could hardly last.[65] In the fall of 1991, it was already apparent that it would be difficult to reach consensus among the Muslim-associated Party of Democratic Action, the Serbian Democratic Party, and the Croatian Democratic Union on what would happen should Croatia secede from Yugoslavia. Without the assent of the Serbian party, the other parties put forward the February 1992 referendum on independence. War, in turn, followed. The constitutions that have followed these wars, including that within the Dayton Accord, reproduce the same nationalism, Hayden argues, that began the war:

> Bosnia's agony was determined by the success of the Slovenian and Croatian rejection of the common state. . . . once Yugoslavia collapsed, the majority of Bosnian-Serbs and Herzegovinian Croats rejected inclusion in a Bosnian state, just as the Slovenes and the Croats in Croatia had rejected Yugoslavia. Far from being illogical or irrational, their rejection of Bosnia represented a very rational recognition of the logic that had won in what had been until then their joint state. Who would wish to be a member of a minority in someone else's state, when instead they could accede to the state of their own ethnic group? (151–52)

Hayden thus reads late and postcommunist social change in Yugoslavia very differently than others have read social change elsewhere. Citizens in civil society were not engaged in self-determination; instead, republics were given the right to embrace national sovereignty (147). By accepting and actually encouraging a nationalism based on republican boundaries without respecting the national self-determination of minorities, or the self-perceived rights of those who felt threatened by these new governments, international actors made force a more likely outcome. As Woodward put it:

> Because it ignored the compromises that Yugoslavia represented in guaranteeing nations the right to self-determination in a nationally mixed area, ignored the security guarantee that Yugoslavia had provided for territories of mixed population, and did little to reassure those relegated to minority status that they would be protected, it could not reverse the downward spiral of suspicion and insecurity that was leading to war (220).

Hayden wonders whether voters in 1990 might have acted differently had they recognized that the national self-determination for which they voted would have led to the mass violence that was ultimately produced (154). Might Western enthusiasts for democracy and self-determination have tempered their advice knowing that constitutional nationalism and ethnic cleansing would be the result of communism's collapse in the former Yugoslavia (161)? Perhaps it was their wishful thinking, rather than their anticipation of unintended consequences, that made war, rather than peaceful transition, the defining feature of social change in southeastern Europe after communist rule (164).

Transition culture may thus be closer to war than we would acknowledge in an account that focuses on nationalism as the motor force of history. The accounts I have outlined do not deny the significance and responsibility of Milošević and the nationalism he cultivated for making war. They only shift our attention to other factors that have facilitated war's making. For Woodward, Bunce, Hayden, and others, some permutation of militarism, sham constitutionalism, and transition itself all helped to make this war. Transition culture, with its presumption of Western universalism and its unexamined nationalism, might facilitate the making of markets out of planned economies. But, at least for some authors, it also helps to make war. For other authors, such a claim is an outrage. If the West is guilty of anything, it is guilty of appeasement and inaction.

Nationalism and Intervention

Another area expert, Sabrina Ramet has little patience for arguments that put any responsibility for the wars in the former Yugoslavia outside Milošević and Serbia proper. She notes that the Bush administration in 1991 was actively propping up the Yugoslav government, asking that the republican governments "negotiate." She has little sympathy for this position, and, in fact, associates it with a kind of Serbian denial of responsibility:

> The only form of "negotiation" compatible with the preservation of Yugoslav unity, as Bush and [Secretary of State James] Baker should have known, would have been the complete surrender of the Slovenian and Croatian governments to Serbian diktat, resulting in the removal of the local democratically elected governments and their replacement by quasi-socialist quislings. It is ironic, in this context, to note that Jović, Šuvar and Lazar Mojsov—and no doubt other Yugoslav leaders as well—unable or unwilling to admit their own culpability, were becoming increasingly obsessed with the notion that the United States and Western Europe were actively plotting the dismemberment of the SFRY [Socialist Federated Republic of Yugoslavia]. Indeed, Šuvar told me in 1997 that, in his view, Milošević's suppression of the autonomous provinces, conquest of Montenegro, dispatch of Serbian secret police into Bosnia, economic embargo against Slovenia and repeated violations of the federal constitution had, in his view, essentially nothing to do with the breakup of Yugoslavia.[66]

Thomas Cushman positions his work alongside that of Ramet, and is among the most forceful on this charge of Serbian responsibility and Western irresponsibility. In no other historical period, he writes, have "Western intellectuals proven themselves so willing and able to offer accounts that occlude, obfuscate or even deny the central historical facts of military aggression and mass killing."[67] For him, the facts of the wars are evident:

> The Balkan war, that is, the use of armed forces to impose noncon-sensual solutions on Slovenia, Croatia and Bosnia-Herzegovina by Serbia and Bosnian Serb forces, was planned and carried out by Ser-bian political elites in Belgrade and Bosnia and was prosecuted with the aid of the full military might of the Yugoslav National Army. This war was waged on the sovereign territories of Croatia and Bosnia-Herzegovina primarily against unarmed civilians. During the invasion of Bosnia-Herzegovina, a project of state-sponsored genocide was carried out against the Muslim citizens of that state by Bosnian Serb leaders and soldiers who were sponsored and equipped by the same elites who had planned and executed the War. According to a leaked CIA report, the Serbian leaders and armies are responsible for 90% of the atrocities committed in this war and 100% of the systematic killing. A UN-sponsored report . . . underscores Serbian official di-rection and their responsibility for the vast majority of war crimes committed. . . . The UN concluded that Serbs committed the vast ma-jority of rapes in Bosnia, and again, did so as an organized systematic policy.[68]

Cushman does not claim that *only* the Serbs are guilty, but he does argue that Serbian atrocities were far more premeditated, extensive, and systematic. Ramet agrees:

> Vladimir Žerjavić, the distinguished Zagreb demographer, has esti-mated that in the years 1992–95, some 215,000 persons died in Bosnia-Herzegovina and that among the dead were about 160,000 Muslims, 30,000 Croats, and 25,000 Serbs. Moreover, although the bitterness of the Croat-Muslim battles cannot be denied, Žerjavić's calculations show that only about 2,000 Muslims were killed by Croatian forces; the remaining 158,000 died at the hands of Serbian forces. Of the 30,000 Croats who lost their lives in Bosnia, 2,000 were killed by Muslims and 28,000 were killed by Serbian forces, accord-ing to Žerjavić. And of the 25,000 Serbs who lost their lives in Bosnia, Žerjavić estimates that about half of them were killed by Muslims and half by Croats. In addition to the dead, at least 2.7 million persons had been reduced to refugees. An estimated 20,000–50,000 Bosnian Muslim women had been raped by Bosnian Serb soldiers in a system-atic campaign of humiliation and psychological terror.[69]

For scholars such as Cushman and Ramet, work that distracts us from these basic facts serves to make relativism more palatable and a real-politik of isolationism more acceptable.

For example, Cushman argues that Bette Denich's account of the sensibilities of Croatian Serbs before the 1990 constitution legitimates Serb ideology.[70] Rather than focusing on how the Serb community amplified the provocation and used it to legitimate "military aggression and military killing in Croatia," Denich gives "moral precedence to an empathetic sociological understanding of the Serbian point of view."[71] Cushman also finds Bakić-Hayden's and Hayden's arguments about Orientalism within the Balkans profoundly misleading.[72] When they focus on Slovenian and Croatian cultural strategies to elevate differences with Serbs, they miss the fact that Serbs dominate politically. Also, contrary to Bakić-Hayden and Hayden, there is nothing wrong when cultural difference is used to establish distinct modern liberal orders.[73] Publications such as these, in leading intellectual journals, are bad enough, Cushman argues, but when it affects policies, it is even worse.

Both Cushman and Ramet identify Charles Boyd as exemplary in his equivocation.[74] If guilt for war crimes can be distributed widely, and victims found everywhere, a good case can be made for Western appeasement and inaction. Intellectual work that raises doubt in such a clear case of moral right and wrong, Cushman argues, is irresponsible. Simply said, "relativism was the driving force for the emergence of a form of revisionism which worked to create an ambiguous definition of the situation and which, in turn, thwarted military intervention. The consequence of knowing the truth is decisive action, while the consequence of doubt, spawned as it is by relativistic thinking, is appeasement."[75] For Cushman, looking squarely at the facts with moral backbone is the foundation for a critical theory of war in Bosnia.

Although she recognizes traditional international affinities (German support for Croats, French support for Serbs, British benign neglect in general, and Americans who are strongly influenced by a Serb-American lobby), Ramet's disgust for this relativism is apparent. She finds relativism evident in complaints about the one-sidedness of media coverage, and in calls for war crimes indictments against Alia Izetbegović or in the rehabilitation of Serbia.[76] She follows J. William Fulbright's admonition that to have power and influence and fail to use them when the situation cries out for it is the worst kind of arrogance.[77] She writes:

> Beyond the sheer human suffering, the war had an impact far greater than skeptics were prepared to believe back in 1991 or even in 1992. To begin with, the West declined to defend either the Helsinki Accord, the Geneva Conventions, or the Genocide Convention of

1948, suggesting that the West either considers it impossible to defend these accords or no longer values them. Second, the established
principle of international law known as *uti possidetis* . . . under
which new states that emerged from the fracturing of larger states
were recognized with their preexisting administrative boundaries,
however they might have been drawn, has now been scuttled in
favor of the principle that aggression should be rewarded. Third,
given NATO's timidity and the eagerness of the West to place it
under U.N. authority, questions have now been raised as to whether
NATO has any practical military utility at all. . . . neither the U.N.
nor the West proved capable of defending either moral principles or
political order, then it is not clear why either the U.N. or the West
should be regarded with respect.[78]

From this point of view, if the West bore responsibility at all for these
wars, it has been because of its weak-kneed approach to recognizing
and challenging tyranny. The Dayton Accord is the clearest example
for Ramet of this limitation. Like Hayden, Ramet views the Dayton
Accord as a failure, but not because it was a constitutional sham. She
argued that those who brought about the war and their nationalist
allies should have been barred from politics altogether, rather than
secured in the peace plan. The media, which did so much to foment
the hatred, should have been censored. Moderates should have been
appointed to power, rather than count on elections to throw out the
nationalists. The Implementation Force (IFOR) should have had the
military muscle to guarantee freedom of movement, and not remain
powerless before nationalists themselves. "The design of the Dayton
system can, at best, serve the short-term interests of [Izetbegović,
Milošević, and Tudjman], the short-term interests of local capitalists,
and the short-term interests of the Great Powers."[79]

Ramet grounds her arguments in the natural law tradition, that
sense of moral law with universal validity, applicable to all equally,
whose postulates can be discerned by "unaided reason."[80] Although it
is part of the Western liberal tradition, it is quite distant from the
underlying normative guidelines of transition culture itself. With its
idealism and moral emphasis, natural law's principles can be at odds
with the technical and empirical grounding of transition culture in
markets. It is also fundamentally at odds with nationalism of any sort.
But in its application, natural law is certainly prepared to focus on that
nationalism which generated the others, and to overlook the ways in
which universalism can generate nationalism itself.[81]

Narratives of Responsibility

Although there are many more specific arguments than I have presented, one might identify three general approaches to the Wars of Yugoslav Succession in the Western literature adjacent to transition culture. One approach fixes on the *nationalist dynamic within* the former Yugoslavia. Primary responsibility is assigned to Serbian nationalism and militarism, while liberalism remains a clear alternative to nationalism or militarism. A second approach extends the field of analysis beyond the Yugoslav lands, and implicates liberalism in war. It complicates the nationalist picture by arguing that other features and other actors are also important to explaining the outbreak of war. This *global* approach assigns responsibility for violence to the collapse of federal authority and the relative strength of the military. Inspired by Western invitation, Slovene nationalism, though certainly more liberal than its Serbian counterpart, was the proximate movement to undo Yugoslavia. A third approach shares the emphasis on Serbian nationalism with the first approach, but focuses its narrative on Western inaction and relativism. This *interventionist* argument emphasizes the disproportionate suffering that has taken place, and the moral obligation for the West to do something about it.

Only the first argument suited transition culture well in the mid-1990s, for it is the only one that keeps a clear distinction between transition culture and nationalism's wars. In each of the other accounts, transition culture is implicated in nationalism's wars, but for very different reasons. In the first case, it at least facilitated the conditions for Yugoslavia's breakup. In the second, transition culture is critiqued for its failure to assume moral responsibility for human suffering.

These alternative positions have been assigned very different locations in nationalism's discursive field. The first and second positions struggle to retain that panoptic view of the wars, differing primarily by how they draw the field of interaction, with the first focusing on the dynamic within Yugoslavia, and the latter focusing on how the global environment shaped these wars. The third position, though grounded in universalist arguments against relativism, does not hesitate to identify arguments by their resonance with Serbian interests and ideologies.[82] Of the authors plausibly associated with the "Serbian interest," Robert Hayden has been the most directly criticized.[83] For his part, Hayden recognizes this:

A study of national conflict will inevitably be invoked by partisans for the parties involved and thus become, wittingly or not, part of one or another nationalist discourse. Such discourse, however, robs people of all identity except that of the nation; as Slavenka Drakulić has noted,[84] one is no longer defined by education, job, ideas or character, but only by national identity. In my case, in regard to Yugoslavia, such an identity would have to be imputed through marriage. (xiii)

While the fracture between Cushman and Ramet, on the one hand, and Hayden, on the other, is more open than most, explanations themselves are embedded in this nationalist contest. To find responsibility in Slovenian liberalism, constitutional nationalism, and German, Austrian, and Vatican support for Slovenian and Croatian independence is coded with Serbian interests. Those who emphasize the reality and consequence of cultural differences within Yugoslavia, the difference between symbolic and physical violence, and the balance sheet of war crimes cannot be accused of Serbian sympathy. Of course, some questions are of broad interest. What would have happened in March 1991, if forty thousand Serbian protesters had been successful in bringing down Milošević?[85] Although this was Ramet's question, Hayden's disgust for the Milošević regime would certainly lead him to appreciate an alternative drawn without Milošević (xiii).[86]

By contrasting Ramet and Hayden, one can clearly see how the field cannot be viewed with the panoptic innocence transition culture enjoys. Even so fundamental a question as whether Yugoslavia could have, and should have, been held together is fraught with national resonances.[87] Ramet indicates that by 1991 Yugoslavia's survival would have only been possible with Serbian "diktat" for "the chances of reviving Yugoslavia died long before the JNA's brutal assault on Slovenia in late June 1991."[88] Hayden, by contrast, admonishes U.S. Secretary of State James Baker for not having read the Federalist Papers 1–10. If he had, he would not have advised Yugoslav Prime Minister Ante Marković that the United States *always* supports democracy over unity (159). Once the JNA failed to prevent Slovenia's secession, Hayden fails to see how anyone could have been surprised by the violence that followed (151, 159).

Could and should the Bosnian Serb community's disinterest in membership in an independent Bosnia-Herzegovina have been respected? In this fractured discursive formation, democracy and the law do not provide an unambiguous answer. Ramet argues that democracy in

Bosnia meant respecting the will of two-thirds of its citizenry in its referendum on independence, and that the Bosnian Serbs illegitimately held the independent country hostage.[89] Hayden argues that the referendum and movement toward independence violated both the letter and the spirit of the republic's 1990 constitution. When Bosnian Serb politicians tried to use constitutional principles to prevent this outcome, Bosnian Muslims and Croats ignored this procedure at the European Union's urging (89–94).

Focusing in this way on the various accounts of the Wars of Yugoslav Succession, one can appreciate the difficulty of putting these wars at the heart of transition culture. Even if one is convinced that intervention is desirable in, or that transition is responsible for, these wars, the mode of explanation just does not fit with transition culture. It is not just that one is about making markets and the other about making peace. Institutional determinism can shape the confidence of transition culture's future focus, but the eventfulness of war demands recurrent reconsiderations of missed opportunities and unintended outcomes. Transition culture can overlook its nationalism, but accounts of war cannot avoid it. And when this eventfulness is combined with standpoints of interpretation, our sense of opportunity structure in transition culture is exploded. This became especially apparent in the spring of 1999.

NATO's War over Kosovë

The spring 1999 bombing of Serbia and the ethnic cleansing of Kosovë were mistakes. They were not inevitable, but the result of miscalculations on all sides. This, at least, was one explanation for how this round of events could have occurred. Tim Judah argued that, on the one hand, it "was widely assumed that if bombing began Milošević would give up after a day or two. . . . There were also real hopes that Milošević would be overthrown in Belgrade in the event of a NATO attack." On the other hand, Milošević

> believed—so all the available evidence suggests—that either NATO's threats were a bluff or, if they were not, the Greeks and Italians would cause such problems that the alliance would split or become paralyzed. With equal lack of judgment, he also believed that the fear of some form of Russian reaction would force a NATO climbdown. Another of Milošević's Rambouillet calculations may have been that if he accepted the deal his power—the only thing he cares

about—would have come under threat from the extreme nationalist leader Vojislav Šešelj, whom Milošević has kept on his side by appointing him Serbian deputy premier.[90]

Mistakes and unintended consequences are central to a critical, cultural, and historical sociology of social change. They suggest that certain cultural formations guide assessments of strategies and their link to outcomes. To understand the choices people and other agents take, one must understand the formation of their identities and the frameworks shaping action. Cultural formations thus mediate social change, but those mediations cannot be understood apart from events that potentially transform them. When events produce unintended results, or even worse, consequences distant from stated or even implicit intentions of the strategies that initiated them, frameworks must be altered. That, in turn, might change cultural formations themselves. These transformations might take place in broader publics, but under conditions of war, the cultural formations shaping the visions and strategies of influentials are most important.

One of the most critical transformations of transition culture has been articulated by the man who represents not only civil society and emancipation of the 1980s, but also the institutionalization of democracy in Central Europe in the 1990s. Václav Havel said in a speech to the Canadian parliament:

> The alliance to which Canada and now the Czech Republic belong is waging a struggle against the genocidal regime of Slobodan Milošević. This struggle is neither easy nor popular, and we can differ on its strategies and tactics. But there is one thing no reasonable person can deny: this is probably the first war that has not been waged in the name of "national interests," but rather in the name of principles and values. If one can say of any war that it is ethical, or that it is being waged for ethical reasons, then it is true of this war. Kosovo has no oil fields to be coveted; no member nation in the alliance has any territorial demands on Kosovo; Milošević does not threaten any member of the alliance. And yet the alliance is at war. It is fighting out of concern for the fate of others. It is fighting because no decent person can stand by and watch the systematic, state-directed murder of other people. It cannot tolerate such a thing. It cannot fail to provide assistance if it is in its power to do so.
>
> This war places human rights above the rights of the state. The Federal Republic of Yugoslavia was attacked by the alliance without a direct mandate from the UN. This did not happen irresponsibly, as an act of aggression or out of disrespect for international law. It happened, on the contrary, out of respect for a law that ranks higher

than the law which protects the sovereignty of states. The alliance acted out of respect for human rights, as both conscience and international legal documents dictate.

This is an important precedent for the future. It has been clearly said that it is simply not permissible to murder people, to drive them from their homes, to torture them, and to confiscate their property. What has been demonstrated here is the fact that human rights are indivisible and that if injustice is done to one, it is done to all.[91]

Havel's support for this war is remarkable, but indicative of a profoundly important shift in the cultural formations emerging from communism's collapse. It was tempting for East Central Europeans to avoid the horrors of war in southeastern Europe, much as transition culture has attempted to write the plot of transition without war's hell in its script. Many leading politicians in Hungary and the Czech Republic, fewer in Poland, argued against NATO's intervention. At least they did not stand up to support it. They would rather focus on their own country's peaceful transition, and to the extent possible, avoid their implication in war. This might make strategic military sense in Hungary, given its border with Yugoslavia, but the question was as much a matter of political contest in the Czech Republic. Neither the liberals' political leader, Václav Klaus of the Civic Democratic Party, nor the leader of the postcommunist Czech social democrats, Miloš Zeman, wanted to disturb the political status quo in their own country. They preferred to avoid comment. Former Foreign Minister Josef Zieleniec, however, challenged his countrymen and their political elites to assert where they stand, and whether those values are sufficiently European, and universal, to extend beyond their borders.[92]

Some of the most serious challenges to the NATO effort came from within Europe and NATO itself, however. The war nearly brought down the German coalition government of Social Democrats and Greens in mid-May. Germans were especially opposed to sending in ground troops. The extraordinary debates that have attended Germany's reconstruction of its cultural and political role in Europe after the horror of Nazi genocide in World War II made it nearly impossible for Germany to participate in a military offensive on the ground in Yugoslavia, especially with Greens in the cabinet.[93] Plans were in place for that ground assault, but fortunately for the German government, and likely the alliance itself, Milošević capitulated before those plans had to be carried out.

Even within Yugoslavia, one can identify dispositions that resonate with the kinds of arguments Havel and his allies made, even if they could not support the bombing. Milo Djukanović and Zoran Djindjić, president of Montenegro and head of the Democratic Party of Serbia, respectively, articulated the centrality of European identity, democracy, and morality alongside an emphasis on getting rid of Milošević:

> We remain committed to Yugoslavia's integration into Europe. . . . Only a democratic and stable Yugoslavia can secure stability in the Balkans. . . . Military intervention in Kosovo has led to new problems, whether or not that was intended. With intervention, the West assumed part of the responsibility for finding solutions to these problems. At the same time, intense efforts will be necessary on the part of Yugoslavs to win the trust of the outside world and recover the moral standing lost because of Kosovo. Even before the end of the war, the international community should state clearly and unequivocally that democratic and economic reconstruction in Yugoslavia represents its official and binding position. Such a statement would give hope to the citizens of our country and encourage the transformation of the political landscape. The cycle of politics that in the past 10 years or more has led our country to this tragedy must be broken. If the war ends with a signature on a peace agreement and the same leadership in power, with Slobodan Milosevic at the helm, the tragedy and the violence will continue.[94]

On September 24, 2000, slightly more than one year after the bombing, Vojislav Koštunica beat Milošević in direct elections for the Yugoslav presidency. However, Milošević insisted that Koštunica did not win the required 50 percent of the popular vote, and insisted that runoff elections between the two take place as scheduled two weeks later. The opposition, broadly aligned like never before in support of Koštunica's candidacy, planned the rebellion.[95] Drawing on the vigorous student movement Otpor (Resistance) and striking workers for the popular mobilization, and on the contacts within the regime held by former military leaders such as Vuk Obradović and local political leaders such as Čačak's mayor Velimir Ilić, Milošević was forced out. On September 29, workers occupied the Kolubara coal mine thirty miles from Belgrade to demand that those election results be honored, and faced down a police challenge on October 4. On October 5, hundreds of thousands of demonstrators flowed into Belgrade from across the country, and some of their number occupied and sacked two symbols of Milošević's power, the federal parliament and Serbian television building. The police shot off some tear gas, but the army decided not to provide reinforcements. By 7 P.M. that evening, the police gave up. The next day, Milošević conceded, and the end of Yugoslavia's isolation from Europe appeared to have begun.[96] Havel's hope that human rights be extended within Serbia might now be realized. The Cold War's end may have seen the making of a new barrier down the middle of the old Yugoslavia. Now, however, the West might aspire once again to a new universality with a new government in Serbia and an infusion of Western aid. Not only does Belgrade have cause for celebration, but the West does too. I attended one such celebration that anticipated this very outcome.

In New York City, just seventeen days before the Yugoslav elections, the American Friends of the Czech Republic, hosted by President Clinton through video and President Havel in person, assembled in a gala affair to recognize the U.S. Secretary of State Madeleine Albright with a "civil society vision award." Havel, whose authority in defining the virtues of civil society can hardly be doubted, and whose leadership in democratic state building is widely acknowledged, risked a great deal to support NATO's bombing of Serbia. That support was certainly offered in the spirit of extending human rights, and in elevating, in the words of Jürgen Habermas, a "society of world citizens" over realpolitik and its absolutist support for state sovereignty.[97] It also, however, was about consolidating the place of the Czech Republic in a Western tradition, secured by its American alliance. Madeleine Albright, the honoree of this dinner, embodied in her person those deep ties between the Czech Republic and the United States of America.

Linkages between the United States and the Czech Republic can be found, the evening's video suggested, in the immigration of Czechs to the United States. Secretary Albright herself celebrated the greatness of the United States with the observation that a "little Czech girl" like her could rise to such a position. President Havel observed that Albright was herself the most powerful Czech woman to have ever lived, and likely the most powerful woman in the world. Communism interrupted that close association between Czechs/Czechoslovakia and the United States, but now the United States and the Czech Republic were tied together like never before. General Wesley Clark elevated the significance of this tie with his observations on the war in Kosovë. He spoke of his pride in commanding troops from the Czech Republic and other countries in transition in this humanitarian intervention. And he had special praise for Albright, whose leadership led to intervention. She was the one who asked what good having all this military might was if it could not be used when necessary.

From my distant seat in the hall, it looked as though one phase in the making of transition culture was over and a new one had begun. NATO secured the ties between East Central Europe and the West. Transition culture, always premised on its opposition to dictatorship, was once defined by a distance from socialism measured by the embrace of the market. When it came to military intervention in Yugoslavia, however, markets could not provide sufficient justification. Human rights, that other side to civil society around which the struggle for emancipation in 1989 was waged, were now more prominent in the definition of Western affiliation. This is more, however, than a shift in emphasis from 1989. Now, rather than civil society emancipating itself, the most powerful woman in the world and the world's most intellectual president stood united in their conviction that the world's most powerful military alliance could bring Serbia into Europe, and ensure the rights of Kosovar Albanians.

Within a month, Albright's gamble, and Havel's vision, appeared to be right. If transition culture is any guide, the contentiousness of this end to history will be written out of the story. It no longer matters whether these were nationalism's wars or a consequence of the Cold War's end. Military intervention in the name of human rights laid the foundation for Serbian civil society to emancipate itself, ten years after the rest of communist-ruled Eastern Europe. Or so might the postscript to that celebration be written.

If Koštunica's government promises what many in the world hope, transition culture will now be extended to Yugoslavia. Much as the International Commission recommended in 1996, the task can be seen as twofold: to facilitate "the transition process from state socialism to market economies" and to deal with the "impact of war and sanctions."[98] Transition culture will be complicated by the legacy of war, but I would expect that transition culture will also be transformed as it confronts the inadequacies of its own cultural formation.

Transition culture depended on the clear conviction that socialism was historically exhausted and that the West was there to help postcommunist countries realize an alternative, and normal, future. Transition culture worked with a teleological sense of time, in which current developments are interpreted within a framework of their fit with a desirable future understood through the institutionalization of a market economy and democratic polity. National differences certainly existed, but in celebration of multicultural variety rather than in the anxiety over competing interests. We began to appreciate the limits of this framework for understanding, and engaging, social change as we moved beyond those national communities and social groups whose cultural association with the West resonated with their own imagined community and future. Estonian Russians from our focus groups wondered whether their own discontinuous history was the result of U.S. strategy rather than the Soviet Union's implosion. Residents in Ukraine wondered whether they lost more than they gained in transition, as they focused more on the past than on some radiant future. Even Polish managers wondered whether mulitnational corporations would keep Polish interests at heart as they managed global transition. These anxieties are likely to be magnified many times over in postwar Yugoslavia.

First of all, it will be hard to imagine that the West, and especially the United States, can be constructed positively, or even neutrally. Although there certainly are accounts that place primary responsibility for the violent end to Yugoslavia on the shoulders of Slobodan Milošević and the nationalism associated with him, these are not the only plausible accounts, and certainly not the only ones that are consequential within Yugoslavia. There is a powerful sense within Serbia, and beyond, that the West *made the crisis* that now needs to be undone. During the spring 1999 bombing campaign, Maria Todorova said:

> They [the West] severely and consistently mishandled the situation in Yugoslavia during the past decade, and instead of contributing to an accommodating and compromising spirit, they have in fact exacerbated (without creating) the process of the ugly disintegration of Yugoslavia. In the concrete recent crisis, they came in unprepared to handle a humanitarian disaster that, according to their own protestations, they knew was going on or was inevitably coming. In fact, they actually created it. When the refugees came pouring in, Emma Bonino, EU Commissioner on Humanitarian Aid, suggested that Romania and Bulgaria should take the bulk of the refugees since this was a regional problem. The West also came in unprepared (not physically but psychologically) to see through its mission to the end. NATO members actually stated firmly their conviction up front, that they were not going to jeopardize the life of a single one of their civilized citizens for any Balkanite. . . . As a result the West has severely destabilized the Balkans.[99]

Transition culture's practitioners associate the West with the rule of law, and the societies in need of transition with its absence. Some within Serbia have even charged that the June 2001 extradition of Milošević to The Hague violated Serbian law. The rule of law can challenge not only those in transition, but also global actors who define transition. During the intervention, some international lawyers charged that NATO's bombing strategy broke international law by focusing on civilian targets.[100]

Beyond the question of law, there is also one of morality. Transition culture associated the socialist past with moral bankruptcy and the denial of freedom. The Milošević regime will certainly be accused of even worse crimes against humanity, but some ethicists have charged that NATO conducted an "unjust war" in its efforts to overthrow Milošević. In a just war, one cannot endanger citizens without putting one's own soldiers at risk.[101] NATO clearly privileged its own pilots' lives over those of innocent Serbian civilians in its strategy to bomb Belgrade, Novi Sad, and other sites, rather than undertake what many thought at the time to be more effective, if riskier, low-flying military sorties over Kosovë.[102] Koštunica's victory and Milošević's extradition might make these questions disappear, but I suspect that that might be wishful thinking. Although wishful thinking, based on a commitment to presumably universal principles, has helped to make some effective "self-fulfilling prophecies" in East Central Europe, that very disposition has been disastrous in the southeast.

Hayden criticized NATO's attack, and the reasoning Havel and other advocates of this intervention offered. He did not deny Serbian war crimes, but he also looked to the contradictions of intervention in regard to international law and constitutional logic, and to intervention's unintended outcomes. As he describes it:

> The Rambouillet document synthesized the least workable features of Yugoslav and post-Yugoslav pseudoconstitutionalism, destroying Yugoslav sovereignty in Kosovo while pretending to acknowledge it, and providing for a transition to "democracy" that would, once again, ensure the complete domination of the majority ethno-national group. In the end, the idea that NATO was supporting a multicultural polity in Kosovo was as believable as Franjo Tudjman's proclamation of Croatia as "the most democratic state on earth" as he presided over the expulsion of that republic's largest minority. To top it all off, NATO itself waged a war of international aggression, mainly against civilians, in order to bring about the situation in which the

ethnic majority of Kosovo would become sovereign in the territory and expel the minority. Perhaps fittingly, Kosovo in 1998–99 presented a recapitulation of the demise of Yugoslavia in the early 1990s: a contradiction between the maintenance of an established state and self-determination for a local minority, addressed by fraudulent constitutional proposals in order to set the stage for massive violence, and ultimately, secession and the ethnic homogenization of seceded territory. (167–68)[103]

Hayden argues for a different ethic of responsibility, especially in light of these contradictions and (unintended) consequences. These wars were the consequence of an international law and practice founded primarily on a commitment to principles. Hayden does not deny their value, but he wonders about their "sufficiency." Certainly, humanitarian principles were not primarily in operation, he notes, when the United States acquiesced in what Richard Holbrooke called "a milder form of ethnic cleansing" in the expulsion of Serbs from Croatia in 1995.[104] They were, rather, following an ethic of responsibility based on an anticipation of long-term consequences. Hayden only wishes that the West had done that earlier, and supported the redrawing of boundaries or the movements of populations following the victory of nationalists in the 1990 democratic elections. The wars began, he argued, because Western diplomats and politicians "acted on what they wished to believe rather than on the evidence of what was most likely to happen" (164).

One of the most critical outcomes of NATO's military intervention in Kosovë has been the redefinition of transition culture itself. Transition culture promised a new world order, open to all so long as they embraced the premise of democracy and markets. It was directed against the partition of Europe, against the Berlin Wall, forever the symbol of the division between the free and the unfree, the prosperous and the oppressed. Entry into the European Union was the institutional expression of this admission to a united Europe. Joining NATO was not, it was argued, an aggressive statement, but rather a principle of admission to an international order whose stability would be reinforced by military alliance. NATO's admission of Poland, Hungary, and the Czech Republic was an expression of transition culture's own effort to be inclusive, and the support of those nations for the entry of the Baltic states, Romania, Slovakia, and other countries reflects that progression. After NATO's intervention, NATO plays a new role, and a new cultural formation is emergent.

Even if transition culture's core principles move from the extension of the market to the defense of human rights, its nationalism becomes simultaneously more apparent. NATO now represents a potential threat. As one Ukrainian diplomat said in the aftermath of the bombing, to win her public's support for NATO's expansion was always difficult, but one strong argument was that NATO was a *defensive* alliance, not an aggressive one.[105] Now, regardless of the justice of the cause, NATO's bombing of Serbia has caused those outside of NATO, especially those with cultural affinities with the Serbs, to worry whether NATO might pose a threat to *them*. The Russians articulate this concern most obviously, but even the Ukrainians, with tens of Ukrainians dead in Novi Sad as a consequence of NATO attacks, wondered what NATO represents, and what transition means. Does it mean a new opportunity for all, where markets and human rights are part and parcel of a new expanded Europe? Or does it suggest a new curtain falling across Europe, with the Slavic orthodox on the poor and endangered side?

Barely one year after this pessimism, a more optimistic interpretation was possible. To ignore Milošević's terror in Kosovë, one might argue, would have represented a worse exclusion than NATO's attack appeared to symbolize. Ignorance of war crimes could have signaled the final exclusion of "the Balkans" from Europe, and the opportunity to overlook developmental possibilities as they have been overlooked in Africa, or as war crimes were overlooked in Rwanda, Somalia, Liberia, Eritrea, and Ethiopia. With the election of Koštunica and the extradition of Milošević, however, there appears to be a new chance for a new Europe. But we can hardly treat the future as a smooth extension of an optimistic present. The history of the years since the fall of communism makes it difficult to treat transition culture's institutional determinism as a substitute for a cultural and historical sociology of postcommunist social change that might, in turn, constitute the analytical core of critical transition culture.

Conclusions

Over the same decade in which the Polish Solidarity movement initiated emancipation from communism, Yugoslavia began its descent into hell. Valerie Bunce nicely recast Timothy Garton Ash's now famous rap of tens in communism's downfall: it took Poland ten years, Hungary ten months, and East Germany ten weeks to end communism, but it took Czechoslovakia only ten days.[106] Yugoslavia, Bunce reminds us, also took about a decade to end communism, from the death of Tito to the collapse of its federal structures.[107] Yugoslavia, however, was rarely considered in the frame of transition. When transition's proponents wrote, "countries have varied in the pace at which they have been able to put in place the components of a successful transformation to a market economy—and in their economic performance,"[108] they hardly had in mind barriers such as the violence described earlier. After NATO's intervention and Koštunica's election, postwar postcommunist capitalism cannot be left out of transition culture. The war-torn must now become a central part of transition culture's plot. But even before this transformation, postcommunist war shaped transition culture.

Transition culture's vision and practice depends on its construction of others, as the preceding chapters have emphasized. The meaning of transition has been defined through its antagonism to socialism and those qualities derived from it. Transition culture has also been formed through its labilities, most notably in relation to nationalism. Although transition culture suggests internationalism with its emphasis on free trade and convertible currencies, we have also seen that it rests in nationalism's discursive formation. In fact, it is quite dependent on it for success. Transition culture can acquire meaning and consequence through its support for a "return to Europe," and its opposition to the return of Russian empire in Eastern Europe. However, in order for transition not to appear as yet another imperial imposition, it has to appear to be of the nation, for the nation. Its relationship to violence like that described earlier is another matter entirely, however.

One powerful, but insufficiently acknowledged, condition of transition's making is the peace with which communism's end was produced throughout most of Eastern Europe. Although transition culture typically emphasizes the system's historical exhaustion, in chapter 1 I argued that its end could have been colored very differently. Instead of negotiating communism's collapse among those who could resolve fundamental differences peacefully, violent confrontations could have accompanied the system's last months in Poland. It is hard to imagine anything so gruesome as what happened in Srebrenica in July 1995 happening in Poland, but before the 1990s, it was hard to imagine anything so horrible happening in Srebrenica. Peaceful change in Poland was a contingent outcome of strategic action by the party, the church, and Solidarity, much as Srebrenica's violence was the result of strategic action among a very different set of actors. Poland's peaceful resolution set into motion the conditions that allowed Poland's transition to take off, whereas ethnic cleansing, systematic rape, and liquidation have put up obstacles to "transition" in the lands of the former Yugoslavia with which Poland has never had to deal. Social peace has been a condition of success among transition's exemplars, but it has remained for the most part an unacknowledged condition. It has not been explicitly theorized to the extent that it ought to be. This chapter has focused on the significance of peace in transition culture by examining how war has been framed in nationalism's terms and distanced from transition itself. War became transition's alternative.

An alternative to transition is different from its opposite. Nationalism's wars work differently in the making of transition culture than socialism does. Within transition culture, socialism is explicitly acknowledged and used to define the problems that need to be overcome, or need to be explained away. Transition culture claims to understand socialism, perhaps even better than it really does. With that understanding in hand, it can treat those in despair as reflections of that past failure. Suitably disempowered within transition culture, those in despair can be treated as a generation lost, or, more generously, left in a safety net.

Nationalism's wars function differently, and in a much more complex way, within transition culture. Until NATO's 1999 bombing and Koštunica's election, they were rarely the subject of explicit analysis in transition culture. Rather, they functioned as a distant threat, belonging to peoples whose own nationalisms are responsible. Transition culture would not only claim innocence before war, but it also would not claim to offer any fix either. At best, it could offer a potential remedy once wars end. Despite that distance, nationalism's wars animated anxieties about transition's alternative modernities, and transition's implication in making those wars. Those anxieties rest, I propose, in the unresolved relationship between transition and war. In psychoanalytic terms, war was at the heart of transition culture, but it could not be looked at directly.

One way to hide its presence in transition culture was to assign the Wars of Yugoslav Succession to a regional cycle of unremitting nationalist warfare. Those approaches that fixed explanation within Yugoslav nationalist dynamics fit easiest with transition culture's innocence, but this was an uneasy resolution. After all, some analysts drew the field of responsibility differently, implicating global social change and Western policy and practice directly in making Yugoslavia's hell. Others denied that association vigorously, arguing that Milošević and his nationalism were to blame, but they also indicted the West for its indifference to crimes against humanity. NATO's war over Kosovë changed the whole debate, however. Intervention now defined the West's relationship to the Wars of Yugoslav Succession, and forced it to redefine the meaning of transition.

Transition culture's interventions have been organized around the assumption of technical superiority in understanding how to make markets and democracy, with little value assigned expertise in history and culture. Transition culture's technical emphasis enabled the feint of political disinterest, and a relative distance from arguments that challenge the culture's core presumptions. Western military intervention in Yugoslavia changed that. *This* intervention could not be guided by technical concerns. Moral claims had to mobilize support and investments. Although technical expertise in war making and peacemaking was critical, expertise in history and culture could not be shunted aside. Contentiousness, rather than being an unfortunate intrusion into a relatively determinist tale, had to be implicated in the task of intervention itself.

Exploring the relationship between intervention and nationalism thus has had to become central to the problematic of transition culture, rather than neatly hidden in appeals to universalism. Addressing the past, rather than fixing on the future, has also become necessarily more important. With the election of Koštunica as president and the "return" of Serbia to Europe, transition culture now must figure out its place in Yugoslavia. And with that engagement, critical transition culture might find its own place, where the claims of those dispossessed by transition are taken to the heart of analysis and intervention, and the contentions over nationalism might become part of transition culture itself. The mantra might even change. From dictatorship to democracy and from plan to market might be extended to include transition as freedom and the accomplishment of peace.

Conclusion

Critical Transition Culture

The cultural formations of postcommunism are no simple reflection of something more real. Transition culture has shaped the strategies and practices of all sorts of actors, from the World Bank to those whose lives have been turned around by the movement "from plan to market." Transition culture has made a radically new process of social change sensible by emphasizing certain processes, competencies, and epistemologies in its elaboration. The study of movement from plan to market, for instance, has privileged not only economic and business expertise in the comparative study and institutional design of transition, but it has also privileged knowledge organized around the remedy of lacks to realize a desired and known future. And transition culture has shaped our sense of postcommunist social change with its focus on institutional design and elite agency in peacetime conditions. Transition culture has itself become possible, however, because it has found its place among preexisting, if variably enduring, cultural formations.

Transition culture has been built upon a global liberalism constituted in opposition to socialism, understood not only as a political-economic but also a cultural system. Although transition culture has been remarkably open to making former communists its proponents, it identifies appeals to socialism and its accompanying competencies and desires as part of a past that must be transcended to realize a radiant future. Transition culture's relationship to nationalism is even more labile, however. In some circumstances, the two reinforce each other, when, for example, Poland and Estonia find their national destinies in transition culture's embrace, and transition culture finds its success in its articulation by exemplary liberals in successful postcommunist societies. In other circumstances, nationalism figures as transition culture's dangerous alternative, in the tardiness of Ukrainian transition, in the threatened return of Russian communists to power, or in nationalism's Wars of Yugoslav Succession.

Transition culture rests on the notion and experience of emancipation, even if the more critical elements of 1989 were excised in its translation into transition. The mobilization of civil society across a wide array of social circumstances provided the constituency for which internationally sanctioned opposition intellectuals negotiated with communist authorities for freedom. Transition culture's freedom has designated, however, the self-reliant middle class, with the support of authorities in alliance with globalization's architects, to be the agents of progress.

In this volume, I have sought to identify and analyze transition culture and its supporting cultural formations. I have analyzed transition culture in theory and practice across different sites of postcommunist social change, and its historical and cultural bookends in 1989's emancipation and in the ensuing Wars of Yugoslav Succession. I have tried to constitute a *critical* transition culture, one that is more "self-conscious about its historicity, its place in dialogue and among cultures, its irreducibility to facts, and its engagement in the practical world."[1] This conclusion will summarize my findings and suggest their relevance to an emergent articulation of inequality, peace, and freedom that might constitute the core of critical transition culture.

Emancipation, Transition, Nationalism, and War

During the 1970s and 1980s in communist-ruled societies, civil society was more than a social location in between the state and the private sphere. Civil society was also a discursive intervention that intellectuals used to bring together a number of disparate activities into a single counterhegemonic movement for which they could be spokespersons. The second economy, the underground cultural world, nationalists of relatively democratic persuasion, labor and other social movements, and other activities "autonomous" from the state were not only bound together by their common enemy in the communist-ruled state. The articulation of civil society gave them a positive reference, something around which their autonomous activities could cumulate in positive struggle. The intellectuals' suffering and struggle to be independent and critical enabled their claim to leadership and empowerment to articulate the common vision. The identification of civil society also enabled the expression of an international alliance that would not be cast so easily as hostile, but rather compatible with emancipatory desires for freedom, and its expressions in pluralism and publicity.

At the same time, however, this intellectual leadership was not a natural expression of civil society's wishes. It was, rather, an expression of hope based on the social mobilization of various capacities within civil society, and rooted within a culture of critical discourse that was the intellectuals' distinction. That distinction, however, had powerful national variants, especially when it came to reconciliation with their communist opponents. Poland's mobilization in Solidarity led the struggle for emancipation, but it also found negotiation with communists morally challenging and politically difficult. Hungary's civil society, if with a more narrowly mobilized class base, nevertheless provided the greater spark for emancipation. It had an easier time negotiating the political architecture of an emancipated Hungary with erstwhile oppressors. Gorbachev's *perestroika* provided the enabling condition for emancipation, and was motivated by an enormously flexible vision of socialism that broke most conventions with which the Communist Party was thought to lead. The interaction of all three led to the emancipation of Eastern Europe. And freedom from communist rule from Moscow came to be understood in terms of transition.

Transition—the movement from plan to market and from dictatorship to democracy—is animated by a particular culture of values and competencies, and centered in transnational organizations and compatible national bodies that promote it. This community of discourse is rife with debate, but its membership is recognizable by the common assumptions and contests in which they engage. Their stories typically revolve around the inadequacies of existing institutions and mentalities. These lacks become the basis for understanding and intervening in the system, based on knowledge of a desirable future organized around a form of global integration dominated by the West and international financial organizations. The culture's analytical rhetoric emphasizes the importance of global transformations and the comparative study of interventions in making social change. Societies are relatively equivalent in this culture, and the successful can become exemplars for the rest. Estonia, for instance, is disciplined and open to the world, while Ukraine is beset by a parliament that obstructs privatization and has an economy grounded in the informal. This general theory of history, its specific mode of comparison, and the particular characters attributed to nations in transition organize not only the interventions of organizations, but even transition culture in practice.

One core activity of transition culture consists in making better business organizations, and through it the entrepreneurial spirit and culture of risk, opportunity-seeking, and self-reliance posed as the disposition of success. In practice, many of the ingredients associated with a multinational transition culture are retained, most notably in the identification of socialist attributes as a thing of the past to be superseded. At the same time, however, practice transforms the ascription of qualities, if not the criteria of assessment. East Europeans struggle to transfer the ownership of transition culture from expatriates to the indigenous in their contest over claims to competence. The opposition between a socialist past and a capitalist future is retained, but the local value added tends to be enhanced when the indigenous do the accounting. East European managers realize some of that emancipatory potential embedded in transition culture when they realize a new fusion of competencies, shifting the locus of innovation out of the core of the multinational world into emerging markets and emancipated nations.

The reach of transition culture is, of course, limited. It is a sine qua non for membership in the multinational corporation. To the extent the owners and managers of other firms must work in a global capitalism, they too will be affected by the terms of transition culture, if less completely defined by them. Beyond the world of business, most appreciate the opening of the public sphere, but when popular culture is vulgar and information is propagandistic, the value of freedom might not be recognized as much of a bargain when despair becomes the principal emotion organizing one's assessment of transition. Embrace of transition culture in the postcommunist world varies considerably by social group, but it is also deeply affected by its articulation with the nation.

Two men from Lviv focus groups were exemplary in this enunciation. Their Ukrainian nation was individualistic and resonant with that entrepreneurial culture that is the radiant future, similar to what they see the Baltic nations to have already. Estonians, however, articulate transition not only as a movement from plan to market, and away from dependency toward self-reliance, but also away from Russia. Even Estonian Russians recognize some value in this geopolitical movement, but they also express resentment for the particular interpretations of openness to the outside world and freedom that accompany communism's end in Estonia. They can critique Estonian nationalism, however, within the bounds of transition culture.

The sense of transition culture is less coherent, more pervasive, and more difficult to escape than was the ideology that accompanied communist rule. At the same time, transition culture's flexibility and contradictoriness offer considerable space for critique along some dimensions of injustice and social problems within the bounds of the discursive community. Poverty, for instance, is an increasingly central theme of the World Bank, even if it has been relatively marginal within transition culture's principal contentions. Estonians are particularly good at expressing the limitations of transition culture and suggesting transformations for reconstructing its practice within its broader framework. Not only, for instance, should the broader international public be concerned about the environmental catastrophes that military pollution has left in its wake, but the public and its local authorities should mobilize in order to take advantage of the global alliances available after communism's end. This articulation of opportunity through transition culture is not, however, widespread, especially in those places racked by ecological, and economic, catastrophe.

In places such as Ivankiv, Sillamäe, Donetsk, and Olexandrivka, it was difficult to articulate the preceding decade's improvements in 1996. Hopelessness, hardly a disposition likely to energize self-reliance in civil society, overwhelmed many in our focus groups. Their sense of the world was much more local, and rooted in national experience, or Soviet times. Appreciation for the Soviet past was relatively great in these conditions. Travel was not only allowed over the relatively vast expanse of the USSR, but life was more secure, and people felt more needed. Indeed, people were, apparently, kinder back in Soviet times. Even those whose national attachments were disposed toward transition and the West—the women of Lviv, for example—could lament the loss of civility in transition's course. Everyone misses something from Soviet days, perhaps, but variable articulations of the nation and of transition enable those expressions of loss to be more and less legitimate. To be an advocate of transition, for instance, means to accept the loss of civility as a cost of the new society. Or it means searching for a way to restore it beyond the bounds of what transition emphasizes.

Few turn to religion per se in our focus groups. A wider number discusses the importance of values, and a return to modeling appropriate behavior in public. It is unfortunate, the women of Narva lamented, that honest men cannot be successful. Indeed, the lack of virtuous character in public office only reinforces the conviction that conspiracy was at work in communism's collapse. Although the advocates of transition might not emphasize the corruption of power and privilege, but rather its systemic inadequacies, those who lament the loss of civility are quick to see that men in search of their own fiefdoms were the cause of crisis. In the vision of the dispossessed, Soviet-type society did not collapse because of its own inadequacies but because its leaders betrayed it and the public for which the system was supposed to function. Few might heed the call for the resurrection of an Adolf Stalin, but the betrayed see little reason to believe in transition either. For transition culture to realize its promise, and to avoid its hell, it must attend to the victims of transition and not wait until violence commands its attention. It might even look to the past to find a better way to translate socialism's virtues into the society made by transition.

Transition, therefore, might actually be facilitated by looking toward the socialist past to discover how its relative strengths, civility apparently among them, might be brought into the fusion of qualities that make transition a more appealing description for the future of the dispossessed. This hermeneutics between the past and the present offers a remarkable complement to the translation of transition that the architects of markets and democratic stabilization emphasize. Instead of segmenting itself from that socialism, instead of identifying the future in terms of the utter negation of the past, transition culture might find a more creative reconciliation with it. We might anticipate, then, a transition made not by negating socialism, but by establishing a more creative fusion with some of those elements that people miss, civility among them. At the same time, transition culture would also profit from the recognition of the lability of its own liberalism with its constructed other in nationalism.

Nationalism's study has typically focused on the demonic part of postcommunist social change. With socialism vanquished and a threat only as a habit to be expunged, transition culture's impetus had to come from a new present or future danger. Nationalism certainly provides that, especially when it leads to war. But nationalism is hardly war's explanation.

Many within transition culture debunk "ancient tribal hatreds" as a sufficient explanation for the Wars of Yugoslav Succession, but they nevertheless implicitly accept the idea that modernity's drive toward national homogenization is the key distinguishing feature explaining war's making in this part of Europe. Others, at a greater distance from transition culture's core, implicate the West itself more in war's making, or at least in the deepening of the conflict. The West has helped to constitute the militarism structuring the end to the Cold War, and it has also provided the exit option for those nations that find the weight of Balkan history too much to bear. It is morally right, and politically expedient, to identify nationalist demons, and certainly Slobodan Milošević did everything he could with his policies to ensure that the peaceful negotiation of fundamental differences could not be realized in Yugoslavia. At the same time, however, the fall of the Berlin Wall and the expansion of Europe made it even more reasonable, and desirable, for Slovenia and Croatia to seek a future in the Europe to their north and west rather than to their south and east. In this sense, the emancipation of Eastern Europe aggravated the nationalism of those left on the poorer side of the emerging Europe, even as it made liberal nationalism apparently benign.

Like its earlier incarnations, the 1999 War of Yugoslav Succession challenges the conceptions of civil society and nation that were at the founding and legitimating moments of transition culture. For some, NATO's bombing of Serbia, and the indictment of Milošević as a war criminal, made the peaceful resolution of fundamental differences impossible. The West's innocence was also directly questioned by challenging the legality and justice of the NATO bombing. This ferocity from a distance and indiscretion toward innocents certainly resonated poorly with the peaceful grassroots struggle for pluralism, legality, and publicity that characterized the emancipatory praxis of civil society in the making of 1989. At the same time, NATO and Europe could have left Milošević alone to expel Kosovar Albanians from their home, and thereby complete the strategy for ethnic cleansing with which he had been associated. In that light, Czech president Václav

Havel declared NATO's military intervention just. This spokesperson for and symbol of civil society's peaceful emancipation from communist rule spoke in favor of the war on Serbia so that the universalism of that emancipatory promise might be more completely realized. Although few Serbs would agree, the Serbian democratic revolution of fall 2000 can be constructed as the vindication of Havel's vision. Without the military humiliation occasioned by Kosovë's occupation in the wake of NATO's bombing, one can argue that Vojislav Koštunica would not have had the shoulders of a mobilized Serbian civil society on which to stand in order to take his place in presidential office, and return his nation to Europe.

Whatever Havel's intentions and history's outcomes, however, the danger of nationalism within the rhetoric of universal hope rings loudly to those who stand indicted for their particularisms. This association between the universal promise and the appearance of national privilege in its utterance is, of course, not at all new for those who have breathed the spirit of Johann Gottfried von Herder. He elaborated his doubt over the French Enlightenment's claims to universalism through his articulation of national distinctions.[2] Likewise, in the articulation both of transition and of military intervention against the Milošević regime, it is difficult, if not impossible, to escape the nationalist trap. Even as Koštunica stepped into presidential office after an election and mobilization of civil society against Milošević, he could not express appreciation for a bombing campaign that affected innocent civilians of his own nation. And certainly the Western alliance cannot easily celebrate the military victory to realize human rights without denying the systematicity of its own violations in NATO's bombing campaign.

I do not mean that transition culture or Havel's broader rhetoric on human rights is a conspiracy of Americans, Zionists, and/or Czechs, as some nationalists might argue. Rather, the language of nationalism is inescapable, and malleable. If one is not of the nation, one is automatically suspect; but if one is of the nation, one can be charged with treason. If one assumes that Estonia and Ukraine are equivalent units in the making of transition, one is trapped by nationalism's false assertion of national equivalence. Size and relational space make Ukraine and Estonia obviously different places. But if one tries to explain why Ukraine cannot succeed so easily as Estonia according to the scales established by the owners of transition culture, accounting can sound like apologia. If one articulates a fear for national survival in the face of great imperial power, as Estonians might, nationalism can leap to the lips of the unsympathetic listener. To dismiss the reasonable security concerns of the small nation, however, means that one likely identifies with a homeland with past, present, or aspiring superpower status.

Nationalism is pervasive, and works in articulation with other cultural formations. Rather than use it as a label with which to stick others, or to distinguish oneself, I have argued that it is more useful to see how nationalism is implicated in the making of other cultural projects and social practices. Indeed, if social explanation is our ambition, it is useful to consider how nationalism, liberalism, and socialism are themselves mutually implicated in transition's making. If direct, rather than passive, intervention is our ambition, we might also explain how these cultural formations might be rearticulated to recognize a wider range of people whose fates matter, and whose voices should count more than they apparently do.

I hope to have contributed to this final effort in this volume, for I have aspired to give voice to those expressions silenced within transition culture. I have elaborated the views of men and women in transition culture's marginal communities, as well as those illegitimate expressions of national resentment within transition culture's core. In that fashion, I have sought to identify some of the limits to transition culture's explicit formulation. I have also endeavored to elaborate the structural logic of its explicit formulation, not only through the enunciations of its *prominenci*, but also by its practices and artifacts. I have thus sought to name the course of transition as a cultural formation, and place this global culture within a particular historical conjuncture between emancipation and war.

In keeping with his record for rhetorical accomplishment, Timothy Garton Ash has described this conjuncture as follows: "If the Solidarity revolution in Poland was the beginning of the end of communism, this [the Serbian democratic revolution of fall 2000] was the end of the end of communism. It was the last of a twenty-year chain of new-style, Central and East European revolutions, each learning from the previous one but also adding new ingredients and variations."[3] One should trace this revolutionary learning, but it would be unfortunate to think about the connection only in terms of the virtuous, and these twenty-some years only in terms of founding moments and forward movement. Emancipations deserve their history, but their implication in postrevolutionary change is even more important.

Emancipation birthed transition culture. It provided indigenous grounding for the global transformation of the nation represented by transition, but emancipation's translation into transition also excised several important features of communism's end. Importantly, emancipation was founded on the extension of civil society, but transition has depended on civil society's contraction and constitution in the middle class and the making of markets. Although war and its making have been distanced from transition culture's explicit enunciation, they invisibly, but necessarily, occupy its core by posing such violence as the hellish alternative to transition's success, or geographical extension. The abiding threat presented by a fourth Russian empire and symbolized by a second Chechen war inspires smaller nations to think of transition as not only a political-economic transformation, but also a security blanket. Transition also neatly overlooks its own nationalisms even while it depends on the nationalisms of others to explain war's making and transition's innocence before the violence in the former Yugoslavia. At the same time, because it distances violence from its own social process, transition culture fails to articulate one of its greatest successes in the *peaceful* quality of its transformation. It therefore focuses on those processes of social change that are linked to the making of markets, and not to the assurance of a broader conception of human security that might be identified through freedom, emancipation's core idea, and peace, its unacknowledged condition.

I have sought, in Bourdieu's words, to realize one of the greatest contributions intellectuals might make: to name those things that are repressed in order to enable a wider public to reflect on their meanings.[4] Although this sociology has focused on intellectual and cultural practices well beyond my discipline and the academy per se, it is also a reflexive enterprise. I have embraced what is, at least for Bourdieu, sociology's properly scientific starting point: to analyze the community of transition's discourse of which I am a part, even if I am on its margins with my cultural emphasis.[5] However, transition culture might not be able to afford culture's marginality for long.

As the United Nations Development Program (UNDP) report argues, inequality has risen dramatically within the postcommunist world, suggesting one profound failure across the board.[6] The UNDP does not reject the fundamental economic recommendations of transition culture, but it does alter its cultural frame significantly. It is not end points, but starting points, not pathological lacks, but existing social problems, that should organize our analysis and intervention into post-communist social change. As the public debate within the West over "who lost Russia" illustrates, there are also many within transition culture itself who argue that transition policies associated with the World Bank and the International Monetary Fund made Russia more corrupt and dysfunctional than it would have been otherwise. It has also led, however, some of those who have been core to transition culture to rethink their ideas about the threat to the good society. George Soros in particular now finds "market fundamentalism" and chaos to be as much a threat to the open society as tradition and dogma.[7] In the wake of NATO's bombing of Serbia and Milošević's fall from power, the nationalisms that were at one time exiled from transition culture's purview have now moved to its analytical and political center as Europe moves into the Balkans, and the Balkans return to Europe. Those contentions and standpoints characteristic of assigning responsibility for war may now migrate to the heart of transition culture. Finally, the very global transformation around which transition culture organized its vision of adaptation has become increasingly political.[8] In the 1990s, globalization and its subset of transition may have been perceived as an economic transformation, but in the new millennium it has become overtly political.

Transition culture faces substantial transformation. It will find itself in crisis if its practitioners fail to recognize and transform the culture organizing their work. And without that reflexivity, transition culture certainly will not realize its potential in emancipation.

The cultivation of critical transition culture can contribute to the realization of that potential in two broad ways. It can work to clarify the cultural formations with political consequences underlying what appear to be transition's academic debates. It also can help to reformulate transition culture's critical edge. Although I have dedicated this volume to that clarification and reformulation of transition culture, I have not worked at the core of my own discipline. Sociology's traditional focus on inequality is not at the center of transition culture because of inequality's complicated location in the cultural formations of postcommunism. However, as the UNDP report suggests, inequality is one of the gravest problems facing postcommunism, and one of the greatest challenges facing transition culture. It is not, however, only a matter of analytical focus. It is also a question of articulating inequality with postcommunism's alternatives, and that takes us directly to critical sociology, this volume's animating impulse.

Postcommunist Inequalities and the Polish Round Table

With its respect for the complexity of difference and the eventfulness of social change, critical sociology is deeply embedded in a tradition of inquiry that searches for how things could have otherwise been. Alternatives within modernity—whether systemic in the distinction among democratic capitalism, fascism, and communism, or more incremental in the focus on the transformations and endurance of patriarchy, racism, and colonialism—provide the animating impulse for inquiry into the conditions of the reproduction and transformation of social life. Critical sociology has also sought to illuminate the lives and possibilities of the oppressed and marginal. By clarifying the conditions of their oppression and the possibilities of their empowerment, critical sociology often expressly allies itself with social movements as a force for social change. Putting these two interests together—in alternatives and praxis—critical sociology has been obliged to focus on the conditions of power, if only to understand better how forms of domination reproduce themselves so that they might be transformed.[9] For some critical sociologists, therefore, the study of postcommunist social change has been a disappointment.[10]

The project has been largely defined as one of variation in, and not alternatives to, capitalism. It has focused on elites designing change or moving around property rather than on publics and classes, men and women, adjusting to and reshaping transition.[11] Sometimes these studies focus on the end point of transition in markets and democratic publics and thus read social change through a lens dictated by that anticipated path. In its more institutionalist expression, the path begins with communism's collapse, and future trajectories are established on the basis of the configurations of communism's initial power and loss. Despite the eventfulness of social change in this world region, paths appear to be institutionally set while the consequences of opportunities are written into the tales privileged by those who focus on big structures. In these ways and more, the study of postcommunist social change appears to be quite distant from critical sociology's cutting edge on the theory and practice of emancipation.

Nevertheless, a significant amount of analytical effort has been devoted to inequality's study, critical sociology's starting point and one of sociology's core concerns. These works typically begin with some variation on Gerhard Lenski's classic question of social stratification: who gets what and why?[12] Two authors go so far as to say that such questions of inequality "have dominated all theoretical discussions among sociologists of postsocialist or reforming-socialist societies."[13] Other sociologists promise to build a theory of social change around questions of stratification.[14] Was it the nomenklatura, those with higher education, or those in the opposition who reaped most of the benefits of communism's end? Knowing who benefited from the change, the argument goes, might help us understand the meaning of the change. If the nomenklatura, we might think about this system as "political capitalism" rather than anything else, given the importance of political power in defining privilege.

This set of questions has spawned an enormous amount of scholarship with terrifically interesting findings. For example, one study reports that it is not the old system's ruling class, but the assistant directors of enterprises, who have profited most from the deals to be made following communism's end.[15] Regionally speaking, one would expect political capitalism to have a strong base in Hungary, where the "small transformation" rested on the transfer of political assets into private capital.[16] Szonya Szelényi finds, however, that "the overwhelming majority of former elites (71.5%) were unable to retain their elite positions, with one-third of them (36.9%) experiencing short-range downward mobility into the professional-managerial sector, and another third (34.6%) experiencing long-range downward mobility into the working class or into forced or voluntary retirement."[17] Political elites have faired especially poorly. In Poland, the data appear to be more mixed, but one leading Polish sociologist, Jacek Wasilewski, argues that "the nomenklatura as a whole neither enfranchised itself within, nor dominates the private sector; and it had not retained its political and bureaucratic positions. At the same time, the nomenklatura cannot be considered the main victim of the revolution."[18] The connotation in Wasilewski's remark hints at the indigenous ideological reference of this inquiry into political capitalism.

These studies of inequality in state socialism always have a regional edge. Of course, data tend to come from some places more than others, Hungary far more often than Ukraine, for example, but the nature of the questions themselves also has a regional inflection, and the results of scholarship have cultural and political consequence.[19] While the normative structure of inequality's study might be generally well articulated in relatively stable cultural formations associated with American society, transition culture's labilities have made the cultural connotations and consequences of inequality's address less obvious.[20] I have already demonstrated the ways in which transition culture's scholarship comes to be implicated in contesting competencies over the direction of firms, and over recollections of social change in communism's collapse and sequels. Scholarship in inequality's study also informs the cultural formations of postcommunism, but not necessarily in ways that are most promising for the development of a critical transition culture that extends peace and freedom. Although this question must certainly be investigated in a variety of contexts, I can rely on the setting I know best to illustrate the complexity of inequality's argument in shaping postcommunism's alternatives.

Writing in 1995, in the wake of Aleksander Kwaśniewski's first defeat of Lech Wałęsa for president, Radek Sikorski, a deputy minister of defense during the earlier Jan Olszewski government, tried to explain how a former communist could beat the Nobel Peace Prize–winning hero of the Solidarity movement.[21] Although, to be sure, Kwaśniewski was charismatic, and Wałęsa bumbled, Sikorski argued that the problem lay in postcommunism's founding moment. He described the Round Table as the "original sin of the opposition" that produced a compromised regime, run by a timid prime minister who was overwhelmed by communists still in charge of defense and internal security. Ultimately, "The Round Table talks between the dictatorship and the pro-democracy forces, held at a mansion outside Warsaw called Magdalenka, had a public facade of antagonism and a secret agenda of collaboration." This charge is made even more compelling by choosing his comparisons carefully.

Sikorski looks with envy to Czechoslovakia, with President Václav Havel as the philosopher king and Prime Minister Václav Klaus as an exemplary leader. He envies their leadership, but Sikorski also laments Poland's lack of revolution. The proper death of communism required a real ritual, he believed, complete with skirmishes with the police and dancing in the streets as they had in Prague. Without mass participation in communism's overthrow, there is too much suspicion that things remain the same. Even without the revolution, lustration could have completed that revolutionary ritual in Poland, just as it had in Czechoslovakia.[22]

For Sikorski and his colleagues, the treachery of the Round Table is not so much that it was intrinsically wrong, but that it allowed the communists to continue their influence in politics, and even win in democratic contest. Consequently, the evil of the Round Table was not just that Solidarity's negotiators compromised with communists, but that after communists held no more power, the negotiators stuck to the deal they forged under conditions of communist rule. In 1988–89, they had to compromise with communists because they had no other choice; but after 1990, when freedom reigned and Eastern Europe was emancipated, they could have moved on and completed the revolution. The treachery of the Round Table was that the negotiations stuck.

Within the cultural formation whose analysis Sikorski exemplifies, proof of the Solidarity "Magdalenka" faction's treachery lies in its support for "nomenklatura capitalism." Those Round Table *prominenci* legitimated this political economic injustice with their publications— *Wprost* and *Gazeta Wyborcza*. The latter's chief editor is Adam Michnik, the man whom the right hates the most in the Magdalenka faction, who is said to have gone out of his way to launder former communists into respectability.[23] Michnik's personal and subsequently publicized conversations with the communist who imposed martial law, General Wojciech Jaruzelski, and his reference to Jaruzelski as "my friend" in public statements inflame the passions of those on the far right.[24] They also alienate those who at one time admired Michnik but now consider him off the mark, and even, sometimes, insufficiently Polish.[25]

Some of these themes reappeared during a conference my colleagues and I organized at the University of Michigan in 1999 to investigate the meaning of the Polish Round Table accords of 1989.[26] Using the transcript from this Polish-language conference, we can treat this public event as we did our focus groups—as an opportunity to learn about variations in the ways in which people account for postcommunist history and social change. Understanding these 1989 agreements as the historical foundation for transition culture (chapter 1), we also can discover ways in which transition culture can be contested using traditional arguments of American critical sociology. The political capitalism thesis, as Sikorski suggests, is one of the most important themes for those who wish to criticize the Round Table, but its political resonance is unlikely to be one that most critical sociologists beyond Eastern Europe would embrace.

One of the conference speakers, Wiesław Chrzanowski, an early Solidarity adviser, one of the founders of the Christian National Union, and a former marshal of the Sejm, argued that the Round Table was a *consequence* of the system's collapse, not a *cause* of the system's decomposition. After all, he notes, "several months after the Round Table, together with the fall of the Berlin Wall, other communist regimes in Central Europe, except for Romania, collapsed peacefully" (28).[27] This Round Table was not, in his opinion, a means to end communism. Like Sikorski, who looked to other regimes that collapsed shortly afterwards, or like Valerie Bunce, whose institutional determinism found communist rule not viable, Chrzanowski argued that communism was on its last legs. The Round Table did not facilitate communism's end; rather, it was a way for some to improve their position in communism's collapse.

For Chrzanowski, the communist authorities developed this idea of the Round Table as a way to co-opt that opposition, and to smooth their anticipated fall from power. The authorities thus tried to shape their partners through negotiation, so that they could get the best possible deal out of communism's end. The opposition also saw this as an opportunity. To be sure, these negotiations would lead to some of the goals of the opposition—"broadening the margin of freedom, restoration of legal Solidarity and preventing some sort of frontal collision" (27). Chrzanowski also saw, however, that this was an opportunity for the "leftist opposition" to "eliminate or limit the influence of the right wing of the opposition," by which he meant nationalist or Christian Democratic elements (ibid.). Alongside this political advantage comes some privilege, some "advantages" (28), what he later called "frosting" (123):

> as a result of the discussed agreement [the Round Table], the pre-June government camp [the communists], instead of capitulation and punishment for the past, found its place smoothly within the new order of parliamentary democracy and retained its material and organizational assets. The accepted formula of state law often serves as a cover from punishing lawlessness. Among gains of the other partner was the ability to make personnel decisions regarding the negotiated one-third of the 1989 Sejm seats. . . . As for taking over important mass

media, it's enough to mention *Gazeta Wyborcza*, presently Mr. Michnik's paper, the publication of which was a concession from the government to Solidarity arranged at the Round Table. (29)

Although Chrzanowski is a conservative lawyer and political leader,
his account draws quite clearly on a "radical" portrait of society in its
linkage of power and privilege.[28] He very clearly identifies a dichoto-
mous view of society, which of course was hardly limited to the right-
wing opposition. But his assessment of the Round Table is more specific to the right wing, and akin to radical pictures of inequality that
link the exercise of power to the quest for privilege. Chrzanowski
quite clearly attributes this motive to the communists' Round Table
participation, but he also implies that his former, more leftist, colleagues in Solidarity had some of the same ambition (123).[29]

Adam Michnik was quite disturbed by Chrzanowski's charge.
Michnik countered that Chrzanowski was creating a "black legend"
associated with the Round Table, by arguing that this agreement was
made for the profit of those who negotiated, rather than for the good
of Poland. It is true that Michnik's newspaper is one of the most successful papers in Poland, and in Eastern Europe, but his witty reply to
Chrzanowski suggests one reason for its success: "You worry that I
have 'frosting' from *Gazeta* and I'm happy that Poland has a good
newspaper. And I'm happy that no other postcommunist country has
a good paper like that. And I wish you and your political friends could
make another such daily and we will have two best newspapers" (126).

Wittiness aside, this exchange cuts to the heart of one of the most
politically delegitimating issues associated with the Round Table, and
to its succeeding transition culture. Was this a "secret deal" cut between communists and certain parts of the Solidarity opposition to
produce advantage for all of the negotiators? Even Bishop Aloyzy
Orszulik, who was most closely associated with the negotiations of
the Round Table, expressed disappointment with inequality's distribution ten years later. After all, he said, the decade's transformations
have hurt workers and peasants the most. They are the victims, they
are the poor, of this transformation. And in contrast,

> Some people from the [communist regime], well, even a lot of them,
> have remained well off, in a good situation, not just because they
> kept their apartments, but also because of their salaries and opportu-
> nities to get employed in some other lucrative work. I remember when
> Mr. Sekuła [a former leading communist] was leaving, immediately

the Japanese offered him the position of an expert, I think 150,000 zlotys a month. Today, I'm looking at myself in retrospect, and, as a seventy-seven-year-old, having been formally employed at the Secretariat of the Episcopate for thirty-three years, I have a pension of, I think, about 430 zlotys before taxes, and after taxes 396 zlotys. So, that's some act of injustice too. (259)

Those who adopt a "radical" perspective on the Round Table negotiations, and examine the link between the interests of the powerful and the process of change, and the link between power and privilege, are likely therefore to find something less than heroic about the Round Table.[30] And they are likely to indict one particular man in the process.

Although Michnik is often painted as a man of the left, he resembles much more a conservative when it comes to the Round Table. He paints the Round Table as a political device that served the values of Poland, not of any one particular group. And he finds embedded within the Round Table's method of transformation an alternative model of society worth emulating.

Of course, Michnik believes that each side had a strategic goal— the communists "sought to gain a new legitimacy for communist rule in Poland and abroad, and allowing some form of legalized opposition was to be the price for that. The strategic goal for the Solidarity opposition, on the other hand, was the legalization of Solidarity and launching the process of democratic transformation" (10). There were no secret deals, as Lech Kaczyński and others also affirmed, but it *was* a compromise. And, as Michnik noted, all compromises produce subsequent accusations of betrayal by "extremists" (16).

Michnik also believes that although this Round Table negotiation did not produce an ethos, it was embedded in a different kind of climate "that made it possible for the two worlds, which spoke two different languages, to communicate" (108). Indeed, he learned in that context that although this communist viewpoint was reprehensible in some ways, it was also far more influential than he or his colleagues had admitted. He argued that even those who

accepted the communist government for their own benefit are a component of the Polish nation, which cannot be excluded from Poland, unless one wants to destroy the Polish national community. And this is what I learned at the Round Table. There are two philosophies. Today, we can either say to those people, who used to be my enemies then, and who used to lock me up in jail . . . we can say: "You have an opportunity either to become friends of democratic independent

Poland, a Poland which is oriented toward the West and has a free market economy, or you can make a conscious choice and opt for the status of an enemy of the new Poland." In other words, there are two philosophies faced by any group reaching out to participate in the government after the times of the communist, totalitarian, or paratotalitarian dictatorship. Two logics. The logic of reconquest and the logic of reconciliation . . . reconquering the country is a deeply antidemocratic logic in the sense that it really undermines the plural-istic character of our society. (109)

In this sense, Michnik seeks to elevate a certain value that he learned at the Round Table, and a different way of thinking, a different identity for the Polish state (234). This identity, based on a philosophy of agree-ment, presumes that "those who fought against the People's Republic and those who served the People's Republic" are both part of a demo-cratic future (16).

This "defense" of the status quo produced by the Round Table is certainly conservative in its broad appeal to a united society. More, it produces a kind of radical resentment not only for the privilege associ-ated with some of those who sat around the Round Table, but equally for those who would turn the Round Table into a heroic legend. If this is pluralism, it is also injustice, argue the radicals on the right. They say that Michnik and his allies are imposing a vision of Poland that is in fact one born at the Round Table, in the deal made between the "reds and the pinkos." And here is the irony. Those who find func-tional value in the Round Table's making are painted as pinkos, while conservatives in Polish politics articulate the critique of power and privilege that has traditionally belonged to the "radical" tradition.

Academic inquiry into political capitalism is clearly important for assessment of the Round Table and the transition culture it produced. If one finds that communists (and in Poland the Solidarity figures with whom they bargained—the "Magdalenka" faction) have been privi-leged in the making of postcommunist capitalism, one also finds support for the arguments that Poland's conservatives make over transition's ille-gitimacy. Of course, if one does not find that kind of privilege, it under-mines the conservatives' argument, but it also misses Michnik's point.

Transition and Peace

If Poland has a chance—and I believe that she does—it lies in
people's ability to talk to each other without hatred or hostility.
                                        Adam Michnik[31]

I know that one has to respect the arguments of others. It's not a question of black versus white but of trying to understand the other side. This doesn't mean that one can reach agreement on every point or identify completely with the other side, but we can understand each other. This is the most important thing.

Wojciech Jaruzlelski[32]

For those who embrace the conservatives' radical critique of the Polish Round Table, such statements aggravate the deep wound made by the 1989 compromise with communists. How could such reasonableness be cultivated with Jaruzelski, whose treachery to the Polish nation was exemplified by his imposition of martial law?

When the University of Michigan invited Jaruzelski, his chief of internal security General Czesław Kiszczak, and former Prime Minister Mieczysław Rakowski to participate in the 1999 conference on the 1989 Round Table, those who embraced this radical critique found a huge political opportunity, and mobilized resentment in both Poland and the United States. Those in Chicago organized a "Not Welcome Committee" that sought to prohibit the arrival of those communists most responsible for crimes against the nation.[33]

As I read letters sent to protest their arrival, I became more convinced that it would be an academic failure if we *failed* to invite communists who negotiated the end of the system if they were as evil as the letters' authors suggested. After all, what transformation of identity could lead those who are accused of being responsible for the deaths of Polish citizens to produce a systemic transformation in which they would give up power peacefully? Nevertheless, the moral certainty of those who wanted to indict communists for past sins despite their involvement in *annus miraclum* unnerved me. Pope John Paul II helped. His Holiness, his secretary of state wrote, hoped that

> this disciplined reflection on the spiritual, cultural and political aspects of Poland's peaceful transition to democracy will highlight their ultimate foundation in a moral imperative arising from man's innate dignity and his transcendent vocation to freedom in the pursuit of truth.[34]

This letter was fundamentally important not only because of its ultimate author, but also for the alternative frame in which it invited us to consider the events of 1989 and their aftermath. Although this fragment invites far more discussion than I can consider now, it is important to note its invocation of peace. Where does this question of

peace sit in sociology's debates over power, privilege, and radical social change?

The radical tradition in inequality's study, whether articulated by
radicals or conservatives, does not place this value at the center. To the
extent that radicalism is associated with revolution, and to the extent
that revolution is defined, as it has been classically, by its association
with violence, radicalism can overlook the violence of praxis in its
focus on the systematic oppression of inequality. Those who emphasize inequality rarely position Michnik's interest in talking without
hate in the same place as those in conservative traditions might. In regard to the Round Table itself, Michnik's critics hardly consider the
potential of violence attending communism's end. But even Michnik's
supporters do not emphasize their peace work. Peace, while underlying the end to communism, is rarely articulated as one of its core
values. And without that, it can hardly be developed as a core concern
of transition culture. That limitation is, I would propose, reinforced
by the articulation of inequality in the radical tradition in global sociology and its potentially consonant conservative currents in the cultural formations of postcommunism.

Consider, for instance, how Chrzanowski's views on communism's
collapse fit with most conventional theories of revolution. On the one
hand, the system was weakening through its own internal contradictions, and on the other hand, the opposition was growing stronger
and stronger. Communism's structural collapse was imminent, and
the measure of the revolution could be assessed by the size of the victory over the oppressors. This simple analogy, however, overlooks the
method by which the opposition sought to grow stronger.

Zbigniew Bujak, a leader of the underground resistance from 1981
through his capture in 1986, described the movement's strategy at the
conference. It was not interested in street confrontations and demonstrations. Each time it tried to "overcome the other side with armed
struggle," it would lose. Hence, it decided that "fighting without violence was best." Of course, there were other possibilities:

> in the very first days of martial law, some young people decided to
> get arms. They tried to take arms away from a policeman, a shot
> rang, and that policeman was dead. The uniformed police were not
> our opponent and we didn't really fight against them. Our real rival
> was the secret police. So that was a dramatic and unnecessary death.
> However, of course, the young people who were active in the under-

ground structures were in fact getting armed. They were simply buying weapons, buying grenades. . . . We did succeed, however, to persuade those young people that that wasn't the right way to follow. If
we entered that path, we would lose, because the other side really
wanted this. And we also know that this provocation to push us into
the terrorist position had been prepared. But we managed to defend
ourselves from this, and I'm going to be honest about it, it took a
real effort. These weapons I've mentioned were actually sunk in the
Vistula River and it was all thanks to [the fact that] the people who
were at the head of those underground structures understood our
strategy. (37)

Bujak identified Mahatma Ghandi and Martin Luther King as the movement's models (39). Of course, it also had national religious inspiration.

Not everyone in the Polish opposition was Roman Catholic, but
the Roman Catholic Church was clearly supporting Solidarity in its
peaceful struggle. The church served as a "witness" to the negotiations, but everyone knew whom the church supported. Pope John
Paul II even supported Solidarity over and above an attempt to introduce unions expressly affiliated with the church, recognizing that the
communists sought to divide and thereby weaken the opposition (38).
Before it would go to Magdalenka to negotiate in private, the opposition, of both Catholic and non-Catholic orientations, would assemble
at the episcopate. Bishop Orszulik recalled, "One time, there we go,
we go downstairs, myself, Bishop Gocłowski, all the others. . . . We
are almost approaching the door and Mazowiecki says, 'Listen, but
we have to go to the chapel first to pray.' And all of us turned back, all
of us knelt down, and all of us prayed. And that was unity. One team,
one squad" (155). This was more than a ritual. Solidarity, as a value,
meant something profound. Orszulik described it:

There was only one value for us, Solidarity. And within Solidarity,
there was everybody, people of various political orientations. Therefore, we took great pains during the early encounters with the government side, when there were attempts to exclude Mr. Michnik and
Mr. Kuroń, to . . . we were against that, just as Wałęsa was at that
time, believing that there was need to create a broader societal spec-
trum, background, so that the success of those talks would be more
real. So, nobody painted the left as Trotskyites, dangerous for the
church, and, by the way, at the Round Table we were not concerned
with the church itself. Our concern was focused on the nation, the
country, changes in the country, improvement of the situation in
Poland, the life of the people. That was our concern and not dividing
people into those we liked and those we didn't like. (148–49)

This was solidarity. Not only a collective organization necessary to advance the cause of the powerless against the powerful, but also a moral value, an ethical principle animating peaceful struggle. Bishop Dembowski illustrated some of that ethic in his recollection on the meaning of "enemies" for the church. He was quite impressed by the words appearing at the beginning of one of John Paul II's pontificates: "The church has no enemies, even though there are many people who consider the church their enemy." The bishop painted the communist authorities likewise: they were not his enemy, but "the authorities placed themselves in opposition to society by imposing a socioeconomic system and atheism" (114). Through this critical sensibility, Solidarity could produce a vision of the future that was open to those who would repent, and join society. In this sensibility, born of Saint Paul and reproduced by Father Józef Tischner, solidarity was understood to "bear one another's burden" (115). In the struggle against communism, it is difficult to imagine bearing the burden of the enemy, but perhaps it was imaginable to bear the burden of compromise in the search for peace and freedom. And that meant establishing dialogue with those who represented, in the logic of revolution, the nemesis of freedom.

I asked Janusz Reykowski to serve on a Round Table conference panel that addressed ethics. This world-renowned social psychologist initially resisted the idea, thinking that his contribution would be negated by the fact that he negotiated for the communists. Those who suffered most, and who look more like saints than he, could hardly give him ground to be ethical, he feared. However, he also understood himself to be one of increasingly few liberals in the Polish United Workers' Party who believed in dialogue during the 1980s. When the authorities imposed martial law in 1981, most reformers left the party, and most of those who remained opposed any compromise with the enemy known as Solidarity. Those who opposed compromise have not, however, disappeared with the Round Table's resolution. They continue to argue that the problem was compromise itself, and the weakness of communist leadership. During the conference, Reykowski recalled the recent observations of one prominent communist:

> "The wrong people were in power. Had we removed them on time, had we got rid of Jaruzelski, Rakowski, and Ciosek, and replaced them with real socialists and real patriots, then the whole Round Table would not have been necessary. Look," he said, "what has

happened, how many people have been pushed into poverty now, and how many fortunes have been made by stealing state property, by both the former nomenklatura and the new nomenklatura."

Reykowski continued, and articulated the possibility of this man's vision becoming a real alternative in 1989:

> there was a moment, that was between June 6 and 8 when people who were thinking along those lines mobilized and flooded the Politburo and the Secretariat with their demands to annul the election results, when they prepared an experts' report that the only solution was to annul elections. And there was a dramatic struggle caused by that report, and an effort to neutralize that kind of thinking. If you say, ladies and gentlemen, as Marshal Chrzanowski has said, that the army would not have supported that kind of demands, I will say, well, it's better that we didn't have to check that out. (112)

This view of the Round Table as treachery, as betrayal, can be found on both the communist and the conservative sides. Both sides believe in the rightness of struggle, and the importance of avoiding compromise with the enemy. Both take the image, if not the reality, of political capitalism and gross inequalities as justification for indicting the value of the Round Table and the transition culture that followed it. Communists and nationalists could produce the very violence that motivated Reykowski to struggle for negotiation and Bujak to throw the weapons in the river. Although Bujak and Reykowski were on opposite sides, they shared an important value: the peaceful resolution of their fundamental differences. Perhaps we should therefore see the legacy of 1989 in terms not only of the road from plan to market, or of the debate over who gets what and why. Perhaps 1989 represents a new way of envisioning social change. As "Solidarity's theologian," Father Józef Tischner, put it:

> For me already, the Round Table was the expression of our own political creativity—like Solidarity. Solidarity had the ideational resources of Christianity. And the Round Table had the resources in Solidarity. These two conceptions—Solidarity and the Round Table—incarnate the very Polish road to a peaceful passage from the world of revolution to the world of peace.[35]

From plan to market or from revolution to peace? Although transition culture is clearly built around the former, the motif of peace, embodied in the Polish Round Table, allows us to recognize an unacknowledged condition of transition and a critical legacy of 1989. The end to communist rule was not only about laying the foundations for markets, or even about opening up the public sphere to plurality and electoral contest. It was also about bearing the burdens of others, about being able to talk with others without hatred or hostility, and about reconciliation. It was about a new culture of communication based on tolerance and inclusion. And this legacy becomes even more important as transition culture increases its implication in *postwar* postcommunism.

This framework for thinking about the Round Table is idealized, and, to be sure, one not likely to be accepted by those for whom the Round Table represents immoral and unnecessary compromise. It does, however, have the virtue of encouraging us to consider how certain kinds of identities and strategies facilitated movement toward the peaceful resolution of fundamental differences, and not only toward the market. It invites us to reconsider those conditions that work toward compromise, and those that work toward confrontation. Indeed, it invites us to compare not only Poland and Czechoslovakia in the race toward completing the anticommunist revolution, but also to compare Poland and Yugoslavia to determine why one country moved to a world of peace and the other to war.

Nationalism provides the easiest answer. Poland's nationalism was directed toward the Soviet Union, and it allowed political opponents at least to recognize one another's common membership in a national community. Yugoslavia did not have an external opponent—or rather, its external opponents could be found within the former Yugoslavia.[36] But this approach, while institutionally sensible, also minimizes the struggle that Bujak, Rejkowski, and others undertook to ensure that no events would spark violent confrontations. In the absence of such events, it is easy to overlook history's eventfulness, and then it is productive to recall the ways in which particular events set up cycles of violence in the Soviet Union.[37] Focus on nationalism also allows one to overlook the constitution of other cultural formations of postcommunism that make some trajectories of social change obvious, while others go unacknowledged and ill conceived.

In this volume, I have worked to name and elaborate transition culture, one of the most significant cultural formations of postcommunism. I have discussed cultural formations around nationalism, war, and emancipation as well, but mainly to clarify the conditions of transition culture. I have also suggested that a focus on the concentration of privilege and on political capitalism contributes, unintentionally for some but deliberately for others, to a radical conservative critique of that transition culture which has developed in Poland, that transition culture also may be facing an important transformation within Poland's elite political culture. Let me be explicit.

Poland's radical conservatives stress the need to continue the struggle against communists. This promises to transform that dimension of transition culture that focuses on the future and treats socialism as something already anachronistic. The radical conservative strategy seeks to bring the past to the present in order to shape an alternative future. Poland's conservative leftists—those who negotiated at the Round Table as well as their political allies—are the mainstays of transition culture, and have in large part defined that course. However, they must develop a new cultural formation with which to defend themselves against the charge of injustice animated by radical conservatives. They must develop an alternative nationalism, defined by a new Poland that embraces pluralism and reconciliation internally and integration globally. Unfortunately, this is also a Poland beset by radical inequalities, the best fodder for mobilizing Poland's radical conservatism. Transition culture could be at risk if these inequalities do not become a central part of the cultural formation inspired by the Round Table. It is at even greater risk beyond Poland, which at least remains an international exemplar of transition culture. Fortunately for transition culture, its leitmotif in freedom has been radically reconceived in ways that promise to realize transition's emancipatory hope, if it can be reworked for critical transition culture.

Transition as Freedom

Before liberalism established its hegemony over discussions of economic change, when socialism was still a viable alternative shaping the critical imagination, we would not be speaking in terms of transition culture at all. The terms of engagement would lie primarily in the contest between capitalism and Soviet-type socialism and the search for a third way. The search for a third way has died many deaths, however. Its first mortal blow came in 1968, when the Prague Spring and the ambitious economic theories of Ota Šik and others were killed by the invasion of Warsaw Pact troops.[38] The third way suffered further when, during the 1970s and 1980s, brilliant East Central European economists became more and more involved in liberal economics, arguing with increasing conviction and power that there could be no third way.[39] The gradual economic collapse of self-managing socialism in Yugoslavia reinforced their position. The last major hope for some kind of third way rested with *perestroika,* and what Tatyana Zaslavskaya called the "second socialist revolution."[40]

Zaslavskaya and her colleagues from Novosibirsk provided Gorbachev and others with an inspiring argument about how Soviet society wasted the human factor and its natural resources. Consistent with democratic-socialist precepts, she argued that the solution rested in the democratization of society and work, while nonetheless compensating people more appropriately for the character of their contributions. Increasing autonomy for enterprises was important, but she also argued that producers needed to be directly connected with each other, rather than subordinated to the mismanagement of state administration.[41] It is not my intention, nor my capacity, to argue whether her ideas could have worked had Gorbachev and his advisers understood better the limits of their own capacities to steer change.[42] I only point out that discussions of the third way, especially in terms of the struggle to develop a vision of democratic socialism, have faded, and have been replaced with a third way based on a new progressivism whose translation into transition is not obvious.[43] Even when the "left" has returned to power, or to influence, in Eastern Europe, it has not produced much of an alternative to transition culture.

Left parties in postcommunist countries have promoted a "social market" approach: they advocate or develop social policies that focus on those hurt most severely by transition. Sometimes, as in Poland, they develop innovative social programs—regarding pension reform, for example. Sometimes, as in Russia, they call more simply for a return to the rights of state socialism, but without much sense of how this might be achieved in the new economic and political environment. When the social-democratic successor parties came to power in Hungary and Poland, they followed relatively liberal political-economic policies, confirming their own location within transition culture. Communist parties in Russia and the Czech Republic are more ideologically opposed to transition, but their arguments reflect opposition to transition culture rather than any serious articulation of a third way. They are not even very social-democratic. As Linda Cook, Mitchell Orenstein, and Marilyn Rueschemeyer concluded in their volume on these parties, "left parties in postcommunist Europe are not advocating . . . social democratic policy. Instead, they have either defended the socialist welfare state against a neoliberal or ad hoc dismantling, or taken a more centrist position, apparently speaking more to the median voter than to a purely left constituency on social policy matters."[44]

Longing for a third way is implicit, however, in some of the critiques inspired by marxist theorists such as Michael Burawoy.[45] Burawoy has demonstrated the irrationality of capitalist transformation in several workplaces, from Hungary to Russia, and argued for the significance of recognizing the value and innovation of greater democracy on the shop floor. This argument, however, cannot move with the kind of confidence that marxist theory once offered, for it does not have behind it an alternative systemic framework with which to challenge the articulation of national economies with capitalism. Its only serious alternative rests in looking at Russia through a China lens, rather than through the Western prism that transition culture highlights.[46] Instead of expanding political freedom at the same time as one introduces market reform in a space as large as China, or Russia, this perspective suggests that one must retain the strong state with a less than democratic spirit. In the case of places with as much space or variety as Russia or China, viable transition might have to be an authoritarian capitalism rather than the complete package that transition culture has promoted.

That might be the third way left in the contest between capitalism and socialism, but it is hardly one that draws on the legacy of the Prague Spring or other democratic socialist perspectives. Although marxism remains a powerful critical lens through which transition might be viewed, and its suffering documented, I have not found within its engagements with the postcommunist world any great sense of emancipatory hope. There is, however, just such an alternative brewing in terrific proximity to transition culture.

Amartya Sen is trying to shift the terms of debate beyond an apparently anachronistic contest between capitalism and socialism toward a more radical critique (if radicalism rests in the potential for consequential intervention and not only distance from core precepts).[47] Rather than developing a core position by accessing different institutional theories, as marxism tends to do, Sen begins his work with an argument for the priority of freedom. Development, he argues, should be understood in terms of "expanding the real freedoms people enjoy," which means that intervention should focus on expanding those substantive freedoms directly, rather than attending to the distant mediating institutions that are supposed to produce it (3). Freedom, he argues, is heterogeneous, or at least it can be constrained in a number of ways. Famine constrains freedom. Inadequate health care or dangerous biophysical environments constrain freedom. Poverty constrains freedom. Gender inequality constrains freedom. The absence of political liberty and civil rights constrains freedom. Cultural repression constrains freedom. Both economic insecurity and physical insecurity constrain freedom. Both inappropriate processes and inadequate opportunities in any of these realms, and presumably more, constrain freedom. With this emphasis, Sen redirects our attention to agency, to the capacity of an individual to bring about change, and to participate in those conditions of life that make both individual and collective conditions of life better (19).

As an economist, Sen works within a theoretical tradition that has focused on income poverty; he suggests that this tradition move to think about capability deprivation more broadly. That tradition also works typically with data that are broad and systemic, as poverty rates are. But he pushes the tradition further, to put mortality, and not just incomes, across gender and region, at the heart of analysis. These indicators are useful to assess how different structures, and policies, shape forms of unfreedom. At the same time, however, Sen is sympathetic, as is James Wolfensohn, president of the World Bank, to a kind of "comprehensive development framework" in which the liberalization of markets is combined with the development of social opportunities and the expansion of freedoms of other kinds (126–27). Sen is therefore very sensitive to how culture and the evaluation of priorities affects individuals and their choices.

Sen rejects, prima facie, the sanctity of tradition over the right of individuals to choose the form of life they pursue (and therefore rejects from the start any argument that denies education to any group or an open media to any subject). However, he also argues that individuals must be given the freedom to discuss, debate, and select the values with which they assess their choices: "It can indeed be argued that a proper understanding of what economic needs are—their content and their force—requires discussion and exchange" (153):

> Extreme inequalities in matters of race, gender, and class often survive on the implicit understanding . . . that "there is no alternative."
> For example, in societies in which antifemale bias has flourished and

been taken for granted, the understanding that this is not inevitable may itself require empirical knowledge as well as analytical arguments, and in many cases, this can be a laborious and challenging process. The role of public discussion to debate conventional wisdom on both practicalities and valuations can be central to the acknowledgment of justice. (287)

Basic civil rights and political freedoms are therefore indispensable, Sen argues, for producing those social values that might allow institutional engagements of injustice. But it is not, as he implies, primarily a question of political and civil rights. It is also about how culture works to enable discussion and exchange to take place.

Culture is deeply entangled in discussions of development as freedom when the capability "to choose a life one has reason to value" are normative guides to inquiry rather than assumptions never to be explored (74). Cultural analysis is also critical to understanding the makers of global public policy, as Sen reminds us in his discussion of how English attitudes toward the Irish contributed to the Irish famine of the 1840s (173–75).

Transition, like English policies on Irish famine, is embedded in culture. The policies of the World Bank, or of national ministries of finance, are rooted in tacit understandings of the cultures that go with markets, that are embedded in nations, and that are left by communist rule. Sen himself reproduces some of that general perspective in his brief remarks about the postcommunist countries even as he criticizes shock therapy and those who were overly enthusiastic about the "magic of allegedly automatic market processes" (264–65). He follows Adam Smith to argue that markets require institutional structures and implicit codes of behavior to make them function properly. But he also follows transition culture when he implies that the cultural problem lies in Eastern Europe and the former Soviet Union.

Sen's intervention in the World Bank's theory and practice represents a significant expansion of the logic of development, in terms through which the Bank itself can work. It offers an immanent critique of the Bank's argument and practice. It does not, however, provide all the assessment the Bank needs to realize the challenge Sen levels. Sen's argument does not address the internal and external power relations that make some kinds of projects feasible while others are left on the shelf. It does not provide all the methodological guidance or technical advice that might enable freedom to become the central guide to the Bank's work. His arguments are also focused on particular parts of the world—or at least they do not address a world in transition from communist rule. I nevertheless find his arguments of incredible value for envisioning a culture of transition that is consistent with the emancipatory hope of 1989. It requires, however, a particular twist to realize its relevance.

Although Sen recognizes the significance of culture for his arguments, his methodological priorities do not invite significant exploration into the hermeneutics of development, or of social change more broadly. He argues against those who elevate tradition in order to restrict the freedom of women and the poor to decide for themselves, but his method does not invite us to consider how those in other spheres of authority constitute cultural formations that shape the ways in which freedom is exercised. I sympathize with his political point, but I find it also extremely helpful to consider how values are shaped in less tradition-laden cultural formations, where cultural power is perhaps less obvious, but even more consequential.

My preference may come from the world on which I have focused, for those who invoke the future, rather than the past, are those who set the terms in which people apparently develop the right to choose. By understanding how transition culture empowers some, and disempowers others, we are more likely to find a way to recover that inclusive vision of civil society articulated in 1989, and to promote development as freedom in ways that not only recognize the injustice of racism, sexism, or class oppression, but also might see how transition culture develops its own forms of cultural authority to limit freedom's expression and expansion.

Sen's argument helps to constitute a new cultural formation in which inequality's address becomes part of freedom's expression, and an extension of that emancipatory promise of 1989. It offers a radically different approach to thinking about transition. Instead of a movement from plan to market, we can address transition as a form of freedom's making. Instead of comparing the progress of nations in their road to the market, we can compare the ways in which the poor are empowered to participate in the course of postcommunist social change. Instead of waiting for wars to end, we can ask how global policies and practices make compromise unnecessary and violence more likely. And with these alternative frames, those marginalized by transition's course can become the analytical center of a new transition culture, which in turn rests on an extension of something indigenous to the emancipatory struggle itself. What would transition look like if the world of peace, rather than the market, were its teleology? And how would transition culture function if, alongside of the empowerment of the responsible, solidarity and bearing the burden of others, even beyond one's nation, were the point of interested scholarship?

With such a focus, transition culture as we know it would come to an end. Its end would not be marked by any particular nation's entry into the European Union, by Serbia's democratic revolution, or by any other institutional marker of global integration on the West's universal terms. Instead, its end would be marked by a new universal premise: the realization that development as freedom is a challenge for all societies, whether marked by a communist past or not. Inequality is central to this problem, but it does not depend on the universalism promised by capitalism's counterculture. Rather, it depends on freedom's extension, the promise of emancipation.

In this sense, the cultural formations of postcommunism, dependent as they are on the opposition between socialism and capitalism as the past and the future, would become an anachronism. Rather than an adjective used to distinguish us from them, nationalism's complex articulation with freedom also could be acknowledged. Instead of presuming peace to be the point of departure, its realization could be the point of focus. With these transformations, we might even find transition's emancipation to rest in its own critical transition culture, and its fulfillment in the extension of its work beyond the lands once ruled by communists.

Appendix A

Interview Schedule for Focus Groups

In May and June 1996, ten colleagues from Estonia, Ukraine, and Uzbekistan—Rein Vöörman, Marika Kirch, Jelena Hellamae, and Aleksander Plotkin from Estonia; Victor Susak, Natalija Salabaj, and Yuliya Yakubova from Ukraine; and Alisher Ilkhamov, Ludmila Hafizova, and Nilufar Egamberdieva from Uzbekistan—worked with colleagues from the University of Michigan to produce a methodology appropriate for the examination of identity formation and social problems in Estonia, Ukraine, and Uzbekistan. The interview schedule for focus groups is reproduced below.

I. Introduction (10 minutes)

Welcome to our meeting. We have invited you here to discuss some problems of our contemporary life. My name is _____. My co-moderator is _____. My notetaker is _____, etc.

We are from the _____ Center/University/Academy of Sciences. We are talking with people in this society and in (name the two other societies) about how their lives have changed over the past ten years or so.

We all know that there have been many important social and economic changes in these years. The goal of our discussion today is to understand how these changes have had an effect on each of you personally, and on people like you.

The discussion is completely voluntary and confidential. We will tape-record this discussion, and my associate, Ted, will be taking notes on our discussion. The transcripts of this study will be used only for scientific research and educational purposes. They will be anonymous, that is, no specific statements will be attached to anyone's name.

The most important rule in this discussion is that we want everyone to be able to feel free to speak as they wish. As a moderator in this group, my main job is to lead discussion with a few questions, but also to make sure people can talk as they wish. If some people are speaking too much, I might have to ask them to say a little bit less so that others have a chance to speak. And if you are not saying much, I might ask you your opinion. And of course there might be disagreements here in this group, and I may have to step in if people are wrestling on the table over their opinion of (some funny thing). But usually I don't have to do these things. Most of the time, people can do their own moderating.

Why don't we begin by writing your names on the pieces of paper we have before you. Write your name as you wish to be addressed here. Let me show you how it can be folded and put in front of you so that the rest of the group can remember your name.

Now that we have all made our name cards, I'd like to ask each of you to say a few words about yourself *(predstavit'sebe)*.

Now let's turn to our discussion questions. As I said, we are here to discuss how the recent social and economic changes of the last ten years have affected your lives.

II. Improvements (15 minutes at most)

Here are some cards. Please write on your card an answer to the following question:

In what ways have these changes of the last ten years improved your life and the lives of people like you?

Please list the three most important ways things have improved.

Please write three answers on this card. We would like to collect these cards at the end of our discussion, so please write them down as neatly you can.

Now, before we discuss what you have all written, let me ask you to do one more thing: if you had to pick only one of these improvements, which would you say is the most important? Please put an X next to this improvement.

OK, let's begin. Who here has a most important improvement that they think others might also have mentioned? Does anyone else have something similar, whether or not it was their most important improvement? (If nobody mentions this) Now that it is mentioned, would anyone here also find this to be a particularly important improvement?

Probes: Are all these improvements felt by everyone? Whose lives have improved the most in these specific areas?

Why are we experiencing these improvements?

Who would like to be next? Who has another important improvement that they think others might also have mentioned?

Probes.

We probably could talk more about this, but let us now collect the cards. That way we can be sure of being able to study all of your ideas. Now we'd like to turn to something similar.

III. Difficulties (30 minutes)

Now, while we have spoken a great deal about improvements, these changes in the last ten years also may have made some things more difficult or worse. (Hand out cards.)

In what ways have changes of the last ten years or so made your life and the lives of people like you more difficult? Please list the three most important difficulties on your card.

Before we discuss what you have written, please look at your list and put an X by the problem or difficulty that you think is most important for you and people like you.

Who here has marked a most important problem that they think someone else here might have mentioned? Does anyone else have something similar, whether or not it was their most important problem? (If nobody mentions this) Now that it is mentioned, would anyone here also find this to be a particularly important problem?

Probes: Are all these difficulties felt by everyone? Whose lives have worsened the most in these specific areas?

Why are we experiencing these difficulties? Do you think any particular person or group has caused these difficulties? Is this problem worse today than it was years ago? Is it getting better? What will it take to improve?

Who would like to be next? Who has another important difficulty that they think others might also have mentioned?

Probes.

IV. Specific Social Issues (20 minutes)

You all have identified many important social issues here. We would like to ask you more directly about a couple issues that you have mentioned and some that you didn't mention very directly, but might be on your cards as less important issues.

1) Have the issues we discussed today affected men and women differently? Are there any particularly important problems, whether or not we mentioned them today, that affect men much more than women, or women more than men?

Probes: Are all men experiencing these difficulties in the same way? Are all women? Which group of men and which group of women has it the worst? Why are we/they experiencing these problems? Do you think any particular person or group has caused these particular problems? Is this problem much worse today than it was years ago? Is it getting better? What will it take to improve?

2) Have the issues we discussed today affected people of various nationalities differently?

Probes: Are all people of nationality X experiencing these difficulties in the same way? All people of nationality Y? Which group has it the worst? Why are we/they experiencing these problems? Do you think any particular person or group has caused these particular problems? Is this problem much worse today than it was years ago? Is it getting better? What will it take to improve?

3) Have the issues we discussed today affected people of various regions differently?

Probes: Are all people of region X experiencing these difficulties in the same way? All people of region Y? Which group has it the worst? Why are we/they experiencing these problems? Do you think any particular person or group has caused these particular problems? Is this problem much worse today than it was years ago? Is it getting better? What will it take to improve?

At this point, collect the cards on which people have written down their list of difficulties.

V. Site-Specific Questions (10 minutes)

VI. At End of Discussion

Thank you very much for your participation today. Your discussion has been really valuable for us. Before you leave, we would like you to answer two final questions on this sheet. We don't want to have discussion of these items now, but we would very much appreciate your comments on them.

1) As part of our research, we want to conduct interviews with some people who are bringing about important changes in this country. Can you suggest the names of one or two people who understand some of the issues which we discussed today and who are involved in bringing about change? Looking around the room at the issues we have discussed, with what social issues are they associated? What is their social position?

2) When we spoke today, we asked you to talk about yourself and about people like you. What groups of people were you thinking of today when you were talking about yourself and people like you?

Would you put your name on this questionnaire, so that if we need to ask you more about a particular person you recommend, we might be able to contact you?

Thank you very much for your participation.

Appendix B

Coding Scheme for
Focus Group Narratives

Our coding scheme for the focus group data was based first of all on the interview schedule that the Ford-project team developed in May–June 1996. In part, the codes reflect the basic organization of the transcript interview schedule, and the subsequent distinctions the coders could identify. These second codes were created by the coders (Lisa Fein and Michael Kennedy, in consultation with Marianne Kamp and Donna Parmelee) after initial readings of a few transcripts. They are designed to capture the major alternative dimensions of discussions of the basic questions (see Appendix A). A few additional codes were introduced after the initial coding sequences were conducted. Any particular line segments could be multiply coded. Transcripts were coded by Fein and Kennedy independently and reviewed together to create a common code for each transcript. These transcripts were subsequently reviewed to ensure that consistent coding schemes were used.

Three codes refer to frames of questions that were necessarily posed in each focus group. They include:

Ethnic refers to the coding of line segments in which discussions of nationality, ethnicity, and citizenship are conducted. This includes discussions of national cultural issues.

Gender refers to the coding of line segments in which discussions of gender issues, explicitly or implicitly, are addressed.

Region refers to the coding of line segments in which conditions of specific regions within the country or abroad are considered and potentially compared. This includes references to other nations or to general regions such as "the West." It also captures discussion of tourism, travel, and emigration.

The following codes were not mandated by the original focus group interview schedule. The coders introduced them to capture salient dimensions of discussion. As such, to the extent that they appear, they are the consequence of focus group interests. There are some exceptions, however, where moderators introduce the subjects rather than allow them to emerge from focus group interests.

Corrupt refers to segments in which profit or privilege from the abuse of power was identified. This occurs among managers, state officials, health-care personnel, and others. Actions may be criminal (in which case they are also coded as crime), but are not necessarily so.

Crime refers to any line segments that discuss crime—robbery, murder, and so on. This sometimes overlaps with corruption.

Ecology refers to environmental concerns. This includes water and air pollution, radioactivity, and the like. This often overlaps with health concerns. In the Kiev-led focus groups (Kiev, Ivankiv, and Donestsk women), Chernobyl was identified in the introductory statement as a concern.

Education refers to line segments discussing schools, teachers, and matters concerning those specifically designated by their measure of education. This code also includes discussions of science and technology.

Employment refers to line segments involving unemployment, underemployment, and group or individual conditions of employment.

Freedom refers to freedom of speech, the press, and so on, as well as freedom of choice and opportunity, and freedom to work as one wishes. It also captures freedom to travel. It does not address religious freedoms, which are coded separately.

Health refers to health-care issues. It also includes corruption among health-care providers and health problems resulting from environmental degradation.

Independence refers to the independence of the state, or the adoption of its constitution.

Language refers to line segments discussing language, or calling attention to the fact of shifting from one language to another in discussion.

Milservice refers to military issues, such as war and peace in other places (notably Chechnya) and soldiers' conditions of work.

Monetary refers to matters of monetary reform and macroeconomic issues accompanying a transition to a market economy. It addresses broad economic questions such as privatization.

Religion refers to matters concerning religion, God, and so on. It includes freedom to practice religion and religion's revival.

Salary refers to the payment of salaries, pensions, or other stipends or benefits.

Standliv is a broad code that refers to general quality-of-life issues such as the price of goods and their availability (refers to inflation and shortages), the availability and quality of infrastructure, and insecurity about the future.

Stratif refers to inequalities and explicit comparisons between groups.

Trade refers to work at the bazaar or selling and buying goods. It can be a problem or an improvement, part of the solution or something to blame. It is not coded as such when a trader or that kind of job title is mentioned.

USSR refers to line segments mentioning the disintegration of the USSR either positively or negatively. It captures all general references to the Soviet period, especially when that past is used to assess the present. It also refers to segments in which control of the economy or regulation of social welfare is discussed.

Values refers to statements regarding mercifulness, courtesy, respect, decency, and care for others or their opposites. It can be a problem or an improvement. It can explain the problem or be part of the solution. It sometimes overlaps with religion.

Notes

Introduction

1. As Zygmunt Bauman, *Socialism: The Active Utopia* (London: Allen and Unwin, 1976), described it.

2. Both former president (1990–95) and leader of Solidarność (1980–90) Lech Wałęsa and President Aleksander Kwaśniewski had to appear before a tribunal in August 2000 to explain their relationship to the secret police. See, for example, Steven Erlanger, "Poland Spy Inquiry Said to Be a Failed Political Tactic," *New York Times,* August 20, 2000, p. 4.

3. See, for example, Ernest Gellner, *Conditions of Liberty: Civil Society and Its Rivals* (New York: Penguin, 1994), and George Soros, *Open Society: Reforming Global Capitalism* (New York: Public Affairs, 2000).

4. Michael D. Kennedy, *Professionals, Power and Solidarity in Poland: A Critical Sociology of Soviet-Type Society* (Cambridge: Cambridge University Press, 1991).

5. Fredric Jameson and Masao Miyoshi, eds., *The Cultures of Globalization* (Durham, N.C.: Duke University Press, 1998).

6. Amartya Sen, *Development as Freedom* (New York: Alfred A. Knopf, 1999), is my reference here, and my protagonist in transition culture's final reconfiguration in the volume's conclusion.

7. In this sense, I build on Ronald Grigor Suny and Michael D. Kennedy, eds., *Intellectuals and the Articulation of the Nation* (Ann Arbor: University of Michigan Press, 1999). Here, however, I focus on the articulation of transition culture and its implication in the nation.

8. Zygmunt Bauman, *Hermeneutics and Social Science* (New York: Columbia University Press, 1978), and Richard Berstein, *The Restructuring of Social and Political Theory* (Philadelphia: University of Pennsylvania Press, 1978), provide some general theoretical arguments on behalf of this orientation. Anthony Giddens, *The Constitution of*

Society (Berkeley: University of California Press, 1984), discusses at length a hermeneutic sociology in which the discursive rendering of unacknowledged conditions of action and unintended consequences of action becomes a central feature of critical inquiry. Jeff Livesay, "Normative Grounding and Praxis: Habermas, Giddens and a Contradiction within Critical Theory" (*Sociological Theory* 3 [1985]: 66–76, p. 70), calls Giddens's sociology a kind of "critical hermeneutics" because it seeks to extend the "discursive penetration of social actors into the unacknowledged conditions and unintended consequences of action." See also John B. Thompson, *Critical Hermeneutics* (Cambridge: Cambridge University Press, 1981).

9. This project is thus different from most "transitological" studies. A great deal of interesting work on transition from communist-ruled societies has been undertaken, but that research tends to be cast in terms of inequality and institution making within the framework of transition culture itself. What shapes market and political outcomes? What are the best strategies for capital accumulation and democratic stabilization? Who wins and who loses? I would also ask how these questions fit with transition itself. See, for example, this review essay: Victor Nee and Rebecca Matthews, "Market Transition and Societal Transformation in Reforming State Socialism," *Annual Review of Sociology* 22 (1996): 401–35.

10. Here I draw on Janet Hart's notion of "mobilizing narrative." See Janet Hart, *New Voices in the Nation: Women and the Greek Resistance, 1941–1964* (Ithaca, N.Y.: Cornell University Press, 1996).

11. Susan Gal and Gail Kligman, *Politics of Gender after Socialism* (Princeton, N.J.: Princeton University Press, 2000); Stephen Crowley, *Hot Coal, Cold Steel: Russian and Ukrainian Workers from the End of the Soviet Union to the Post-Communist Transformations* (Ann Arbor: University of Michigan Press, 1997); Lewis H. Siegelbaum and Danile J. Walkowitz, eds., *Workers of the Donbass Speak: Survival and Identity in the New Ukraine, 1989–1992* (Albany: State Universtiy of New York Press, 1995); Kimita-ka Matsuzato, ed., *Regions: A Prism to View the Slavic-Eurasian World. Towards a Discipline of 'Regionology'* (Sapporo: Slavic Research Center, 2000).

12. See especially Raymond Williams, *Marxism and Literature* (Clarendon: Oxford University Press, 1977). Subsequent references are given in the text.

13. Nicholas Dirks, Geoff Eley, and Sherry Ortner ("Introduction," in *Culture/Power/History: A Reader in Contemporary Social Theory* [Princeton, N.J.: Princeton University Press, 1994], pp. 3–45) represent their own collective project in this spirit, seeking to "understand the ways in which the subject is culturally and historically constructed in different times and places, as a being with a particular kind of affective organization, particular kinds of knowing and understanding, particular modes of gender and sexual ordering, and so forth. At the same time we seek to highlight efforts to understand the ways in which culturally and historically constituted subjects become agents in the active sense—how their actions and modes of being in the world always sustain, and sometimes transform the very structures around them" (12). One can also link this disposition to Bourdieu and his conceptions of field, but here I wish rather to emphasize the play in the cultural system that formation, rather than field, signifies. See the discussion by Dirks, Eley, and Ortner on p. 16.

14. This approach to culture is not typical, however, in either the sociology of culture or East European studies. Very often, when scholars in either of these areas invoke culture, they are likely to refer to the more structural and relatively enduring system of norms or beliefs across time and space, with particular boundaries, often national, in play. This approach to culture is especially oriented to those epistemologies that focus on the internalization of culture and its mental structures rather than on their more

communicative and event-sensitive practices. Jeffery C. Alexander and Philip Smith, "The Discourse of American Civil Society: A New Proposal for Cultural Studies" (*Theory and Society* 22 [1993]: 151–207) elaborate both approaches to the cultural/action relationship, but ultimately focus more on how deeply the civil society code has structured American political action over more than a century. See also Jeffery Alexander, "Citizen and Enemy as Symbolic Classification: On the Polarizing Discourses of Civil Society," in Michele Lamont and Marcel Fournier, eds., *Cultivating Differences: Symbolic Boundaries and the Making of Inequality* (Chicago: University of Chicago Press, 1992). For a rather more sustained emphasis on the structural, see Michele Lamont, "Introduction: Beyond Taking Race Seriously," in *The Cultural Territories of Race: Black and White Boundaries* (Chicago: Russell Sage Foundation, 2001). Ann Kane, "Theorizing Meaning Construction in Social Movements: Symbolic Structures and Interpretation during the Irish Land War" (*Sociological Theory* 15:3 [1997]: 249–76), recommends this structural approach independent of practice, but note how dependent the argument is for its a priori notion of national boundaries.

Rather than focus on mental structures, culture can be studied around narratives or stories, sequences of events designed to communicate a certain meaning. Peggy Somers understands these to be the foundations of identity itself: "Narrative identities are constituted by a person's temporally and spatially variable place in culturally constructed stories composed of (breakable) rules, (variable) practices, binding (and unbinding) institutions and the multiple plots of family, nation, or economic life." See Margaret R. Somers, "The Narrative Constitution of Identity: A Relational and Network Approach," *Theory and Society* 23:5 (1994): 605–50, p. 625. Narratives are not the only elements of cultural formations—symbols, musical formations, and other elements are an important part of the cultural formation on which nations are built. Note especially Karen A. Cerulo, *Identity Designs: The Sights and Sounds of a Nation* (New Brunswick, N.J.: Rutgers University Press, 1995). I find the narrative part of transition culture most compelling, especially in that it depends less on a narrative of being, and more one of mobilization. For this distinction, see Hart, *New Voices in the Nation*.

15. For instance, Iván Szelényi, Szonja Szelényi, and Winifred Poster, "Interests and Symbols in Post-Communist Political Culture: the Case of Hungary" (*American Sociological Review* 61 [1996]: 466–77) rely on a notion of "social democratic sentiment" to explain the return of postcommunist parties to power. For a discussion of this general approach, see Mabel Berezin, "Politics and Culture: A Less Fissured Terrain," *Annual Review of Sociology* 23 (1997): 361–83. For a substantial discussion of Hungarian national identity, see György Csepeli, *National Identity in Contemporary Hungary* (New York: Columbia University Press, 1997).

16. For example, Michael Burawoy, Joshua Gamson, and Alice Burton, *Ethnography Unbound: Power and Resistance in the Modern Metropolis* (Berkeley: University of California Press, 1992), and Michael Burawoy, Joseph A. Blum, Sheba George, Zsuzsa Gille, Teresa Gowan, Lynne Haney, Maren Klawiter, Steven H. Lopez, Sean Riain, and Millie Thayer, *Global Ethnography: Forces, Connections and Imaginations in a Postmodern World* (Berkeley: University of California Press, 2001).

17. For example, Sonya Rose, *Limited Livelihoods: Gender and Class in 19th Century England* (Berkeley: University of California Press, 1992).

18. See, for example, Alain Touraine, *The Voice and the Eye: An Analysis of Social Movements* (Cambridge: Cambridge University Press, 1981), for a discussion of sociological interventionism.

19. I might have chosen to identify transition culture as a discursive formation, following the work of Michel Foucault (*The Archaeology of Knowledge,* trans. A. M.

Sheridan Smith [New York: Pantheon, 1969]), or as a knowledge culture, as Margaret Somers ("Narrating and Naturalizing Civil Society and Citizenship Theory: The Place of Political Culture and the Public Sphere," *Sociological Theory* 13:3 [1995]: 229–74) has suggested in her work. Transition culture is better characterized as a cultural formation because it is less specified and institutionalized than the knowledge cultures Somers builds her theories around. I do work with Foucault's notion of discursive formation later, especially in my discussion of nationalism. As Craig Calhoun (*Nationalism* [Buckingham: Open University Press, 1997], p. 3) describes it, a discursive formation is "a way of speaking that shapes our consciousness, but also is problematic enough that it keeps generating more issues and questions, keeps propelling us into further talk, keeps producing debates over how to think about it." In general, it is useful to think about nationalism as a discursive formation, but in its articulation with transition, I find it more useful to analyze its grounding in the cultural formations attending postcommunism's social formation.

20. Kennedy, *Professionals, Power and Solidarity in Poland.*

21. Craig Calhoun, *Critical Social Theory: Culture, History and the Challenge of Difference* (Oxford and Cambridge: Blackwell, 1995), p. 11.

22. On marxism, see Michael D. Kennedy and Naomi Galtz, "From Marxism to Postcommunism: Socialist Desires and East European Rejections," *Annual Review of Sociology* 22 (1996): 437–58. There are many engagements of the articulation of feminism between Western and East European gender politics. For one of the earlier explorations of this difficulty, see Nanette Funk and Magda Mueller, *Gender Politics and Post-Communism: Reflections from Eastern Europe and the Former Soviet Union* (New York: Routledge, 1993). For reflections on the progress that has been made, see Gal and Kligman, *Politics of Gender after Socialism,* and Sabrina Ramet, ed., *Gender Politics in the Western Balkans: Women and Society in Yugoslavia and the Yugoslav Successor States* (State College: Pennsylvania State University Press, 1999). On postmodernism, see the essays in Aldona Jawłowska and Marian Kempny, eds., *Cultural Dilemmas of Post-Communist Societies* (Warsaw: IfiS, 1994), for a discussion of that potential fit. For my sense of the issue, see "An Introduction to East European Ideology and Identity in Transformation," in Michael D. Kennedy, ed., *Envisioning Eastern Europe: Postcommunist Cultural Studies* (Ann Arbor: University of Michigan Press, 1994), pp. 1–45.

23. See Martin Jay, "For Theory," *Theory and Society* 25 (1996): 167–83; Michael D. Kennedy, "For Theory and Its Others: A Comment on Jay," *Theory and Society* 25 (1996): 185–92.

24. Seyla Benhabib, *Critique, Norm and Utopia* (New York: Columbia University Press, 1986); Pierre Bourdieu, *In Other Words: Essays Towards a Reflexive Sociology,* trans. Matthew Adamson (Stanford, Calif.: Stanford University Press, 1990), p. 149.

25. See Jonathan Turner, *The Structure of Sociological Theory* (Belmont, Calif.: Wadsworth, 1991), pp. 9–11; Turner's exemplar in this stream of theory is Anthony Giddens, *The Constitution of Society* (Berkeley: University of California Press, 1984). See William H. Sewell Jr., "A Theory of Structure: Duality, Agency, and Transformation," *American Journal of Sociology* 98:1 (1992): 1–29, for illustrations of its application.

26. John Guidry, Michael D. Kennedy, and Mayer Zald, "Globalizations and Social Movements," in John Guidry, Michael D. Kennedy, and Mayer Zald, eds., *Globalizations and Social Movements: Culture, Power and the Transnational Public Sphere* (Ann Arbor: University of Michigan Press, 2000), pp. 1–32; Benhabib, *Critique, Norm and Utopia,* p. 225.

27. Giddens, *The Constitution of Society,* makes this "double hermeneutic" one of the foundational points in his sociological theory.

28. I find the following particularly compelling for not only critical but also transition theory: William Connolly (*Identity/Difference: Democratic Negotiations of Political Paradox* [Ithaca, N.Y.: Cornell University Press, 1991], p. 191) writes, "Social critique must become more attentive to generic sources of suffering (arguably) rooted in the human condition itself if its institutional criticisms are to sink more deeply into the texture of public life."

29. See, for example, Nancy Fraser, *Justice Interruptus: Critical Reflections on the "Postsocialist" Condition* (New York: Routledge, 1997), or Calhoun, *Critical Social Theory.*

30. Thomas McCarthy, *The Critical Theory of Jürgen Habermas* (Cambridge: MIT Press, 1978), p. 319.

31. Alvin W. Gouldner, *The Future of Intellectuals and the Rise of the New Class* (New York: Seabury Press, 1979), pp. 83–85.

32. Consider Theda Skocpol and Margaret Somers, "The Uses of Comparative History in Macrosocial Inquiry," *Comparative Studies in Society and History* 22 (1980): 174–97. One might use this to distinguish Weberian and Durkheimian sociologies as do Charles Ragin and David Zaret, "Theory and Method in Comparative Research: Two Strategies," *Social Forces* 61 (1983): 731–54. Ragin has subsequently tried to supersede this opposition with his Boolean algebraic approach (elaborated in *The Comparative Method* [Berkeley: University of California Press, 1989]), but the distinctions remain rather viable for marking most sociology. Also, like comparative and historical sociology, critical sociology is more eventful and conjunctural, than it is Humean and probablistic, in its causal reasoning. Here one excellent illustration of this difference in approach can be found in the critique by Gerhard E. Lenski, "History and Social Change," *American Journal of Sociology* 82 (1976): 548–64, in Robert Nisbet's *Social Change and History* (Oxford: Oxford University Press, 1969).

33. Here, I draw from William H. Sewell Jr., "Three Temporalities: Toward an Eventful Sociology," in Terrence J. McDonald, ed., *The Historic Turn in the Human Sciences* (Ann Arbor: University of Michigan Press, 1996), pp. 245–81.

34. Sewell, "Three Temporalities," pp. 247–50, takes world-systems theorist Immanuel Wallerstein (*The Modern World System,* vol. 1, *Capitalist Agriculture and the Origins of the European World Economy in the Sixteenth Century* [New York: Academic Press, 1974]) to task for failing to recognize the contingencies in history that enabled capitalism's emergence, for instance. Why did Portugal succeed as the exploring state? Why did the Hapsburgs fail to gain political hegemony? What enabled the success of the Dutch revolt, whose consequence was so great because it enabled new institutions particularly suited to finance capitalism to emerge. Many of Charles Tilly's "pernicious postulates" fall precisely within such a teleological framework. See his *Big Structures, Large Processes, Huge Comparisons* (New York: Sage, 1984).

35. Theda Skocpol, *States and Social Revolutions: A Comparative Study of France, Russia and China* (Cambridge: Cambridge University Press, 1979).

36. For example, see Michael Burawoy, "Two Methods in Search of History: Skocpol vs. Trotsky," *Theory and Society* 18 (1989): 759–805.

37. Sewell, "Three Temporalities, pp. 256–59. Subsequent references are given in the text.

38. Mark Traugott, *Armies of the Poor: Determinants of Working-Class Participation in the Parisian Insurrection of June 1848* (Princeton, N.J.: Princeton University Press, 1985); Howard Kimeldorf, *Reds or Rackets? The Making of Radical and Conservative Unions on the Waterfront* (Berkeley and Los Angeles: University of California Press, 1988).

39. This is one reason, for instance, why Liah Greenfeld, *Nationalism: Five Roads to Modernity* (Cambridge: Harvard University Press, 1992), has been so critically received in the field: originating differences in nation making insufficiently explain perennial qualities of nations. This is also why Rogers Brubaker's *Citizenship and Nationhood in Germany and France* (Cambridge: Cambridge University Press, 1992) and *Nationalism Reframed: Nationhood and the National Question in the New Europe* (Cambridge: Cambridge University Press, 1996) have carried so much more appeal; he seeks to explain how initial differences are reproduced over time. For elaboration, see Michael D. Kennedy, "What Is 'the Nation' after Communism and Modernity?" *Polish Sociological Review* 1:105 (1994): 47–58.

40. Exemplified by Barrington Moore, *Social Origins of Dictatorship and Democracy* (Boston: Beacon Press, 1966), and carried forward by, among others, Jeffery Paige, *Coffee and Power* (Cambridge: Harvard University Press, 1997), and Gale Stokes, "The Social Origins of East European Politics," *East European Politics and Societies* 1 (1987): 30–74.

41. See E. P. Thompson, *The Making of the English Working Class* (London: Golloncz, 1963); Sonya Rose, *Limited Livelihoods: Gender and Class in 19th Century England* (Berkeley: University of California Press, 1992); Reinhard Bendix, *Kings or People: Power and the Mandate to Rule* (Berkeley: University of California Press, 1978); Julia Adams, "The Familial State: Elite Family Practices and State-making in the Early Modern Netherlands," *Theory and Society* 23 (1994): 505–39.

42. Michael Burawoy, "Neoclassical Sociology: From the End to Socialism to the End of Classes," *American Journal of Sociology* 106:4 (2001): 1099–1120.

43. *From Plan to Market: World Development Report, 1996,* published for the World Bank (New York: Oxford University Press, 1996), p. iii.

44. Ibid., pp. iii–iv.

45. Ibid.

46. Michael Burawoy, "The State and Economic Involution: Russia through a China Lens," *World Development* 24:6 (1996): 1105–17, identifies this particular theoretical strategy, but is able to do so because he is grounded in another intellectual tradition. Normally, the constitutive power of transition narratives is nearly invisible (Kennedy and Galtz, "From Marxism to Postcommunism") and those mobilized within the transition narrative have powerful cultural tools with which to diminish those who challenge the transition to the market.

47. David Stark, "The Great Transformation? Social Change in Eastern Europe," *Contemporary Sociology* 21:3 (1992): 299–320; Valerie Bunce, "Should Transitologists Be Grounded?" *Slavic Review* 54 (1995): 111–27.

48. Nee and Matthews ("Market Transition and Societal Transformation in Reforming State Socialism," p. 403) define the paradigm this way: "The integrating idea of the new institutionalist paradigm is the assumption that actors identify and pursue their interests in opportunity structures shaped by custom, cultural beliefs, social norms and networks, market structures, formal organizations and the state. The new institutionalist paradigm is well suited for studies of transition societies because it focuses analytical attention on institutional change, its causes and its effects."

49. Ákos Róna-Tas, *The Great Surprise of the Small Transformation* (Ann Arbor: University of Michigan Press, 1996).

50. Here I draw on passages from my "Postcommunist Institutional Design," *Contemporary Sociology* 28:2 (1999): 207–9, in which I reviewed Jon Elster, Claus Offe, and Ulrich Preuss, *Institutional Design in Post-Communist Societies: Rebuilding the Ship at Sea* (Cambridge: Cambridge University Press, 1998), and David Stark and László

Bruszt, *Postsocialist Pathways: Transforming Politics and Property in East Central Europe* (Cambridge: Cambridge University Press, 1998).

51. See Burawoy, "The State and Economic Involution," and Michael Burawoy and Pavel Krotov, "The Soviet Transition from Socialism to Capitalism: Worker Control and Economic Bargaining in the Wood Industry," *American Sociological Review* 57 (1992): 16–38.

52. Kennedy and Galtz, "From Marxism to Postcommunism."

53. Jan Švejnar, Katherine Terrell, and Daniel Munich, "Unemployment in the Czech and Slovak Republics," in *The Czech Republic and Economic Transition in Eastern Europe* (San Diego: Academic Press, 1995).

54. Burawoy, "Neoclassical Sociology," p. 1118. Also see many of the contributions in Michael Burawoy and Katherine Verdery, eds., *Uncertain Transition: Ethnographies of Change in the Postsocialist World* (Lanham, Md.: Rowman and Littlefield, 1999).

55. Hence, both works tend to assume that panoptic view of a representative of an international culture, that view from nowhere that allows the problem of transition's success and failure to be posed. See Calhoun's comments on this in *Critical Social Theory*, p. 53.

56. See Michael D. Kennedy, "Postcommunist Capitalism, Culture and History," *American Journal of Sociology* 106:4 (2001): 1138–51.

57. Gil Eyal, Iván Szelényi, and Eleanor Townsley, *Making Capitalism without Capitalists: The New Ruling Elites in Eastern Europe* (London: Verso, 1998).

58. Ibid., p. 17.

59. That power bloc uses three rituals—purification, sacrifice, and confession—initially to purge postcommunists from power and later society from socialist pollution in order to build the rational economy and capitalist alternative. Following Bourdieu, Eyal, Szelényi, and Townsley treat culture as a form of capital, and use the dominance of different types of capital to distinguish social structures. But this Bourdieuian notion of capital fails to recognize its mediating function in the constitution of actors or in the coordination of action (Calhoun, *Critical Social Theory*, 155). For instance, the complicated biographies one might find in life histories are reduced to *categories* of actors. Eyal, Szelényi, and Townsley distinguish dissidents, whose degrees of opposition go unmarked, from socialist technocrats and managers, each with different allocations of cultural capital. Their kinship ties, friendship networks, early career trajectories, and personal memories during communist rule and its end go unmarked before their class classification, which in turn shapes the action that gets theorized.

60. Eyal, Szelényi, and Townsley, *Making Capitalism without Capitalists*, p. 39.

61. Robert Brenner's critique of Wallerstein exemplifies this tendency. See Robert Brenner, *The Brenner Debate: Agrarian Class Structure and Economic Development in Pre-Industrial Europe* (Cambridge: Cambridge University Press, 1985).

62. Valerie Bunce, *Subversive Institutions: The Design and Destruction of Socialism and the State* (Cambridge: Cambridge University Press, 1999).

63. Most notably in "Should Transitologists Be Grounded?"

64. Bunce, *Subversive Institutions*, p. 71.

65. Ibid., p. 132.

66. Mark Beissinger, "Nationalist Violence and the State: Political Authority and Contentious Repertoires in the Former USSR," *Comparative Politics* (July 1998): 401–22.

67. For Beissinger's additional reflections on contingency and necessity in nationalism, see Mark Beissinger, "Nationalisms That Bark and Nationalisms That Bite: Ernest Gellner and the Substantiation of Nations," in John A. Hall, ed., *The State of the*

Nation: Ernest Gellner and the Theory of Nationalism (Cambridge: Cambridge University Press, 1999), pp. 169–90, and "Nationalism and Violence," in Alexander Motyl, ed., *The Encyclopedia of Nationalism* (forthcoming). See also Beissinger's *Nationalist Mobilization and the Collapse of the Soviet State: A Tidal Approach to the Study of Nationalism* (Cambridge: Cambridge University Press, 2002).

68. See, for instance, Rogers Brubaker and David Laitin, "Ethnic and Nationalist Violence," *Annual Review of Sociology* 24 (1998): 423–52.

69. This attention requires a kind of cultural expertise that works against broad and representative research. In its quantitative form, even eventful approaches tend to frame culture, and identity in particular, in instrumental rather than phenomenological ways. In the language of nationalism studies, "culturalist" explanations tend to be rather uneventful and primordial. See Beissinger, "Nationalism and Violence." This need not, and in fact should not, be. Cultural studies has, in the past decade, become much more attentive not only to the eventful, but also to the discursive framing involved in an object's study. See, for instance, Nicholas B. Dirks, Geoff Eley, and Sherry Ortner, "Introduction" to *Culture/Power/History* (Princeton, N.J.: Princeton University Press, 1994). For its application to the study of nationalism, see Geoff Eley and Ronald Grigor Suny, eds., *Becoming National: A Reader* (New York: Oxford University Press, 1996).

70. Bunce, *Subversive Institutions*, pp. 83–84.

71. Ibid., p. 104.

72. Brubaker, *Nationalism Reframed*, p. 61.

73. For an important demonstration on why omitting liberalism from an explanation of nationalism is problematic, see Susan Woodward, *Balkan Tragedy: Chaos and Dissolution after the Cold War* (Washington, D.C.: Brookings Institution, 1995).

74. Beissinger, *Nationalist Mobilization and the Collapse of the Soviet State*.

75. Bunce, *Subversive Institutions*, pp. 92.

76. Ibid., p. 145.

77. Katherine Verdery, *What Was Socialism and What Comes Next?* (Princeton, N.J.: Princeton University Press, 1996), pp. 10–11. Subsequent references are given in the text.

78. Gerhard Lenski, *Power and Privilege* (New York: Macmillan, 1966).

79. See William A. Gamson and David S. Meyer, "Framing Political Opportunity," in John McCarthy, Douglas McAdam, and Mayer Zald, eds., *Comparative Perspectives on Social Movements: Political Opportunities, Mobilizing Structures and Cultural Framings* (Cambridge: Cambridge University Press, 1996), pp. 275–90, for one example of how contentiousness and polysemy might be built into the meaning of political opportunity itself.

80. Verdery, *What Was Socialism and What Comes Next?*, pp. 1–9; see also her intellectual autobiography, and those of others in East European studies, in Ronald Grigor Suny and Michael D. Kennedy, *Intellectuals and the Articulation of the Nation* (Ann Arbor: University of Michigan Press, 1999).

81. Michael Burawoy, "Marxism after Communism," *Theory and Society* 29:2 (2000): 151–74.

82. My contrast of contexts works therefore in the tradition of Reinhard Bendix, at least in the categories of Skocpol and Somers, "The Uses of Comparative History in Macrosocial Inquiry."

83. Here I find Burawoy's comparison of Skocpol and Trotsky instructive ("Two Methods in Search of History").

84. Pierre Bourdieu, *In Other Words: Essays Towards a Reflexive Sociology*, trans. Matthew Adamson (Stanford, Calif.: Stanford University Press, 1990), p. 177.

85. See, for instance, Calhoun, *Critical Social Theory*, p. 53.

86. Bunce, *Subversive Institutions*, is especially good for developing this logic of comparison.

87. Homi K. Bhabha, "Narrating the Nation," in Homi K. Bhabha, ed., *Nation and Narration* (London: Routledge, 1990).

88. Michael D. Kennedy, *Professionals, Power and Solidarity in Poland: A Critical Sociology of Soviet-type Society* (Cambridge: Cambridge University Press, 1991).

89. Georg Simmel, "The Stranger" (1906), in Georg Simmel, *Individuality and Social Forms* (Chicago: University of Chicago Press, 1971). Because I have no Polish blood, nobody has accused me of being a traitor to the nation. Because of my in-betweenness, I hope I can recognize qualities of engagement that others may have trouble seeing owing to the mobilization of morality in which the Round Table was made. I am working on a much more in-depth historical sociology of the Round Table based in part on the conference "Communism's Negotiated Collapse: The Polish Round Table Talks Ten Years After" at the University of Michigan, April 7–10, 1999. See http://www.umich.edu/ ~iinet/PolishRoundTable.

90. Skocpol and Somers, "The Uses of Comparative History in Macrosocial Inquiry."

91. Although I did not include the Uzbek data in this project, my association with my colleagues there has been enormously rewarding and beneficial, notably with Alisher Ilkhamov. For elaboration of this paradigm for international research, see Michael D. Kennedy, "Internationalizing Social Science in Eastern Europe," *Items: Social Science Research Council* 52:2–3 (1998): 44–47. This strategy for comparative research also animates the University of Michigan International Institute project "Rethinking Area Studies." See http://www.umich.edu/~iinet.

92. Václav Havel, "The Politics of Hope," in *Disturbing the Peace: A Conversation with Karel Hvížd'ala*, trans. Paul Wilson (London: Faber and Faber, 1990).

1. Emancipation and Civil Society

Earlier versions of this chapter were presented to the Chicago Humanities Institute conference "Beyond Civil Society" in 1996 and at the Institute of Historical Studies, Lviv University, Ukraine, in 1993. I thank those who commented on my presentations in those contexts, and hope that they can see evidence of their contribution in this chapter. In this chapter, I also draw on ideas and passages from earlier works: "The Intelligentsia in the Constitution of Civil Societies and Post-Communist Regimes in Hungary and Poland," *Theory and Society* 21:1 (1992): 29–76; "Istorychna spadshchyna ta hromadians'ke suspil'stvo: al'ternatyvni natsiji v Sxidnij Jevropi" (Historical legacies and civil societies: Alternative nations in Eastern Europe), in Yaroslav Hrytsak and Mykola Krykun, eds., *Ukraina Moderna* (Modern Ukraine), vol. 1 (Lviv: Lviv State University, 1996); and (with Daina Stukuls) "The Narrative of Civil Society in Communism's Collapse and Postcommunism's Alternatives: Emancipation, Polish Protest and Baltic Nationalisms," *Constellations: An International Journal of Critical and Democratic Theory* 5:4 (1998): 541–71.

1. The essays in Jon Elster, ed., *The Roundtable Talks and the Breakdown of Communism* (Chicago: University of Chicago Press, 1996), provide important accounts of how communist leaders in Poland, Hungary, East Germany, Czechoslovakia, and Bulgaria worked with opposition leaders to fashion the Round Table exit from communism. The first chapter of David Stark and László Bruszt, *Postsocialist Pathways: Transforming Politics and Property in East Central Europe* (Cambridge: Cambridge University Press, 1998), addresses the sequential significance of these transformations. This approach extends the theoretical range of rational choice and other academic expressions,

but it implicitly depends on knowing a great deal about the context of action and how to establish the first- and second-order preferences of those who would negotiate (Valerie Bunce, *Subversive Institutions: The Design and Destruction of Socialism and the State* [Cambridge: Cambridge University Press, 1999], p. 151; subsequent references are given in the text). For an extended critique of rational choice approaches to East European change, see Michael Bernhard, "Institutional Choice after Communism: A Critique of Theory-Building in an Empirical Wasteland," *East European Politics and Societies* 14:2 (2000): 316–47.

2. William H. Sewell, Jr., "Three Temporalities: Toward an Eventful Sociology," in Terrence J. McDonald, ed., *The Historic Turn in the Human Sciences* (Ann Arbor: University of Michigan Press, 1996), p. 263.

3. This redefinition "is precisely the story in a nutshell of the fall of socialism and the state" (Bunce, *Subversive Institutions,* p. 18).

4. Raymond Williams, *Marxism and Literature* (Clarendon: Oxford University Press, 1977), p. 115.

5. Janet Hart, for example, in "Reading the Radical Subject: Gramsci, Glinos and Paralanguages of the Modern Nation," in Ronald Grigor Suny and Michael D. Kennedy, eds., *Intellectuals and the Articulation of the Nation* (Ann Arbor: University of Michigan Press, 1999), p. 194, scours "the historical record for analogous moments, comparable in terms of scene, emplotment and protagonists; and maintaining a critical consciousness about past events" in order to craft future praxis.

6. Michael D. Kennedy, *Professionals, Power and Solidarity in Poland: A Critical Sociology of Soviet-Type Society* (Cambridge: Cambridge University Press, 1991). For a discussion of normative penumbrae, see John Guidry, Michael D. Kennedy, and Mayer Zald, eds., *Globalizations and Social Movements: Culture, Power and the Transnational Public Sphere* (Ann Arbor: University of Michigan Press, 2000).

7. Pierre Birnbaum and Ira Katznelson, "Emancipation and the Liberal Offer," in Pierre Birnbaum and Ira Katznelson, eds., *Paths of Emancipation: Jews, States and Citizenship* (Princeton, N.J.: Princeton University Press, 1995), p. 4, where their reference is Jews but with whose emancipation they identify "slaves unshackled from bondage, colonized subjects freed from imperial domination, or serfs liberated from neo-feudalism."

8. Ibid.

9. William J. Sewell, "Ideologies and Social Revolutions: Reflections on the French Case," *Journal of Modern History* 57:1 (1985): 57–85; Andrew Arato, "Revolution, Restoration and Legitimation: Ideological Problems of the Transition from State Socialism," in Michael D. Kennedy, ed., *Envisioning Eastern Europe: Postcommunist Cultural Studies* (Ann Arbor: University of Michigan Press, 1994).

10. Steven Lukes, "Emancipation," in Tom Bottomore, ed., *A Dictionary of Marxist Thought* (Cambridge: Harvard University Press, 1983), pp. 146–47, p. 146.

11. Ferenc Feher, Agnes Heller, and György Markus, *Dictatorship over Needs* (New York: St. Martin's Press, 1983), especially the discussion of *ius supplicationis* and denunciation (pp. 175–76).

12. Alvin W. Gouldner, *The Future of Intellectuals and the Rise of the New Class* (New York: Seabury Press, 1979), pp. 83–85.

13. Jean Cohen and Andrew Arato, *Civil Society and Political Theory* (Cambridge: MIT Press, 1992), p. ix. A virtue of the Cohen and Arato book is that, although not developed extensively in this very abstract text on political theory, much of Arato's theory is based on his analysis of the Hungarian experience. One of his insightful applications

of civil society theory to postcommunist society can be found in "Revolution, Restoration and Legitimation."

14. For a historical account of the variety of civil society's invocations, see Dominique Colas, *Civil Society and Fanaticism: Conjoined Histories* (Stanford, Calif.: Stanford University Press, 1997). Among other things, he discusses Christian debates during the Middle Ages about the relative powers of spiritual and temporal swords; Luther's and especially Melanchthon's opposition to the iconoclasts and to peasant revolts; Albrecht Dürer's paintings, which make the difference, and mediation, between civil society and the City of God explicit; Spinoza, who signals Reason's centrality in civil society's form of mediation; and Leibniz, who casts civil society as the effect of scientific progress and a mirror of the City of God.

15. For elaboration of how the utopia of normality functions in social transformation of Soviet-type societies, see Daina Stukuls, "Imagining the Nation: Campaign Posters of the First Postcommunist Elections in Latvia," *East European Politics and Societies* 11:1 (1997): 131–54, and *Imagining the Nation: History, Modernity and Revolution in Latvia* (State College: Pennsylvania State University Press, 2002).

16. Nicolae Harsanyi and Michael D. Kennedy, "Between Utopia and Dystopia: The Labilities of Nationalism in Eastern Europe," in Kennedy, *Envisioning Eastern Europe*, pp. 149–79.

17. For one such expansive critique, see Isaac D. Balbus, *Marxism and Domination: A Neo-Hegelian, Feminist, Psychoanalytic Theory of Sexual, Political and Technological Liberation* (Princeton, N.J.: Princeton University Press, 1982).

18. See, for example, Nancy Fraser, *Justice Interruptus: Critical Reflections on the "Postsocialist" Condition* (New York: Routledge, 1997), and Craig Calhoun, *Critical Social Theory: Culture, History and the Challenge of Difference* (Oxford and Cambridge: Blackwell, 1995).

19. Alain Touraine's critical sociology, in the search to claim historicity, has been organized around this vision. See, for instance, *Return of the Actor*, trans. Myrna Godzich (Minneapolis: University of Minnesota Press, 1988).

20. Zygmunt Bauman makes the strong case for this position in *Socialism: The Active Utopia* (London: Allen and Unwin, 1976).

21. Michael D. Kennedy and Naomi Galtz, "From Marxism to Postcommunism: Socialist Desires and East European Rejections," *Annual Review of Sociology* 22 (1996): 437–58.

22. The critical theoretical potential of civil society to those places such as Central Asia where emancipation and domination are framed in very different terms is more complicated. See Roger D. Kangas, "State Building and Civil Society in Central Asia," in V. Tismaneanu, ed., *Political Culture and Civil Society in the Soviet Successor States* (New York: M. E. Sharpe, 1995), pp. 271–91.

23. Ernest Gellner, *Conditions of Liberty: Civil Society and Its Rivals* (London: Penguin, 1994). Subsequent references are given in the text. Of course, Gellner is not alone. George Soros was one of his most important allies in this process, establishing with the Central European University one of those places where such ideas could be elaborated. For some of Soros's own theoretical vision, see George Soros, *Underwriting Democracy* (New York: Free Press, 1991), and *Open Society: Reforming Global Capitalism* (New York: Public Affairs, 2000).

24. One might instead say that this was their commitment, not their ideology, for ideology was something distant from civil society and rather associated with communist dogmatism. See Michael D. Kennedy, "An Introduction to East European Identity and Ideology in Transformation," in Kennedy, *Envisioning Eastern Europe*, pp. 1–45.

25. Adam Michnik, for instance, argued that civil society's empowerment depended very much on the choice of the U.S. government to identify its partner in international diplomacy as Polish society (embodied in Lech Wałęsa, Adam Michnik, and other opposition figures) rather than the Polish state. See Adam Michnik, *Letters from Freedom: Post–Cold War Realities and Perspectives* (Berkeley: University of California Press, 1998), p. 103. For a more general discussion of the importance of political opportunity structures in enabling 1989, see Anthony Oberschall, "Opportunities and Framing in the Eastern European Revolts of 1989," in Doug McAdam, John D. McCarthy, and Mayer N. Zald, eds., *Comparative Perspectives in Social Movements: Political Opportunities, Mobilizing Structures and Cultural Framings* (Cambridge: Cambridge University Press, 1996), pp. 93–121.

26. David Ost, "Polish Labor before and after Solidarity," *International Labor and Working Class History* 50 (1996): 29–43, and *The Politics of Anti-Politics* (Philadelphia: Temple University Press, 1990); Kennedy, *Professionals, Power and Solidarity in Poland.*

27. See Tomasz Maštnak, "Civil Society in Slovenia: From Opposition to Power," *Studies in Comparative Communism* 23 (1990): 305–17.

28. Anatol Lieven, *The Baltic Revolution: Estonia, Latvia and Lithuania and the Path to Independence* (New Haven and London: Yale University Press, 1993), p. 220.

29. For an excellent overview of the East European region, see Ivo Banac, ed., *Eastern Europe in Revolution* (New York: Cornell University Press, 1992).

30. For a description of this Lockean version, see Charles Taylor, "Modes of Civil Society," *Public Culture* 3:1 (1990): 95–118.

31. Ákos Róna-Tas, *The Great Surprise of the Small Transformation* (Ann Arbor: University of Michigan Press, 1996).

32. Analysts of Romania hesitate to use the term "civil society," illustrating the difficult relationship between Romanian political developments under communism and civil society theory. See Gail Kligman, "Reclaiming the Public: A Reflection on Creating Civil Society in Romania," *East European Politics and Society* 4:3 (1990): 393–439, and Katherine Verdery and Gail Kligman, "Romania after Ceausescu: Post-Communism Communism?" in Banac, *Eastern Europe in Revolution*, pp. 117–47.

33. László Bruszt, "Without Us but for Us? Political Orientation in Hungary in the Period of Late Paternalism," *Social Research* 44 (1988): 43–76.

34. For a variety of interpretations on this broad stroke, see Alain Touraine, *Solidarity 1980–81* (Cambridge: Cambridge University Press, 1983); Kennedy, *Professionals, Power and Solidarity in Poland*; Ost, "Polish Labor before and after Solidarity."

35. Stephen Crowley, *Hot Coal, Cold Steel: Russian and Ukrainian Workers from the End of the Soviet Union to the Post-Communist Transformations* (Ann Arbor: University of Michigan Press, 1997); Lewis H. Siegelbaum and Daniel J. Walkowitz, eds., *Workers of the Donbass Speak: Survival and Identity in the New Ukraine, 1989–1992* (Albany: State University of New York Press, 1995).

36. Nicolae Harsanyi and Michael D. Kennedy, "Between Utopia and Dystopia: The Labilities of Nationalism in Eastern Europe," in Kennedy, *Envisioning Eastern Europe*, pp. 149–79; Veljko Vujacić, "Historical Legacies, Nationalist Mobilization, and Political Outcomes in Russia and Serbia: A Weberian View," *Theory and Society* 25:6 (1996): 763–801; Katherine Verdery, *National Ideology under Socialism: Identity and Cultural Politics in Ceausescu's Romania* (Berkeley and Los Angeles: University of California Press, 1991).

37. Gale Stokes, "The Devils Finger: The Disintegration of Yugoslavia," in *Three Eras of Political Change in Eastern Europe* (Oxford: Oxford University Press, 1997),

pp. 109–43, esp. pp. 127–29. One should not, of course, assume that civil society and nationalism are mutually exclusive. See Susan Woodward's important assessment of how Slovene liberalism contributed to the Wars of Yugoslav Succession in *Balkan Tragedy* (Washington: Brookings Institution, 1995).

38. Elster, *The Roundtable Talks,* provides important accounts of how communist leaders in Poland, Hungary, East Germany, Czechoslovakia, and Bulgaria worked with opposition leaders to fashion the Round Table exit from communism. For an especially detailed treatment of Hungarian communist leaders in this effort, see Rudolf Tökés, *Hungary's Negotiated Revolution* (Cambridge: Cambridge University Press, 1996).

39. See Arato, "Revolution, Restoration and Legitimation."

40. Katherine Verdery, "Civil Society or Nation? 'Europe' in Romania's Post-Socialist Politics," in Ronald Grigor Suny and Michael D. Kennedy, eds., *Intellectuals and the Articulation of the Nation* (Ann Arbor: University of Michigan Press, 1999).

41. Tökés, *Hungary's Negotiated Revolution,* 313; see also László Bruszt's comments at the conference on the Polish Round Table, April 6, 1999, University of Michigan.

42. See, for example, Norman M. Naimark, "Ich will hier raus": Emigration and the Collapse of the German Democratic Republic," in Banac, *Eastern Europe in Revolution,* pp. 72–95. If the Soviets had insisted, however, that the Hungarians deny this exodus, things might well have been different. See Jacques Levesque, *The Enigma of 1989: The USSR and the Liberation of Eastern Europe* (Berkeley: University of California Press, 1997), p. 154.

43. The Soviets also supported and found the developments in Poland and Hungary appealing (see Levesque, *The Enigma of 1989,* pp. 116, 137). Former Hungarian communist leader Károly Grósz argues to the contrary, however: the erosion of Leninism in the USSR undermined the conditions for the reproduction of communist rule in Eastern Europe (p. 214).

44. The literature on the East European intelligentsia is huge. For a discussion, see Kennedy, "The Intelligentsia in the Constitution of Civil Societies," pp. 31–36, and Michael D. Kennedy, "Eastern Europe's Lessons for Critical Intellectuals," in Charles Lemert, ed., *Intellectuals and Politics: Social Theory in a Changing World,* Key Issues in Sociological Theory, vol. 5 (Boulder, Colo.: Sage Press, 1991), pp. 94–112. For a subsequent elaboration of this approach to the sociology of intellectuals, see Suny and Kennedy, *Intellectuals and the Articulation of the Nation.* For an important comparative analysis of the autonomy of intellectuals, see Jeffery Goldfarb, *On Cultural Freedom* (Chicago: University of Chicago Press, 1982).

45. See Katherine Verdery, *National Ideology under Socialism.*

46. For a discussion of this thesis, see Kennedy, *Professionals, Power and Solidarity in Poland.*

47. György Konrád and Iván Szelényi, *The Intelligentsia on the Road to Class Power* (New York: Harcourt Brace Jovanovich, 1979).

48. Consider, for instance, the evolution of Iván Szelényi's own appreciation for the thesis in "The Prospects and Limits of the East European New Class Project," *Politics and Society* 15 (1986–87): 103–44; Iván Szelényi and Bill Martin, "The Three Waves of New Class Theories and a Postscript," in Charles Lemert, ed., *Intellectuals and Politics: Social Theory in a Changing World* (Newbury Park, Calif.: Sage, 1991), and Michael D. Kennedy, "An Interview with Iván Szelényi," videotaped interview, seminar on the topic "The Cold War and Its Aftermath," Advanced Study Center, University of Michigan, 1994.

49. Tökés, *Hungary's Negotiated Revolution,* p. 326.

50. For a discussion of how the Messner and Rakowski governments attempted

this economic reform and rule by experts without consultation with Solidarity, see Jan Skorzyński, *Ugoda i Rewolucja: Władza i Opozycja 1985–89* (Warsaw: Presspublica, 1995).

51. See Kennedy, *Professionals, Power and Solidarity in Poland*; Kennedy, "The Intelligentsia in the Constitution of Civil Societies."

52. János Kis, "Can 1956 Be Forgotten?" reprinted in *Politics in Hungary: For A Democratic Alternative* (New York: Columbia University Press, 1989), p. 28.

53. János Kis, "The 1956–57 Restoration," in *Politics in Hungary*, p. 81.

54. János Kis, "The Present Crisis and Its Origins," in *Politics in Hungary*, pp. 85–96, p. 95.

55. János Kis, "The End and the Beginning, " in *Politics in Hungary*, p. 22.

56. Kis, "Can 1956 Be Forgotten?" pp. 23–39, esp. 26–27.

57. Kis understands Kádárism in that period as three planks: the public display of party unity, the political neutralization of society, and the refusal to recognize any extra-party negotiating partner. See János Kis, "After the Fall Session of the National Assembly," in *Politics in Hungary*, pp. 153–74. See also János Kis, "The 1956–57 Restoration in a Thirty Years Perspective," in *Politics in Hungary*, pp. 31–84.

58. Kis, "The 1956–57 Restoration in a Thirty Years Perspective," p. 47.

59. Grzegorz Ekiert and Jan Kubik, *Rebellious Civil Society: Popular Protest and Democratic Consolidation in Poland, 1989–93* (Ann Arbor: University of Michigan Press, 1999), provide an important account of the vitality of protest in Poland.

60. For a substantial elaboration of the significance of various experiences of 1956, see Grzegorz Ekiert, *The State against Society: Political Crises and Their Aftermath in East Central Europe* (Princeton, N.J.: Princeton University Press, 1996).

61. See, for instance, how the Polish case is treated in Jon Elster, Claus Offe, and Ulrich Preuss, *Institutional Design in Postcommunist Societies: Rebuilding the Ship at Sea* (Cambridge: Cambridge University Press, 1998). See also Michael Burawoy and János Lukács, *The Radiant Past: Ideology and Reality in Hungary's Road to Capitalism* (Chicago: University of Chicago Press, 1992). For a thoughtful extension to the East German case, see Linda Fuller, *Where Was the Working Class? Revolution in Eastern Germany* (Urbana: University of Illinois Press, 1999).

62. Tökés, *Hungary's Negotiated Revolution*, p. 316.

63. Ibid., p. 261.

64. See Burawoy and Lukács, *The Radiant Past*.

65. These accounts draw on several sources, including Nigel Swain, "Hungary's Socialist Project in Crisis," *New Left Review* 176 (1989): 3–31; Pierre Kende, "Functions and Prospects of the Democratic Opposition in Hungary," in Aleksander Smolar and Pierre Kende, eds., *The Role of Opposition*, Study Number 17–18 (Research Project on Crises in Soviet-type Systems, Munich, 1989); László Bruszt, "The Roundtable Negotiations in Hungary and Poland: A Comparison" (Lecture at the University of Michigan, November 10, 1989), and "1989: The Negotiated Revolution in Hungary," *Social Research* 57:2 (1990): 365–88; László Urban, "Hungary in Transition: The Emergence of Opposition Politics," *Telos* 79 (1989): 108–18; Mitchell Cohen, "The Withering Away of the Communist State," *Dissent* (fall 1989): 455–61. George Schöpflin, lecture on Hungary at the University of Michigan, November 6, 1989; József Szayer, interview, February 15, 1989; and Tökés, *Hungary's Negotiated Revolution*.

66. Schöpflin, lecture on Hungary at the University of Michigan, November 6, 1989.

67. See Tökés, *Hungary's Negotiated Revolution*, for more elaborate accounts of the various groups and political leaders at the time.

68. György Konrád, *Antipolitics* (New York: Harcourt Brace Jovanovich, 1984), pp. 53–54.

69. Jószef Szayer, "Law and Political Change in Hungary: the Case of FIDESZ," lecture at the University of Michigan, February 15, 1989.

70. József Szayer, interview, February 15, 1989.

71. Bruszt, "1989"; Janet Fleischman, "New Independent Youth and Trade Union Organizations: An Emerging Civil Society?" *Across Frontiers* (winter/spring 1989): 28.

72. Tamás Bauer, "Hungarian Economic Reform in East European Perspective," *East European Politics and Society* 2:3 (1988): 418–32, esp. 425–26.

73. Swain, "Hungary's Socialist Project in Crisis," p. 17.

74. Urban, "Hungary in Transition."

75. Schöpflin, lecture on Hungary at the University of Michigan, November 6, 1989.

76. Beyond the groups already discussed, the Independent Small Holders Party, the Hungarian Social Democratic Party, the Hungarian People's Party, the Christian Democratic People's Party, and the Endre Bajcsy-Zsilinszky Society composed the ORT. For a discussion of these groups, see Tökés, *Hungary's Negotiated Revolution*, pp. 308–14.

77. Ibid., p. 313.

78. Bruszt, "1989"; Tökés, *Hungary's Negotiated Revolution*, pp. 314, 394.

79. Indeed, "Without the initiation on February 6, 1989 and the successful conclusion on April 5, 1989 of the Polish National Roundtable, Károly Grósz and the PB [Politburo] would have hesitated to initiate a similar process in Hungary" (ibid., p. 307).

80. In October 1989, Pozsgay tried to take over the party, but he discovered that the reformist wing had only two-fifths of the votes necessary. The party was instead dissolved, and the reformists formed the Hungarian Socialist Party (Schöpflin, lecture on Hungary at the University of Michigan, November 6, 1989).

81. Károly Grósz said in 1993 that "we rejected that which existed, but did not know what else might come to replace it" (cited in Tökés, *Hungary's Negotiated Revolution*, p. 285). Aleksander Kwaśniewski told me on October 14, 1998, that had the party and its international allies known what was to come, no agreement could ever have been reached at the Round Table.

82. Tökés, *Hungary's Negotiated Revolution*, p. 208. See also the discussion about how, in May 1988, Hungarian Minister of Interior István Horváth refused to deploy force against nonviolent political dissent (ibid., p. 296).

83. I introduce this argument in "Contingencies and the Alternatives of 1989: Toward a Theory and Practice of Negotiating Revolution," *East European Politics and Society* 13:1 (1999): 301–10.

84. In this section, I rely on Aleksander Smolar's detailed discussion of the Polish opposition in "The Polish Opposition," in Smolar and Kende, *The Role of Opposition*; Jerzy Holzer and Krzysztof Leski, *Solidarność w Podziemniu* (Łódź: Wydawnictwo Łodzkie, 1990).

85. Maciej Łopiński, Marciń Moskit, and Mariusz Wiłk, *Konspira: Solidarity Underground*, trans. Jane Cave (Berkeley: University of California Press, 1990), presents these debates very well.

86. Smolar, "The Polish Opposition."

87. Interview with Zbigniew Bujak, November 23, 1998.

88. David Mason, "Poland's New Trade Unions," *Soviet Studies* 39 (1987): 489–508, esp. 502.

89. Smolar, "The Polish Opposition," p. 19.

90. Ibid., p. 14.

91. Andrzej Walicki, "Liberalism in Poland," *Critical Review* 2 (1988): 8–38.

92. Smolar, "The Polish Opposition."

93. Interview with Zbigniew Bujak, November 23, 1998.

94. For a discussion of the intellectual politics of WiP, see Michael D. Kennedy, "The Constitution of Critical Intellectuals: Polish Physicians, Peace Activists and Democratic Civil Society," *Studies in Comparative Communism* 23:3/4 (1990): 281–304.

95. Interview with Wojciech Jaruzelski, October 7, 1998.

96. Interview with Janusz Rejkowski, October 10, 1998.

97. Walicki, "Liberalism in Poland."

98. See David Ost, "The Transformation of Solidarity and the Future of Central Europe," *Telos* 79 (1989): 69–94, esp. 76. General Kiszczak claimed in an interview that he could have imprisoned Bujak before Bujak was finally arrested on May 31, 1986, but that he would have been more trouble as another martyr than as an underground leader. Interview, October 8, 1998.

99. Interview with Zbigniew Bujak, November 23, 1998.

100. As in Bronisław Geremek's proposal for an anticrisis pact co-organized by Solidarity and the authorities in *Konfrontacje* 2 (1988). See the discussion in Skorzyński, *Ugoda i Rewolucja,* pp. 58–60.

101. Interview with Janusz Rejkowski, October 10, 1998.

102. János Kenedi, *Do It Yourself* (London: Pluto Press, 1982).

103. William A. Gamson and David S. Meyer, "Framing Political Opportunity," in McCarthy, McAdam, and Zald, *Comparative Perspectives on Social Movements.* See also Oberschall, in ibid.

104. See Ronald Grigor Suny, *The Soviet Experiment: Russia, the USSR and the Successor States* (New York: Oxford University Press, 1998), pp. 449–68, and "Nationalism and Nation-States: Gorbachev's Dilemmas," in *The Revenge of the Past: Nationalism, Revolution and the Collapse of the Soviet Union* (Stanford, Calif.: Stanford University Press, 1993), pp. 126–60.

105. Levesque, *The Enigma of 1989,* p. 29. Subsequent references are given in the text.

106. Printed originally in *Pravda,* June 28, 1988; cited in ibid., p. 80 n. 11.

107. For the specific forms of nonintervention and their consequences, see Levesque, *The Enigma of 1989,* pp. 155–56 for East Germany, p. 174 for Bulgaria, and pp. 187–88 for Czechoslovakia.

108. Gorbachev believed that the East European regimes "made their choice" in favor of socialism, and hence he could not believe that they would opt out. See Mikhail Gorbachev, *Perestroika: Vues neuves sur notre pays et le monde* (Paris: Flammarion, 1987), p. 280, and Levesque, *The Enigma of 1989,* p. 47, for discussion.

109. See Gorbachev, *Perestroika,* p. 301.

110. Ronald Grigor Suny, "Elite Transformation in Late-Soviet and Post-Soviet Caucasia, or What Happens when the Ruling Class Can't Rule?" in Timothy J. Colton and Robert C. Tucker, eds., *Patterns in Post-Soviet Leadership* (Boulder, Colo.: Westview, 1995), pp. 141–67, illustrates that one of the critical factors enabling the formation of a stable political elite in postcommunist states is "the willingness of the old political elite to surrender power and accept the new rules of the political game" (144). Sometimes, of course, the communists cannot find common ground, as in Georgia, where the April 1989 killings of peaceful demonstrators in Tblisi radicalized the opposition and made compromise with communists impossible (156, 161).

111. As Janusz Reykowski stated in *Trybuna Ludu,* February 11–12, 1989; cited in Skorzyński, *Ugoda i Rewolucja,* p. 204.

112. Skorzyński, *Ugoda i Rewolucja,* pp. 89, 92, 118–19.

113. Theda Skocpol, *States and Social Revolutions* (Cambridge: Cambridge University Press, 1979), is known for this state-centered conjunctural emphasis, but Valerie Bunce's *Subversive Institutions* extends that theme directly to the issues considered here.

114. Jadwiga Staniszkis, *The Dynamics of Breakthrough in Eastern Europe: The Polish Experience* (Berkeley: University of California Press, 1991), p. 1.

115. "Polaków mniej interesuje 'okrągly stól,' a bardziej suto zastawiony stól," "Konferencja prasowa Mieczysława F. Rakowskiego," *Trubuna Ludu,* October 15–16, 1988; cited in Skorzyński, *Ugoda i Rewolucja,* p. 112.

116. Andrzej Paczkowski, "Polska 1986–1989: od kooptacji do negocjacji: Kilka uwag o wchodzeniu w procesu zmiany systemowej," Instytut Studiów Politycznych Polskiej Akademii Nauk, Warsaw, 1997.

117. Skorzyński, *Ugoda i Rewolucja,* p. 128. Subsequent references are given in the text.

118. Interviews with Andrzej Gdula, October 10, 1998, and Janusz Rejkowski, October 11, 1998.

119. Interview with Wojciech Jaruzelski, October 7, 1998.

120. Skorzyński, *Ugoda i Rewolucja,* pp. 142–47.

121. Staniszkis, *The Dynamics of Breakthrough in Eastern Europe,* p. 201. See also Skorzyński, *Ugoda i Rewolucja,* p. 162

122. Quoted in Sergiusz Kowalski, *Narodziny III Rzeczpospolitej* (Warsaw: Wydawnictwa Szkolne i Pedagogiczne, 1996), p. 10.

123. See, for instance, the remarks of the president and cofounder of the Christian-National Union, Wiesław Chrzanowski, in *Pól Wieku Polityki: czyli rzecz o obronie czynnej. Z Wiesławem Chrzanowskim rozmawiali Piotr Mierecki I Bogusław Kiernicki* (Warsaw: Inicjatywa Wydawnicza «ad astra», 1997).

124. F. Felicki (P. Pacewicz), "Na posiedzeniu KKW," *Tygodnik Mazowsze,* January 25, 1989; cited in Skorzyński, *Ugoda i Rewolucja,* p. 179.

125. Jan Gross discusses this dilemma, and the obligation of Bishop Alojzy Orszulik to deny that any secret deals were made in Magdalenka. See "Poland: From Civil Society to Political Nation," in Banac, *Eastern Europe in Revolution,* pp. 56–71, esp. 58–59 n. 5.

126. Jacek Kuroń, "Okrągly Stól z lotu ptaka," *Tygodnik Mazowsze,* November 23, 1988; cited in Skorzyński, *Ugoda i Rewolucja,* p. 154.

127. Remarks made at "Communism's Negotiated Collapse: The Polish Round Table Talks, Ten Years Later," April 7–10, 1999, University of Michigan, Ann Arbor.

128. This, of course, carried some risk for the church, for these were difficult and delicate politics. One of the most extraordinary documents of these politics can be found in Peter Raina, *Rozmowy z Władzami PRL: Arcybiskup Dąbrowski w Służbie Kosciołu i Narodu* (Warsaw: Książka Polska, 1995).

129. Participants in these Magdalenka meetings included Lech Wałęsa, Tadeusz Mazowiecki, Bronisław Geremek, Zbigniew Bujak, Władysław Frasyniuk, Adam Michnik, Andrzej Stelmachowski, and Lech Kaczyński from the side of Solidarity; Czesław Kiszczak, Aleksander Kwaśniewski, Janusz Reykowski, Andrzej Gdula, Ireneusz Sekuła, Kazimierz Cypryniak, Józef Czyrek, and Stanisław Ciosek from the authorities (Wiktor Osiatyński, "The Roundtable Talks in Poland," in Elster, *The Roundtable Talks and the Breakdown of Communism,* p. 65 n. 22). The clergy included Archbishop Tadeusz Gocłowski, Archbishop Bronisław Dąbrowski, and Father Alojzy Orszulik.

130. Ibid.

131. Janusz Reykowski, "Ład symetryczny. Z prof. Januszem Reykowskim, psychologiem, członkiem Biura Politycznego KC PZPR rozmawiają Leszek Bedkowski i

Daniel Wojtowicz," *Przegląd Tygodniowy,* February 12, 1989; cited in Skorzyński, *Ugoda i Rewolucja,* p. 201.

132. Osiatyński, "The Roundtable Talks in Poland," discusses this briefly on pp. 53–54. Although this proposal appealed to the Solidarity negotiators as an opportunity for extending the logic of competitive elections, it had not been previously discussed among the communist side. In a meeting among communist decision makers on the following Friday, arguments for and against Kwaśniewski's proposal were aired, though Jaruzelski himself never took a position. It was not clear to Janusz Reykowski, at least, whether Jaruzelski would ultimately support the proposal. Before the committee could meet again, government spokesman Jerzy Urban announced that there would be such elections, and the decision was thus made for them. Interview with Janusz Reykowski, April 10, 1999.

133. Remarks made by Janusz Reykowski at "Communism's Negotiated Collapse: The Polish Round Table Talks, Ten Years Later."

134. Osiatyński, "The Roundtable Talks in Poland," p. 54.

135. Timothy Garton Ash, "Revolution in Hungary and Poland," *New York Review of Books,* August 17, 1989, pp. 9–15, p. 10.

136. Marek Henzler, "Wygrali w Prawyborach," *Polityka* 48 (May 27, 1989): 3.

137. Osiatyński, "The Roundtable Talks in Poland," pp. 37–38.

138. Skorzyński, *Ugoda i Rewolucja,* p. 100.

139. Timothy Garton Ash, *The Magic Lantern* (New York: Random House, 1990).

140. Tőkés, *Hungary's Negotiated Revolution,* p. 314.

141. Ibid., p. 384; and David Lane, *Soviet Society under Perestroika* (Boston: Unwin Hyman, 1990), p. 66.

142. This is a very common theme in my interviews with communist reformers in Poland; for Hungary, see Tőkés, *Hungary's Negotiated Revolution,* p. 306.

143. Tőkés, *Hungary's Negotiated Revolution,* p. 307.

144. For a comparison of the Round Tables, see ibid., pp. 333–34, and David Stark and László Bruszt, "Remaking the Political Field: Strategic Interactions and Contingent Choices," in *Postsocialist Pathways,* pp. 15–48.

145. Tőkés, *Hungary's Negotiated Revolution,* pp. 361–98; Stark and Bruszt, "Remaking the Political Field."

146. Tőkés, *Hungary's Negotiated Revolution,* p. 336.

147. Although this was probably a majority position in the party, the negotiating team was not so sure of the future, according to Janusz Reykowski. After the first meeting of the political roundtable, high party officials as well as the negotiating team debated whether these were only mock negotiations. Solidarity, one person argued, did not want real negotiations, and would not negotiate in good faith. Party officials concluded that this might in fact be right, but that there was no peaceful alternative. If they did not negotiate now, in three to five years there would be no chance for a peaceful resolution of differences. Even if the negotiations meant giving up power, they would at least avoid the danger of civil war.

148. In fact, part of the communists' problem was that they chose a particular kind of electoral system—majority runoff rather than a single transferable vote system—that magnified the communist defeat. See Marek Kamiński, "Jak Komuniści Mogli Zachować Wladze po Okrągłym Stole: Rzecz o (nie)Kontrolowanej Odwilzy, Sondazach Opinii Publicznej i Ordynacji Wyborczej," *Studia Socjologiczne* 145:2 (1997): 5–34.

149. Interview with Janusz Reykowski, April 10, 1999.

150. Interview with Andrzej Gdula, October 10, 1998.

151. Adam Michnik, "Your President, Our Prime Minister," in *Letters from Freedom,* pp. 129–31.

152. Róna-Tas, *The Great Surprise of the Small Transformation,* is very effective in this argument.

153. John Borneman, *Settling Accounts: Violence, Justice and Accountability in Post-socialist Europe* (Princeton, N.J.: Princeton University Press, 1997), has made a strong case for the importance of "settling accounts" in postcommunist Europe. He was moved by the demands of the East German public to hold people accountable for the crimes they committed under communist rule. Borneman focuses on how retributive justice might be won whereby the criminals are punished and the dignity of victims is restored. He concentrates especially on Germany, but also attends somewhat to other East European countries. He argues, ultimately, that trials of retributive justice might not only be morally right, but also "necessary to prevent cycles of retributive violence" (7). This is a way of instantiating the rule of law into a society's sense of justice, and to establish the state as a moral agent (23).

2. Transition Culture and Transition Poverty

I wish to thank the audience of the Vocabularies of Identity Conference at the University of Michigan in 1998 and its organizer, Brian Porter, for their comments on earlier parts of this chapter. I also wish to thank Barbara Anderson and our students specifically, for our collaboration in teaching a course comparing Estonia, Ukraine, and Uzbekistan in fall 1996 produced my initial idea for comparing transition culture with transition poverty. My students in subsequent classes on East European societies and institutions helped me elaborate the sense of transition culture. I hope that they can see evidence of their contributions in this chapter. I also wish to express my thanks to my associates at the Center for Russian and East European Studies, notably Marga Miller, whose expertise in technical assistance in Russia contributed significantly to my ideas on this topic, to M. Dierkes and D. Denison for their helpful comments on an earlier version of this chapter, and to Ashraf Ghani on a later version. This essay significantly expands on the introduction to "A Cultural Analysis of Homosocial Reproduction and Contesting Claims to Competence in Transitional Firms," in Daniel R. Denison, ed., *Organizational Change in Transitional Economies* (Mahwah, N.J.: Lawrence Erlbaum Associates, 2001).

1. This is the introduction to the World Bank's Web site, "Europe and Central Asia" regional discussion. See http://www.worldbank.org/html/extdr/offrep/eca/eca.htm, May 17, 1999.

2. http://www.worldbank.org/html/extdr/forngos.htm and *The State in a Changing World: World Development Report, 1997,* published for the World Bank (New York: Oxford University Press, 1997), reflect the broader concerns of transition culture, and show how the preeminent organization within transition culture, the World Bank, can change. As Ashraf Ghani has argued ("Transformations of Expertise in the World Bank," videotaped lecture at the International Institute, University of Michigan, February 8, 2000), the World Bank itself is in the midst of a powerful contest over the substantive foci and epistemological and methodological grounding of its work. For an external assessment of how the World Bank changes, in particular with its growing attention to governance, see Charles Myers, "International Policy Organizations and Post-Communist Politics," unpublished paper, Department of Political Science, University of Michigan, 1999. As Myers points out, the World Bank is stuck: it seeks to present itself as a "learning, flexible and responsive organization," but this very disposition, especially in the publication of its own self-criticism, can "assist its critics and support other views of development" (10).

3. For elaboration, see Michael D. Kennedy and Daina Stukuls, "The Narrative of Civil Society in Communism's Collapse and Postcommunism's Alternatives: Emancipation, Polish Protest and Baltic Nationalisms," *Constellations: An International Journal of Critical and Democratic Theory* 5:4 (1998): 541–71. See also George Soros, *Open Society: Reforming Global Capitalism* (New York: Public Affairs, 2000).

4. Jerzy Szacki, *Liberalism after Communism* (Budapest: Central European Press, 1995), described the Solidarity movement as *proto*liberal, because it elevated civil society over individualism, and subordinated the latter to various collectivist impulses from "society" writ large.

5. John Keane, *Václav Havel: A Political Tragedy in Six Acts* (New York: Basic Books, 2000).

6. Szacki, *Liberalism after Communism.* For a good account of Poland's economic transformations, see Kazimierz Z. Poznański, *Poland's Protracted Transition: Institutional Change and Economic Growth, 1970–1994* (Cambridge: Cambridge University Press, 1996).

7. Jeffrey Sachs, *Poland's Jump to the Market Economy* (Cambridge: MIT Press, 1995), exemplifies this centering of the Polish experience.

8. Although Raymond Williams emphasizes that cultural formations are fluid and multiple, I find it helpful to approach that fluidity after elaborating the more structural features within which historical variability and practice-induced transformations take place. Transition culture, in particular, has an identifiable structure that can be rendered through semiotic analysis. For an elaboration on these distinctions, see Jeffery Alexander, "Analytic Debates: Understanding the Relative Autonomy of Culture," in Jeffery Alexander and Steven Seidman, eds., *Culture and Society: Contemporary Debates* (Cambridge: Cambridge University Press, 1990), pp. 1–30.

9. See Michael D. Kennedy, "The Labilities of Liberalism and Nationalism after Communism: Polish Businessmen in the Articulation of the Nation," in Ronald Grigor Suny and Michael D. Kennedy, eds., *Intellectuals and the Articulation of the Nation* (Ann Arbor: University of Michigan Press, 1999). For an important discussion of how the cultural productions of businessmen have redrawn the imagination of the market economy, see Pauline Gianoplus, "The Business of Identities: Remaking the Polish Bourgeoisie," Ph.D. dissertation, University of Michigan, 1999.

10. I prefer not to engage in discussions of who is, and who is not, intellectual on the basis of their proximity to power. It is, however, important to consider how such discursive moves to identify who is and who is not an intellectual—or a sociologist, for that matter—work to preserve certain boundaries and certain status hierarchies with limited enclaves of knowledge production. For a broader discussion of these issues, see Michael D. Kennedy and Ronald Grigor Suny, "Introduction," in Suny and Kennedy, *Intellectuals and the Articulation of the Nation.*

11. Mirosław Dzielski, "Szefczyk Dratewka na pomysł," in *Duch nadchodzącego Czasu* (Warsaw: Wektory, 1989), p. 206; cited in Szacki, *Liberalism after Communism,* p. 131.

12. Szacki, *Liberalism after Communism,* pp. 143–44.

13. Kennedy, "The Labilities of Liberalism and Nationalism after Communism."

14. Poznański, *Poland's Protracted Transition,* p. 164.

15. Robert Wuthnow, *Communities of Discourse: Ideology and Social Structure in the Reformation, the Enlightenment and European Socialism* (Cambridge: Harvard University Press, 1989), provides the original reference for "community of discourse." Ashraf Ghani has suggested that this might be better conceived as a "universe" of discourse. I retain the reference to community because I want to emphasize the peopling of

this transition culture, a connotation that community nicely implies. I do not, however, want to imply with this term that community involves a singularity of belief or commonality of values. Transition culture is more complicated than that.

16. Peter Hamilton, *Talcott Parsons* (London: Tavistock, 1983), identified three phases of Parsons's work, with the second epitomized by *The Social System* (New York: Free Press, 1951), and his dedication to elaborating pattern variables.

17. Hamilton, *Talcott Parsons,* pp. 104–9, provides a concise introduction to these Parsonian oppositions:

1. affectivity versus affective neutrality—degree of emotion
2. diffuseness versus specificity—scope of obligations
3. universalism versus particularism—generality of evaluation
4. achievement versus ascription—criteria of evaluation
5. self versus collectivity—breadth of interest informing

18. Sachs, *Poland's Jump to the Market Economy,* p. 5.

19. Soros, *Open Society,* pp. 208–34.

20. *From Plan to Market: World Development Report, 1996,* published for the World Bank (New York: Oxford University Press, 1996).

21. Given that this is such a potentially dynamic culture, it is difficult to predict what is enduring and what is not. Based on what the World Bank represented on its Web site in May 1999, one could argue that it endured through the decade's end. (See http://www.worldbank.org/html/extdr/offrep/eca/eca.htm.) However, this overlooks the tensions within transition culture and in the World Bank itself, a subject to which I return in the end of this volume.

22. This report, and transition culture more generally, struggle to take into account the lessons offered by China and Vietnam. In many ways, Vietnam and especially China are much more successful in economic change than other parts of the postcommunist world. Their success is not, however, easily digested within the framework of transition because of their rejection of political democratization alongside economic liberalization and stabilization. In this volume, I do not take into account their place in transition culture but focus rather on those places that struggle to combine the political and economic aspects of transition culture, especially in East Central Europe. For a discussion of why a China lens, rather than a transition culture lens, might be more appropriate for reading Russian change, see Michael Burawoy, "The State and Economic Involution: Russia through a China Lens," *World Development* 24:6 (1996): 1105–17.

23. *From Plan to Market: World Development Report, 1996,* p. 2. Subsequent references are given in the text.

24. Another way to draw the distinction is to identify the former as a form of analysis and praxis based on the vision of an end point, while the latter focuses on the origins or dynamics of the systems in question. See Burawoy, "The State and Economic Involution."

25. The World Bank has made the addressing of poverty prominent in its self-representation. Its 1999 annual report assesses, for instance, the impact of the Asian crisis on global poverty, and recommends that programs be developed to provide social safety nets, with unemployment insurance, subsidized school fees, job creation, and food subsidies as part of the strategy ("Poverty Forecast Grim: World Bank: Asian Slump Leaves Millions Poor," *Ann Arbor News,* June 3, 1999, p. A4). In the same article, the World Bank's image is reproduced, despite the point of the bank's news conference: "The Bank's underlying purpose always has been to cut poverty, but it has been

criticized for lending programs that stress long term development over dealing more directly with the suffering."

26. These countries include Poland, Hungary, the Czech Republic, and Slovakia.

27. Indeed, the tradition of identifying Ukraine as exemplary in failure continues in the 1997 report, *The State in a Changing World: World Development Report, 1997,* published for the World Bank (New York: Oxford University Press, 1997). Ukraine is specifically identified in a discussion of policy making. Where policy making is weak and fragmented in Africa, and can be addressed by a more professional civil service, in Central and Eastern Europe and the Commonwealth of Independent States, expertise seems satisfactory. Instead, the region apparently has "confused and overlapping responsibilities and multiple rather than collective accountability." Ukraine exemplifies the problem (1997, p. 85). Judges' dependence on local authorities for their housing is another illustration of bad government in Ukraine, for this dependency limits judicial independence (1997, p. 100).

28. http://www.worldbank.org/data/countrydata/aag/estaag.pdf (May 1999).

29. http://www.worldbank.org/ecspf/final/html/estonia.htm (May 1999).

30. The World Bank explains one reason for Ukraine's failure by its leaders' preoccupation with questions of national identity (11). Its citizens recognize this problem in a different way. In one focus group, to be discussed in chapter 5, Andriy from Ivankiv, proud to speak Ukrainian, lamented that "Everyone knows when the Soviet Union was falling apart, Ukraine was the richest country in it" but that 80 percent of the crisis Ukraine faces is because "those who have power think more about themselves than about the country as a whole" (2174, 2185).

31. *The State in a Changing World: World Development Report, 1997,* p. 85.

32. This dependency limits judicial independence (ibid., p. 100).

33. http://www.worldbank.org/ecspf/final/html/ukraine.htm (May 1999).

34. Contrary to what many have felt to be the logic of transition, the desirable state is not the minimalist state, according to James Wolfensohn, president of the World Bank. Wolfensohn asserted that the desirable state should be constructed to play "a catalytic, facilitating role, encouraging and complementing the activities of private businesses and individuals" (*The State in a Changing World: World Development Report, 1997,* p. iii). Indeed, drawing on the strength of its broad comparative and empirical approach, the report argues quite directly that "good government (understood as both policy and institutional capability) helps explain the income gap between East Asia and Africa" (32). See Myers, "International Policy Organizations and Post-Communist Politics," for an extended discussion of the World Bank's changing appreciation for governance issues.

35. Vladimir Popov, Paul Gregory, Catalin Zamfir, Carol Scott Leonard, Asta Sendonaris, Susan Linz, Stephen Batsone, Nada Kobeissi, Giovanni Andrea Cornia, Victor Rodwin, Harley Balzer, and Omar Noman, *Poverty in Transition* (Regional Bureau for Europe and the CIS. United Nations Development Program, 1998). This report is not officially endorsed by the UNDP, but rather reflects the views of the authors. Subsequent references are given in the text.

36. Back cover of *Poverty in Transition.*

37. This is exemplified in the discussion of the box on the alternative models of the welfare state (105), and alternative types of industrial policy (133).

38. Estonia, however, has not remained so quick in implementing its reforms of education systems.

39. Originally published in "Point-Counterpoint: Should the State Help the Post-

Soviet Poor" (1998), www.ijt.cz/transitions/shouldl.html, adapted in *Poverty in Transition*, p. 104.

40. Understood here as one hundred dollars in purchasing power parity per month per person; see pp. 12–14.

41. Here again I focus only on cases with relatively firm assignments of virtue or failure to their examples, and do not include the numerous examples, especially pertaining to microfinance development, that link international agencies across the region. Here the focus is on the exemplary international agency less than the country per se.

3.1–2: Health-care reform: the message in these two boxes is not so clearcut. Both emphasize the crisis of adult male mortality, but the Russian case in intervention earns more positive commentary. The problem is addressed by a UNDP project, whereas the Hungarian efforts are apparently less well elaborated, perhaps less well understood.

Learning from Positive Efforts/Russian Federation box: this refers to progress in the development of such a class.

Dangers Needing Address/Russian Federation box: this refers to the cultural resistance to discuss inequality and the formation of such a class.

5.5: Unemployment policy box: this exemplary effort is also a UNDP project in collaboration with the European Union and Japan.

Dangers Needing Address/Poland box: this box was not so much a danger as it mostly described the history of reform, but it was hardly positive in comparison to the Kazakhstani account. It was rather used to show that a failure to address pension reform adequately can cause political troubles, and even downfalls of governments.

42. Raymond Williams, *Marxism and Literature* (Oxford: Clarendon, 1977), p. 116.

43. It is almost too clear. I hope my use of artifacts is sufficiently convincing that this structure lies in the data, or that at least this structure does not only reflect my own predisposition toward transition culture.

44. For elaboration of how the utopia of normality functions in the social transformation of Soviet-type societies, see Daina Stukuls, "Imagining the Nation: Campaign Posters of the First Postcommunist Elections in Latvia," *East European Politics and Societies* 11:1 (1997): 131–54, and *Imagining the Nation: History, Modernity and Revolution in Latvia* (State College: Pennsylvania State University Press, 2002); as well as Nicolae Harsanyi and Michael D. Kennedy, "Between Utopia and Dystopia: The Labilities of Nationalism in Eastern Europe," in Michael D. Kennedy, ed., *Envisioning Eastern Europe: Postcommunist Cultural Studies* (Ann Arbor: University of Michigan Press, 1994), pp. 149–79.

45. This was, after all, the value of utopia in enabling the future to be imagined as something other than a smooth extension of the present. "As Theodor Adorno put it, society can become 'problematic' (i.e. an object of intellectual and practical criticism) only if people can conceive of one which is different from it" (Theodor Adorno, "Zur Logik der Sozialwissenschaften," *Kölner Zeitschrift für Soziologie* 14 [1962]: 262; cited in Zygmunt Bauman, *Socialism: The Active Utopia* [London: Allen and Unwin, 1976], p. 36).

46. Williams, *Marxism and Literature*, pp. 132–34.

47. See Ann Swidler, "Culture in Action: Symbols and Strategies," *American Sociological Review* 51:2 (1986): 273–86.

48. For an application of this to nationalism, see Ronald Grigor Suny and Michael D. Kennedy, eds., *Intellectuals and the Articulation of the Nation* (Ann Arbor: University of Michigan Press, 1999).

49. Williams, *Marxism and Literature*, p. 123.

3. Transition Culture in Business Practice

Pauline Gianoplus, Naomi Roslyn Galtz, and Margaret Foley met with me in the 1995–96 academic year in a "bizculture" salon where the materials and ideas for this paper were developed. I wish to thank them and the various audiences where earlier versions of this chapter have been presented: the Vocabularies of Identity Conference at the University of Michigan in 1998, the Organizational Change in Transition Economies conference at the William Davidson Institute in 1997, the University of Wisconsin, Madison, and UCLA in 1997, the 1995 meeting of the American Sociological Association, and presentations at the Center for International Business Education, the Center for Research on Social Organization, and the Advanced Study Center of the International Institute at the University of Michigan. I also wish to express my thanks to my associates at the Center for Russian and East European Studies, notably Marga Miller, whose expertise contributed significantly to my ideas on this topic, and to M. Dierkes and D. Denison, for their helpful comments on an earlier version of this chapter. This particular project was supported by a grant from the William Davidson Institute; previous work on the subject was also supported by the National Council for Soviet and East European Research and the Rackham Graduate School and the Center for International Business Education at the University of Michigan. This essay draws on several other publications of mine, including "The Labilities of Liberalism and Nationalism after Communism: Polish Businessmen in the Articulation of the Nation," in Ronald Grigor Suny and Michael D. Kennedy, eds., *Intellectuals and the Articulation of the Nation* (Ann Arbor: University of Michigan Press, 1999), and "A Cultural Analysis of Homosocial Reproduction and Contesting Claims to Competence in Transitional Firms," in Daniel R. Denison, ed., *Organizational Change in Transitional Economies* (Mahwah, N.J.: Lawrence Erlbaum Associates, 2001).

1. I draw on several data sources for this chapter. Beginning in 1990, I have advised American business experts who visit Eastern Europe. In particular, since 1995, I have been a research associate of the William Davidson Institute at the University of Michigan Business School, an institute dedicated to facilitating the transition to a market economy across the world. Attending the institute's lectures, workshops, and conferences has contributed enormously to my sense of transition culture. More formally, along with five former graduate students—Pauline Gianoplus, Dina Smeltz, Naomi Roslyn Galtz, Magdalena Szaflarski, and Margaret Foley—between 1991 and 1995 I have collected more than one hundred semistructured interviews on the cultural encounter between Western, and especially American, business experts and East European entrepreneurs and managers. I draw on these interviews in this chapter. The interviews we have collected are ethnographic, but derived from semistructured interview schedules. We do not pretend that they are in any sense "representative" of the total of business entrepreneurs or managers developing postcommunist capitalism, nor are they representative of the experts who have gone to advise business in Eastern Europe. These interviews are highly skewed toward exemplary businessmen and women, those who can win the subsidized attention of business consultants grounded in academic institutions. Likewise, the interviews with Americans are skewed away from those working in private consulting firms, and toward those still in school. Many of them, but not all, had internships with the William Davidson Institute, and before that, the Michigan Business Assistance Corps under the direction of Marian Krzyzowski. "Experts" therefore work in the region with varying degrees of experience and credentials—from MBA students on a summer internship and MBA graduates who have worked in the region for several years, to

retired American businessmen advising for a year. The East European businessmen and women we interviewed have been entrepreneur-owners of small firms, indigenous consultants, and managers in state-owned firms, multinational firms, and firms in movement toward private ownership. Various kinds of expatriate managers are located in between the expert consultants and indigenous businesspeople: some knew little about their new country before they arrived, others grew up in the country.

Although my research assistants and I have interviewed entrepreneurs, consultants, and managers from China, Russia, Ukraine, Hungary, Estonia, the Czech Republic, Slovakia, and Poland, most of the interviews have been conducted with Polish businesspeople. We have interviewed business consultants or advisers from the Peace Corps, the International Service Executive Corps, the Enterprise Corps of the University of North Carolina at Chapel Hill, the University of Michigan MBA Corps, and interns with the William Davidson Institute at the University of Michigan.

In this chapter, I rely mostly on a series of fifty-six in-depth interviews with both Western experts and East European managers and entrepreneurs conducted in 1994 and 1995. All but three of the twenty-seven 1994 interviews were conducted in Poland. All but six of the interviews were with Polish managers and entrepreneurs, given that most of my previous work relied on interviews with Western experts (Michael D. Kennedy and Pauline Gianoplus, "Entrepreneurs and Expertise: A Cultural Encounter in the Making of Post-Communist Capitalism in Poland," *East European Politics and Societies* 8:1 [1994]: 56–91). The twenty-four interviews with Polish managers and entrepreneurs represented fifteen different firms. Eight of my informants were employed in consulting firms. Four interviews were conducted with representatives of manufacturing firms, three interviews with those employed in mass media, and three in communications. I interviewed one person from the government side of business support, and one person from a service establishment.

Apart from one interview in Russia, the twenty-nine interviews in 1995 took place in Ann Arbor, Michigan, and were conducted with participants in the William Davidson Institute's summer projects. The William Davidson Institute organizes projects in which a team of American MBA, and occasionally area studies MA, students work with an indigenous firm's management to resolve a particular problem identified by that management as one in need of improvement. Out of this group, nine interviews were conducted with American interns and the balance with East European consultants, managers, or interns from the region who were associated with eleven different firms. Fifteen of the interviews were with people associated with the Polish projects, although people who worked in Hungary, Russia, Romania, and Slovakia were also interviewed. These firms included two communications, two consulting, five manufacturing, and two light manufacturing/retail firms.

Each interview lasted from one to three hours. Four researchers conducted the interviews. We relied on a common interview schedule for each type of respondent (manager, intern, and "local fellow"—an indigenous person who has had training in Western business management techniques) to guide our semistructured interviews and ensure that we covered the same ground, if not in exactly the same fashion. Those who seek clarity on the distribution of values and other qualities of mental structures will not find what they need with these data and this chapter's presentation. Those interested in culture in action should find what they seek.

2. Craig Calhoun, *Nationalism* (Buckingham: Open University Press, 1997), pp. 92–95.

3. The numbers following references designate my own coding system for the par-

ticular interview conducted. In order to encourage our subjects to speak freely, we guaranteed them anonymity. In order to preserve that anonymity, I have had to alter quotations slightly so that anonymity would be preserved. Given that there were relatively few non-Polish interviews, I have had to mask the nationality of the comment. For example, where it is not critical to the sense of the quotation, I replace Polish or Romanian with "East European" and American or German with "Westerner" or the country's name with "my country."

4. Indeed, some authors have suggested that the relationship should not be so obvious. The relationship between national, transition, and socialist cultures ought to be conceived in terms of lability, where the relationship between these systems of cultural practices is *assumed* to be unstable and contested. See Nicolae Harsanyi and Michael D. Kennedy, "Between Utopia and Dystopia: The Labilities of Nationalism in Eastern Europe," in Michael D. Kennedy, ed., *Envisioning Eastern Europe: Postcommunist Cultural Studies* (Ann Arbor: University of Michigan Press, 1994), pp. 149–79.

5. This framework of transition and cultural transformation is so powerful that it distracts people from considering the similarities between American and East European experiences, as a marxist perspective, for instance, might encourage. Only one American adviser emphasized the similarity: "these guys are as advanced or more advanced than some of my customers used to be when I worked at GE." Nevertheless, he still interpreted the majority of his firm in terms of the transition culture narrative. They lacked the "drive to or the initiative that is required to do something above and beyond their day-to-day responsibilities," something he attributed to their formation under socialism (977).

6. One might find some precedent for these managerial politics of assimilation in the Western corporate firm. In general, managers tend to promote those who resemble themselves in manner and style. Kantor calls this "homosocial reproduction" (Rosabeth Moss Kantor, *Men and Women of the Corporation* [New York: Basic Books, 1977]). In the West, homosocial reproduction is not a consequence of simple racism or sexism, but is indirectly a product of organizational uncertainty and managerial discretion. The significance of trust and communication among corporate managers and the difficulty of evaluating management activities all push toward a form of homosocial reproduction. Homosocial reproduction is also implicated in managerial efficacy. To be noticed as a superior manager, one must undertake activities that are extraordinary, visible, and relevant to solving the most pressing organizational problem (177). But to solve these problems, one must have power, and power over subordinates depends on having credibility with one's superiors (169–70). Whether to realize management goals or to get promotions, Kantor argues that cultural identification with one's superiors is important. The problem of homosocial reproduction is also a key issue facing firms in transitional economies, and especially multinational firms. In many ways, one could argue that Kantor's argument applies directly. Given the greater organizational uncertainty of the early stages of firm development, homosocial reproduction is more likely. Given the uncertainty of the business environment, the pressure to practice homosocial reproduction is greater. And given the push toward a stricter gender division of labor in the larger social structure, the impetus toward the gendering of homosocial reproduction is perhaps even stronger. For one of the most important initial statements on this, see Peggy Watson, "The Rise of Masculinism in Eastern Europe," *New Left Review* 198 (193): 71–82. For a later systematic statement, see Susan Gal and Gail Kligman, *Politics of Gender after Socialism* (Princeton, N.J.: Princeton University Press, 2000).

7. Kennedy and Gianoplus, "Entrepreneurs and Expertise."

8. Many of the advisers we interviewed had read Janos Kornai, *The Socialist Sys-*

tem: The Political Economy of Communism (Princeton, N.J.: Princeton University Press, 1992), from which this and other analytical statements could be taken.

9. Much as in Kantor's analysis (*Men and Women of the Corporation,* pp. 63–67).

10. Estonian business adviser Alexander Plotkin emphasizes that Estonian and Russian managers are particularly unable to recognize this inadequacy. See Michael D. Kennedy, "The Value of Business Expertise in Eastern Europe," *Journal of the International Institute* 4:1 (1996): 10.

11. I suspect that this adequacy has less to do with the quality of translation than with the "can-do" attitude cultivated among Western businesspeople. I find that Western advisers focus on problems that can be solved and not with issues that have no direct solution as the philosophical challenge in translation can imply.

12. This difference tends to be minimized in most of the interviews we conducted. And it should be. Most of the people we interviewed were working within firms exemplifying transition culture, and were, in one way or another, working with Westerners to improve their own business practices. Indeed, the interviews were themselves part of the overall transition culture practice, for Americans were interviewing East Europeans and Americans about their collaboration. Within the very framework of the research, therefore, transition culture was privileged. At the same time, however, during interviews, we specifically probed for those moments where East European difference might be less easily assimilated into transition culture.

13. Kennedy, "The Value of Business Expertise in Eastern Europe."

14. Debates over the value of expatriate appointments are common in multinational discussions. On the one hand, it is clear that expatriates facilitate communication with the home office of the multinational. On the other hand, a five-year appointment is usually understood as a three-year job—the first year is learning, and the last year is preparing to leave. One of the major initiatives in multinational development is to create genuinely multinational managements in the core. Multinational corporations wishing to demonstrate their multinational commitments flag this dimension of career promotions. See, for example, C. K. Prahalad and Kenneth Lieberthal, "The End of Corporate Imperialism," *Harvard Business Review* (July–August 1998): 69–79.

15. See ibid.

16. József Böröcz, "Social Change by Fusion?" Paper presented at the Thirty-second Conference of the International Institute of Sociology, Università degli Studi, Trieste— Gorizia, July 3–6, 1995. Böröcz has subsequently elaborated on this in Hungarian in *Fúziók: Társadalmi átalakulás és intézményi kreativitás* (Budapest: Osiris, forthcoming).

17. Amartya Sen, *Development as Freedom* (New York: Alfred A. Knopf, 1999), pp. 173–75.

4. Transition, Freedom, and Nationalism

Earlier versions of this chapter were presented to Harvard University's Center for European Studies and Center for Russian Studies in 1997, to the University of Michigan's Center for Russian and East European Studies in 1997, and to the University of Michigan's Social Psychology group in 1998. I thank these audiences for their helpful comments. This research has been generously supported by both the Ford Foundation (Ford Foundation Grant No. 950–1163) and the National Council for Soviet and East European Research (NCSEER) (Research Contract 812–11). Neither organization is responsible for the findings presented in this report. I am grateful to all of our colleagues who have worked on this project with me, most especially and immediately to Lisa Fein, who worked with me in coding the data.

1. Mart Laar, "Estonia's Success Story," *Journal of Democracy* 7:1 (January 1996): 97.

2. Ernest Gellner, *Nations and Nationalism* (Ithaca, N.Y.: Cornell University Press, 1983), p. 1.

3. Ibid., p. 126.

4. Craig Calhoun, *Nationalism* (Buckingham: Open University Press, 1997).

5. Benedict Anderson, *Imagined Communities: Reflections on the Origin and Spread of Nationalism*, 2d ed. (London: Verso, 1991), p. 6.

6. Calhoun, *Nationalism*, p. 5.

7. Nationalism is a discursive formation, "a way of speaking that shapes our consciousness, but also is problematic enough that it keeps generating more issues and questions, keeps propelling us into further talk, keeps producing debates over how to think about it" (ibid., p. 3).

8. Roman Szporluk, *Communism and Nationalism: Karl Marx versus Friederich List* (New York: Oxford University Press, 1988), p. 93. He bases his ideas on Anthony Smith, *Theories of Nationalism* (New York: Harper and Row, 1993), p. 21. See also Roman Szporluk, Gale Stokes, Miroslav Hroch, and Ernest Gellner, "Discussion," *East European Politics and Societies* 4:1 (1990): 77–97; Elie Kedourie, *Nationalism* (London: Hutchinson, 1960).

9. *From Plan to Market: World Development Report, 1996,* published for the World Bank (New York: Oxford University Press, 1996), p. 11.

10. Calhoun, *Nationalism*, pp. 45–46.

11. For a general argument about comparative social science along these lines, see Craig Calhoun, *Critical Social Theory: Culture, History and the Challenge of Difference* (Oxford: Blackwell, 1995), pp. 53–55.

12. David Laitin, *Identity in Formation: The Russian-Speaking Populations in the Near Abroad* (Ithaca, N.Y.: Cornell University Press, 1998).

13. Many other works deal with this subject as well, including Jeff Chinn and Robert Kaiser, *Russians as the New Minority: Ethnicity and Nationalism in the Soviet Successor States* (Boulder, Colo.: Westview Press, 1996).

14. Lowell Barrington, "The Domestic and International Consequences of Citizenship in the Soviet Successor States," *Europe-Asia Studies* 47 (1995): 731–63.

15. Vello Pettai, "Contemporary International Influences on Post-Soviet Nationalism: The Cases of Estonia and Latvia" and "Emerging Ethnic Democracy in Estonia and Latvia," papers presented to the "Identity Formation and Social Issues in Estonia, Ukraine and Uzbekistan" project at the University of Michigan, September 1996.

16. Pettai, "Contemporary International Influences on Post-Soviet Nationalism," pp. 12–13.

17. Andrew Wilson, *Ukrainian Nationalism in the 1990s: A Minority Faith* (Cambridge: Cambridge University Press, 1997).

18. Laada Bilaniuk, "The Politics of Language and Identity in Post-Soviet Ukraine" (Ph.D. diss. in anthropology, University of Michigan, 1998), argues, however, that the dominant ideology is not nationalism per se, but purism. People rank well-spoken Ukrainian, and well-spoken Russian, over what they perceive to be a mixture, or *"surzhyk."* Indeed, Yuriy 1 from our Ivankiv focus group provides a nice illustration of the power of this nationalism in language: "I served in West Ukraine. There I got some language. I studied in a Ukrainian school only half a year, till my father went to Germany and sent my mother and me to Berdyansk. I do not blame anybody. I understand the language in principle, but cannot speak it. It is like being a dog: you cannot say anything. No, I mean, I can speak, but I do not want to make mistakes. So, I speak Russian" (871–82).

19. For a broad survey of the languages of the Soviet Union, identifying their structural features as well as their classification, see Bernard Comrie, *The Languages of the Soviet Union* (Cambridge: Cambridge University Press, 1981).

20. Laitin, *Identity in Formation,* pp. 360–61.

21. Ibid., p. 102.

22. Ibid.; originally from Ivan Drach, "Ukraina i Rossiia: perspektivy vzaimootnoshenii," *Nezavisimaia Gazeta* (Moscow, in Russian), February 3, 1994.

23. This emphasis is provided by Karen Fields in her introduction to Émile Durkheim, *Elementary Forms of Religious Life* (New York: Free Press, 1995).

24. Aksel Kirch, ed., *The Integration of Non-Estonians into Estonian Society: History, Problems and Trends* (Tallinn: Estonian Academy of Sciences, 1997), p. 151.

25. Consider, for the sake of contrast to Laitin's viewpoint, Rein Taagepera, *Estonia: Return to Independence* (Boulder, Colo.: Westview Press, 1993), or Orest Subtelny, *Ukraine: A History* (Toronto: University of Toronto Press, 1994), pp. 573–95.

26. Laar, "Estonia's Success Story," p. 97.

27. Address to the Estonian parliament by Estonian Foreign Minister Siim Kallas on May 30, 1996, in FBIS SOV 96–107 June 3, 1996, p. 68.

28. Press conference on June 17, 1996, GMT 12–00 on Tallinn Radio Tallinn Network FBIS SOV 96–119–19. This anxiety is not limited to the Baltics, but is shared by many in small nations who "know" Russian notions of national security. Václav Havel, for instance, expressed his concerns about Russia's recognition of its own national boundaries ("Kosovo and the End of the Nation-State," an address given to the Canadian Senate and House of Commons in Ottawa on April 29, 1999, reprinted in *New York Review of Books,* June 10, 1999, pp. 4, 6).

29. Michael Specter, "Russian Minority Fearful in Estonia," *New York Times,* May 26, 1996, p. 4.

30. I made a similar argument in regard to Jan Krzysztof Bielecki in "The Labilities of Liberalism and Nationalism after Communism: Polish Businessmen in the Articulation of the Nation," in Ronald Grigor Suny and Michael D. Kennedy, eds., *Intellectuals and the Articulation of the Nation* (Ann Arbor: University of Michigan Press, 1999).

31. Of course, the European Union and other European agencies, such as the Council of Europe, have actively lobbied Estonia to soften its language requirements for citizenship.

32. Michael D. Kennedy, "Postcommunist Institutional Design," *Contemporary Sociology* 28:2 (1999): 207–9.

33. Janet Hart, *Women and the Greek Resistance: 1941–1964* (Ithaca, N.Y.: Cornell University Press, 1996), p. 50.

34. Laar, "Estonia's Success Story," p. 97.

35. The formulation "concentrated bursts of data" is from focus group methodologist David Morgan, in the seminar "Narrative Analysis, Oral History and Focus Groups," University of Michigan, June 1996. One especially useful collection on focus group research is David Morgan, ed., *Successful Focus Groups: Advancing the State of the Art* (Thousand Oaks, Calif.: Sage, 1993); see also David Morgan, *Focus Groups as Qualitative Research,* 2d ed. (Thousand Oaks, Calif.: Sage, 1997), and "Focus Groups," *Annual Review of Sociology* 22 (1996): 129–52. Focus groups have been used in the former Soviet Union; see, for instance, Judith S. Kullberg, "The Ideological Roots of Elite Political Conflict in Post-Soviet Russia," *Europe/Asia Studies* 46:6 (1994): 929–53.

36. Focus groups are typically conducted within a single language, or at least within a single society, and have rarely been used for cross-cultural research. For one of the earliest uses of this methodology in cross-cultural research, see John Knodel, "Focus Groups as a Qualitative Method for Cross-Cultural Research in Social Gerontology,"

Journal of Cross-Cultural Gerontology 10 (April 1995): 7–20, and "Conducting Comparative Focus Group Research: Cautionary Comments from a Coordinator," *Health Transition Review* 4:1 (winter 1993): 99–104. The original project included Uzbekistan along with Estonia and Ukraine. For a variety of reasons, I have decided to limit the comparison in this book to Estonia and Ukraine.

37. It is important to emphasize here that this total project was comparative and collaborative from the beginning. Our starting team at the University of Michigan included Barbara Anderson, Ted Hopf, Marianne Kamp, Oksana Malanchuk, and Donna Parmelee. I also had the pleasure of working with many scholars from Estonia, Ukraine, and Uzbekistan who were involved in the collection and production of these data, nine of whom worked with us in Ann Arbor for forty-eight days in May–June 1996 in the design of this study. They included Rein Vöörman, Marika Kirch, Jelena Hellamae, and Aleksander Plotkin from Estonia; Victor Susak, Natalija Salabaj, and Yuliya Yakubova from Ukraine; and Alisher Ilkhamov, Nilufar Egamberdieva, and Ludmila Hafizova from Uzbekistan. Without their multiple contributions, our subsequent analysis of these data would, of course, not have been imaginable.

38. These sites are described in greater detail in the next chapter.

39. This was not always successful. It was most problematic for the focus groups conducted in Uzbekistan, notably in Ferghana. There, the only way the group could be assembled was by visiting the market square and finding willing participants.

40. Not every transcript could be transcribed verbatim, and few could be transcribed perfectly well. Moynak men from Uzbekistan, for instance, had to be treated entirely non-verbatim, whereas Lviv men was rendered nearly perfectly from tape to paper.

41. After recording these sessions, the tapes were transcribed and translated on site and subsequently checked for quality at the University of Michigan. The analysis of these transcripts has been sorted through a program called Ethnograph. This program allows for the coding of qualitative data fragments across thousands of pages of text. Codes can overlap. A data fragment discussing an ethnic division of labor in one particular area might be coded simultaneously as employment, region, ethnicity, and gender. Some of the codes appeared in each transcript. For instance, we asked each group to address whether women and men suffered equally through the problems of post-Soviet transition. There were other topics, however, which were not introduced by the moderators, and which could only emerge if the focus groups themselves thought it an important problem, virtue, or solution. For instance, only a few groups identified values as either a problem or a potential solution to the problems that they faced. But even if a code had to be addressed, the amount of time each group spent talking about the issue varied considerably.

42. See Michael D. Kennedy, "The Spatial Articulation of Identity and Social Issues: Estonia, Ukraine and Uzbekistan through Focus Groups," in Kimitaka Matsuzato, ed., *Regions: A Prism to View the Slavic-Eurasian World. Towards a Discipline of 'Regionology'* (Sapporo: Slavic Research Center, 2000).

43. For a specific critique of this work attending to the particular problem associated with variable moderator influence, see Marianne Kamp, "Voluntary and Elicited Discourses: Comparing Moderator Influence on Focus Groups" (http://www.umich.edu/~iinet/crees/fsugrant).

44. As John Knodel noted in his commentary on an earlier paper using these data, one cannot say whether attention to an issue denotes importance, salience, or even comfort for discussing that issue. I do not mean to skirt the issue, but it is sufficiently challenging to merit extended discussion elsewhere.

45. The numbers following quotes refer to numbered passages in that particular focus group.

46. Nevertheless, they discussed it more than any other group in Estonia or Ukraine, suggesting that although they almost forgot about it, they ultimately did not, and once raised, it was relatively important in comparison to other focus groups.

47. For a discussion of the various strategies to interpret focus group data, and especially the utility of such counting procedures for relatively large numbers of focus groups, see Richard A. Krueger, *Analyzing and Reporting Focus Group Results* (Sage, 1998), especially the essay by David Morgan, "Computerized Analysis," pp. 89–93.

48. For a valuable discussion of how the open public sphere discusses social problems in Estonia and other countries around the Baltic Sea, see Mikko Lagerspetz, *Social Problems in Newspapers: Studies around the Baltic Sea* (Helsinki: Nordic Council for Alcohol and Drug Research, 1994), and "Social Problems in the Estonian Mass Media in 1975–1991," *Acta Sociologica* 36 (1993): 357–69.

49. For arguments along these lines, see Michael D. Kennedy, "An Introduction to Ideology and Identity After Communism," in Michael D. Kennedy, ed., *Envisioning Eastern Europe: Postcommunist Cultural Studies* (Ann Arbor: University of Michigan Press, 1994).

50. *From Plan to Market: World Development Report, 1996,* published for the World Bank (New York: Oxford University Press, 1996), p. 126.

51. For instance, note Victor's caution in the focus group from Narva: "In general, the appearance of the chance to choose is positive. But the choice is not always . . . Let's say that a possibility to choose does not always correspond to the realization of a choice" (823–37).

52. Vladimir from Tallinn reinforced this point (328–38).

53. This means that they have gone back to school to obtain additional certifications of proficiency.

54. Anya is quite critical about the lack of professional opportunities in Ukraine. Later, she does not limit the point to women, but she does emphasize that the apparent freedom is not producing the kind of individualism and responsibility that it is supposed to. It is not an "open society, in reality we end up with something that is psychologically closed" (1127–28).

55. This concern over the demographic fate of the nation is an important feature of Baltic discourse on gender. For elaboration, see Daina Stukuls, "Body of the Nation: Mothering, Prostitution, and Women's Place in Postcommunist Latvia," *Slavic Review* 58:3 (1999): 537–58.

56. Katherine Verdery is especially good at showing how the nation can serve as a master symbol organizing gender, or subverting civil society (*What Was Socialism and What Comes Next?* [Princeton, N.J.: Princeton University Press, 1997]).

57. Laitin, *Identity in Formation.*

58. Of course, Estonians may have been better informed and more internationally oriented than were Ukrainians even before *perestroika,* but I would expect that transition has only magnified their relative disparities of international attention.

59. Tallinn women (380–94).

60. Laitin, *Identity in Formation,* p. 60.

61. At the same time, they showed their commitments to transition culture not only with their rationales for why open borders, and not only open societies, are valuable. The Narvan men, at least, blamed the Russians for many of the problems with this international travel.

62. C. Wright Mills, *The Sociological Imagination* (London: Oxford University Press, 1959), p. 8.

63. Michael Burawoy and Janos Lukacs, *The Radiant Past: Ideology and Reality in Hungary's Road to Capitalism* (Chicago: University of Chicago Press, 1992), argue that the obvious discrepancy between ideology and reality in socialism was what made ideological critique and class-consciousness more likely than in capitalism, where consent, and not only goods, is manufactured.

64. Deniz Kandiyoti, "End of Empire: Islam, Nationalism and Women in Turkey," in Deniz Kandiyoti, ed., *Women, Islam, and the State* (Philadelphia: Temple University Press, 1991) and Hart, *Women and the Greek Resistance.*

65. See, however, Lynne Haney, "'But We Are Still Mothers': Gender, the State and the Construction of Need in Postsocialist Hungary," in Michael Burawoy and Katherine Verdery, eds., *Uncertain Transition: Ethnographies of Change in the Postsocialist World* (Lanham, Md.: Rowman and Littlefield, 1999), pp. 151–87, and Stukuls, "Body of the Nation."

5. Environmental Problems, Civility, and Loss in Transition

Earlier versions of this chapter were presented in several settings: "Beyond State Crisis: The Quest for the Efficacious State in Africa and Eurasia" at the University of Wisconsin, Madison, March 11–14, 1999; the Workshop on Identity Formation and Social Issues in Estonia, Ukraine, and Uzbekistan held in Kiev, August 4–8, 1997; and in lectures at Hokkaido University's 1998 conference on Regionology, and at the University of Kansas the same year. I thank those who commented on my presentations in those settings. This research has been generously supported by both the Ford Foundation (Ford Foundation Grant No. 950–1163) and the National Council for Soviet and East European Research (NCSEER) (Research Contract 812–11). Neither organization is responsible for the findings presented in this report. I am grateful to all of our colleagues who have worked on this project with me, most especially and immediately to Lisa Fein, who worked with me in coding the data and analyzing environmental problems.

1. On a television broadcast, on Moscow Russian Public Television, First Channel Network in Russian 0440 GMT, July 1, 1996, reprinted from the "Elections '96 Program," in FBIS SOV 96–127, July 1, 1996, p. 11.

2. Despite a new president and a new Chechen war begun in 1999, the West continues to treat Russia specially.

3. See, for example, Janine Wedel, *Collision and Collusion: The Strange Case of Assistance to Central and Eastern Europe* (New York: St. Martin's Press, 1998).

4. Peter J. Stavrakis, "The East Goes South: International Aid and Convergence in Africa and Eurasia," presented at the conference "Beyond State Crisis: The Quest for the Efficacious State in Africa and Eurasia" at the University of Wisconsin, Madison, March 11–14, 1999. See also Peter J. Stavrakis, "Bull in a China Shop: USAID's Post-Soviet Mission," *Demokratizatsiya* 4:2 (spring 1996), and Wedel, *Collision and Collusion.*

5. The principal point of departure for much hermeneutic sociology is Hans-Georg Gadamer, *Truth and Method* (London: Sheed and Wart, 1975). For elaborations, see Zygmunt Bauman, *Hermeneutics and Social Science* (New York: Columbia University Press, 1978); Josef Bleicher, *The Hermeneutic Imagination* (London: Routledge and Kegan Paul, 1982); John B. Thompson, *Critical Hermeneutics* (Cambridge: Cambridge University Press, 1981); Michael D. Kennedy, "Hermeneutics, Structuralism and the Sociology of Social Transformation in Soviet-Type Society," *Current Perspectives in Social Theory* 8 (1987): 47–76.

6. For this theoretical emphasis, see Stephen White, *Political Theory and Post-*

modernism (Cambridge: Cambridge University Press, 1991), and my review of it in *Critical Sociology* 19:2 (1992): 124–28.

7. Ernest Gellner, *Conditions of Liberty: Civil Society and Its Rivals* (London: Penguin, 1994), esp. pp. 137–49.

8. Elżbieta Skotnicka-Illasiewicz and Włodzimierz Wesołowski, "The Significance of Preconceptions: Europe of Civil Societies and Europe of Nationalities," in Sukumar Periwal, ed., *Notions of Nationalism* (Budapest: Central European University Press, 1995), pp. 208–27.

9. Pope John Paul II sees the same difference between Polish religiosity and West European secularism, but he supports Poland's entry to Europe with the hope that Polish spirituality might influence that secularism. He told Polish bishops on June 11, 1999, "Europe needs a Poland that believes deeply and is culturally creative in a Christian way, conscious of the role that providence has entrusted to it" (Alessandra Stanley, "Pope, Hurt in Fall, Tells Poles to Resist Secularism," *New York Times*, June 13, 1999, p. A6).

10. Skotnicka-Illasiewicz and Wesołowski, "The Significance of Preconceptions," p. 210.

11. *From Plan to Market: World Development Report, 1996*, published for the World Bank (New York: Oxford University Press, 1996), p. 11.

12. Even the most successful societies in transition culture can have these threats. Exemplary of this threat to transition culture in late 1990s Poland is Andrzej Lepper and his peasants' movement Samo-Obrona (self-defense). In an interview on television (Graffiti, broadcast on Polsat in the United States on May 27, 1999), Lepper defended his movement's blockades of roads and other illegal protests with the rhetoric of victimization. He argued that Minister of Finance Leszek Balcerowicz, an exemplar of transition culture, was running the country, and that the World Bank was behind him. His movement seeks to publicize the real plight of the dispossessed of transition—not only farmers, but also health-care workers and other public-sector employees. Even Pope John Paul II does not understand how bad things are, he says.

13. Consider the World Bank's Web page dedicated to civil societies and nongovernmental organizations: http://www.worldbank.org/html/extdr/forngos.htm.

14. *The State in a Changing World: World Development Report, 1997*, published for the World Bank (New York: Oxford University Press, 1997), pp. 14–15. Subsequent references are given in the text.

15. The World Bank went beyond platitudes. A vital civil society and public opinion can serve as an important pressure for minimizing corruption (ibid., pp. 102–8, esp. 107–8). To win civil society's trust, corruption should be addressed by providing civil society with better tools for monitoring and punishing the corrupt in the courts (9). In particular, privatization should be made more legitimate by making it more transparent to civil society (6). Social capital (here understood as "the informal rules, norms and long-term relationships that facilitate coordinated action and enable people to undertake cooperative adventures for mutual advantage" [114]) is also found to be important to overall well-being and development in society.

16. Michael D. Kennedy, "Postcommunist Institutional Design," *Contemporary Sociology* 28:2 (1999): 207–9.

17. Despite transition culture's evocation of civil society as a globally relevant idea, it might not be the appropriate concept for discussing the state–society relationship in Africa. See, for example, Achille Mbembe, "Provisional Notes on the Postcolony," *Africa* 62:1 (1992): 1–35.

18. Craig Calhoun and John Ritzer, "Social Problems," in Craig Calhoun and George Ritzer, eds., *Social Problems: A Critical Approach* (New York: McGraw-Hill, 1993).

19. Although social problems might be discussed as if they exist independently of social perceptions and power relations, most analysts of social problems recognize that problems cannot be properly interpreted unless their social construction is analyzed too. See, for example, Kristin Luker, *Abortion and the Politics of Motherhood* (Berkeley: University of California Press, 1984); James A. Holstein and Gale Miller, eds., *Reconsidering Social Constructionism: Debates in Social Problems Theory* (New York: Aldine de Gruyter, 1993). In particular, analysts recommend that the making and resolution of problems be understood from various points of view. For instance, when assessing social policy, one should consider whether actors speak from the point of view of clients or of policy makers (Pekka Sulkunen, *White Collar Vernacular: Individuality and Tribalism of the New Middle Class* [Aldershot: Avebury Academic Publishers, 1992]). When assessing state efficacy or Soviet abnormality, one therefore should consider its making from different points of view, based on class, nationality, gender, and types of expertise.

20. Michael D. Kennedy, "The End of Soviet-Type Societies and the Future of Post-Communism," in Calhoun and Ritzer, *Social Problems.*

21. Western analysts have, of course, also identified a set of social problems in post-communist Eastern Europe and the former Soviet Union. See, for example, Ian Bremmer and Ray Taras, eds., *Nations and Politics in the Soviet Successor States* (Cambridge: Cambridge University Press, 1993); Mark Beissinger, "How Nationalisms Spread: Eastern Europe Adrift the Tides and Cycles of Nationalist Contention," *Social Research* (spring 1996): 1–50; Ke-Young Chu and Sanjeev Gupta, "Protecting the Poor: Social Safety Nets during Transition," *Finance and Development* 30 (1993): 24–27; Michael Ellman, "The Increase in Death and Disease under 'Katastroika,'" *Cambridge Journal of Economics* 18 (1994): 329–55; Murray Feshbach, *Ecological Disaster: Cleaning Up the Hidden Legacy of the Soviet Regime* (New York: Twentieth Century Fund, 1995); Murray Feshbach and Alfred Friendly Jr., *Ecocide in the USSR: Health and Nature under Siege* (New York: Basic Books, 1992); Rensselaer W. Lee III and Scott B. MacDonald, "Drugs in the East," *Foreign Policy* (spring 1993): 89–107; Richard F. Kaufman and John P. Hardt, *The Former Soviet Union in Transition,* edited for the Joint Economic Committee, U.S. Congress (Armonk, N.Y.: M. E. Sharpe, 1993); Radio Free Europe/ Radio Liberty, "Health Care Crisis," *Radio Free Europe/Radio Liberty Research Reports* 2, October 8, 1993, pp. 31–62; Iliana Zloch-Christy, *Eastern Europe in a Time of Change: Economic and Political Dimensions* (Westport Conn.: Praeger, 1994); James R. Millar, ed., *Social Legacies of Communism* (Cambridge: Cambridge University Press, 1994); Richard Lotspeich, "Crime in the Transition Economies," *Europe-Asia Studies* 47:4 (1995): 555–89; Mikko Lagerspetz, "Social Problems in the Estonian Mass Media 1975–1991," *Acta Sociologica* 36 (1993): 357–69.

22. Daina Stukuls, "Imagining the Nation: Campaign Posters of the First Postcommunist Elections in Latvia," *East European Politics and Societies* 11:1 (1997): 131–54, and *Imagining the Nation: History, Modernity and Revolution in Latvia* (State College: Pennsylvania State University Press, 2002).

23. Resonating here with Craig Calhoun's proposal that we study identity and topical debate in tandem (*Critical Social Theory* [Oxford: Blackwell, 1995], p. 247).

24. Jane Dawson, *Eco-Nationalism: Anti-Nuclear Activism and National Identity in Russia, Lithuania and Ukraine* (Durham, N.C.: Duke University Press, 1996); Roman Szporluk, "National Awakening: Ukraine and Belorussia," in Uri Ra'anan, ed., *The Soviet Empire* (Lexington, Mass.: Lexington Books, 1990); and Anatol Lieven, *The Baltic Revolution: Estonia, Latvia and Lithuania and the Path to Independence* (New Haven and London: Yale University Press, 1993), p. 220.

25. Barbara Anderson and John Romani, "Estonian Attitudes Towards Environmental Pollution on the Eve of Independence," paper presented at the Conference on Population and Environment, Rome, October 1996.

26. Dawson, *Eco-Nationalism.*

27. Jaan-Mati Punning, "Aspects of Ecological Security: A Case Study of Estonia," in Peeter Vares and Gunnar Lassinantti, eds., *Ecological Security of the Baltic States, Nordic Countries and North-West Russia* (Tallinn: Institute of International and Social Studies, Academy of Sciences, 1995), pp. 49–58.

28. Rein Ratas, "Towards Ecological Security," in Vares and Lassinantti, *Ecological Security of the Baltic States,* pp. 7–11.

29. Vladimir Nosov, "Environmental Problems in Sillamäe," in Vares and Lassinantti, *Ecological Security of the Baltic States,* pp. 64–68. Most of the text that follows draws on this article.

30. Estonians constitute only 1–2 percent of the local population.

31. For a discussion of the coding strategies we used, see Appendix B.

32. The effect of moderators is a more significant issue than we expected, based on our training in focus groups. This, unfortunately, affects our ability to interpret not only independence, but also the relative salience of ecology. In several of the Ukrainian cases, the moderators introduced an ecological theme from the beginning by noting that ten years earlier was the year the Chernobyl catastrophe happened. The moderators have said that to fail to mention Chernobyl, when asking about change over the preceding decade, would only strike Ukrainians as bizarre, or that there was some kind of ignorance or hidden agenda. We cannot be the judge of what was best to do in this regard, but only note the trade-off. In general, to the degree one tries to increase the resonance of discussion with any particular focus group, the potential for more standardized comparison is reduced. And here we can see the price: we cannot tell how much focus groups would emphasize the environment without having had it mentioned by the moderator. We might, however, examine this problem briefly by comparing those focus groups where Chernobyl was used as a prompt by the moderators and those where it was not.

Chernobyl was mentioned by the moderator in initial statements among Ivankiv men and women, Russian-speaking men from Kiev and Ukrainian-speaking women from Kiev, and not mentioned in the initial statements among Russian-speaking women from Kiev, Lviv men or women, Donetsk men, or Olexandrivka women or men. But for Olexandrivka women, Donetsk and Ukrainian-speaking women from Kiev, Chernobyl was used to introduce the question of the environment (1403–7 and 2762–63). In none of these cases, however, did Chernobyl's mention prompt discussion as it did in the Ivankiv groups. Nevertheless, its introduction seems to have led to slightly more discussion of the environment than what we would have seen otherwise. Note that those groups where Chernobyl was not used as a prompt were also the groups where the environment received the least attention: Lviv men and women and Donetsk men. From this we conclude that the unevenly distributed Chernobyl prompts magnify differences, but overall patterns are not disrupted. It is a more salient issue in Kiev and especially Ivankiv than in Donetsk or Lviv. Olexandrivka is in the middle, where other environmental issues, especially among men, are of concern.

33. Indeed, the moderator himself apparently feared that the men's group might not come up within anything positive to say. He said in response to a cue in the group, "Well, if you think that there was absolutely nothing good in your life . . . that may be, of course. But let me tell you one thing. If you think well, you definitely will find something good there" (452–58).

34. Although the moderators expected this group to be composed of Ukrainian speakers, many of the participants admitted, in the course of discussion, that they really could not speak Ukrainian, and rather asked if they could speak in Russian, including this Mykola.

35. Andriy argues that it is worse in Ukraine because although the West has the same problems, there "they try to deal with such problems somehow" (1386–87). In Ukraine, they do not address them.

36. In general, these women find that men are affected most directly by the nuclear reactor crisis because of the proximity of their work (1519–38).

37. For a provocative discussion of Soviet civil society, see Naomi Roslyn Galtz, "Space and the Everyday: An Historical Sociology of the Moscow Dacha," Ph.D. dissertation, Department of Sociology, University of Michigan, 2000.

38. This category plays on the name of the Ukrainian president of the time, and refers to traders.

6. Transition Culture and Nationalism's Wars

I wish to thank my colleagues of the Working Group in Southeast European Studies at the University of Michigan for their association and in particular for the fine programming and visiting speakers they have enabled to attend the university. Their workshop "Doing History in the Shadow of the Balkan Wars," University of Michigan, January 17, 1997, was especially helpful in the conception of this chapter. I wish to thank them, as well as Bob Donia, Andy Markovits, and Floyd Kennedy Jr., who have read earlier versions and portions of this chapter. My colleague at the Center for Russian and East European Studies, Donna Parmelee, has been extremely helpful. Her expertise in the region served as a good "reality check" on my own less grounded theoretical explorations.

1. I wrote these passages as I followed the news that week from the *New York Times* (July 12–17, 1995). For more substantial elaborations of the case, with the advantage of historical distance, see Jan Willem Honig and Norbert Both, *Srebrenica: Record of a War Crime* (London: Penguin, 1996), and David Rohde, *Endgame: The Betrayal and Fall of Srebrenica, Europe's Worst Massacre since World War II* (New York: Farrar, Straus and Giroux, 1997). Rohde estimated that 7,079 men were confirmed missing through this massacre (p. xvi). See also Chuck Sudetić, *Blood and Vengeance* (London: Penguin, 1998), for the portrait of one Muslim family's experience in these days.

2. Stephen Kinzer, "Refugees' Accounts Back Atrocity Charges," *New York Times,* July 17, 1995, p. A5. For an argument about the systematicity of these crimes in the Kosovë war, see Human Rights Watch, "Kosovo: Rape as a Weapon of Ethnic Cleansing," vol. 12, no. 3(D) (March 2000).

3. Stephen Kinzer, "Muslims Tell of Atrocities as Safe Town Fell," *New York Times,* July 14, 1995, p. A5. Susan Woodward points out similar difficulties regarding the safe areas in *Balkan Tragedy: Chaos and Dissolution after the Cold War* (Washington, D.C.: Brookings Institution, 1995), pp. 320–21.

4. Leo Tindemans, Lloyd Cutler, Bronisław Geremek, John Roper, Theo Sommer, Siomone Veil, and David Anderson, *Unfinished Peace: Report on the International Commission on the Balkans* (Washington: Carnegie Endowment for International Peace, 1996), p. 1.

5. Ibid., pp. 2–3.

6. I might simply follow the tides of war and name this region Kosova, and not

Kosovo, to follow the Albanian rather than Serb expression. Instead, I follow Victor Friedman's practice in naming Kosovë to signify that even in titling a place, one implicates an argument in a particular narrative. See Victor Friedman, "The History of Macedonian Identity and the Balkan Wars of 1991–94," prepared for "Doing History in the Shadow of the Balkan Wars," University of Michigan, January 17, 1997.

7. Mark Danner, "Endgame in Kosovo," *New York Review of Books,* May 6, 1999, p. 8.

8. Ibid. See Leo Tindemans et al., *Unfinished Peace,* p. 42.

9. Timothy Garton Ash, "Anarchy and Madness," *New York Review of Books,* February 10, 2000, pp. 48–53.

10. Cited in William J. Buckley, *Kosovo: Contending Voices on Balkan Intervention* (Grand Rapids, Mich.: Eerdmans, 2000), p. 17

11. Maria Todorova, "The Balkans from Invention to Intervention," in ibid., pp. 159–69.

12. Buckley, *Kosovo,* lists more than 180 Web sites devoted to the war around Kosovë.

13. *Before the Rain* (Macedonia-France-UK), 1994, directed by Milcho Manchevski. Of the films I have seen set during these Wars of Yugoslav Succession, this is the most compelling and interesting, as it shows how difficult it is to stand outside, or beyond, the conflict between Albanians and Macedonians in the same village. I am told by Albanian colleagues and analysts grounded in their community, however, that this film is distressingly distant from their perspective on cycles of violence.

14. Stjepan G. Meštrović, *The Balkanization of the West: The Confluence of Postmodernism and Postcommunism* (London: Routledge, 1994), p. 85.

15. Ibid., p. 84.

16. Ibid., p. 97. For a much more focused assessment on the gendering of this war, see Alexandra Stiglmayer, ed., *Mass Rape: The War against Women in Bosnia-Herzegovina* (Lincoln and London: University of Nebraska Press, 1994).

17. Meštrović, *The Balkanization of the West,* p. 106.

18. Of course, the West *did* back Milošević, and Croatian leader Franjo Tudjman and Bosnian leader Alia Izetbegović, in a certain sense through the Dayton Accords by assigning them responsibility for "agreement." See James Gow, *Triumph of the Lack of Will: International Diplomacy and the Yugoslav War* (New York: Columbia University Press, 1997).

19. Slavoj Žižek, *Tarrying with the Negative* (Durham, N.C.: Duke University Press, 1993), p. 200.

20. Susan Woodward, *Balkan Tragedy: Chaos and Dissolution after the Cold War* (Washington, D.C.: Brookings Institution, 1995), p. 1.

21. Of course, not all parts of the former Yugoslavia are equally distant. Some have argued that Slovenia's motive for leaving Yugoslavia was informed by its recognition that the conditions of entry to the European Union would be far easier to meet without the southeast part of the federal republic than with it. See ibid. and Milica Bakić-Hayden and Robert Hayden, "Orientalist Variations on the Theme 'Balkans': Symbolic Geography in Yugoslav Politics, 1987–90," *Slavic Review* 51:1 (spring 1992): 1–15.

22. Maria Todorova, "The Balkans: From Discovery to Invention," *Slavic Review* 53:2 (1998): 453.

23. See Dina Iordanova, "Narrating the Balkans in Film: Indigenous Images or Mirroring Stereotypes," workshop on the topic "Doing History in the Shadow of the Balkan Wars," Working Group on Southeast European Studies, University of Michigan, January 17, 1997.

24. Anthony Giddens, *Introduction to Sociology* (New York: Norton, 1991), p. 463.

25. Even marxist scholars critical of the "neoclassical" sociology of postcommunist social change overlook the barbaric alternative of postcommunist war. See Michael Burawoy, "Neoclassical Sociology: From the End to Socialism to the End of Classes," *American Journal of Sociology* 106:4 (2001): 1099–1120, and my response (Michael D. Kennedy, "Postcommunist Capitalism, Culture and History," *American Journal of Sociology* 106:4 [2001]: 1138–51).

26. One of the most prominent scholars of southeastern Europe, Ivo Banac, has summarized his own position on nationalism's significance by arguing that the wars have their roots in the political cultures of national groups, most specifically in the very different nationalist ideologies. See Ivo Banac, Foreword to Sabrina Ramet, *Balkan Babel* (Boulder, Colo.: Westview Press, 1999), p. xvii.

27. Tindemans et al., *Unfinished Peace*, p. 27.

28. Gale Stokes, "The Devil's Finger: The Disintegration of Yugoslavia," in *Three Eras of Political Change in Eastern Europe* (Oxford: Oxford University Press, 1997), pp. 109–43. Subsequent references are given in the text.

29. Kosovë and Albania were united under the fascists. It was the only area in Yugoslavia that did not support the Partisans and the only place where communism was militantly imposed and resisted. See Branka Magaš, *The Destruction of Yugoslavia: Tracing the Break-up 1980–92* (London: Verso, 1993), p. 34.

30. See also Ramet, *Balkan Babel*, p. 160.

31. Warren Zimmermann, "Milosevic's Final Solution," *New York Review of Books*, June 10, 1999, p. 41.

32. Ibid., p. 42.

33. As Banac and Ramet have; see Ramet, *Balkan Babel*, pp. 162–63.

34. Ibid., p. 167.

35. Gale Stokes, "Nationalism, Responsibility, and the People-As-One: Reflections on the Possibilities of Peace in the Former Yugoslavia," in *Three Eras of Political Change in Eastern Europe* (Oxford: Oxford University Press, 1997), pp. 144–53.

36. Ibid., pp. 145–48.

37. Ibid., p. 151.

38. Gale Stokes, John Lampe, and Dennison Rusinow, with Julie Mostov, "Instant History: Understanding the Wars of Yugoslav Succession," *Slavic Review* 55 (1996): 160.

39. See Bogdan Denitch, *Ethnic Nationalism: The Tragic Death of Yugoslavia* (Minneapolis: University of Minnesota Press, 1994), and *Limits and Possibilities: The Crisis of Yugoslav Socialism* (Minneapolis: University of Minnesota Press, 1990). For a more recent text located more within the institutionalist tradition, see Valerie Bunce, *Subversive Institutions: The Design and Destruction of Socialism and the State* (Cambridge: Cambridge University Press, 1999). This argument about nationalism filling vacuums in postcommunist societies is argued quite broadly. For one exemplary statement, see Ernest Gellner, "Nationalism in the Vacuum," in Alexander Motyl, ed., *Thinking Theoretically about Soviet Nationalities* (New York: Columbia University Press, 1992), pp. 243–54.

40. Bunce, *Subversive Institutions*, pp. 130–33.

41. Ibid., p. 132.

42. Tindemans et al., *Unfinished Peace*, p. 57.

43. C. Wright Mills, *The Causes of World War III* (New York: Simon and Schuster, 1958), p. 47.

44. E. P. Thompson, "Notes on Exterminism: The Last Stage of Civilization," in *Exterminism and Cold War* (London: Verso, 1982).

45. Sam Marullo, *Ending the Cold War at Home: From Militarism to a More Peaceful World Order* (New York: Lexington, 1994).

46. Daniel Chirot, "What Happened in Eastern Europe in 1989?" in Daniel Chirot, ed., *The Crisis of Leninism and the Decline of the Left: The Revolutions of 1989* (Seattle: University of Washington Press, 1991).

47. Tindemans et al., *Unfinished Peace*, p. 7.

48. See Charles Tilly, "War and the Power of Warmakers," in Peter Wallensteen, Johan Galtung, and Carlos Portales, eds., *Global Militarization* (Boulder, Colo.: Westview, 1985), for a more general account of the significance of arms supply, and Mark Beissinger, "Nationalist Violence and the State: Political Authority and Contentious Repertoires in the Former USSR," *Comparative Politics* 1 (July 1998): 401–22, for a more specific application to the former Soviet Union.

49. For one remarkably concise text, see Dilip Hiro, *Between Marx and Muhammad: The Changing Face of Central Asia* (Glasgow: HarperCollins, 1994).

50. Woodward, *Balkan Tragedy*, pp. 26–27.

51. Tim Judah, "Inside the KLA," *New York Review of Books,* June 10, 1999, pp. 19–23.

52. Of course, its future was made by its own politics too. Throughout the 1980s, its unity was undermined by its wish to diminish the autonomy of the Territorial Defense Forces. It believed that a more centralized military would be a more effective military defense against NATO invasion. And, facing economic pressures, it undertook policies that particularly alienated Slovenia, including the closing of its regional headquarters in Ljubljana and exporting arms to places such as Libya, a policy that alienated Slovene civil society activists. See James Gow, *Legitimacy and the Military: The Yugoslav Crisis* (London: Pinter, 1992), cited in Stokes, Lampe, and Rusinow, "Instant History," p. 138.

53. Some even suggest that the use of effective military force by the JNA to prevent Slovenia's secession was the last moment in which war could have been averted. See, for example, Robert Hayden, *Blueprints for a House Divided: The Constitutional Logic of the Yugoslav Conflicts* (Ann Arbor: University of Michigan Press, 1999), p. 151.

54. Bunce, *Subversive Institutions*, pp. 107–10.

55. Ibid., p. 95.

56. Todorova, "The Balkans from Invention to Intervention," p. 161.

57. Robert Gary Minnich, "Reflections on the Violent Death of a Multi-Ethnic State: A Slovene Perspective," *Anthropology of East Europe Review* 11:1–2 (1993): 90–99. I draw on Minnich's narrative to produce the following account. See also Jill Benderly and Evan Kraft, eds., *Independent Slovenia: Origins, Movements, Prospects* (New York: St. Martin's Press, 1994).

58. Even more, they were indignant over the failure of the West and the United States to assure their right to self-determination. They were more liberal than the West itself. After independence, the Slovenes have continued to persevere, even with the additional challenge of taking care of seventy thousand war refugees, about 4 percent of the Slovenian population. The Slovene government also paid more attention to minority rights than the other states, and to the rule of law, in contrast to the more belligerent policies of Serbia and Croatia. See Minnich, "Reflections on the Violent Death of a Multi-Ethnic State," p. 95.

59. Ibid.

60. From the collapse of the entire Soviet bloc, to the crisis of governance in the first world associated with identity politics and the expansion of the impoverished classes,

Yugoslavia's breakup could be seen as a variation on this theme. See Woodward, *Balkan Tragedy.* Subsequent references are given in the text.

61. This account of war resonates with Beissinger's emphasis on violence in the former Soviet Union ("Nationalist Violence and the State").

62. *The State in a Changing World: World Development Report, 1997,* published for the World Bank (New York: Oxford University Press, 1997); Jon Elster, Claus Offe, and Ulrich Press, *Institutional Design in Post-Communist Societies: Rebuilding the Ship at Sea* (Cambridge: Cambridge University Press, 1998).

63. Jeffery Alexander, "Bringing Democracy Back In: Universalistic Solidarity and the Civil Sphere," in Charles Lemert, ed., *Intellectuals and Politics: Social Theory in a Changing World* (Boulder, Colo.: Sage, 1992), p. 169.

64. Robert Hayden, *Blueprints for a House Divided: The Constitutional Logic of the Yugoslav Conflicts* (Ann Arbor: University of Michigan Press, 1999). Subsequent references are given in the text.

65. Robert J. Donia and John V. A. Fine Jr., *Bosnia and Herzegovina: A Tradition Betrayed* (New York: Columbia University Press, 1994); Tone Bringa, *Being Muslim the Bosnian Way: Identity and Community in a Central Bosnian Village* (Princeton, N.J.: Princeton University Press, 1995).

66. Ramet, *Balkan Babel,* pp. 64–65.

67. Thomas Cushman, *Critical Theory and the War in Croatia and Bosnia,* Donald W. Treadgold Papers in Russian, East European, and Central Asian Studies, Henry M. Jackson School of International Studies, University of Washington, July 1997, no. 13, p. 10.

68. Ibid., pp. 11–12.

69. Ramet, *Balkan Babel,* p. 239.

70. He critiques Bette Denich ("Dismembering Yugoslavia: Nationalist Ideologies and the Symbolic Revival of Genocide," *American Ethnologist* 21:2 [1994]: 367–90), but these comments might also be extended to Hayden, *Blueprints for a House Divided.*

71. Cushman, *Critical Theory and the War in Croatia and Bosnia,* p. 21.

72. Milica Bakić-Hayden and Robert Hayden, "Orientalist Variations on the Theme 'Balkans': Symbolic Geography in Recent Yugoslav Politics, 1987–90," *Slavic Review* 51:1 (1992): 1–15.

73. Cushman, *Critical Theory and the War in Croatia and Bosnia,* p. 29.

74. Charles Boyd, "Making Peace with the Guilty: The Truth about Bosnia," *Foreign Affairs* 74:5 (1995): 22–38, was discussed in ibid., pp. 30–35, and Ramet, *Balkan Babel,* p. 220.

75. Cushman, *Critical Theory and the War in Croatia and Bosnia,* p. 42.

76. With her characteristic flair, Ramet writes: "No doubt there were those who, in World War II, considered it 'biased' that the American media devoted so little attention to discussing the 'atrocities' perpetrated by the Polish resistance against Nazi occupation forces"(*Balkan Babel,* p. 219).

77. Ibid., p. 221.

78. Ibid., pp. 239–40.

79. Ibid., p. 293.

80. Sabrina P. Ramet, "Eastern Europe and the Natural Law Tradition," Donald W. Treadgold Papers in Russian, East European and Central Asian Studies, Henry M. Jackson School of International Studies, University of Washington, August 2000, no. 27.

81. The romantic reaction to the Enlightenment, especially within Central Europe, is the classic example. See Roman Szporluk, *Communism and Nationalism: Karl Marx versus Friederich List* (Oxford: Oxford University Press, 1988).

82. I have already discussed Cushman's arguments against scholarship that distracts

us from Serbian responsibility in the wars. Ramet's positioning is more subtle. She does not write about sympathizers of the Croatian or Slovenian causes the way she describes those sympathetic to the Serbian one. She refers to Magaš, *The Destruction of Yugoslavia,* in this account: her "firm criticism of Milošević and Serbian nationalists in general has not won her applause from those quarters sympathetic to the Serbian cause" (351). Ramet also refers to "Belgrade's friends in the West," but they are not only those relativists who fail to see moral responsibility. She includes those whom Serb-Americans have influenced, including Congressman Lee Hamilton, who "is said to have received nearly $50,000 in itemized contributions from leading figures in the Serb American and Greek American communities in the years 1993–1995" (219).

83. Ramet is most critical of Hayden's review of Thomas Cushman and Stjepan Meštrović, *This Time We Knew: Western Responses to Genocide* (New York: New York University Press, 1996), in "The Tactical Uses of Passion," *Current Anthropology* 38:5 (1997): 924–25.

84. He refers to Slavenka Drakulić, *The Balkan Express* (New York: Norton, 1993).

85. Ramet, *Balkan Babel,* p. 60.

86. See Mirjana Prosić-Dvornić, "Enough! Student Protest '92: The Youth of Belgrade in Quest of 'Another Serbia,'" *Anthropology of East Europe Review* 11:1 and 2 (1993): 127–37, for another account of Serbian protest.

87. Scholars more competent in southeast European area studies than I am have explored what has been termed the inevitability and evitability thesis. I am indebted to Denny Rusinow's point in his paper "Some Reflections on the Impact of Yugoslavia's Disintegration and Wars of Succession on Historical Research and Writing" for the workshop "Doing History in the Shadow of the Balkan Wars," Working Group on Southeast European Studies, University of Michigan, January 17, 1997.

88. Ramet, *Balkan Babel,* pp. 64–65, 66.

89. Ramet, *Balkan Babel,* p. 240.

90. Judah, "Inside the KLA," p. 22.

91. Václav Havel, "Kosovo and the End of the Nation-State," address given to the Canadian Senate and House of Commons in Ottawa on April 29, 1999, *New York Review of Books,* June 10, 1999, p. 6.

92. "Exministr Zieleniec: Mlcenim ke Kosovu nas politic tahnou na Vychod," *Dnes,* May 11, 1999, p. 6.

93. For a general discussion of this anxiety over Germany's role in international affairs, see Andrei S. Markovits and Simon Reich, *The German Predicament: Memory and Power in the New Europe* (Ithaca, N.Y.: Cornell University Press, 1996). Its German translation is even more relevant in light of the NATO bombing of Serbia: *Das Deutsche Dilemma: Macht und Machtverzicht in der Berliner Republik* (Berlin: Alexander Fest Verlag, 1998), with a foreword by Joschka Fischer, the foreign minister and Green leader. See also Andrei S. Markovits, "The Identity Crisis of the German Left: A Report from Berlin" *Dissent* (summer 1999): 17–19, for a discussion of the impact of the war on the German left.

94. Milo Djukanović and Zoran Djindjić, "Toward a New Start for Yugoslavia, with Outside Help," *International Herald Tribune,* May 10, 1999, p. 8.

95. Happening as I concluded this volume, I rely on Steven Erlanger and Roger Cohen, "From a Summons to a Slap: How the Fight in Yugoslavia Was Won," *New York Times,* October 15, 2000, p. 12.

96. There remains significant disagreement, at the time of this writing, about whether Milošević's extradition for war crimes will affect that integration. For example, Kenneth Roth, executive director of Human Rights Watch, wrote in a letter to the *New*

York Times (October 15, 2000) that Richard Haas, a former National Security Council official, was wrong when he said, "I would not make coughing up Milosevic the No. 1 priority. After all, he was largely killing his own people, and he can be tried for that in his own country," to which Roth responded: "In fact, the vast majority of Mr. Milosevic's victims were not 'his own people.' They were residents of Bosnia and Croatia. Even his victims in Kosovo, a part of Yugoslavia, were mostly ethnic Albanians rather than the ethnic Serbs who dominate the Yugoslav federation. Given the nature of his crimes and the feeble state of the Yugoslavian judiciary, an international tribunal is the appropriate forum."

97. Jürgen Habermas, "Bestiality and Humanity: A War on the Border between Law and Morality," in Buckley, *Kosovo*, pp. 306–16.

98. Tindemans et al., *Unfinished Peace*, p. 144.

99. Todorova, "The Balkans from Invention to Intervention," pp. 167–68.

100. Jonathan Miller, "Be Careful, Waging War against Civilians Is against the Law," *International Herald Tribune*, May 13, 1999, p. 6. See also the documentation offered by Human Rights Watch: "Civilian Deaths in the NATO Air Campaign," Vol. 12, No. 1(D) (February 2000).

101. Jean Bethke Elshtain, "Can Kosovo Conflict Be a Just War?" *Long Island Newsday*, May 16, 1999, p. B5.

102. Zimmermann, "Milosevic's Final Solution," p. 43.

103. Hayden subsequently discusses the Rambouillet Accords in detail.

104. Richard Holbrooke, *To End a War* (New York: Random House, 1998), p. 160, cited in Hayden, *Blueprints for a House Divided*, p. 162.

105. Natalia Zarudna, counselor, embassy of Ukraine to the United States, "Ukraine as an Emerging Central European Nation," at the conference "Eastern Europe at the Dawn of the New Millennium," Center for International Business Studies, Wayne State University, Detroit, May 18, 1999.

106. Timothy Garton Ash, *The Magic Lantern: The Revolution of 1989 Witnessed in Warsaw, Budapest, Berlin and Prague* (New York: Random House, 1990).

107. Bunce, *Subversive Institutions*, pp. 71–72.

108. This is the introductory statement to the World Bank's Web site on the "Europe and Central Asia" regional discussion. See http://www.worldbank.org/html/extdr/offrep/eca/eca.htm (May 17, 1999).

Conclusion

1. Craig Calhoun, *Critical Social Theory: Culture, History and the Challenge of Difference* (Oxford and Cambridge: Blackwell, 1995), p. 11, uses this to describe critical social theory in general.

2. *J. G. Herder on Social and Political Culture*, trans., ed., and intro. F. M. Barnard (Cambridge: Cambridge University Press, 1969), p. 7. For an important elaboration of these ideas, see Roman Szporluk, *Nationalism and Communism: Karl Marx versus Friederich List* (New York: Oxford University Press, 1988), esp. p. 92.

3. Timothy Garton Ash, "The Last Revolution," *New York Review of Books*, November 16, 2000, p. 14.

4. Pierre Bourdieu, *In Other Words: Essays Towards a Reflexive Sociology*, trans. Matthew Adamson (Stanford, Calif.: Stanford University Press, 1990), p. 149.

5. Ibid., p. 177.

6. Vladimir Popov, Paul Gregory, Catalin Zamfir, Carol Scott Leonard, Asta Sendonaris, Susan Linz, Stephen Batsone, Nada Kobeissi, Giovanni Andrea Cornia, Victor Rodwin, Harley Balzer, and Omar Noman, *Poverty in Transition*, Regional Bureau for

Europe and the Commonwealth of Independent States (New York: United Nations Development Program, 1998).

7. George Soros, "Who Lost Russia?" in *Open Society: Reforming Global Capitalism* (New York: Public Affairs, 2000), pp. 235–64.

8. See, for example, Fareed Zakaria, "Globalization Grows Up and Gets Political," *New York Times, Week in Review,* December 31, 2000, p. 9.

9. Michael D. Kennedy, *Professionals, Power and Solidarity: A Critical Sociology of Soviet-Type Society* (Cambridge: Cambridge University Press, 1991), was written in this tradition.

10. See, for example, Michael Burawoy, "Neoclassical Sociology: From the End to Socialism to the End of Classes," *American Journal of Sociology* 106:4 (2001): 1099–1120.

11. See, for example, Michael D. Kennedy, "Postcommunist Institutional Design," *Contemporary Sociology* 28:2 (1999): 207–9.

12. Gerhard Lenski, *Power and Privilege: A Theory of Social Stratification* (Chapel Hill: University of North Carolina Press, 1984 [1966]).

13. Yu Xie and Emily Hannum, "Regional Variations in Earnings Inequality in Reform-Era Urban China," *American Journal of Sociology* 101 (1996): 951.

14. Gil Eyal, Iván Szelényi, and Eleanor Townsley, *Making Capitalism without Capitalists: The New Ruling Elites in Eastern Europe* (London: Verso, 1998), is exemplary, but not alone, here. See Michael D. Kennedy, "Postcommunist Capitalism, Culture and History," *American Journal of Sociology* 106:4 (2001): 1138–51.

15. Eric Hanley, "Cadre Capitalism in Hungary and Poland: Property Accumulation among Communist-Era Elites," *East European Politics and Societies.* The degree to which *(a)* the nomenklatura is the beneficiary of the changes, and *(b)* the agent of change is an entrepreneur/manager or some kind of political capitalist organization has been identified as a key debate in the sociology journals. Among others, see Victor Nee, "Social Inequalities in Reforming State Socialism: Between Redistribution and Markets in China," *American Sociological Review* 56 (1991): 267–82; Ákos Róna-Tas, "The First Shall Be Last? Entrepreneurship and Communist Cadres in the Transition from Socialism," *American Journal of Sociology* 100 (1994): 40–69; Victor Nee, "The Emergence of a Market Society: Changing Mechanisms of Stratification in China," *American Journal of Sociology* 101 (1996): 908–49; Iván Szelényi and E. Kostello, "The Market Transition Debate: Towards a Synthesis?" *American Journal of Sociology* 101 (1995): 1082–96; Andrew Walder, "Local Governments as Industrial Firms: An Organizational Analysis of China's Transitional Economy," *American Journal of Sociology* 101 (1995): 263–301; József Böröcz and Ákos Róna-Tas, "Small Leap Forward: Emergence of New Economic Elites," *Theory and Society* 24 (1995): 751–81.

16. Ákos Róna-Tas, *The Grand Surprise of the Small Transformation: The Demise of Communism and the Rise of the Private Sector in Hungary* (Ann Arbor: University of Michigan Press, 1997).

17. Szonja Szelényi, *Equality by Design: The Grand Experiment in Destratification in Socialist Hungary* (Stanford, Calif.: Stanford University Press, 1998), pp. 115–16.

18. Jacek Wasilewski, "The Old Apparatus in the New System: The Case of the Communist Nomenklatura in Poland," in Ursula van Beek, ed., *South Africa and Poland in Transition: A Comparative Perspective* (Pretoria: HSRC Publishers, 1995), p. 278. The nomenklatura's political influence, of course, could increase in the wake of parliamentary victories after the time when Wasilewski collected his data.

19. These studies are always regionally constrained, and can get lost in the generation of generalization. Hungary is much more prominent in generalizations about transition than Ukraine, for example. These cuts also encourage relatively parsimonious theories, manifest in simple but testable hypotheses that are then applied across many

points in time and places of change, partially compensating for the contextual origins of the original questions with new data points. However, the originating question still shapes the inquiry. See Michael D. Kennedy, "Postcommunist Capitalism, Culture and History."

20. See, for example, Herman Strasser, *The Normative Structure of Sociology: Conservative and Emancipatory Themes in Social Thought* (London: Routledge and Kegan Paul, 1976). These normative themes in inequality's study have also been addressed in Lenski, *Power and Priviliege,* and Stanisław Ossowski, *Class Structure in the Social Consciousness* (New York: Free Press of Glencoe, 1963).

21. Radek Sikorski, "How We Lost Poland: Heroes Do Not Make Good Politicians," *Foreign Affairs* 75:5 (September–October 1996): 15–22. Brian Porter drew this article to my attention after one of the Polish-American E-mail networks put it up on the Web to provide intellectual ammunition for denouncing the 1999 University of Michigan conference on the Polish Round Table. The election was a major defeat for the Catholic church. In the second round, the electorate chose Kwaśniewski despite the church's best efforts. The Polish primate, for instance, said that anyone who voted for the candidate of the Union of the Democratic Left was a "neopagan." See Martin Krygier, "The Polish Political Miracle: Communists to Communists in Six Short Years," *Quadrant* (June 1996): 52. I do not find Sikorski's main explanations for the relative success of the former communist in this presidential contest, and in the earlier parliamentary elections, unreasonable. He writes that the former communists were "led by ambitious, pragmatic, morally flexible individuals—exactly the sort that make successful democratic politicians these days." Wałęsa's defeat requires its own explanation. Sikorski, like most people I know, blames Wałęsa for his own loss. His erratic performance during his first term as president and his crude behavior during the campaign itself drove many people long sympathetic to Solidarity into Kwaśniewski's constituency. More generally, however, Sikorski argues that the leaders of ex-Solidarity parties were filled with heroes who would rather stand on principle and become media showmen than build coalitions.

22. In Hungary, in contrast, the ritual was completed by a quick apology and it was over. See Eyal, Szelényi, and Townsley, *Making Capitalism without Capitalists.* Lustration promises to cleanse the political scene of those whose past action compromises them for present service. It appeared to some, however, that lustration was not to be used to cleanse those who were complicit with the secret police under communist rule. The Jan Olszewski government, with Antoni Macierewicz at the helm of the ministry of interior, appeared ready to use files of dubious accuracy to undermine the claims of those who might lead the country. Certainly, President Kwaśniewski might have been excluded from his position were such a law put into effect. What really shook the political stage, however, was that then-President Wałęsa was to have been portrayed as too willing under communist rule to comply (or feign compliance, for we cannot know the difference) with the police to pursue his own interests. Wałęsa marshaled his own forces and forced the Olszewski government to step down.

23. By contrast, Ira Katznelson has called Michnik "Eastern Europe's emblematic democratic intellectual" (*Liberalism's Crooked Circle: Letters to Adam Michnik* [Princeton, N.J.: Princeton University Press, 1996], p. 11).

24. Adam Michnik, "We Can Talk without Hatred: A Conversation with Wojciech Jaruzelski," in Adam Michnik, *Letters from Freedom: Post–Cold War Realities and Perspectives* (Berkeley: University of California Press, 1998), pp. 260–85.

25. After *Rzecpospolita,* one of Poland's leading dailies, reprinted the accusation by some in the Polish diaspora that I was "narzędzie w rękach Adama Michnika" (a tool in

the hands of Adam Michnik) (see Jan Palarczyk, "Sezon Myśliwski," *Rzeczpospolita,* March 13–14, 1999, p. 18), Polish colleagues have more often asked me about my assessment of Michnik. One colleague said that Michnik is damaging Poland's image abroad, reinforcing the notion that Poles are anti-Semitic. He continued by saying that Poles are no more anti-Semitic than other peoples. My colleague reminded me that Michnik's father and brother were communists, as if to suggest a genetic link between betrayal and national loyalty. It is difficult to escape the trap of anti-Semitism, especially in the critique of the Round Table. And that difficulty of escape only increases resentments among those who were excluded not only from negotiations, but also from the riches available through political capitalism.

26. Together with colleagues Brian Porter, Marysia Ostafin, Piotr Michałowski, Ewa Juńczyk-Ziomecka, and Zbigniew Bujak, I helped organize a conference at the University of Michigan on the Polish Round Table of 1989. For materials surrounding this conference, see www.umich.edu/~iinet/PolishRoundTable. I draw on that conference in what follows. See also Michael D. Kennedy, Brian Porter, Margarita Nafpaktitus, and Donna Parmelee, eds., *Negotiating Radical Change: Poland's Round Table Talks* (Ann Arbor: Center for Russian and East European Studies, University of Michigan, 2001), and www.umich.edu/~iinet/PolishRoundTable/html, for analytical extensions of that conference. I also draw on my essay for that collection, "Power, Privilege and Ideology in Communism's Negotiated Collapse," in what follows.

27. Page numbers refer to those in the conference's printed volume.

28. For concise and surprisingly enduring portraits of conservative and radical approaches to inequality's study, see Lenski, *Power and Privilege.*

29. Chrzanowski acknowledges that these subsequent advantages were not "foreseen" at the time (123).

30. Some have argued that it is important to distinguish between the results of the Round Table and the making of that negotiated revolution. For example, another conference participant, Lech Kaczyński, spoke about the Round Table in terms similar to those of Bishop Orszulik. Both the bishop and the politician would agree that the Round Table was a very positive means to develop, peacefully, an independent and democratic Poland. It legalized Solidarity and it opened the way to democratic elections. On that foundation, Solidarity succeeded and won the elections. It even managed to form a government, led by Tadeusz Mazowiecki. But after communism collapsed in the rest of the region, Kaczyński believes that the Solidarity government should have moved quickly to deepen changes, to privatize industry more rapidly, to introduce civil liberties and democratic procedures more quickly, to build a new state, and to restructure society more fundamentally. He argues after the collapse of communism throughout the region, there should have been a more aggressive move to establish justice, to punish those who committed gross crimes under communist rule, and certainly to end their privileges (238–39).

This perspective might be identified with Chrzanowski's radicalism, but Kaczyński clearly sees this Round Table compromise as "necessary." With communism's collapse throughout the region, however, that compromise should have been lifted and those who were privileged in the old system should not have received privilege in the new. In this sense, Kaczyński is more like Lenski than Chrzanowski, for he argues that we must view the conditions in which power and privilege are distributed. Sometimes inequality might be for the good of the society, but at other times it is the result of injustice. Compromise with communists was good once it was unclear whether communism could return; once it was dead and gone, those deals should have been rendered invalid.

31. Michnik, in "We Can Talk without Hatred," p. 285.

32. Jaruzelski, in ibid.

33. In the end, neither Jaruzelski nor Kiszczak could attend the conference for health reasons. Although placards were plastered across campus, denouncing these two and Rakowski as genocidal mass murderers, no protest demonstrations took place during the conference.

34. This letter, which references Encyclical Letter Centesimus Annus 23–24, was sent from the Vatican on March 5, 1999, to University of Michigan president Lee Bollinger.

35. Adam Michnik, Józef Tischner, and Jacek Żakowski, *Między Panem a Plebanem* (Cracow: Spoleczny Instytut Wydawniczy Znak, 1995), p. 558. Tischner is depicted as "Solidarity's theologian" on the cover of his book *The Spirit of Solidarity* (San Francisco: Harper and Row, 1984).

36. Valerie Bunce provides among the most sophisticated, and concise, of such accounts (*Subversive Institutions: The Design and Destruction of Socialsim and the State* [Cambridge: Cambridge University Press, 1999]).

37. Mark Beissinger, *Nationalist Mobilization and the Collapse of the Soviet State: A Tidal Approach to the Study of Nationalism* (Cambridge: Cambridge University Press, 2002).

38. Ota Šik, *The Third Way: Marxist-Leninist Theory and Modern Industrial Society* (London: Wildwood House, 1976).

39. Tamas Bauer, "Hungarian Economic Reform in East European Perspective," *East European Politics and Society* 2:3 (1988): 418–32, esp. 425–26.

40. Tatyana Zaslavskaya, *The Second Socialist Revolution* (Bloomington: Indiana University Press, 1990).

41. Ibid., p. 65.

42. As Jacques Levesque, *The Enigma of 1989: The USSR and the Liberation of Eastern Europe* (Berkeley: University of California Press, 1997), argues, and as I elaborate in chapter 1.

43. See Anthony Giddens, *The Third Way: The Renewal of Social Democracy* (Cambridge: Polity Press, 1998).

44. Linda J. Cook, Mitchell A. Orenstein, and Marilyn Rueschemeyer, "Conclusions" in Linda J. Cook, Mitchell A. Orenstein, and Marilyn Rueschemeyer, eds., *Left Parties and Social Policy in Postcommunist Europe* (Boulder, Colo.: Westview, 1999), pp. 242–43.

45. See, for example, Michael Burawoy, "Neoclassical Sociology"; "Marxism after Communism," *Theory and Society* 29:2 (2000): 151–74; "Afterword," in Michael Burawoy and Katherine Verdery, eds., *Uncertain Transition: Ethnographies of Change in the Postsocialist World* (Lanham, Md.: Rowman and Littlefield, 2000), pp. 301–12; and "Marxism as Science: Historical Challenges and Theoretical Growth," *American Sociological Review* 55 (1990): 775–93.

46. Michael Burawoy, "The State and Economic Involution: Russia through a China Lens," *World Development* 24:6 (1996): 1105–17.

47. Amartya Sen, *Development as Freedom* (New York: Alfred A. Knopf, 1999), draws on his work with the Human Development Reports of the United Nations Development Program and is based on a series of lectures given at the invitation of the president of the World Bank, James Wolfensohn. Subsequent references are given in the text.

Index

MICHAEL D. KENNEDY is vice provost for international affairs, director of the International Institute, and professor of sociology at the University of Michigan. He serves on the executive committee for the Center for International Business Education and is the former director of the Center for Russian and East European Studies. He is author of *Professionals, Power, and Solidarity in Poland: A Critical Sociology of Soviet-Type Society*; editor of *Envisioning Eastern Europe: Post-communist Cultural Studies*; and coeditor (with John A. Guidry and Mayer N. Zald) of *Globalizations and Social Movements: Culture, Power, and the Transnational Public Sphere* and (with Ronald Grigor Suny) of *Intellectuals and the Articulation of the Nation*.